Disruptive Trends in Automation Technology

Disruptive Trends in Automation Technology

Editors

Seppo Sierla
David Hästbacka
Kai Zenger

MDPI

Basel • Beijing • Wuhan • Barcelona • Belgrade • Novi Sad • Cluj • Manchester

Editors
Seppo Sierla
Aalto University
Aalto
Finland

David Hästbacka
Tampere University of Technology
Tampere
Finland

Kai Zenger
Aalto University
Espoo
Finland

Editorial Office
MDPI
St. Alban-Anlage 66
4052 Basel, Switzerland

This is a reprint of articles from the Special Issue published online in the open access journal *Applied Sciences* (ISSN 2076-3417) (available at: https://www.mdpi.com/journal/applsci/special_issues/Trends_Automation_Technology).

For citation purposes, cite each article independently as indicated on the article page online and as indicated below:

Lastname, A.A.; Lastname, B.B. Article Title. *Journal Name* **Year**, *Volume Number*, Page Range.

ISBN 978-3-7258-1211-0 (Hbk)
ISBN 978-3-7258-1212-7 (PDF)
doi.org/10.3390/books978-3-7258-1212-7

Contents

Yohan A. Aparicio and Manuel Jimenez
Mathematical Modeling of SOIC Package Dynamics in Dielectric Fluids during High-Voltage Insulation Testing
Reprinted from: *Appl. Sci.* **2024**, *14*, 3693, doi:10.3390/app14093693 1

Arnak Poghosyan, Ashot Harutyunyan, Edgar Davtyan, Karen Petrosyan and Nelson Baloian
A Study on Automated Problem Troubleshooting in Cloud Environments with Rule Induction and Verification
Reprinted from: *Appl. Sci.* **2024**, *14*, 1047, doi:10.3390/app14031047 25

Yuemin Zheng, Zelin Fei, Jin Tao, Qinglin Sun, Hao Sun, Zengqiang Chen and Mingwei Sun
Intelligent Trajectory Tracking Linear Active Disturbance Rejection Control of a Powered Parafoil Based on Twin Delayed Deep Deterministic Policy Gradient Algorithm Optimization
Reprinted from: *Appl. Sci.* **2023**, *13*, 12555, doi:10.3390/app132312555 40

Henri Pörhö, Jani Tomperi, Aki Sorsa, Esko Juuso, Jari Ruuska and Mika Ruusunen
Data-Based Modelling of Chemical Oxygen Demand for Industrial Wastewater Treatment
Reprinted from: *Appl. Sci.* **2023**, *13*, 7848, doi:10.3390/app13137848 59

Antonio Rosales and Tapio Heikkilä
Analysis and Design of Direct Force Control for Robots in Contact with Uneven Surfaces
Reprinted from: *Appl. Sci.* **2023**, *13*, 7233, doi:10.3390/app13127233 81

Tuomo Sipola, Tero Kokkonen, Markku Puura, Kalle-Eemeli Riuttanen, Kari Pitkäniemi, Elina Juutilainen and Teemu Kontio
Digital Twin of Food Supply Chain for Cyber Exercises
Reprinted from: *Appl. Sci.* **2023**, *13*, 7138, doi:10.3390/app13127138 99

Teemu Pätsi, Markku Ohenoja, Harri Kukkasniemi, Tero Vuolio, Petri Österberg, Seppo Merikoski, et al.
Comparison of Single Control Loop Performance Monitoring Methods
Reprinted from: *Appl. Sci.* **2023**, *13*, 6945, doi:10.3390/app13126945 112

Rakshith Subramanya, Seppo Sierla and Valeriy Vyatkin
From DevOps to MLOps: Overview and Application to Electricity Market Forecasting
Reprinted from: *Appl. Sci.* **2022**, *12*, 9851, doi:10.3390/app12199851 130

Jesse Miettinen, Riku-Pekka Nikula, Joni Keski-Rahkonen, Fredrik Fagerholm, Tuomas Tiainen, Seppo Sierla and Raine Viitala
Whitening CNN-Based Rotor System Fault Diagnosis Model Features
Reprinted from: *Appl. Sci.* **2022**, *12*, 4411, doi:10.3390/app12094411 161

Ioannis Manthos, Thomas Sotiropoulos and Ioannis Vagelas
Is the Artificial Pollination of Walnut Trees with Drones Able to Minimize the Presence of *Xanthomonas arboricola* pv. *juglandis*? A Review
Reprinted from: *Appl. Sci.* **2024**, *14*, 2732, doi:10.3390/app14072732 183

applied sciences

Article

Mathematical Modeling of SOIC Package Dynamics in Dielectric Fluids during High-Voltage Insulation Testing

Yohan A. Aparicio * and Manuel Jimenez

Electrical and Computer Engineering Department, University of Puerto Rico Mayagüez, Mayagüez, PR 00681, USA; manuel.jimenez1@upr.edu
* Correspondence: yohan.aparicio@upr.edu

Abstract: The efficient testing and validation of the high-voltage (HV) insulation of small-outline integrated circuit (SOIC) packages presents numerous challenges when trying to achieve faster and more accurate processes. The complex behavior these packages when submerged in diverse physical media with varying densities requires a detailed analysis to understand the factors influencing their behavior. We propose a systematic and scalable mathematical model based on trapezoidal motion patterns and a deterministic analysis of hydrodynamic forces to predict SOIC package misalignment during automated high-voltage testing in a dielectric fluid. Our model incorporates factors known to cause misalignment during the maneuvering of packages, such as surface tension forces, sloshing, cavity formation, surface waves, and bubbles during the insertion, extraction, and displacement of devices while optimizing test speed for minimum testing time. Our model was validated via a full-factorial statistical experiment for different SOIC package sizes on a pick-and-place (PNP) machine with preprogrammed software and a zero-insertion force socket immersed in different dielectric fluids under controlled thermal conditions. Results indicate the model achieves 99.64% reliability with a margin of error of less than 4.78%. Our research deepens the knowledge and understanding of the physical and hydrodynamic factors that impact the automated testing processes of high-voltage insulator SOIC packages of different sizes for different dielectric fluids. It enables improved testing times and higher reliability than traditional trial-and-error methods for high-voltage SOIC packages, leading to more efficient and accurate processes in the electronics industry.

Keywords: high-voltage testing; surface-mount devices (SMDs); dielectric fluid hydrodynamics; SOIC package misalignment

Citation: Aparicio, Y.A.; Jimenez, M. Mathematical Modeling of SOIC Package Dynamics in Dielectric Fluids during High-Voltage Insulation Testing. *Appl. Sci.* **2024**, *14*, 3693. https://doi.org/10.3390/app14093693

Academic Editor: Ernst Gockenbach

Received: 19 February 2024
Revised: 16 April 2024
Accepted: 23 April 2024
Published: 26 April 2024

1. Introduction

The automated testing and validation of high-voltage (HV) integrated circuits (ICs) has enabled unprecedented growth and efficacy in the power electronics industry. Despite the advances made in the last decade, there still exist multiple avenues that hold promise in further improving the testing processes of HV reinforced insulating barrier IC packages [1]. The demand for efficient testing methods for electronic devices operating at voltages up to 20 kV has experienced significant growth in recent years, particularly in low-profile power electronics devices [2,3]. The prevention of arcing in the narrow gaps of small-outline integrated circuit (SOIC) packages during high-voltage tests is an essential requirement to meet the International Electrotechnical Commission (IEC) VDE 0884-11 standard [4]. This necessity has heightened the interest in efficient testing methods for the introduction of new-generation insulating materials. Controlled HV testing of small components has required submerging the device under test (DUT) in a dielectric fluid to prevent electric arcs [5]. However, optimizing the maneuverability of small components under such conditions is a challenging task due to the myriad of factors that come into play when attempting to predict their dynamic behavior [6].

Recent research in electronics manufacturing and testing has made significant strides, particularly in dielectric fluids and IC manipulation studies. Azmi et al. studied the breakdown voltage of dielectric oils and underscored the superior performance of FR3 over mineral and vegetable oils in high-voltage applications [7]. Haegele et al. complemented this finding with research on the aging of natural vegetable oils, demonstrating that oils like FR3 possess greater dielectric strength and better dissipation factors, albeit with susceptibility to changes due to humidity, oxidation, and viscosity over time [8]. As for integrated circuit testing, Kamath et al. delved into the resilience of insulators in FR3 fluid, a crucial step in preventing electrical arcing and IC damage [2].

Likewise, the employment of pick-and-place machines in the manipulation of electronic components has been the focus of numerous studies in technical literature, underscoring the importance of precision, timelines, and speed engineering algorithm manipulation [9–14]. Parallel advancements in micromanipulation technologies have also helped improve the field. Masood et al. worked on the development of thermodynamic microgrippers, which have played a pivotal role in precise component placement within fluids [15]. Their work sparked further interest in precision studies, such as those led by Nally et al., who explored the integration of vision systems in pick-and-place systems for parallel system assembly [16].

Together, these studies highlight the crucial need for ongoing innovation and refinement in high-voltage IC testing methods, underscoring the importance of material properties, precision engineering, and advanced test methods for reliable and efficient IC test and electronic systems development. The previously reviewed studies, however, do not provide information on how to establish a speed at which a package can travel in a dielectric fluid without exceeding the maximum allowed misalignment to guarantee successful insertion into the test socket or for successful removal, preventing detachment from the pneumatic holder.

Our research addresses the challenges posed by the automation of the manufacturing and validation processes, especially in SOIC package handling capable of withstanding high stresses. The proposed study aims to improve the efficiency and accuracy of high-stress testing methods by addressing the complex hydrodynamic interactions that develop during the movement of these packages in dielectric fluids and optimizing the testing process.

We addressed the problem of establishing the maximum speed at which a DUT can be displaced to prevent exceeding the maximum misalignment allowed for SOIC packages during automated insertion and removal from a zero-insertion force (ZIF) socket immersed in a dielectric fluid. Our approach was to understand and quantify the factors affecting such a misalignment, focusing on the interactions occurring during the DUT movement into, inside, and out from the fluid. We characterized stress forces, splashes, cavity formation, and surface waves that limit the speed and precision of their manipulation. We hypothesize that it is possible to predict the resulting misalignment based on an analysis of the physical properties of the dielectric fluid and its interaction with the SOIC packages.

This research used a methodology that involves the creation of an innovative mathematical model for the automated testing of SOIC packages in dielectric fluids, integrating mechanical and hydrodynamic aspects with standardized test procedures and thorough reliability assessments. It includes a comprehensive evaluation of the insertion, extraction, and displacement processes for SOIC packages in various dielectric fluids. The methodology involves the construction of a specialized automated mechanical platform designed for precision testing, incorporating thermal control of the dielectric fluids. It also involves meticulous data collection and the application of comprehensive statistical methods, such as analysis of variance and frequency distribution, through a full factorial experimental design to confirm the validity of the model.

This research is an important step forward in high-voltage IC testing, particularly in automated SOIC package handling in dielectric fluids. This study achieves an exceptional reliability of 99.64% with a margin of error of less than 4.78%. This study is notable for the implementation of a forward automated system that achieves vertical movements at a speed of 0.2882 m/s and is characterized by its ability to consistently manipulate packages quickly and accurately. In addition, this research contributes significantly to the standardization of calculations for optimum test speeds and highlights the limitations of high-speed package handling.

The rest of this document is organized as follows: Section 2 establishes the theoretical foundations for the model. Section 3 describes the development of the mathematical model for hydrodynamic force analysis. The following section discusses the statistical model validation and the results from the model application and assesses model consistency and repeatability. The final sections compare misalignment speeds across various models and summarize the essential conclusions and implications.

2. Mathematical Preliminaries

In this section, we present the mathematical concepts used for the scalable formulation leading to the generation of the proposed mathematical model.

2.1. *Effects of Dielectric Fluids*

The physical properties of dielectric fluids, such as surface tension, mass density, volume, temperature, and viscosity, can significantly impact the dynamics of packages undergoing a submerged high-voltage testing process. This statement takes particular significance for small-outline integrated circuit (SOIC) packages, as even small shifts have the potential to cause misalignment before they reach their intended position. Dielectric fluids undergo molecular property changes due to the pressure exerted by the surface topology of a device under test (DUT). Although there is no static friction between a solid and a liquid, even a small force can result in a transfer of momentum with slight acceleration, causing the fluid's velocity to increase linearly with depth [8].

2.1.1. Interfacial Tension

Molecular attraction at the solid–liquid interfaces, particularly between the DUT and the dielectric fluid's surface, causes interfacial tension (IFT). Surface tension influences several factors, including the dielectric fluid's characteristics, environmental conditions, viscosity–temperature coefficient (VTC), and the DUT's contact area.

Surface tension induces fluid movement, generating additional reflected forces acting both normally and tangentially on the device's surface. The excess reflected forces introduce surface energy, which gradually causes the DUT to deviate from its initial position [17].

Two main factors, the drag coefficient (or resistance) and the drag force the device exerts on the fluid, influence the flow around a SOIC package. The friction factor represents the ratio between the fluid's kinetic energy per unit volume of the SOIC and the drag force exerted per unit area:

$$f \cdot K_e = \frac{F_f}{A}, \tag{1}$$

where F_f represents the force resulting from the fluid's motion, A is the characteristic area of the wet surface projected on a plane perpendicular to the fluid's approach velocity, and K_e denotes the characteristic kinetic energy per unit volume [18]. K_e is obtained as

$$K_e = 0.5 \cdot \rho \cdot \vec{v}^2, \tag{2}$$

where $\vec{v}$ represents the fluid's approximate external velocity and ρ represents its density.

2.1.2. Dynamics of the Conservation of Mass and Momentum

The mass, density, and volume dynamics directly influence the behavior of an IC package submerged in a dielectric fluid. Unlike the DUT, the dielectric fluid can change its shape, but the volume of liquid displaced by the DUT remains constant. As the DUT mass remains constant, the product of density and volume also remains unchanged. When the fluid changes direction upon contact with the moving DUT, a force acts from the center to the corners of the DUT where the fluid bends [19]. To calculate the displaced fluid amount, multiply the device's submerged volume (V) by the fluid's density (ρ). Laminar turbulence occurs and bends the fluid at contact points where the displaced fluid exceeds the device's contact angles by 180 degrees, altering the device's original position. Determining the force that the DUT can withstand before misalignment occurs is crucial.

Various factors determine the resulting thrust force on the IC. These include the device's weight, the interaction between the friction coefficient and fluid pressure in the horizontal direction, and the frictional forces that oppose rectilinear movement. This analysis requires a flow control model in a coordinate axis system, as referenced in [20–22]. Figure 1a shows a model that analyzes the dielectric flow around the base of a SOIC package, illustrating the force variation from laminar flow as the package moves within the fluid. Similarly, Figure 1b demonstrates the interaction between the laminar flow and the lower IC surface during downward movement. A grid representation of the lower part of the IC enables the identification of consecutive velocity and pressure values, which aids in solving the steady-state incompressible Navier–Stokes equations by treating the flow as compressible [23]. Each analysis yields a new speed, which helps to determine the consecutive values of the resulting forces. The force in the x direction is equivalent to the rate of mass change, as expressed in Equation (3),

$$\vec{F}(\partial x) = \frac{\partial \vec{m}}{\partial t}(v_2 cos\theta_2 - v_1 cos\theta_1), \tag{3}$$

where v_1 and v_2 are speeds in a defined position.

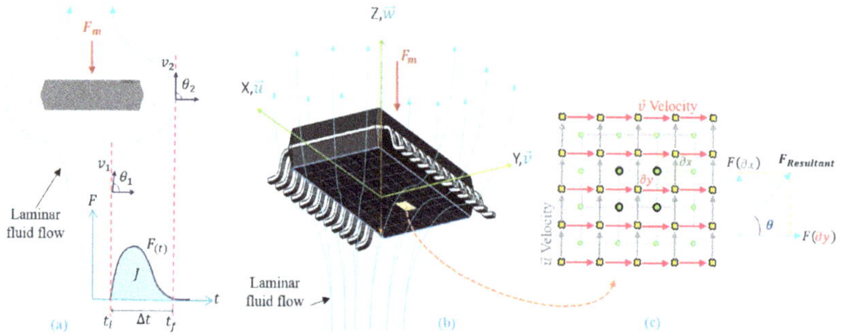

Figure 1. Analysis of linear momentum: (**a**) pressure coefficient and velocity contours, (**b**) IC isometric model with laminar flow fluid behavior, and (**c**) resulting force from stream function by the pressure and speed grid model.

In a collision between the DUT and the dielectric fluid, the impulse (J) acting on the DUT is equal to the change in the device's linear momentum in time $\Delta t = t_f - t_i$ and can be expressed as the area under the curve of the function $\vec{F}(t)$ [24]. The impulse (J) is given by

$$J = \int_{t_i}^{t_f} \vec{F}(t)dt \tag{4}$$

Utilizing Newton's second law of motion [25], the net force acting on an object is determined as the summation of all vector forces applied to it, expressed by the following equation:

$$\vec{F_{net}} = \Delta\vec{P} * (\Delta t)^{-1}, \tag{5}$$

where the net force ($\vec{F_{net}}$) in the DUT is directly associated with the change in fluid momentum $\vec{P}$ over time (t). Evaluating the momentum between the initial moment $\vec{P_i}$ and the final moment $\vec{P_f}$ in Equation (4), we obtain the change in fluid momentum $\vec{P}$:

$$\Delta\vec{P} = J = \vec{P_f} - \vec{P_i} \tag{6}$$

The momentum remains constant if no external forces act over the DUT. Internal forces ($\vec{F_{net}}$) can change the momentum $\Delta\vec{P} * (\Delta t)^{-1} \rightarrow \vec{P_f} = \vec{P_i}$ on parts of the system, but they cannot change the total momentum of the entire system.

The strain rate in a fluid over time depends on the discrete applied shearing stress and its relation to the velocity gradients. This relationship is given by

$$\vec{F_{net}} = m\vec{a} = m * \Delta\vec{v}/(\Delta t) \tag{7}$$

Here, the product of the mass of the device (m) and its velocity ($\vec{v}$) at a specific time (t) determines the momentum of the fluid, which can be expressed through three scalar values representing the vector relationships along the X, Y, and Z axes. Figure 1c shows a staggered grid model that stores velocity components at its center. Pressure differences between corner nodes drive the rate of mass change in this configuration. Each grid analysis yields a new speed, which helps determine the successive values of the resulting forces. The force in the X direction is equivalent to the rate of mass change, written as:

$$\vec{F}(\partial x) = \frac{\partial \vec{m}}{\partial t}(v_2 cos\theta_2 - v_1 cos\theta_1) \tag{8}$$

where v_1 and v_2 are speeds in a defined position. Speed change in the X direction and the force in the Y direction are analogous to the mass change rate from the speed change in the Y direction, shown below:

$$\vec{F}(\partial y) = \frac{\partial \vec{m}}{\partial t}(v_2 sin\theta_2 - v_1 sin\theta_1) \tag{9}$$

The individual resultant force for the flow grid model is given by

$$F_{Resultant} = \sqrt{\vec{F}(\partial x)^2 + \vec{F}(\partial y)^2} \tag{10}$$

Hence, the total force exerted on the fluid equals the momentum change rate through the DUT volume and can be calculated with Equation (11).

$$F = \frac{\partial \vec{m}}{\partial t}(\vec{v}_{out} - \vec{v}_{in}), \tag{11}$$

where $\vec{v}_{out}$ and $\vec{v}_{in}$ are speeds in a defined time range. Analysts reviewed each grid to derive new speeds and consecutive values of resulting forces. The rate of mass change determines the forces acting in the x and y directions. Consequently, the momentum rate of change through the DUT volume dictates the total force on the fluid, which comprises three vector components in the velocity direction. The total force F_T equals the sum of these forces:

$$F_T = F_m + F_B + F_D \tag{12}$$

Here, the device's base area exerts the machine force (F_m) on the fluid. The fluid exerts the buoyant force (F_B) on the device's area in contact with it. Similarly, the fluid pressure exerts the drag force (F_D) on the device's contour. Vectors F_B and F_D oppose the velocity and are represented with a negative sign as:

$$F_B = -\rho V_g, \tag{13}$$

$$F_D = -0.5 * \rho * \mu A * \vec{v}^2_{max}, \tag{14}$$

where ρ is the fluid density and V_g is the DUT volume, $\vec{v}^2_{max}$ is the maximum velocity along the Z-axis, μ is the fluid friction coefficient, and A is the device's area in contact with the fluid.

The resulting force on the Z-axis depends on the weight in the vertical mechanism parallel to the central axis of the screw, the horizontal friction coefficient in the screw, and the forces opposing linear motion [26]. Figure 2 illustrates the variables and parameters involved in the vertical load movement of our load model using the lead-screw drive [27]. A stepper motor provides the required torque to move the load through the lead screw against the thrust load on the ball nut. The necessary torque needed to move the load is given by

$$T = T_{w1} + T_{w2}, \tag{15}$$

where T_{w1} represents the torque against the external force and T_{w2} is the torque against the friction force. Hence, the required basic torque can be expressed as

$$T = P_t \frac{F_m + \mu m g}{2\pi} \quad \text{expressed in} \quad \mathrm{N \cdot m} \tag{16}$$

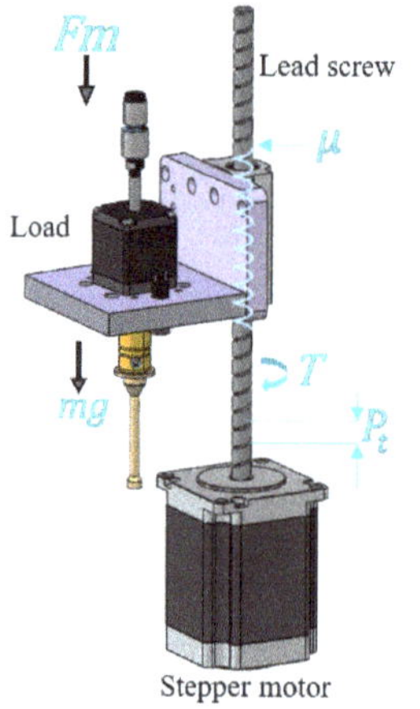

Figure 2. Vertical movement of a load using a lead-screw drive.

Isolating (F_m) from (16), we obtain the machine force on the Z-axis, given as

$$F_m = \frac{2\pi T}{P_t} - \mu m g, \tag{17}$$

where P_t is the lead screw pitch (m), μ is the friction coefficient on the sliding surface, m is the overall load mass (Kg), and g is the gravity 9.81 m/s^2.

2.2. Electronic Components Assembly

In the advanced electronic component assembly industry, automated machinery places surface-mount devices (SMDs) using pick-and-place machining centers. Testing industrial isolation SOIC packages focuses on aligning components and preventing disturbances during their three-dimensional navigation. Precisely positioned nozzles, aided by vacuum systems for suction pressure, meticulously transport surface-mount components. Typically, the production team maintains a clean, disturbance-free environment. In the industrial process of testing SOIC package isolation, The primary focus in testing SOIC package isolation is on component alignment and disturbance prevention while maneuvering within a dielectric fluid [11]. An integrated vision system with cameras ensures accuracy, validating the correct placement of devices in Cartesian X and Y coordinates.

2.2.1. Assembly in the Presence of Dielectric Fluids

Performing procedures in the presence of a dielectric fluid is crucial in the high-voltage testing process of small-outline integrated circuit (SOIC) packages. Optimizing such an operation necessitates a predictive model for assessing package misalignment when manipulated by a pick-and-place system. Figure 3 illustrates a model of a high-voltage

(HV) testing setup for SOIC packages inserted into and extracted from a zero insertion force (ZIF) socket submerged in dielectric fluid. Figure 3 shows a model depicting the high-voltage (HV) testing setup, where a system inserts and extracts SOIC packages into and from a zero-insertion force (ZIF) socket submerged in dielectric fluid.

When an automatic pick-and-place machine transports an integrated circuit through a dielectric fluid, the DUT encounters additional forces influenced by various factors such as IC volume, fluid characteristics, travel speed, and reached depth. Upon submergence, the fluid's viscosity reduces the cohesion between the nozzle and the DUT. This viscosity effect primarily applies to the thin region adjacent to the solid boundary (surface layer), where forces are significant.

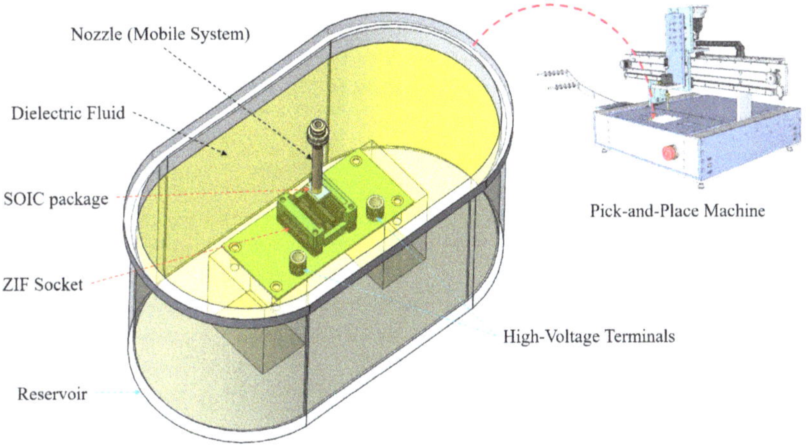

Figure 3. High-voltage testing manipulation model.

Higher viscosity in a dielectric fluid creates a large surface layer next to the IC, increasing the fluid's surface tension from the device's edges to its center. Higher viscosity indicates lowest fluidity, but this fluidity increases with rising temperature. The changes in fluid behavior due to temperature affect the forces exerted on the DUT.

Friction building up on the IC surface can cause turbulent flow between the pin spaces, around the device's encapsulation, and at the junction between the nozzle and the DUT. This phenomenon arises due to the device's shape and the changes in fluid pressure. Energy builds up unevenly at the device's edges, sometimes overcoming the vertical resistance that maintains alignment and altering the device's horizontal position in both the X and Y components [28].

2.2.2. Physical Characteristics of SOIC Packages

We selected three different SOIC packages to meet the research requirements, adhering to the dimensions and specifications set by the Solid State Technology Association (JEDEC 300 mil). Table 1 list the physical and physic characteristics of three models of selected SOIC packages (small-outline package plus the number of pins).

Table 1. SOIC packages' physical and physic characteristics.

SOIC Package	Length mm	Width mm	Height mm	Equivalent Diameter mm	Area mm^2	Volume mm^3	Mass Kg	Weight N
SOP-16	10.49	10.64	2.65	10.57	111.68	296.61	1.36×10^{-4}	1.33×10^{-3}
SOP-20	12.60	10.64	2.65	11.54	134.13	355.60	4.99×10^{-4}	4.89×10^{-3}
SOP-24	15.60	10.64	2.65	12.65	166.00	440.81	6.35×10^{-4}	6.23×10^{-3}

2.2.3. Physical Characteristics of Selected Dielectric Fluids

The physical properties of dielectric fluids, such as viscosity, surface tension, and density, significantly affect the performance of HV testing processes. FR3 vegetable oil (Plymount, MN, USA), DPMS (DMS-T23) silicone (Morrisville, PA, USA), and DTE-150 (LVO-330) mineral oil (Irving, TX, USA) are industrial electrical insulators with similar densities and surface tensions [29–31]. The kinetic viscosity directly affects the mobility of a DUT submerged in a dielectric fluid, particularly when there are temperature variations. Generally, as the temperature increases, the kinetic viscosity of the fluid tends to decrease. This reduction in viscosity enhances the mobility of the DUT in the fluid, as a lower viscosity implies less resistance to the movement of the DUT within the fluid. To maintain a consistent viscosity of the dielectric fluid during tests, the temperature was controlled at 25 °C ± 0.25 °C. This control was achieved using a C206T temperature controller, equipped with a 6.56 FT sensor and a 20 Watts/120 VAC halogen bulb for heating [32]. Once the dielectric fluid reached the target temperature, it consistently stayed within this range, eliminating the need for an additional cooling system. Table 2 details the characteristics of the chosen dielectric fluids, allowing us to evaluate the device under mobility test with three different viscosity ranges.

Table 2. Constants of the physical characteristics of dielectric fluids.

Dielectric Medium	Density Kg/m^3	Viscosity at 25 °C cSt	Surface Tension mN/m
Air	1.17	16.92	N/A
FR3	922.99	40.00	23.99
DTE-150	856.00	150.00	22.26
DPMS	967.99	350.00	21.10

3. Mathematical Model Development

In this section, we conduct an analytical assessment of the trapezoidal movement pattern to ascertain the SOIC package's trajectories, speed, acceleration, and test duration. Subsequently, we perform a deterministic analysis of the hydrodynamic forces and physical factors influencing the SOIC package's positional deviation when immersed in a dielectric fluid.

3.1. Motion Profile Analysis of the Characterization

Developing mathematical models that combine mass and momentum conservation principles for energy conservation in movements through varying densities requires a comprehensive analysis of the trapezoidal movement pattern [33]. Such analysis is pivotal in understanding SOIC package trajectories, considering essential factors like speed, acceleration, and test time. It also requires a deterministic evaluation of dielectric fluids' physical and dynamic properties. This evaluation leads to an examination of hydrodynamic forces and physical dependencies. These factors determine how a SOIC package moves and positions itself in a dielectric fluid.

The nozzle holds the package at its original position along the Z-axis, where the analysis begins. Figure 4 illustrates the complete time–speed trapezoidal motion pattern for the entire process divided in twenty stages represented by the Roman numbers (I–XX). The detailed analysis examines the device's insertion and extraction displacements along the Z-axis, which the nozzle holds. The movement sequence involves first moving downwards through the air, then submerging into the dielectric fluid until reaching the upper surface of the zero-insertion force (ZIF) socket. The insertion process slows down and continues moving until the ZIF socket activates and stops it.

Subsequently, the process allocates a specific time to release the SOIC package and then moves the Z-axis back to the ZIF socket's surface at a reduced speed. Once in position, the system increases the speed to the maximum allowed and then halts again upon reaching the home position. For extracting the SOIC package from the ZIF socket, the system replicates the same operational sequence in reverse order. A programmed speed ratio, tailored to the distance between each step, governs each travel time, featuring instant transitions with constant acceleration or deceleration. While inserting and removing the package are the most critical movements for the IC, technicians must remove the nozzle from the dielectric fluid to conduct high-voltage tests. Figure 5 showcases the trapezoidal motion pattern for either the insertion or extraction of the SOIC package selected from the twenty process stages represented by the Roman numbers.

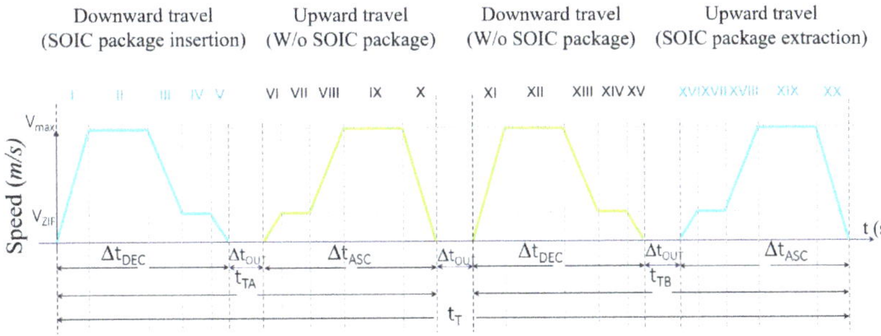

Figure 4. Trapezoid movement pattern: time–speed complete.

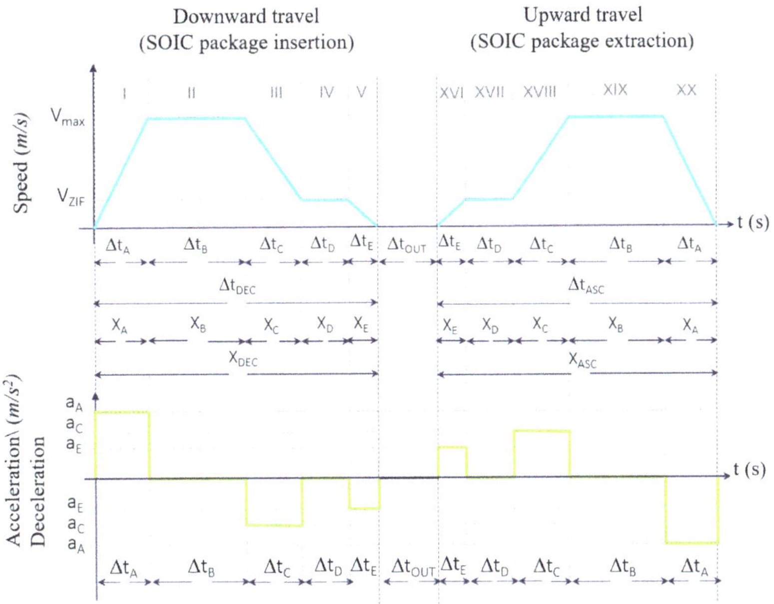

Figure 5. Trapezoid movement pattern: time–speed.

The insertion or extraction procedure requires a total time (t_T), which includes the sum of the downward travel time (Δt_{DEC}), the upward travel time (Δt_{ASC}), and a waiting period (t_{OUT}) to activate or deactivate the pneumatic system that releases or retains the SOIC package. Each downward or upward travel phase is segmented into periods with constant transitions, resulting in five distinct travel periods in each direction. The total time for each completed characterization process is $2t_T$. In a single characterization process, the total travel distance X_0 equals twice the sum of the descent distance X_{DEC} and the ascent distance X_{ASC}.

A mathematical analysis of the trapezoidal pattern for downward travel requires motion with a constant acceleration function $\Delta X = V_0\Delta t + \frac{1}{2}a\Delta t^2$ $(constant\ a)$, where X is the final position, V_0 is the initial velocity, Δt is the time interval, V is the final velocity, and a is the acceleration to evaluate each segment [34]. Tables 3 and 4 show the equations of the intervals covered and accelerations obtained.

Table 3. Equations of the intervals covered.

Stage	Downward Period Distance Covered	Stage	Upward Period Distance Covered
I	$X_A = \frac{1}{2}a_A\Delta t_A{}^2$	XVI	$X_E = \frac{1}{2}a_E\Delta t_E{}^2$
II	$X_B = V_{max}\Delta t_B$	XVII	$X_D = V_{ZIF}\Delta t_D$
III	$X_C = V_{max}\Delta t_C - \frac{1}{2}a_C\Delta t_C{}^2$	XVIII	$X_C = V_{ZIF}\Delta t_C + \frac{1}{2}a_C\Delta t_C{}^2$
IV	$X_D = V_{ZIF}\Delta t_D$	XIX	$X_B = V_{max}\Delta t_B$
V	$X_E = V_{ZIF}\Delta t_E - \frac{1}{2}a_E\Delta t_E{}^2$	XX	$X_A = V_{max}\Delta t_A - \frac{1}{2}a_A\Delta t_A{}^2$

Table 4. Equations of acceleration or deceleration on trapezoid pattern.

Stage	Accel–Decel	Stage	Accel–Decel	Stage	Accel–Decel
I and XX	$a_A = \frac{V_{max}}{\Delta t_A}$	III and XVIII	$a_C = \frac{V_{max}-V_{ZIF}}{\Delta t_C}$	V and XVI	$a_E = \frac{V_{ZIF}}{\Delta t_E}$

The total distance (X_T) required to complete a test corresponds to the sum of four distances traveled on the Z-axis. Each vertical run covers a distance of 78.994 mm. This comprises a 75.819 mm path from the Z-axis origin to the top surface of the ZIF socket, along with a 3.175 mm path for inserting or removing the SOIC package into the ZIF socket. The distance covered at maximum speed is the sum of distances X_A, X_B, and X_C, while the ZIF socket operating distance is the sum of distances X_D and X_E. The equation for the total distance traveled is as follows:

$$X_T = 4 \cdot [X_A + X_B + X_C + X_D + X_E] \quad (18)$$

Replacing the values obtained from the motion trapezoidal pattern, we obtained a total distance traveled as a function of time–speed, as shown in Equation (19):

$$X_T = 2V_{max}(\Delta t_A + 2\Delta t_B + \Delta t_C) + 2V_{ZIF}(\Delta t_C + 2\Delta t_D + \Delta t_E) \quad (19)$$

The total time required to complete a test is equal to the sum of the partial times Δt_{DES}, Δt_{ASC}, and Δt_{OUT}, as shown below:

$$t_T = 2\Delta t_{DEC} + 2\Delta t_{ASC} + 3\Delta t_{OUT} \quad (20)$$

3.2. Behavioral Analysis of Forces Exerted on DUT

Analyzing the forces acting on the SOIC package, especially near its contour, the complexity increases due to the variety of forces encountered in different fluid environments.

To understand a device's behavior in different fluids, we must deduce the forces acting during its linear displacement. Understanding these forces helps determine the SOIC package's maximum permissible speed while maintaining its alignment [35].

Table 5 lists the mechanical and physical parameters necessary for force analysis in the Z-axis. The impact of forces in the dielectric fluid requires considering the friction coefficients (μ), obtained from Equations (22) and (23), and Reynold's number (Re), obtained from Equation (21).

Tables 6 and 7 provide a breakdown of the Reynold numbers for each medium through which the SOIC packages moved and the corresponding coefficients of friction.

$$R_e = \frac{\rho * S_d * V_{Mmax}}{\eta} \quad (21)$$

$$\mu_{air} = \frac{24 * (1 + 0.15 * R_{e_{air}}^{0.687})}{R_{e_{air}}} \ (Re < 500) \quad (22)$$

$$\mu_{oil} = \frac{24}{R_{e_{oil}}} + \frac{6}{1 + \sqrt{R_{e_{oil}}}} + 0.4 \left(0.2 < Re < 10^5\right) \quad (23)$$

Table 5. Summary of parameters' Z-axis characteristics.

Symbol	Description	Value	Units
T	Motor torque on the Z-axis	0.8054	N·m
P_t	Lead screw pitch	0.01	m
μ	Friction coefficient on the sliding surface	0.15	
m	Overall load mass	1	Kg
F_m	Machine force on the Z-axis from Equation (17)	318	N
j	Rotor inertia	1.172×10^{-5}	Kg·m^2
RPS	Revolutions per second	0.547	rev/s
a_a	Angular acceleration	43,373.56	rad/s^2
V_{Mmax}	Maximum linear velocity on the Z-axis	0.288	m/s
X_{air}	Air travel distance	0.045	m
X_{oil}	Oil travel distance	0.030	m
X_f	Final travel distance in the oil	0.003	m
X_T	Total travel distance	0.078	m
D_n	Nozzle contact end diameter	0.0036	m
a_n	Nozzle contact end suction area	1.02×10^{-5}	m^2
$a_{n_{cyl}}$	Nozzle contact end cylinder area	3.02×10^{-5}	m^2
P_{Sm}	Measured maximum suction pressure	9997.40	Pa·N/m^2
F_{Smax}	Maximum suction force is equal	0.102	N

Table 6. Reynold's number for each media and SOIC package.

SOIC Package	Dielectric Medium			
	Air	FR3	DTE-150	DPMS
SOP-16	211.04	70,222.13	17,366.60	8416.66
SOP-20	230.48	76,689.88	18,966.13	9191.87
SOP-24	252.74	84,095.12	20,797.52	10,079.44

Table 7. Friction coefficients for each media and SOIC package.

SOIC Package	Dielectric Medium			
	Air	FR3	DTE-150	DPMS
SOP-16	0.788	0.423	0.447	0.464
SOP-20	0.760	0.422	0.445	0.461
SOP-24	0.732	0.421	0.442	0.458

For force analysis exerted on the DUT, we maintained a constant maximum speed in two different mediums (air and dielectric fluid), each with varying densities. Assuming near-zero instantaneous acceleration concerning the displacement of the SOIC package, we analyzed the resulting forces during its trajectory and the associated energy losses for each density, including transitions between different fluids. Figure 6 shows the force models we developed for each medium, detailing how we moved the SOIC package and facilitating the analysis of static and dynamic force behaviors.

The force analysis depicted in Figure 6 reveals a model for the initial moment without vertical movement in Figure 6a. In this scenario, the machine force (F_m), drag force ($F_{d_{air}}$), and normal force (N) are all zero. Therefore, the initial suction force (F_S) must be equal to or greater than the weight of the SOIC package (W_{SOIC}).

The resulting force, considering the machine force (F_m), acceleration, and an initial velocity of zero, is given by Equation (24):

$$-F_s + W_{SOIC} - N - Fd = 0 \tag{24}$$

Here, the normal force (N) results from multiplying the air density (ρ_{air}), gravity acceleration (g), and the volume of the SOIC package base (γ_{SOIC}). The drag force (f_d) depends on the normal force, and we multiply it by the friction coefficient (μ_{air}).

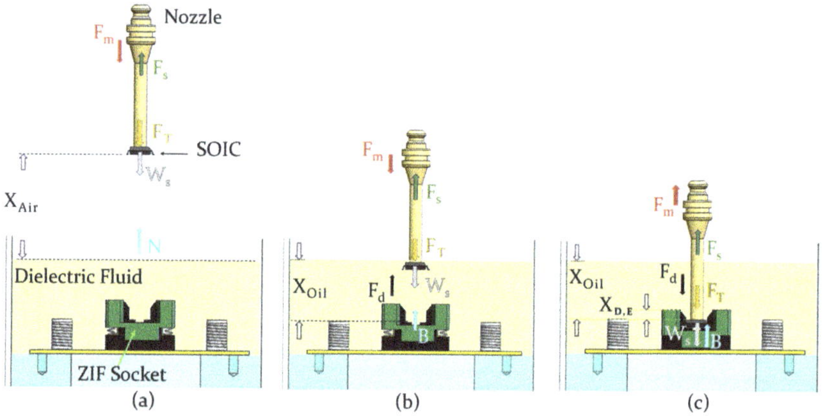

Figure 6. (**a**) Analysis for SOIC package moving down in the air, (**b**) air–dielectric fluid interface, and (**c**) SOIC package moving up in a dielectric fluid.

To determine the maximum velocities for each medium, we use Newton's second law for force analysis and apply the principle of conservation of energy to symmetric temporal translation [36]. In this case, the Z-axis moves vertically, holding a SOIC package under suction pressure.

The drag force exerted by the fluid medium depends on the square of the velocity and the area of the SOIC package (a_{SOIC}) in contact with the dielectric fluid, given by Equation (25):

$$F_d = \frac{V_{max}^2 * \rho * \mu * a_{SOIC}}{2} \tag{25}$$

By substituting the drag force into Equation (24), we can derive the maximum speed for downward displacement in the air, as shown in Equation (26):

$$|V_{max_{Air_D}}| = \sqrt{\frac{2(F_s + N - W_{SOIC})}{\mu \cdot \rho_{air} \cdot a_{SOIC}}} \tag{26}$$

We considered the velocity as an absolute value and denote its direction with the suffix $D = downward$ and $U = upward$.

Moving on to Figure 6b, which represents a constant velocity, zero acceleration, and downward displacement in a dielectric fluid, we obtained Equation (27):

$$-F_s + W_{SOIC} - B = 0 \tag{27}$$

Here, the buoyant force (B) is equal to the dielectric fluid density (ρ_{oil}) multiplied by gravity acceleration (g) and by the volume of the SOIC package base (γ_{SOIC}). The drag force (F_d) is proportional to the buoyant force and the friction coefficient (μ_{oil}).

The maximum velocity (V_{max}) for downward displacement in the dielectric fluid can be determined using Equation (28):

$$|V_{max_{Oil_D}}| = \sqrt{\frac{2(F_s + B - W_{SOIC})}{\mu \cdot \rho_{oil} \cdot a_{SOIC}}} \tag{28}$$

In the context of upward displacement in the dielectric fluid, as depicted in Figure 6c, the drag force (f_d) exhibits an inverse direction about the flotation force, acting only over the upper areas of the SOIC package (excluding the area under the nozzle $a_{n_{cyl}}$). This results in Equation (29):

$$-F_s + W_{SOIC} - B + Fd = 0 \tag{29}$$

By substituting the equivalent values for the drag force, the maximum speed for upward displacement in the dielectric fluid can be expressed using Equation (30):

$$V_{max_{Oil_U}} = \sqrt{\frac{2(F_s + B - W_{SOIC})}{\mu \cdot \rho \cdot (a_{SOIC} - a_{n_{cyl}})}} \tag{30}$$

Behavioral Analysis of Suction Force

The minimum suction force (F_s) required to securely hold the SOIC package during vertical movement, as described in Equation (31), is directly linked to several factors. These include the mass of the SOIC package (m_{SOIC}), the acceleration due to gravity (g), the linear machinery acceleration (a_L), a minimum safety factor (S_f) typically set at 1.5 or 2.0 (which accounts for the secure holding of rigid surfaces with minimal porosity), the nozzle diameter of 3.607 mm, and the reciprocal of the drag coefficient (μ) of the dielectric fluid [37]. The formula for calculating the minimum suction force is given as follows:

$$F_s = m_{SOIC} \cdot (g + \frac{a_L}{\mu}) \cdot S_f \tag{31}$$

The maximum linear machinery acceleration obtained was 40.77 m/s^2. For the experimentation and analysis, a minimum safety factor of 1.5 was selected.

Table 8 presents the values of the pneumatic line's minimal pressure and the corresponding suction force necessary to ensure the secure attachment of the SOIC package to the nozzle.

Table 8. Minimum suction force and vacuum pressure for each SOIC package.

Dielectric Medium	SOIC Package	Minimum Suction Force N	Vacuum Pressure N/m^2
AIR	SOP-16	0.0138	458.78
	SOP-20	0.0471	1560.70
	SOP-24	0.0613	2031.89
FR3	SOP-16	0.0239	791.59
	SOP-20	0.0790	2617.87
	SOP-24	0.0999	3309.28

Table 8. *Cont.*

Dielectric Medium	SOIC Package	Minimum Suction Force N	Vacuum Pressure N/m^2
DTE-150	SOP-16	0.0227	753.53
	SOP-20	0.0754	2496.94
	SOP-24	0.0955	3162.83
DPMS	SOP-16	0.0220	727.74
	SOP-20	0.0729	2414.89
	SOP-24	0.0925	3063.13

After determining the suction force values, we substituted them into Equations (26), (28) and (30) to calculate the maximum speed of continuous displacement along the Z-axis during testing.

The results of these calculations are presented in Table 9, which provides the maximum speed values required for transporting the DUT through two different media, namely air and oil. These speed values account for constant acceleration and are essential for the testing process.

Table 9. Maximum Z-axis velocity calculated (downward and upward).

Dielectric Medium	SOIC Package	Downward m/s	Upward m/s
AIR	SOP-16	29.735	18.132
	SOP-20	26.581	30.197
	SOP-24	27.820	30.757
FR3	SOP-16	1.073	1.257
	SOP-20	1.721	1.955
	SOP-24	1.741	1.925
DTE-150	SOP-16	1.055	1.235
	SOP-20	1.697	1.928
	SOP-24	1.720	1.901
DPMS	SOP-16	0.922	1.080
	SOP-20	1.472	1.673
	SOP-24	1.494	1.652

To calculate the maximum speed (V_{ZIF}) needed to close the ZIF socket, we applied a force to the spring-loaded mechanism until the spring shifted to a position that corresponds to the total distance $(X_D + X_E)$, as shown in Figure 5. We can determine the magnitude of this force using Equation (32), where (K) denotes the spring's elasticity constant, following Hooke's law [38].

$$F_Z = K \cdot (X_D + X_E) \quad (32)$$

The work performed by the spring (W_{Spring}), as calculated in Equation (33), is directly proportional to the potential energy (E_p) stored in the spring. It is important to note that this calculation neglects energy losses due to vibration.

$$W_{Spring} = 0.5 \cdot K \cdot (X_D + X_E)^2 \quad (33)$$

The potential energy (E_p) stored in the spring, as expressed in Equation (34), is proportional to the square of the maximum speed used to close the ZIF socket (V_{ZIF}).

$$E_p = 0.5 \cdot m_{load} \cdot V_{ZIF}^2 \quad (34)$$

The equation for determining the maximum speed required to close the ZIF socket, V_{ZIF}, is derived from equating the work performed by the spring (W_{Spring}) to the potential energy (E_p) stored in the spring, as shown in the equation below:

$$V_{ZIF} = \sqrt{\frac{K \cdot (X_D + X_E)^2}{m}} \quad (35)$$

Using the mechanical specifications of the ZIF socket, a force of 1.7 Kgf , equivalent to 16.67 N, is required for compression. Applying Newton's law for forces, where force equals mass times acceleration due to gravity, we find a mass of 0.0044 Kg.

To determine the spring constant (K) of the ZIF socket, the mechanical specifications indicate a force of 0.39 N (40 gmf) per pin. In the case of the 28-pin ZIF socket model, the total applied force is 11 N for a travel distance of 0.003 m. Substituting these values into Equation (32), we find that the elasticity constant of the ZIF socket is equivalent to 9.485 Kg/s^2. By substituting these values into Equation (36), we determine the maximum operating speed of the ZIF socket to be:

$$V_{ZIF} = 0.14 \text{ m/s} \quad (36)$$

4. Behavioral Analysis of Surface Tension, Capillarity, Cavitation, and Splash

Dynamic surface tension affects the splatter. It increases during surface expansion and decreases as waves move in the newly formed interface [39]. Further analysis of surface tension strength, along with considerations of capillarity, cavitation, and splash effects, enabled the establishment of a more precise mathematical model. This model can now predict deviations with different DUT sizes, various dielectric fluids with other characteristics, and different operational speeds of pick-and-place machines.

4.1. Behavioral Analysis of Surface Tension Force

The force that exists due to the surface tension of the dielectric and the forces that arise from the contact of a DUT when immersed in the dielectric fluid can generate significant deviations in the final insertion position of the SOIC package. The force between the DUT and the surface of the dielectric fluid changes as the size of the DUT increases, the temperature varies, the impact velocity increases, and the physical characteristics of the dielectric make it denser. The surface tension force F_{ST} depends on the device's side length L_{SOIC}, its width Wd_{SOIC}, the capillarity C_a, and the surface tension coefficient σ. Surface tension force equation is given by Equation (37).

$$F_{ST} = (2 \cdot L_{SOIC} + W_{dSOIC}) \cdot \sigma \cdot (1 - C_a) \quad (37)$$

Table 10 shows the values of the net surface tension force values on SOIC packages when they are submerged in the dielectric fluid.

Table 10. Surface tension force (N/m) for each dielectric and SOIC package.

SOIC Package	Dielectric Medium		
	FR3	DTE-150	DPMS
SOP-16	39.929	43.957	49.561
SOP-20	37.127	40.805	46.058
SOP-24	35.025	38.528	43.431

4.2. Cavitation and Capillarity Analysis

Cavitation during the insertion of the SOIC package into the dielectric fluid at the initial impact speed could lead to the formation of splashes at the edges of the SOIC package. However, cavity formation becomes dependent on the physical properties of the SOIC package, the pin contours, the wettability of the material, and the impact speed. Using approximations of the Froude model that describe the surface behavior of the dielectric fluid when it receives disturbances at the moment of contact with an object, we analyzed each of the SOIC packages concerning the maximum operating speed of the pick-and-place machine [40]. The nondimensional Froude's number is given by $f_r = V_{Mmax} \cdot (g \cdot D)^{-1/2}$, where V_{Mmax} is the maximum velocity at the moment of contact with the dielectric fluid, g is the gravity acceleration, and D is the equivalent diameter of SOIC package. The Froude numbers exhibit variation across different SOIC packages, with values of 0.8946 for the 16-pin, 0.8561 for the 20-pin, and 0.8175 for the 24-pin.

The air cavity's hydrodynamics and the device's geometry, resulting from vertical immersion, exhibit relatively low Froude numbers near the cavity $(F_r \leq 0)$. However, the nozzle holding the SOIC package prevents the air cavity on the DUT from completely closing. Therefore, analyzing the effects of viscosity and surface tension near the air cavity closure due to capillarity on the SOIC package's surface using the Weber model (W_e) [41]. We evaluated the role of surface tension and the drag force of the capillarity (C_a) on the device's surface as follows:

$$W_e = \frac{\rho \cdot V_{Mmax}^2 \cdot D}{\sigma} \tag{38}$$

$$C_a = \frac{W_e}{R_e}, \tag{39}$$

where ρ is the dielectric fluid density, D is the equivalent diameter of the SOIC package, σ is the surface tension coefficient, and V_{Mmax} is the maximum velocity of the pick-and-place machine. Table 11 shows the nondimensional values of capillarity at the surface of SOIC packages when they change between the air interface and the dielectric fluid.

Table 11. Capillarity for each dielectric and SOIC package.

SOIC Package	Dielectric Medium		
	FR3	DTE-150	DPMS
SOP-16	2.4×10^{-4}	9.687×10^{-4}	2.498×10^{-3}
SOP-20	2.4×10^{-4}	9.687×10^{-4}	2.498×10^{-3}
SOP-24	2.4×10^{-4}	9.687×10^{-4}	2.498×10^{-3}

We used the values in Table 11 to predict the cohesion between the surfaces of different SOIC packages and a similar dielectric fluid. This capillary action contributes to the formation of microdroplets and bubbles. We deduced that the maximum capillary action depends on the dielectric's viscosity below a certain microunit threshold, allowing negligible cavitation.

4.3. Splash Analysis

To calculate the percentage and splash threshold of the dielectric fluid, we need to relate the surface tension and inertial forces, taking into account the viscosity's impact. By applying Equation (40), we can obtain the splash percentage (% Splash). Furthermore, the nondimensional Ohnesorge number (Oh), as defined in Equation (41), allows us to relate surface tension with viscous and inertial forces. This correlation estimates the splash threshold constant K_s, which we can calculate using Equation (42), as modeled by Brown (2008) [42].

$$Splash = \frac{100 \cdot W_e}{W_e + 10^6} \tag{40}$$

$$Oh = \frac{\sqrt{W_e}}{R_e} \tag{41}$$

$$K_s = W_e \cdot Oh^{0.4} \tag{42}$$

Table 12 shows the dimensionless values of the percentage of the splash and dimensionless values of the splash threshold between the air interface and the dielectric fluid when making contact with the base area of the SOIC package.

Drawing on Murphy's comparative analysis of different oils, we compared the splash percentages of dielectric fluids [43]. Our findings indicate that the splash heights range approximately from 0.533 μm to 1.974 μm.

Table 12. Splash threshold and sloshing percentage for selected dielectric fluid interfaces and SOIC packages.

Dielectric Medium	SOIC Package	Splash Percentage (%)	Splash Threshold
FR3	SOP-16	0.169	0.063
	SOP-20	0.168	0.110
	SOP-24	0.210	0.167
DTE-150	SOP-16	0.184	0.064
	SOP-20	0.184	0.112
	SOP-24	0.230	0.170
DPMS	SOP-16	0.200	0.065
	SOP-20	0.202	0.114
	SOP-24	0.252	0.174

5. Results and Analysis

We present the results obtained to establish the correlation between the final position of a SOIC package manipulated in a dielectric fluid and its vertical travel speed during pick-and-place machine-assisted tests. These experimental results determine the probability distribution of the observed profiles, showcasing the repeatability, reproducibility, and robustness of the overall setup employed in this study.

5.1. Statistical Validation of Samples

To validate our proposed solution, we first examined the behavior of the extracted data and identified the relationships between variables. We performed 450 measurements in total across three different SOIC packages and three different dielectric fluids. For each possible combination, we completed 50 measurements and reported the sample deviations for each set in X and Y coordinates. To identify the direction of measurements, we assigned a negative sign to deviations to the left on the X-axis and the front on the Y-axis. We assigned implicit positive values to deviations to the right on the X-axis and backward on the Y-axis. The model did not permit deviations in the Z direction, so we did not consider them in the analysis.

Figure 7 shows boxplots of the X and Y axes, respectively, illustrating the median, the highest significance percentiles, and the minimum and maximum values of the deviation of the SOIC packages in Cartesian X and Y coordinates for each type of dielectric fluid.

In each boxplot, the ends of the vertical lines indicate the minimum and maximum data values. The Points outside the extremes indicated by the symbol (*), present outliers up to a maximum of 1.5 times the interquartile range. We observed a conservative quartile concentration trend around the maximum alignment point in the box plots, with minimal variations in the upper and lower quartiles not exceeding 0.1 mm. The SOP16 packages showed minor deviations from other SOIC packages but did not maintain symmetric behavior across different dielectric fluids. Conversely, SOP24 packages had a symmetrical deviation ratio in various dielectric fluids and a higher concentration of deviations than

SOP16 and SOP20 packages. Significantly, we recorded the lowest concentration of deviations with the dielectric fluid FR3. The higher friction coefficient and greater contact area of SOP24 with the dielectric fluid likely caused a thinner cohesion layer and higher surface tension at the edges.

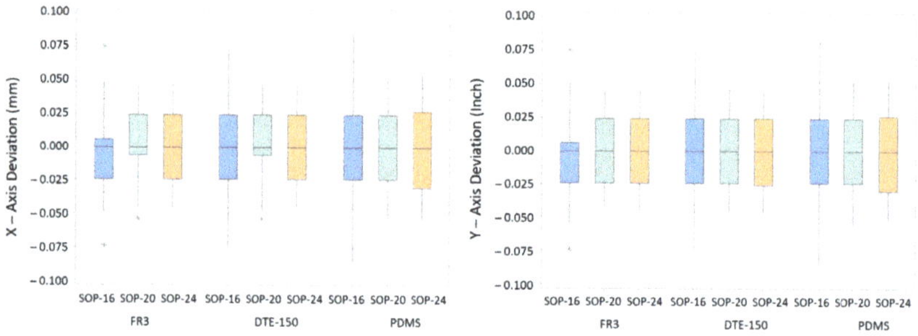

Figure 7. Boxplot of X and Y axes SOIC packages deviation on dielectric fluid.

5.2. Consistency and Repeatability

We estimated the overall reliability of the results by evaluating them at a confidence level of 95% or higher, using the acceptable internal consistency indicator. Cronbach's alpha showed an overall reliability of 99.64%, confirming the high reliability of the collected data. Figures 8 and 9 show the frequency values within the deviation range of the SOIC packages on a set of histograms with the variance dispersion correlation at 25% of the total deviation range.

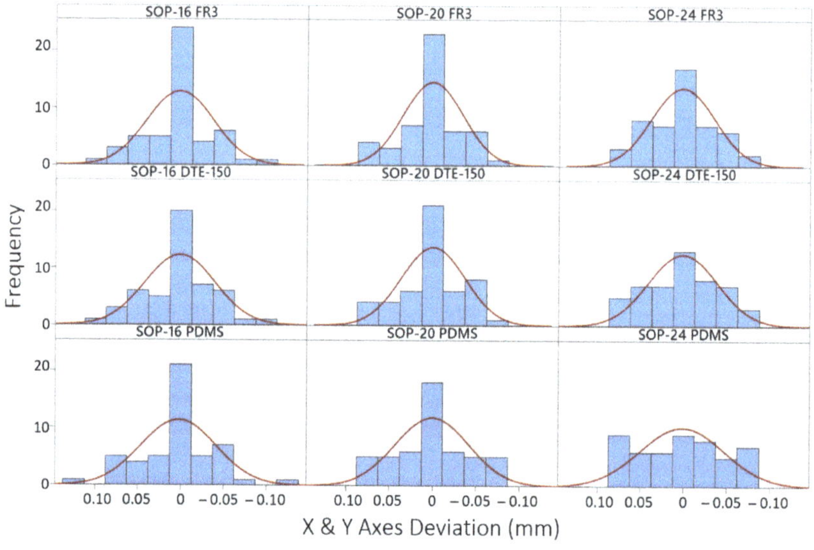

Figure 8. Histogram with a normal curve of SOIC packages on dielectric fluids.

The histogram analysis of Figure 8 revealed a Gaussian curve with a center frequency trend and uniform dispersion around most results. Notably, dielectric fluid FR3 exhibited a higher center alignment frequency for SOP16 packages, while SOP24 packages showed the lowest center alignment frequency.

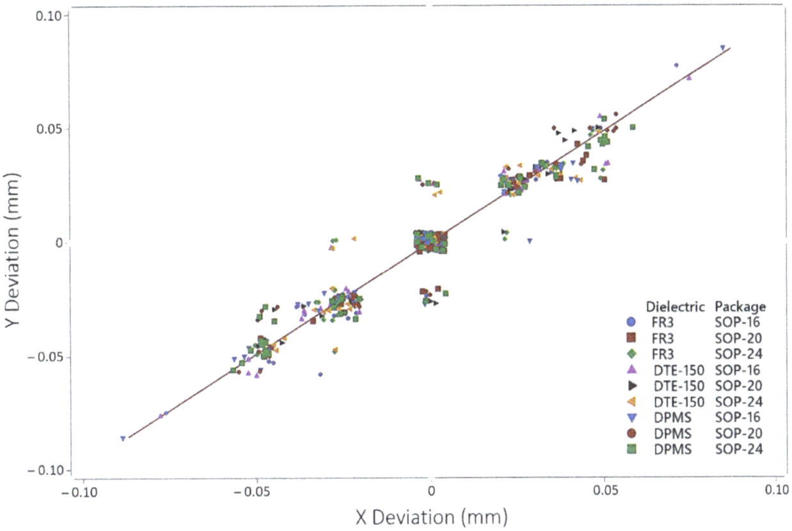

Figure 9. Correlation of dispersion matrix plot: X and Y axes deviation.

Examining the dispersion matrix plot in Figure 9, we observed linear correlations between deviations in both negative and positive directions. Median and mode results for each sample set consistently equaled zero. To assess data consistency, we determined the sample arithmetic mean, maximum, and minimum deviation values and sampled standard dispersion around the mean, standard deviation, median, and mode for each set of samples, thereby reducing limitations.

We observed that the SOP24 packages had the lowest misalignment values at the minimum and maximum end points relative to the SOP16 and SOP20 packages. However, their standard deviations recorded in tests on all dielectric fluids were the largest. We also observed that SOP16 packages had the highest maximum and minimum misalignment values for the DPMS dielectric fluid and the highest misalignment range in all tested dielectrics. The testing results of the SOP20 packages were compared and recorded as the lowest standard deviation for the FR3 dielectric fluid.

5.3. *Misalignment Velocity Analysis*

Our factorial analysis determined that the relative standard error margin was less than 4.78%, ensuring an overall reliability of 99.64%. As shown in Figure 10, the pick-and-place machine achieved a maximum test speed of 0.288 m/s. We found the average deviation to be 0.0711 mm, which is about 25.14%, significantly lower than the error tolerance limit of 0.2829 mm. Our probability assessments revealed that the mean velocity probability for misalignment is 0.832 m/s, and the median probability for maintaining the IC within 0.2829 mm alignment at maximum velocity is 1.5466 m/s. We identified that dielectric fluids with lower viscosity, such as FR3, DTE-150, and PDMS , allow better alignment of ICs at maximum speeds of 1.778 m/s, 1.727 m/s, and 1.499 m/s, respectively.

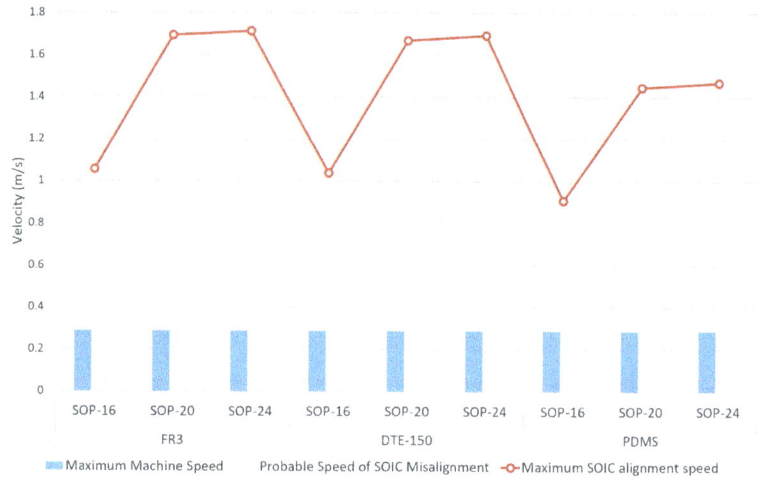

Figure 10. Maximum velocity for testing SOIC packages aligned.

Figure 11 shows the cumulative deviation statistics of a SOIC package model as it moves through a specific dielectric fluid. We calculated the maximum deviation using the test pick-and-place machine's maximum velocity. We then compared these data with the permitted maximum alignment on both the X and Y axes.

We determined each set's maximum alignment speed by multiplying the deviation frequencies with the test's velocity, assuming linear dispersion correlation.

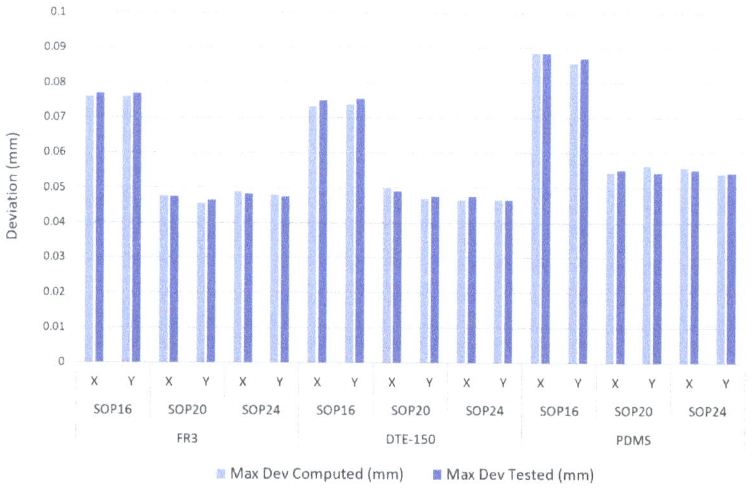

Figure 11. Accumulated deviation in the results obtained.

The results obtained present margins of relative standard errors lower than 4.78%, as shown in Figure 12. It was observed that the SOP24 package presented more deviations in the test with DPMS dielectric fluid. The SOP20 package maintained the most stable behavior, with the least deviation in the different dielectric fluids.

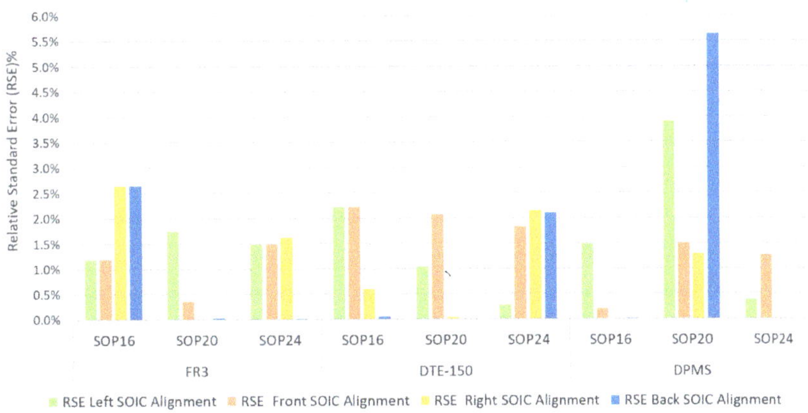

Figure 12. Descriptive statistics of the relative standard errors.

5.4. Additional Parameters Analyzed during the Tests

We observed no perceptible levels of splashing in the dielectric fluid during the SOIC package insertion. Dielectric fluid dripped and leaked during nozzle removal and testing of the SOIC package. We compared the dielectric fluid losses for every 150 tests with about 19.89 mL of FR3, 34.1 mL of DTE-150, and 51.14 mL of DPMS.

We observed that during the release of the SOIC package from the nozzle after testing, the DPMS dielectric fluid exhibited higher adhesion to the surface, in contrast to FR3, which exhibited less adherence and prevented the IC's release due to its weight.

We detected the presence of dielectric fluid in the vacuum pneumatic lines after each set of tests. However, these minimal levels of dielectric fluid did not obstruct the airflow.

6. Conclusions

We have presented the development of a systematic and scalable mathematical model to predict SOIC package misalignment during automated high-voltage IC testing in a dielectric fluid, achieving an impressive reliability of 99.64%, with a margin of error below 4.78%. This model comprehensively analyzes mechanical and hydrodynamic factors, including the crucial aspects of misalignment during the insertion and extraction of SOIC packages from ZIF sockets.

This study furthered the knowledge in the development of an energy model for high-voltage test speed calculation that seeks to improve the handling of SOIC packages in dielectric fluids in an advanced automated system, offering vital information on the rate-limiting hydrodynamic effects and precision in handling of SOIC packages.

A thorough analysis of the physical properties of dielectric fluids, including viscosity, surface tension, and density, was conducted to understand their influence on the misalignment experienced by the packages during the insertion and removal process. The proposed configuration was evaluated consistently across three types of certified dielectric fluids (FR3 vegetable oil, DPMS silicone, and DTE-150 mineral oil) and different SOIC packages, which included SOP16, SOP20, and SOP24, aligned to JEDEC's standard MC-012 [44], significantly defining the understanding of fluid dynamics and ensuring the reliability and repeatability of the results.

This study introduced novel knowledge by analyzing the forces acting on SOIC packages in air and dielectric fluid environments, including the interface between these two mediums. It developed a model to quantify energy losses in each environment where SOIC packages operate. This research highlighted the advantages and limitations of various trapezoidal motion patterns, particularly in high-speed operations, emphasizing their potential to expedite automated high-voltage testing processes.

This research also explored the mechanics of the ZIF socket and the potential effects of cavitation and splash formation when inserting the SOIC package into the dielectric fluid. This study evidenced that the DUT geometry and fluid properties significantly influence these phenomena.

This study applied Cronbach's alpha for robust statistical reliability validation, effectively confirming Gaussian distribution patterns and linear deviation correlations. It also analyzed and comprehensively evaluated misalignment probabilities, analyzing factors such as surface tension, sloshing, cavity formation, and bubble dynamics during DUT handling.

This study represents a significant contribution to the semiconductor industry in the field of high-voltage IC testing, providing an advanced model for predicting SOIC package misalignment with a resource-efficient approach that outperforms traditional trial-and-error models, improving the automated handling and validation of high-voltage isolation tests for SOIC packages.

Author Contributions: Conceptualization, Y.A.A. and M.J.; methodology, M.J.; writing—original draft, Y.A.A.; review and editing, Y.A.A. and M.J.; experimentation, Y.A.A.; data treatment and statistical analyses, Y.A.A.; tables and figures preparation, Y.A.A. All authors have read and agreed to the published version of the manuscript.

Funding: This research was supported in part by Texas Instruments, Inc. under the UPRM-TI Collaborative Program. Any opinions, findings, conclusions, or recommendations expressed in this article are those of the authors and do not necessarily reflect the views of the sponsor.

Institutional Review Board Statement: Not applicable.

Informed Consent Statement: Not applicable.

Data Availability Statement: The data presented in this study are openly available in [Data Testing deviation HV-SOIC.csv] at [https://github.com/YAAMNAY/Data_SOIC_DF_deviation.git] (accessed on 29 March 2024).

Conflicts of Interest: The authors declare no conflicts of interest. The authors declare that this study received funding from Texas Instruments, Inc. under the TI-UPRM Partnership. The funder was not involved in the study design, collection, analysis, interpretation of data, the writing of this article or the decision to submit it for publication.

References

1. Bonifield, T. *High-Voltage Isolation Quality and Reliability for amc130x*; SSZY024; Texas Instruments Incorporated: Dallas, TX, USA, 2016.
2. Kamath, A.; Soundarapandian, K. *High-Voltage Reinforced Isolation: Definitions and Test Methodologies*; Texas Instruments White Paper; Texas Instruments Incorporated: Dallas, TX, USA, 2014.
3. Thawani, V.; Reghunathan, A. *Fully Integrated Signal and Power Isolation—Applications and Benefits*; SLYY112; Texas Instrument Incorporated: Dallas, TX, USA, 2017.
4. Bonifield, T. *Enabling High Voltage Signal Isolation Quality and Reliability*; Application Note SSZY028; Texas Instruments, Inc.: Dallas, TX, USA, 2017.
5. Geng, J. The development of high-voltage repetitive low-jitter corona stabilized triggered switch. *Rev. Sci. Instrum.* **2018**, *89*, 044705. [CrossRef] [PubMed]
6. Kamath, A.; Bhardwaj, N.; Soundarapandian, K. *Understanding Failure Modes in Isolators*; Texas Instruments Incorporated: Dallas, TX, USA, 2018.
7. Azmi, K.; Jamil, M.; Ahmad, M. Breakdown voltage characteristics of RBD Palm Olein and Envirotemp FR3 mixture under quasi-uniform electric field. In Proceedings of the 2011 IEEE Colloquium on Humanities, Science and Engineering, Penang, Malaysia, 5–6 December 2011; pp. 421–424.
8. Haegele, S.; Vahidi, F.; Tenbohlen, S.; Rapp, K.; Sbravati, A. Investigation of interfacial surface creep breakdown at oil-pressboard interfaces in natural ester liquid and mineral oil. In Proceedings of the 2017 IEEE 19th International Conference on Dielectric Liquids (ICDL), Manchester, UK, 25–29 June 2017; pp. 1–5.
9. Bourbonnais, F.; Bigras, P.; Bonev, I. Minimum-time trajectory planning and control of a pick-and-place five-bar parallel robot. *IEEE/ASME Trans. Mechatron.* **2015**, *20*, 740–749. [CrossRef]
10. Bai, L.; Yang, X.; Gao, H. Corner Point-Based Coarse–Fine Method for Surface-Mount Component Positioning. *IEEE Trans. Ind. Inform.* **2018**, *14*, 877–886. [CrossRef]

11. Gokulnath, A.; Chandrakumar, S.; Sudhakar, T. Open Source Automated SMD Pick-and-Place Machine. *Procedia Comput. Sci.* **2018**, *133*, 872–878.
12. Hesse, C.; Deubel, H. Advance planning in sequential pick–and–place tasks. *J. Neurophysiol.* **2010**, *104*, 508–516. [CrossRef] [PubMed]
13. Li, X.; Yang, X.; Gao, L.; Su, Z.; Wei, X.; Lv, Z.; Liang, J.; Li, H.; Fang, F. Rapid Measurement and Identification Method for the Geometric Errors of CNC Machine Tools. *Appl. Sci.* **2019**, *9*, 2701. [CrossRef]
14. Hagel, O. Electronic Device and Method of Making the Same Using Surface Mount Technology. U.S. Patent Application 20190059160, 21 February 2019.
15. Masood, M.; Saleem, M.; Khan, U.; Hamza, A. Design, closed-form modeling and analysis of SU-8 based electrothermal microgripper for biomedical applications. *Microsyst. Technol.* **2019**, *25*, 1171–1184. [CrossRef]
16. Nally, A.; VanNorden, J.; Urquhart, J. Robotic Placement Machine for Optical Bonding, System and Method of Use Thereof. US20120234459A1, 6 February 2018.
17. Kalil Coelho, Y. Pore-scale modeling of oil mobilization trapped in a square cavity. *IEEE Lat. Am. Trans.* **2016**, *14*, 1800–1807. [CrossRef]
18. Crowe, C.T. *Multiphase Flows with Droplets and Particles*; CRC Press: Boca Raton, FL, USA, 2011; pp. 67–93.
19. Huh, C.; Scriven, L. Hydrodynamic model of steady movement of a solid/liquid/fluid contact line. *J. Colloid Interface Sci.* **1971**, *35*, 85–101. [CrossRef]
20. Vaudor, G. A consistent mass and momentum flux computation method for two phase flows. Application to atomization process. *Comput. Fluids* **2017**, *152*, 204–216. [CrossRef]
21. Özkaya, N.; Leger, D.; Goldsheyder, D.; Nordin, M.; Özkaya, N.; Leger, D.; Goldsheyder, D.; Nordin, M. Impulse and momentum. In *Fundamentals Of Biomechanics: Equilibrium, Motion, and Deformation*; Springer: New York, NY, USA, 2017; pp. 253–278
22. Langtangen, H.; Mardal, K.; Winther, R. Numerical methods for incompressible viscous flow. *Adv. Water Resour.* **2002**, *25*, 1125–1146. [CrossRef]
23. Kumar, M.; Kumar, R. On some new exact solutions of incompressible steady state Navier–Stokes equations. *Meccanica* **2014**, *49*, 335–345. [CrossRef]
24. Gresho, P.; Sani, R.; Engelman, M. *Incompressible Flow and the Finite Element Method: Advection-Diffusion and Isothermal Laminar Flow*; John Wiley & Sons: Hoboken, NJ, USA, 1998; pp. 707–847.
25. Welty, J.; Rorrer, G.; Foster, D. *Fundamentals of Momentum, Heat, and Mass Transfer*; John Wiley & Sons: Hoboken, NJ, USA, 2020; pp. 398–488.
26. Pritschow, G. Ball screw drives with enhanced bandwidth by modification of the axial bearing. *Cirp Ann.* **2013**, *62*, 383–386. [CrossRef]
27. Omron, Industrial Automation. Technical Explanation for Servomotors and Servo Drives. Servo TGE21. Available online: https://www.ia.omron.com/support/guide/14/introduction.html (accessed on 1 December 2023).
28. Devauchelle, O. Stability of bedforms in laminar flows with free surface: From bars to ripples. *J. Fluid Mech.* **2010**, *642*, 329–348. [CrossRef]
29. Cargill Inc. *Envirotemp FR3 SDS Fluid, Datasheet*; Cargill Inc.: Plymount, MN, USA, 2017. Available online: https://vantran.com/wp-content/uploads/2020/12/Envirotemp-FR3-SDS.pdf (accessed on 29 March 2024).
30. Gelest Inc. *DMS-T23 High Temperature Silicone Heat Transfer Fluid, D. Datasheet*; Gelest Inc.: Morrisville, PA, USA, 2014. Available online: https://s3.amazonaws.com/gelest/sds/DMS-T23_GHS+US_English+US.pdf (accessed on 29 March 2024).
31. Exxon Mobil Corporation. *Mobil DTE Mineral Oil Extra Heavy, IP-346. Datasheet*; Exxon Mobil Corporation: Irving, TX, USA, 2016. https://msds.exxonmobil.com/Download.aspx?ID=1005960&docFormat=PDF (accessed on 29 March 2024).
32. Inkbird Tech. *Heating Output Temperature Controller C206T User Manual*; Inkbird Tech. C.L: Shenzhen, China, 2016; pp. 1–10. Available online: https://data2.manualslib.com/pdf6/141/14053/1405273-inkbird/c206t.pdf?40b598a40d1f1d87461d5e37026 27575&take=binary (accessed on 29 March 2024).
33. Voss, W. *A Comprehensible Guide to Servo Motor Sizing*; Copperhill Media: Spring, TX, USA, 2007.
34. William, M. Quantifying Measurement. *University Physics*; Morgan & Claypool Publishers: San Rafael, CA, USA, 2016; Volume 1, pp. 105–150.
35. EADmotors. *Linear Stepper with Threaded Screw LA23ECK-N200U. Datasheet*; EADmotors: Dover, NH, USA, 2014; pp. 23–24. Available online: https://www.electrocraft.com/files/legacy/ead_step.pdf (accessed on 29 March 2024).
36. Scheck, F. *Mechanics: From Newton's Laws to Deterministic Chaos*; Springer: Berlin/Heidelberg, Germany, 2014.
37. Volodymyr, S. Modeling of Bernoulli gripping device orientation when manipulating objects along the arc. *Int. J. Adv. Robot. Syst.* **2018**, *15*, 1729881418762670.
38. Pluta, Z.; Hryniewicz, T. A developed version of the Hooke's law. *Int. Lett. Chem. Phys. Astron.* **2013**, *2*, 49–59. [CrossRef]
39. Richardson, E. The impact of a solid on a liquid surface. *Proc. Phys. Soc.* **1948**, *61*, 352. [CrossRef]
40. Yan, H. *Cavity Dynamics in Water Entry at Low Froude Numbers*; Cambridge University Press: Cambridge, UK, 2009.
41. Bormashenko, E. Wetting of flat gradient surfaces. *J. Colloid Interface Sci.* **2018**, *515*, 264–267. [CrossRef] [PubMed]
42. Brown, A.; Jepsen, R.; Yoon, S. *Modeling Large-Scale Drop Impact: Splash Criteria and Droplet Distribution*; Sandia National Lab. (SNL-NM): Albuquerque, NM, USA, 2008.

43. Murphy, D. Splash behavior and oily marine aerosol production by raindrops impacting oil slicks. *J. Fluid Mech.* **2015**, *780*, 536. [CrossRef]
44. *JEDEC's Standard MC-012*; Solid State Product Outline MS-012 Standard; Plastic Dual Small Outline Gull Wing, 1.27 mm Pitch Package. JEDEC: Arlington, VA, USA, 2020. Available online: https://www.jedec.org/system/files/docs/MS-012G-02.pdf (accessed on 22 April 2024).

applied sciences

MDPI

Communication

A Study on Automated Problem Troubleshooting in Cloud Environments with Rule Induction and Verification

Arnak Poghosyan [1,2,*], Ashot Harutyunyan [1,3,4,*], Edgar Davtyan [5], Karen Petrosyan [6] and Nelson Baloian [7]

1. VMware Inc., Palo Alto, CA 94304, USA
2. Institute of Mathematics NAS RA, Yerevan 0019, Armenia
3. ML Laboratory, Yerevan State University, Yerevan 0025, Armenia
4. Institute for Informatics and Automation Problems NAS RA, Yerevan 0014, Armenia
5. Picsart, Miami, FL 33009, USA; edgar.davtyan@picsart.com
6. College of Science and Engineering, American University of Armenia, Yerevan 0019, Armenia; karen_petrosyan2@edu.aua.am
7. Department of Computer Science, University of Chile, Santiago 8330111, Chile; nbaloian@dcc.uchile.cl

* Correspondence: arnak@instmath.sci.am (A.P.); harutyunyan.ashot@ysu.am (A.H.)

Abstract: In a vast majority of cases, remediation of IT issues encoded into domain-specific or user-defined alerts occurring in cloud environments and customer ecosystems suffers from accurate recommendations, which could be supplied in a timely manner for recovery of performance degradations. This is hard to realize by furnishing those abnormality definitions with appropriate expert knowledge, which varies from one environment to another. At the same time, in many support cases, the reported problems under Global Support Services (GSS) or Site Reliability Engineering (SRE) treatment ultimately go down to the product teams, making them waste costly development hours on investigating self-monitoring metrics of our solutions. Therefore, the lack of a systematic approach to adopting AI Ops significantly impacts the mean-time-to-resolution (MTTR) rates of problems/alerts. This would imply building, maintaining, and continuously improving/annotating a data store of insights on which ML models are trained and generalized across the whole customer base and corporate cloud services. Our ongoing study aligns with this vision and validates an approach that learns the alert resolution patterns in such a global setting and explains them using interpretable AI methodologies. The knowledge store of causative rules is then applied to predicting potential sources of the application degradation reflected in an active alert instance. In this communication, we share our experiences with a prototype solution and up-to-date analysis demonstrating how root conditions are discovered accurately for a specific type of problem. It is validated against the historical data of resolutions performed by heavy manual development efforts. We also offer experts a Dempster–Shafer theory-based rule verification framework as a what-if analysis tool to test their hypotheses about the underlying environment.

Keywords: automated troubleshooting; real-time product activity detection; problem root cause analysis; machine learning; explainable AI; proactive SaaS support

Citation: Poghosyan, A.; Harutyunyan, A.; Davtyan, E.; Petrosyan, K.; Baloian, N. A Study on Automated Problem Troubleshooting in Cloud Environments with Rule Induction and Verification. *Appl. Sci.* **2024**, *14*, 1047. https://doi.org/10.3390/app14031047

Academic Editors: Seppo Sierla, David Hästbacka and Kai Zenger

Received: 30 November 2023
Revised: 18 January 2024
Accepted: 24 January 2024
Published: 26 January 2024

1. Introduction

With the intensive evolution of IT ecosystems, such as the cloud computing infrastructures and the Internet of Things (IoT), in complexity and sophistication, automated management methods are becoming increasingly important for the industry. Performance surveillance and root cause analysis (RCA) of issues using traditional monitoring tools, dashboarding of such environments, and operator-driven correlation of occurring atomic events for inference are not sufficient to effectively derive sources of misbehaviors. Providers of cloud services, including VMware, are continuously researching novel solutions and product features with machine intelligence to address this challenge. It concerns the diagnosis of customer data centers and the products managing those assets. In particular, when a problem has been detected (reflected in an alert with related symptoms) within an application service, in most cases, it is not self-explainable in terms of its underlying reasons. Whether it comes from a machine learning (ML) module that senses an atypical or anomalous behavior (in a performance metric or a super-metric representing its health status) or user-defined conditions, identifying the potential causes of such an event among a lot of other co-occurring events remains a hard task to be delegated to another ML engine. There are no generic resolutions to this challenge in the cloud space because of the diversities and specificities in those applications with various constraints and limitations, especially when it comes to the issue of unavailability of annotated datasets for supervised learning purposes. Approaches vary on a use case basis, some of which are outlined in the related discussion in Section 2. In this regard, our goal in the current study is to design an interpretable ML approach and related system for identifying conditions of occurrence of major performance problems in the service with simple rules that are easily comprehensible for human operators. For such a goal, therefore, we have to deal with a supervised ML while finding sources of labels associated with the performance issue. In this scenario, each problem type has its special RCA model.

Currently, *Problem/Alert troubleshooting* or RCA in cloud services remains a permanent headache for product engineers despite the extensive efforts, developed concepts, and toolsets, including Aria management platform [1–4] authors working towards its enhancement with AI Ops capabilities.

Figure 1 shows a typical chain (shared with us by the partner colleagues in the relevant department) of activities that a product engineer faces across his/her troubleshooting journeys:

a. Aria Ops (former vR Ops) generates a mission-critical alert, and a customer/user cannot diagnose or even understand the situation.
b. Site Reliability Engineering (SRE) or Global Support Services (GSS) teams are involved in the issue resolution.
c. If the issue necessitates, development teams are included in the process.
d. Development spends hours and days performing root cause analysis.
e. Development provides the fix for the problem.
f. Participating engineers gain valuable domain knowledge/expertise.

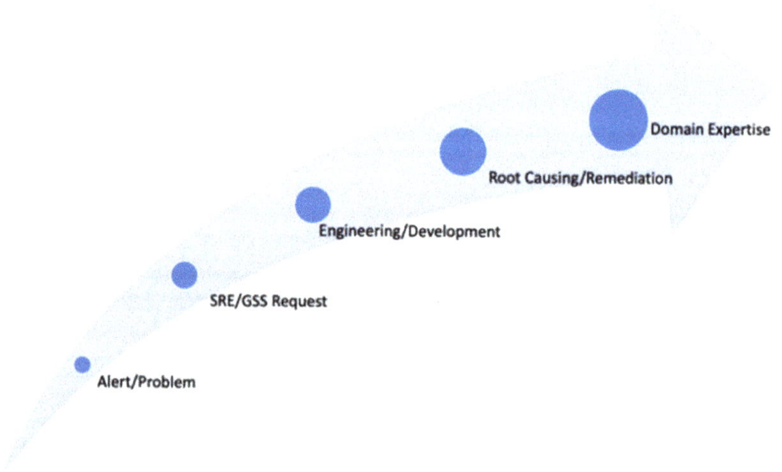

Figure 1. Typical flow in a problem resolution.

Overall, this process chain consumes varying amounts of time and human resources and implies impacts on customer business application loyalty.

At the same time, because of such intensive efforts, the knowledge gained during this process largely remains unsystematized for faster and more machine-based facilitation of handling the next cases to save critically important development resources and relocating them to the delivery of the core solutions/features in the roadmap of off-the-shelf product releases. Of course, in specific cases, when domain expertise is well developed and available, just by inspecting some performance metrics (time series) and log messages, it is quite straightforward to fix the problem with such a manual RCA. Our SRE partners in this study exemplify such situations from their experience. However, from the product perspective, the development teams have no mechanism for automatic knowledge sharing and RCA, which eventually could help the customer to quickly resolve the issue without involvement of third parties.

Our proposal is motivated by the above-mentioned traditional and inefficient ways of problem troubleshooting in such real-time services of business-critical importance and addresses the related lack of capabilities with a recommendation engine (ProbRCA), which is AI-driven and explainable for human operators. Users can easily approve/decline those recommendations for action frameworks and/or enrich related alert definitions with resolution recipes.

This paper focuses on an explainable AI Ops approach [5] (see also survey [6] on RCA methods) to automatically identify conditions that recommend the roots of a specific type of problem occurring across the customer base. Thus, separate ML models need to be trained and continuously improved with additional factual data for trending issues within the provider services. This will allow providers to fix the problems in a timely manner, and even automatically, within a global analytics service/recommender system, especially where the software-as-a-service (SaaS) delivery model is concerned (with the related opportunity to generalize cross-customer patterns based on available self-monitoring metrics of the cloud product). As previously mentioned, human ground truths are unavailable in our use case. Therefore, explainable ML methodologies become attainable with a self-labeling technique we adopt in our research while using system performance indicators (which might be a time series metric) as sources of generating labels. We recently validated this kind of self-supervised learning in the data center administration contexts in other research initiatives on cloud observability tasks (based also on log and trace data).

We also incorporate into our study a rule validation mechanism based on the Dempster–Shafer theory (DST) of evidence [7] with uncertainty modeling, which essentially provides a "what-if" analysis framework for diagnosing the underlying system and its phenomena. This allows cloud users or developers of services to rigorously verify their hypotheses about the system behavior using a recently proposed interpretable classifier [8] with expert encoded rule conditions on system features. It enables owners/experts of the cloud infrastructure or application services to build a troubleshooting knowledge base that systemizes their professional wisdom with scientifically grounded theory and explainable ML mechanisms for more effective and automated diagnosis of business-critical software for which they are responsible for healthy availability. This is another novelty aspect we incorporate into our study since, as stated in the survey [6], no specific learning algorithm was found in the literature on DST.

2. Related Research

As noted in the introduction, real-time diagnostics of offered services remains a challenge. Assistive frameworks, such as Troubleshooting Workbench (TW) by Aria Operations [1], which provide intelligent event/alert consolidation methods of guessing the origin of issues, target this critical task from different angles. TW relies on discovery of important and relevant changes occurring within a delta time-and-topology scope of the cloud infrastructure hierarchy that might provide evidence about the source of the problem, while the alert grouping concepts rely on helping users to focus on the larger incidents to make inference of the root issues easier, as well as helping to look into the problem in relation to co-occurring events across time and infra/app topology axes. However, all these methods are too inherently limited in automation capacities and intelligence power to perform deep and targeted RCA for alerts.

Other event management vendors, such as Big Panda (Redwood City, CA, USA) [9], Moogsoft (San Francisco, CA, USA) [10], and Pager Duty (San Francisco, CA, USA) [11], have adopted the consolidated insight and incident discovery strategy but also built a vision of human-driven guidance of alerts and incidents consisting of those atomic events for training supervised RCA models. An important related approach in the industry is represented by InfoSight (Miami Lakes, FL, USA) [12] by HPE, an AI-powered autonomous operations service applying analytics from global learning with a self-managing, self-healing, and self-optimizing vision for cloud applications. In this regard, ProbRCA was proposed to realize self-support for cloud management offerings with explainable features. It applies cross-customer user and developer feedback and trains accurate models over time to use them to recommend problem resolutions while interpreting/justifying those measures.

In various research initiatives (see [13]), ML methods underly the automation of the management of complex data center applications (built upon many networked objects such as virtual machines (VMs), hosts, datastores, etc.) based on large volumes of data measured from those environments for complete monitoring and observability. At the same time, cloud services must be furnished with efficient self-diagnostics capabilities for business continuity and availability to avoid/eliminate time-consuming analysis of issues by product support specialists. This is a critical problem within self-driving data centers [14]. Moreover, interpretable models (see [15,16]) in RCA are preferable compared to their black-box versions to produce justified recommendations to users and mitigate potential impacts and risks induced by those recommendations. There are specific use cases (e.g., [17–20]) recently modeled by researchers in the domain of intelligent cloud applications relevant to our current study. In some related areas, such as cellular networks [21] and cloud databases [22], authors perform domain-specific modeling for similar problem solutions, which, in our use cases, are not readily achievable because of many factors, including a lack of labeled/annotated datasets, which are hard to obtain for cloud infrastructures. In this regard, we investigate more universal ways to build RCA models while adopting self-supervised strategies in training those models.

3. Materials and Methods for ProbRCA

As an automation solution to the resource-expensive issue of managing problems in product troubleshooting, we suggest ProbRCA, an analytics system with AI Ops that builds and maintains ML models capable of learning explainable and causative patterns (remediation rules) for alert/problem types. In the Aria Ops integration scenario, this approach can automatically check the existence of those rules and proactively provide appropriate recommendations for the resolution of a problem that is not even reported yet or reflected in the alerts stream. As a result, a user quickly obtains valuable data for comprehending the problem and its possible fix, without including additional resources and avoiding the need for time-intensive investments. ProbRCA essentially supports the pipeline in Figure 2 with the building blocks summarized in the following items (reflected in the process diagram of Figure 3):

a. Aira Ops generates mission-critical alerts.
b. ProbRCA sets its general scope to the alert-related other impacted key performance indicators (KPIs) and their monitoring data for trainings.
c. Related time series metrics preprocessing, e.g., smoothing, min/max normalization, thus making the data ready for an accurate analysis.
d. Executing rule induction learning.
e. Discovered rules are added to the library of rules.
f. Relevant rules are tracked and recommended for alert resolution.

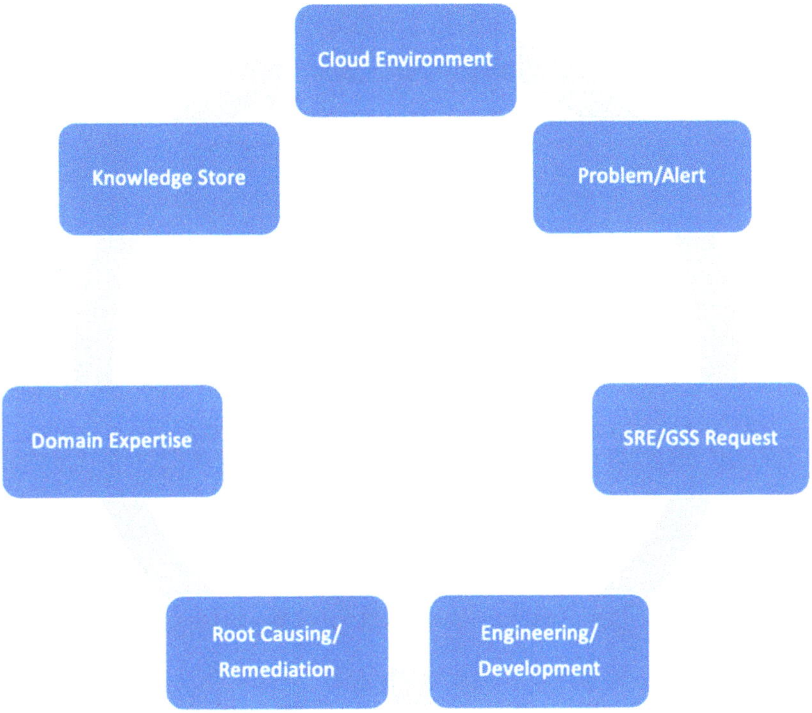

Figure 2. Proposed system (ProbRCA) with AI Ops.

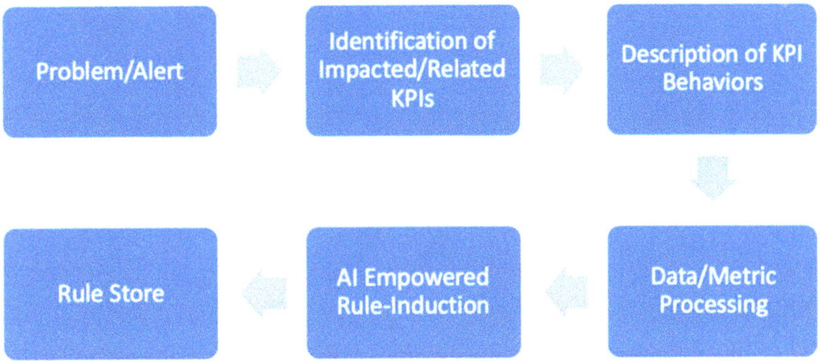

Figure 3. AI empowered rule induction.

Within the SaaS offering model, the self-monitoring metrics for Aria Ops components are owned and managed by the provider, which means that there is a huge and extremely valuable dataset from different customers to be utilized for training the ML models underlying ProbRCA and delivering real-time troubleshooting.

However, Figure 3 can make an expression in which our goal is to design a system that will automatically detect and remediate all types of IT issues. Unfortunately, that is not feasible in general. The same KPI degradations may correspond to totally different IT issues, especially in different customer environments. Figure 4 indicates that the main goal of our system is to generalize, explain, and store the experience of experts for a specific problem and with specific KPI behavior, and automate the process of the proactive detection of similar issues for potentially impacted customers with similar cloud environments. Our system also supports the knowledge transfer from experienced experts who worked for specific customer escalations and stores this information in Knowledge Datastores for further utilization by other specialists.

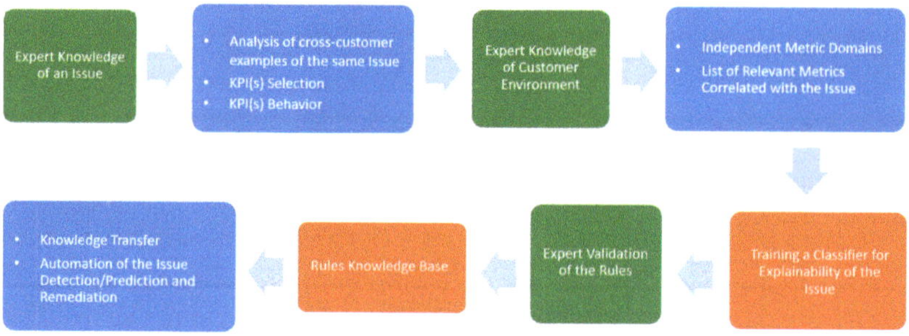

Figure 4. Expert-centric architecture of the system.

This also means that even without the most advanced AI-driven intelligence, ProbRCA may still represent problem solving, a common knowledge sharing/extraction system leveraging cross-customer insights, and a troubleshooting center relying on the basic conceptual and architectural components, as depicted in Figure 5, where reactive and proactive problem resolution depends on the availability of relevant ML models trained on the datasets identified according to the above-mentioned items and the pipeline in Figures 3 and 4.

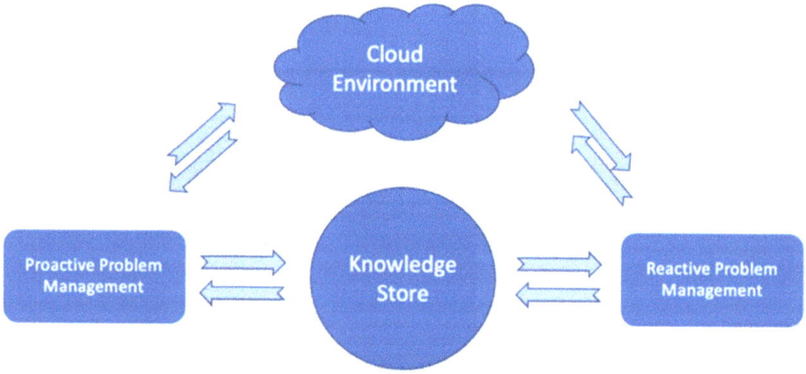

Figure 5. Knowledge-based proactive/reactive problem resolution.

Analysis of specific issues by developers at a serviced cloud eco-system with the Aria Ops management solution and the objective of finding their root causes have resulted in the following interesting lessons:

- Aria Ops collects and stores data with some monitoring intervals. The traditional monitoring interval is 5 min. This means that Aria Ops averages the available values of a metric within this interval and stores them with a time stamp corresponding to the end of that interval. As a result, the average can vary from the actual value corresponding to that specific time stamp, and the difference may be very large, especially in the case of many outliers. We noticed that due to these random fluctuations, some correlated metrics are no longer detectable by the correlation analytics in Aria Ops based on the Pearson coefficient. Hence, this effect makes the correlation engine of the product unfairly useless.
- This synchronization problem can only be resolved by the application of proper data-smoothing techniques. In our experiments, we apply a well-known min–max

smoothing technique that Aria Ops uses in UI for visualizing many data points on a small window. It takes a time window (say, 6 h), finds the minimum and maximum values of a metric, and puts them in the middle and at the end of that interval in the same order as they appeared in that interval. For example, if the minimum occurred earlier than the maximum, then the value of the minimum should be put in the middle and the value of the maximum at the end. Then, it shifts the window by 6 h and reiterates the procedure until the end of the metric.

- Aria Ops collects a vast number of metrics from cloud infrastructures and a number of self-generated metrics constructed by domain experts. The final monitored datasets contain thousands of metrics with highly correlated subsets describing the same process. As a result, the metric correlation engine, or TW, can detect hundreds of other metrics with the same behavior. However, it will be very hard to separate the metrics that describe the same process from the metrics related to different ones for the detection of possible causations. This problem can be resolved only by users with some expertise. They need to manually separate the possible domains of interrelations and skip analysis within the same areas. That is why we work separately with three different datasets below, thus manually decreasing the total number of possible correlations.
- Alerts/alarms are another source of uncertainty in Aria Ops. Many alerts are not directly connected to a problem, as user-defined ones are not always sufficiently indicative. Conversely, many problems have appeared without proper alert generation. In our example below, the problem is not connected to a known alert–the "Remote Collector Down" metric does not trigger any alert due to its fast oscillations. We found that a problem analysis always starts from the corresponding KPI and its behavior. Even if the problem description starts from an alert, the set of appropriate KPI metrics should be identified and described.
- Finally, as we mentioned before, the expert knowledge of Aria Ops engineers remains hidden in internal departments among a small number of specialists. As a rule, this knowledge is not systemized, not shared appropriately, and cannot be used for consistent and proactive management or a fast resolution of similar issues, especially in cross-customer mode.

4. Trending Problem Scenarios

Let us describe a specific trending problem for a period that has impacted many user environments (within several weeks, leading to multiple customer excavations):

Customers did not configure their firewall for Aria Ops Cloud Proxy [23] properly, which means ensuring outgoing traffic to various sub-services.

vR Ops Cloud Proxy is a primary component for data collection. In the case of the SaaS offering, it is the only appliance deployed in the customer environments and the only means of data collection. Because of this, over time, a big set of different functionalities were added to it. All this means is that whenever there is a problem with Cloud Proxy-to-vR Ops cluster communication, the data collection, alerts stream, etc., are all stopped to be serviced; in other words, vR Ops actually is not available.

Cloud Proxy basically contains two major services: the collector service, which is responsible for the collection of data from the endpoints and sending them to the vR Ops cluster, and CaSA (cluster and slice administration), which is responsible for the management of the Cloud Proxy, i.e., initial deployment, upgrade, configuration, etc. For both, as well as for the CP VM, vR Ops collects self-monitoring metrics. All the communication from Cloud Proxy to the vR Ops cluster goes out from HAproxy.

From the engineers' experience, whenever there is a problem on the customer side, e.g., deployment was not performed properly, or the network and firewall were not configured properly, tremendous efforts are required to root out the cause of the situation and validate the resolution. This is especially true in cases related to the firewall, as they require the involvement of different departments and third parties, the customer's network team, the security team, the firewall support team, and development. This results in exhausting communication back and forth and time-consuming activities. We omit listing here SRs that provide evidence for this and contain private information.

In all these cases, the situation is rather simple. It takes time until a customer notices the issue. Then GSS becomes involved, and later, developers join the investigations. Finally, it becomes clear that the cause is the customer's firewall configuration. In the best case, according to our SRE partners' estimate, it takes a week to identify and fix it, but there were cases when it took longer. Additionally, it requires much effort to prove and convince the customer that the problem is not vR Ops-related. This is a common story in practice. Furthermore, in all these cases, Cloud Proxy goes down periodically, and the cloud proxies deployed within the same network and firewall act with the same periodicity. Another observation is that a service can have issues sending the data to the vR Ops cluster in the case of a product bug. In this use case scenario, the developer's investigations lead to the discovery of a common sequence of patterns:

a. An issue with the collector service in the cloud proxy is reported;
b. The CaSA service is also not sending self-metrics;
c. However, whenever the cluster starts receiving (self-monitoring) metrics data, it is found that the cloud proxy VM was not down during the span of the issue;
d. These patterns happen periodically and synchronously.

It is then becoming clear that the problem is network-/firewall-related. We collected datasets on the problem instances of cloud proxy failures detailed above to train and validate interpretable ML algorithms capable of discovering the conditions or causes of those failures (which are already established by the developers as the ground truth of such poor performance).

5. Experiments and Discussions

According to the system diagram of ProbRCA, we conducted initial research on the above-mentioned trending problem and related identification of impacted KPIs. The status of cloud proxy down was chosen. We identified the periodicity and the same behavior for the KPI metrics in case cloud proxies share the same network and firewall. Later, we identified components that can be useful to include in our analysis with their self-monitoring metrics (i.e., collector, CaSA, and Cloud Proxy).

5.1. Data

We utilize three different datasets synchronized by the time stamps. The first dataset contains the metrics from CaSA. It has 36 metrics (columns) and 7530 metric values (rows) with a 5 min monitoring interval. Some of the metrics are "API Calls Avg Response Time", "Free Physical Memory", "Garbage Collector PS Scavenge Collection Time", "Max Heap Size", and "System Attributes Original Total Alert Count".

The second dataset contains the metrics of the collector, with 138 columns and 7530 rows (5 min monitoring interval). Engineers removed some of the redundant metrics. This dataset is composed of metrics such as "Control To Collector Task Action Status Elapsed Time Summary", "Controller To Collector Perform Action Tasks Receive", "Collector To Controller Get Adapter Ids Elapsed Time Summary".

The third dataset is a collection of cloud proxy metrics with 151 columns and 7530 rows (5 min monitoring interval). Some of the names of metrics are "Net TCP CP Close Wait", "Data Receiving Status", "Disk File System Storage DB Files Free", "Disk File System Write Bytes", "Net All Inbound Total".

5.2. Specific Results

According to our general planning, we start with identifying the KPI. For this specific problem, the corresponding alert is missing, but the "Remote Collector Down" KPI has a typical behavior shown in Figure 6. It started to oscillate, going up and down rather frequently, indicating a problem. The same behavior of the same KPI has been detected for a series of customers with totally independent cloud environments. We apply min–max smoothing with a 6 h time interval before applying more intelligent solutions. Figure 7 confirms the oscillating behavior of the KPI after the smoothing. It reduces the number of metric values from 7530 to 208.

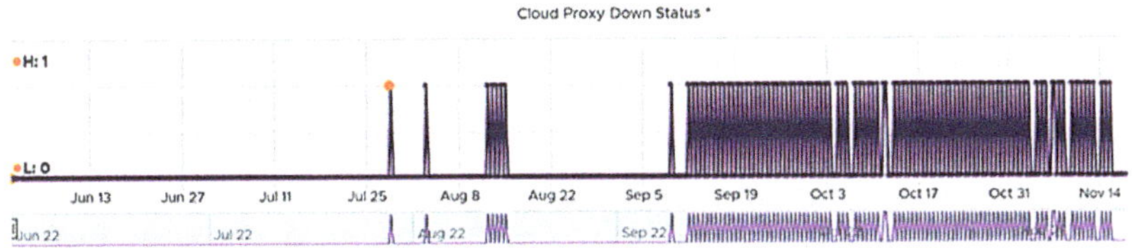

Figure 6. The oscillating behavior of the "Remote Collector Down" KPI.

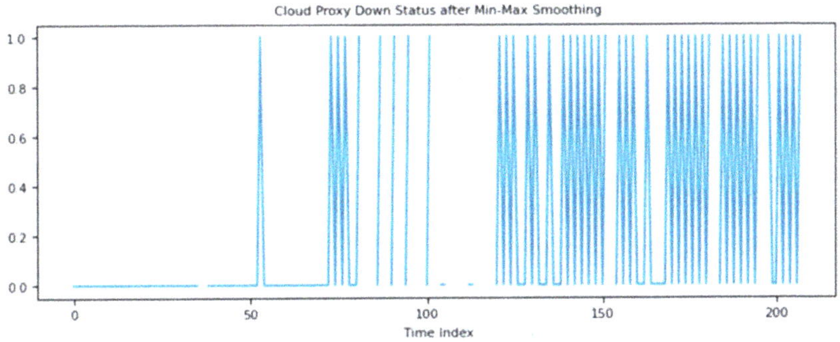

Figure 7. "Remote Collector Down" KPI metric after the min–max smoothing.

We separately analyze connections between the KPI and other indicative metrics for CaSA, collector, and Cloud Proxy. Since our research focuses on interpretable ML strategies, we apply the classification rule-induction system RIPPER (see the related literature [24,25]), which reveals rules containing the names of important metrics with some thresholds combined in conditions. The labeling of datasets is performed via the values of KPI (labels = 0, 1), where label = 1 indicates the "down" status of the cloud proxy. We detected 44 down conditions from 208 available data points.

Applying RIPPER to the CaSA dataset exposed the following rule (Rule 1):

$$\text{(CaSA API Calls Total Requests} \leq 0.1) \text{ and}$$
$$\text{(CaSA Garbage Collector Aggregated Coll. Time} \geq 0.03) \rightarrow \text{KPI} = \text{Down (23/1).}$$

The fraction at the end of the rule characterizes the importance. The number 23 shows how often the rule has been fired, and the denominator indicates the number of misclassifications. The coverage of the rule is

$$22/44 \times 100\% = 0.5\%$$

and the accuracy is

$$22/23 \times 100\% = 96\%$$

Applying RIPPER to the collector dataset detects the second rule (Rule 2):

$$(\text{Collector To Controller Lookup Resource Elapsed Time Summary} \geq 0.002) \\ \rightarrow \text{KPI} = \text{Down}\ (42/5)$$

This rule has 84% coverage and 88% confidence.

Applying RIPPER to the Cloud Proxy dataset returns the third rule (Rule 3):

$$(\text{Net TCP Listen} = 0) \rightarrow \text{KPI} = \text{Down}\ (47/9)$$

which has 86% coverage and 80% accuracy.

These rules and the KPI's specific behavior can be stored as the knowledge that can be used to identify and quickly resolve similar issues. Aria Ops engineers have verified Rules 1–3, which, in combination, indicate firewall problems.

5.3. Experimental Setup

The explainability of predictions (KPI = Up/Down) is critically important for systems owned/managed by experts. AI recommendations must be transparent and trusted, allowing experts to validate and adopt the solutions. Explainable AI (XAI) has many powerful methods with internal (built-in) and external interpretability capabilities. These can reveal the important set of features and sometimes also unveil the ranges of those features, providing a more detailed understanding of specific predictions. These recommendations, given as a set of rules, are known to provide the highest level of explainability that can be easily consumed by domain experts. Modern rule-learning methods contain several powerful classifiers. Two well-known classical approaches known as C5 rules and RIPPER are the state-of-the-art rule induction. RIPPER is especially powerful for large and noisy datasets as it scales linearly with the number of observations. However, we can equally apply both approaches as our datasets are rather small. In those cases, they show similar performance. The selection of RIPPER is simply connected with its efficient implementation in WEKA 3 machine learning software (https://www.cs.waikato.ac.nz/ml/weka/, accessed on 29 November 2023). The corresponding implementation is known as JRip (Java RIPPER).

Let us show how JRip provides the recommendations. We apply it to the first dataset (CaSA) and obtain a set of rules, as in Figure 8. The first two rules explain the positive class (KPI is Down), and the final one labels all the remaining observations from the negative class (KPI is Up). RIPPER rules have hierarchical importance. The first has the largest coverage. After removing the observations (negative and positive) that fire the first rule, we can use the second rule to explain the labels of the remaining instances. Then, we remove the observations that fire the second rule, and all the remaining instances are labeled from the negative class. Our experiments showed only the first rules, although the others can be stored as relevant. We see that RIPPER is very fast for such small datasets. It generated those three rules in 0.03 s.

JRip's output also reveals the classification measures in Figure 9. The accuracy is 86.2% for the first dataset. The corresponding evaluation is very important, as we cannot rely on the rules that eventually result in small accuracy. Similar analysis we performed for all three datasets evaluates the models' performance, calculates the precisions and recalls of the rules, and enables an expert validation if the corresponding scores are acceptable. We cannot control the number of rules. These rules can be simple or complex. Moreover, the experts can reject even very confident rules if the conclusions are frustrating or if they cannot validate them.

```
Test mode:   10-fold cross-validation
=== Classifier model (full training set) === JRIP rules ===

(CaSA API Calls Total Requests ≤ 0.1) &
(CaSA Garbage Collector Aggregated Collection Time ≥ 0.03) →
KPI = Down (23/1)

(CaSA Free Physical Memory ≥ 0.7) &
(CaSA Garbage Collector PS MarkSweep Collection Time ≥ 0.3) →
KPI = Down (17/4)

 → KPI = Up (134/9)

Number of Rules : 3
Time taken to build model: 0.03 seconds
```

Figure 8. JRip rules for the first dataset (CaSA).

```
=== Summary ===
Total Number of Instances          174
Correctly Classified Instances     150          86.2 %
Incorrectly Classified Instances    24          13.8 %

=== Detailed Accuracy By Class ===
TP Rate  FP Rate  Precision  Recall  F-Measure  MCC    ROC Area  PRC Area  Class
 0.954    0.409    0.873      0.954   0.912      0.611  0.669     0.718     Up
 0.591    0.046    0.813      0.591   0.684      0.611  0.797     0.693     Down
Weighted Avg.
 0.862    0.317    0.858      0.862   0.854      0.611  0.701     0.712

=== Confusion Matrix ===

  a    b  ←  classified as
 124   6 |  a = Up
  18  26 |  b = Down
```

Figure 9. JRip classifier performance for the first dataset (CaSA).

5.4. Rule Validation with Dempster-Shafer Theory

To generalize expert views or knowledge gained over larger contexts and measured data horizons related to various scales of product ecosystems and the workloads they manage, we alternatively study a special rule verification framework and the corresponding classifier proposed in [8]. This takes expert hypotheses as rules defined on features (and their combinations) to assess their quality, thus realizing an interpretable what-if analysis for further utilization in the knowledge store and real-time remedial executions. This framework utilizes DST of evidence or plausibility as additional assistance to help experts validate their observations about the environmental conditions in the classification setting. Thus, if their experience tells them that some patterns or behaviors of specific features within particular ranges might lead to the system misbehaving, they plug those hypotheses (in other words, rules) into the DS classifier and obtain validation of their quality, including uncertainty estimates to account for. Moreover, the classical rule induction algorithms and DS rule verification approach can be leveraged and combined, while feeding the automatically learned rules from the first strategy to be estimated with the second. In particular, Rule 1, discovered by RIPPER, obtains a low uncertainty estimate through DS rule testing:

$$\text{(CaSA API Calls Total Requests} \leq 0.1\text{) and}$$
$$\text{(CaSA Garbage Collector Aggregated Collection Time} \geq 0.03\text{)}$$

with a probability of positive class 0.943 and uncertainty 0.057.

For Rules 2 and 3 learned by RIPPER, DST results in the following estimates:

$$\text{Collector To Controller Lookup Resource Elapsed Time Summary} \geq 0.002$$

with a probability of positive class 0.861 and uncertainty 0.139; and

$$\text{Net TCP Listen} = 0$$

with a probability of positive class 0.763 and uncertainty 0.237. In the above, we see a higher uncertainty in the last rule compared to the previous ones, which indicates that there is less evidence for such a condition leading to a KPI breach.

The user of this framework can simply break value ranges (rule intervals) of all the data frame features to verify how they can be indicative, standalone, or in any combination. Here is a set of rules validated with splitting features into two ranges, which in several cases surprisingly results in high-quality rules:

$$\text{CaSA API Calls Total Requests} < 0.424,$$

with a probability of positive class 0.998 and uncertainty 0.002;

$$\text{CaSA Threads} = 0.5,$$

with a probability of positive class 0.993 and uncertainty 0.067;

$$\text{CaSA Free Physical Memory} > 0.397,$$

with a probability of positive class 0.859 and uncertainty 0.141;

$$\text{CaSA Garbage Collector PS Mark Sweep collection Time} > 0.218,$$

with a probability of positive class 0.857 and uncertainty 0.143.

Another complex rule enforced by the user obtains the following estimate:

$$\text{(CaSA GarbageCollector PS MarkSweep Collection Count} = 1\text{) and}$$
$$\text{(CaSA GarbageCollector PS Scavenge Collection Count} = 0\text{),}$$

with a probability of positive class 0.973 and uncertainty 0.027.

The two-interval split is just motivated by the simplicity of rules that experts can expect from the DS rule verification. It also has cheap performance in terms of the algorithm execution. The probability of the positive class and the uncertainty level in the rule estimated by the DST are the main factors the expert user could take into account in approving it for the Knowledge Base and linking it to the troubleshooting procedures and action frameworks. As an expert tool, the DST rule verification allows users to discover patterns/conditions that affect the KPI state, thus guiding them to focus on the corresponding attributes of the environment in root cause identification or prevention of potential misbehaviors. In one of the above rules obtained by DST rule induction, we observe that a free physical memory attribute above some level (0.397) leads to "KPI down" with high probability; thus, the user needs to take care of its tuning accordingly in order to prevent reoccurrence of the issue.

6. Evaluation of Results

We apply available knowledge to an unknown issue in our further evaluation analysis. Aria Ops detected similar problems in other customer environments. We analyze one of those problems. The "Remote Collector Down" KPI inspection showed the same behavior as in Figures 6 and 7. We detected 46 cases when the cloud proxy was down. Verification of rules showed that in the case of Rule 1, the rule was correctly fired in 31 of the cases. In the case of Rule 2, the rule was correctly fired in 32 of the cases. In the case of Rule 3, the rule was correctly fired in 38 of the cases. We can confirm the matching of the problem pattern stored in the rules' library. These highly accurate results on unseen data demonstrate the feasibility of the chosen approach and the quality of the explainable ML models trained. Figures 10 and 11 present the behavior of some of the metrics that participated in the rules in combination with the "Remote Collector Down" KPI after min–max smoothing to clarify the correlations.

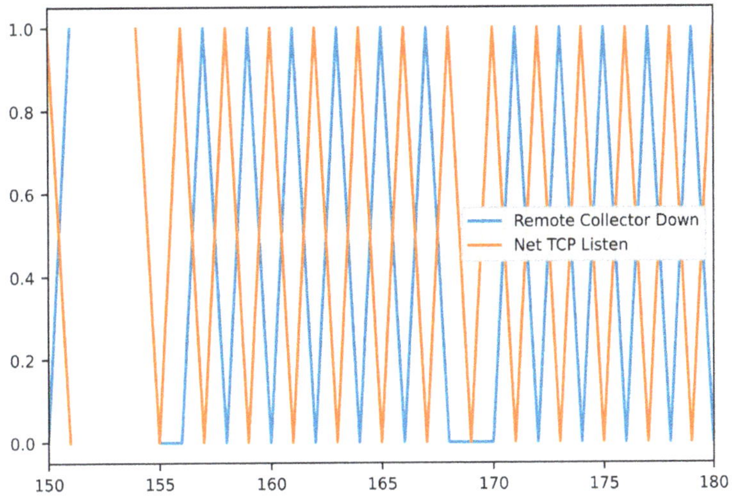

Figure 10. Behaviors of "Remote Collector Down" and "Net TCP Listen" metrics.

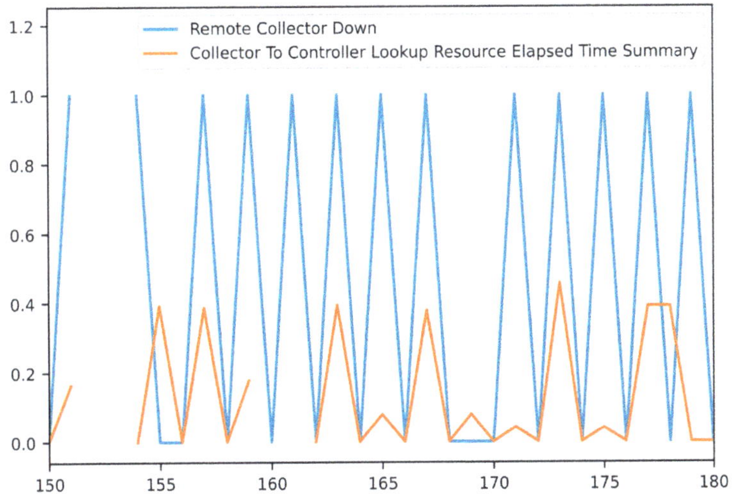

Figure 11. Behaviors of "Remote Collector Down" and "Collector to Controller . . ." metrics.

7. Conclusions and Future Work

Our study proposes an explainable ML framework for automated troubleshooting of cloud services, validating it for several trending problem use cases. It incorporates rule induction methods to learn conditions or sources of anomalous behaviors for application KPIs. Machine-detected causality conditions can enrich the alert definitions in cloud operations services, thus enhancing their event management capabilities with AI-driven problem resolution assistance as an easily achievable implication of this work. We also described our larger vision of building a real-time self-diagnostic system and RCA tool based on global learning across the customer eco-systems within the SaaS cloud delivery model. Our method demonstrated accurate predictions of the root causes of those problem types. We plan to extend our analysis to other problem types and derive insights and quality metrics from larger experimental test beds.

Architecting an end-to-end ProbRCA service requires substantial development work. Within this study, our objective was to prove the viability of such a system from a data science perspective. There are several aspects to work on for a consistent benchmarking solution design, improvement, and evaluation. Continuously retraining ML models for problem types while performing the relevant data labeling in a pipeline, performance analysis of rule induction methods for real-time recommendations, and their validation over time with user feedback mechanisms or indirect means of tracking their actions are several of those aspects. We also plan to put effort into adopting DST-based approaches to better understand this theory's frontiers and its practical significance as an apparatus for characterizing and comprehending managed services.

This communication relates to and builds upon our prior research [26,27] on various specific tasks in cloud diagnostics and administration comprising time series forecasting, anomaly and change detection in not only such structured data, but also in logs and traces, as well as abnormality root cause inference from these types of information sources. Based on these solutions, our outlook for the future of intelligent cloud management includes designing comprehensive AI-driven systems for self-driving data centers.

8. Patents

The study is supported by a filed (2023) US patent.

Author Contributions: A.P. and A.H. conceptualized ProbRCA and worked on automated rule induction, evaluation, and paper drafting. N.B. proposed the DST framework extension of ProbRCA, while E.D. and K.P. produced the corresponding experimental results. All authors contributed to the revision of the paper. All authors have read and agreed to the published version of the manuscript.

Funding: The research was supported by ADVANCE Research Grants from the Foundation for Armenian Science and Technology.

Data Availability Statement: The data presented in this study are available on request from the corresponding author. The data are not publicly available due to their proprietary and business-sensitive nature.

Acknowledgments: The authors are thankful to the anonymous reviewers for very constructive recommendations and comments, which helped improve the presentation of this material.

Conflicts of Interest: A. Poghosyan and A. Harutyunyan were employed by VMware, E. Davtyan was employed by Picsart. The remaining authors declare that the research was conducted in the absence of any commercial or financial relationships that could be construed as a potential conflict of interest.

References

1. VMware Aria Operations. Available online: https://www.vmware.com/products/vrealize-operations.html (accessed on 29 November 2023).
2. VMware Aria Operations for Applications. Available online: https://www.vmware.com/products/aria-operations-for-applications.html (accessed on 29 November 2023).

3. VMware Aria Operations for Logs. Available online: https://www.vmware.com/products/vrealize-log-insight (accessed on 29 November 2023).
4. VMware Aria Operations for Networks. Available online: https://www.vmware.com/products/vrealize-network-insight.html (accessed on 29 November 2023).
5. AI Ops by Gartner. Available online: https://www.gartner.com/en/information-technology/glossary/aiops-artificial-intelligence-operations (accessed on 29 November 2023).
6. Sole, M.; Muntes-Mulero, V.; Rana, A.I.; Estrada, G. Survey on models and techniques for root-cause analysis. *arXiv* **2017**, arXiv:1701.08546v2.
7. Shafer, G. *A Mathematical Theory of Evidence*; Princeton University Press: Princeton, NJ, USA, 1976.
8. Peñafiel, S.; Baloian, N.; Sanson, H.; Pino, J.A. Applying Dempster–Shafer theory for developing a flexible, accurate and interpretable classifier. *Expert Syst. Appl.* **2020**, *148*, 113262. [CrossRef]
9. Big Panda. Available online: https://www.bigpanda.io/ (accessed on 29 November 2023).
10. Moogsoft. Available online: https://www.moogsoft.com/ (accessed on 29 November 2023).
11. Pager Duty. Available online: https://www.pagerduty.com/ (accessed on 29 November 2023).
12. HPE InfoSight. Available online: https://www.hpe.com/us/en/solutions/infosight.html (accessed on 29 November 2023).
13. Josefsson, T. Root-Cause Analysis through Machine Learning in the Cloud. Master's Thesis, Uppsala University, Uppsala, Sweden, 2017. Available online: https://uu.diva-portal.org/smash/get/diva2:1178780/FULLTEXT01.pdf (accessed on 23 January 2024).
14. Realize the AI/ML Fundamentals of the Self-Driving Data Center with vRealize AI. 2020. Available online: https://blogs.vmware.com/cloud/2020/07/07/realize-ai-ml-fundamentals-self-driving-datacenter-vrealize-ai/ (accessed on 23 January 2024).
15. Arrieta, A.B.; Díaz-Rodríguez, N.; Del Ser, J.; Bennetot, A.; Tabik, S.; Barbado, A.; Garcia, S.; Gil-Lopez, S.; Molina, D.; Benjamins, R.; et al. Explainable Artificial Intelligence (XAI): Concepts, taxonomies, opportunities and challenges toward responsible AI. *Inf. Fusion* **2020**, *58*, 82–115. [CrossRef]
16. Ribeira, M.T.; Singh, S.; Guestrin, C. Why Should I Trust You?: Explaining the Predictions of Any Classifier. 2016. Available online: https://arxiv.org/pdf/1602.04938v1.pdf (accessed on 29 November 2023).
17. Chen, Z.; Kang, Y.; Li, L.; Zhang, X.; Zhang, H.; Xu, H.; Zhou, Y.; Yang, L.; Sun, J.; Xu, Z.; et al. Towards intelligent incident management: Why we need it and how we make it. In Proceedings of the 28th ACM Joint Meeting on European Software Engineering Conference and Symposium on the Foundations of Software Engineering (ESEC/FSE 2020), Virtual Event, 8–13 November 2020; pp. 1487–1497.
18. Lyu, Y.; Rajbahandur, G.K.; Lin, D.; Chen, B.; Jiang, Z.M. Towards a consistent interpretation of AIOps models. *ACM Trans. Softw. Eng. Methodol.* **2021**, *31*, 1–38. [CrossRef]
19. Lyu, M.R.; Su, Y. Intelligent Software Engineering for Reliable Cloud Operations. In *System Dependability and Analytics*; Wang, L., Pattabiraman, K., Di Martino, C., Athreya, A., Bagchi, S., Eds.; Springer Series in Reliability Engineering: Piscataway, NJ, USA, 2023.
20. Wang, W.; Chen, J.; Yang, L.; Zhang, H.; Wang, Z. Understanding and predicting incident mitigation time. *Inf. Softw. Technol.* **2023**, *155*, 107119. [CrossRef]
21. Mdini, M. Anomaly Detection and Root Cause Diagnosis in Cellular Networks. Ph.D. Thesis, IMT Antlantique, Rennes, France, 2019.
22. Ma, M.; Yin, Z.; Zhang, S.; Wang, S.; Zeng, C.; Jiang, X.; Hu, H.; Luo, C. Diagnosing root causes of intermittent slow queries in cloud databases. *PVLDB* **2020**, *13*, 1176–1189. [CrossRef]
23. Configuring VMware Cloud Proxies. Available online: https://docs.vmware.com/en/vRealize-Operations/Cloud/getting-started/GUID-7C52B725-4675-4A58-A0AF-6246AEFA45CD.html (accessed on 29 November 2023).
24. Cohen, W. Fast effective rule induction. In Proceedings of the 12th International Conference on Machine Learning, Tahoe City, CA, USA, 9–12 July 1995; pp. 115–123.
25. Fürnkranz, J.; Gamberger, D.; Lavrac, N. *Foundations of Rule Learning*; Springer: Berlin/Heidelberg, Germany, 2012.
26. Poghosyan, A.V.; Harutyunyan, A.N.; Grigoryan, N.M.; Kushmerick, N. Incident management for explainable and automated root cause analysis in cloud data centers. *J. Univers. Comput. Sci.* **2021**, *27*, 1152–1173. [CrossRef]
27. Harutyunyan, A.; Poghosyan, A.; Grigoryan, N.; Kushmerick, N.; Beybutyan, H. Identifying changed or sick resources from logs. In Proceedings of the 2018 IEEE 3rd International Workshops on Foundations and Applications of Self* Systems (FAS*W), Trento, Italy, 3–7 September 2018; pp. 86–91. [CrossRef]

applied sciences

MDPI

Article

Intelligent Trajectory Tracking Linear Active Disturbance Rejection Control of a Powered Parafoil Based on Twin Delayed Deep Deterministic Policy Gradient Algorithm Optimization

Yuemin Zheng [1], Zelin Fei [2], Jin Tao [3,*], Qinglin Sun [1,*], Hao Sun [1], Zengqiang Chen [1] and Mingwei Sun [1]

[1] College of Artificial Intelligence, Nankai University, Tianjin 300350, China; zhengyueminylm@163.com (Y.Z.); sunh@nankai.edu.cn (H.S.); chenzq@nankai.edu.cn (Z.C.); smw_sunmingwei@163.com (M.S.)
[2] Beijing Institute of Spacecraft Environment Engineering, Beijing 100081, China; feizelin0901@163.com
[3] Silo AI, 00100 Helsinki, Finland
* Correspondence: taoj@nankai.edu.cn (J.T.); sunql@nankai.edu.cn (Q.S.)

Abstract: Powered parafoils, known for their impressive load-bearing capacity and extended endurance, have garnered significant interest. However, the parafoil system is a highly complex nonlinear system. It primarily relies on the steering gear to change flight direction and utilizes a thrust motor for climbing. However, achieving precise trajectory tracking control presents a challenge due to the interdependence of direction and altitude control. Furthermore, underactuation and wind disturbances bring additional difficulties for trajectory tracking control. Consequently, realizing trajectory tracking control for powered parafoils holds immense significance. In this paper, we propose a trajectory tracking method based on Twin Delayed Deep Deterministic Policy Gradient (TD3) algorithm-optimized Linear Active Disturbance Rejection Control (LADRC). Our method addresses the underactuation issue by incorporating a guiding law while utilizing two LADRC methods to achieve decoupling and compensate for disturbances. Moreover, we employ the TD3 algorithm to dynamically adjust controller parameters, thus enhancing the controller performance. The simulation results demonstrate the effectiveness of our proposed method as a trajectory tracking control approach. Additionally, since the control process is not reliant on system-specific models, our method can also provide guidance for trajectory tracking control in other aircraft.

Keywords: trajectory tracking control; powered parafoil system; linear active disturbance rejection control; twin delayed deep deterministic policy gradient

Citation: Zheng, Y.; Fei, Z.; Tao, J.; Sun, Q.; Sun, H.; Chen, Z.; Sun, M. Intelligent Trajectory Tracking Linear Active Disturbance Rejection Control of a Powered Parafoil Based on Twin Delayed Deep Deterministic Policy Gradient Algorithm Optimization. *Appl. Sci.* **2023**, *13*, 12555. https://doi.org/10.3390/app132312555

Academic Editors: Seppo Sierla, David Hästbacka and Kai Zenger

Received: 5 September 2023
Revised: 8 November 2023
Accepted: 16 November 2023
Published: 21 November 2023

1. Introduction

The parafoil unmanned aerial vehicle (UAV) is a type of flexible aircraft. A conventional parafoil comprises a canopy, parachute, and payload, enabling it to carry out tasks such as airdrops and aircraft recovery. With the development of autonomous aircraft technology, powered parafoils appeared, incorporating thrust devices into the traditional parafoil design, thus enhancing their endurance capabilities [1]. Hence, powered parafoils possess the capability to execute precise tasks, such as stationary airdrops, and effective trajectory tracking control is paramount for mission success. Nevertheless, the challenges of trajectory tracking control encompass wind disturbances, underactuation, coupling, and unexpected dynamics.

A mathematical model is necessary for analyzing the motion characteristics of a parafoil system given the limitations imposed by actual flight tests, which involve substantial preparation work, time, and expenses. Currently, there are numerous ways to express models of powered parafoils. From a dynamics standpoint, this includes three-degree-of-freedom (DOF) modeling [2], four-DOF modeling [3], six-DOF modeling [4], eight-DOF modeling [5], and nine-DOF modeling [6]. Among them, the eight-DOF model takes into account the slew, sway, yaw, heave, pitch, and roll motions, as well as the relative pitch and relative yaw motion between the parafoil canopy and the payload, which effectively describe the motion state of the actual parafoil [7].

Trajectory tracking control of powered parafoils is a challenging task. The main difficulties arise from three aspects. Firstly, the actual model is more intricate than the constructed model, and there are unmodeled dynamics. Secondly, parafoil trajectory control is achieved by controlling the steering gear during flight, while altitude control is achieved through thrust, resulting in coupling and underactuation between these two control processes. Thirdly, during flight, the system is susceptible to wind disturbances, potentially leading to severe loss of control. Taking into account the issues mentioned above, research has been conducted. However, most of the literature only addresses the problem of path following [8,9]. In our opinion, the main difference between implementing trajectory tracking and path following lies in the design of the guidance law. The guidance law plays a crucial role in expressing the tracking error in alternative forms and effectively addressing the challenges of underactuation. However, in path following control, the guidance law typically overlooks the consideration of forward tracking errors [10]. For example, Sun et al. [11] formulated the guidance law as a sliding mode surface and employed linear extended state observer (LESO) to decouple horizontal path following and height tracking. Subsequently, they accomplished a three-dimensional path following control by utilizing sliding mode controllers (SMCs). Similarly, Li et al. [12] also utilized an SMC for path following control. Guo et al. [13] utilized the barrier Lyapunov function and backstepping method, and developed an adaptive path-following controller. Zheng et al. [14] introduced a horizontal path following guidance law that utilized the lateral tracking error and yaw angle, enabling control of lateral tracking and the yaw angle through flap deflection. However, the study overlooked the parafoil's sideslip angle. There are very few research results on parafoil trajectory tracking control. Li et al. [15] transformed tracking errors into guidance commands for the yaw angle and glide slope angle and employed PID controllers to achieve trajectory tracking control. For a powered parafoil without forward thrust, we proposed a new guidance law and initially realized trajectory tracking control [16]. When selecting a controller, apart from the aforementioned SMCs and PID controllers, other control methods are available, such as LADRC. LADRC is a control method that has been developed based on PID. It operates independently of model information, possesses inherent decoupling capabilities, and is straightforward to implement in engineering applications [17,18]. As a result, LADRC has demonstrated favorable outcomes in path-following control [19–21].

Parameter selection is a vital aspect of the controller configuration process as it directly impacts the tracking accuracy of the controller. Researchers commonly rely on manual tuning of controller parameters, which presents challenges in achieving optimal system performance. Consequently, there has been a continuous emergence of various optimization algorithms aimed at addressing this issue. For example, the heuristic algorithm, exemplified by particle swarm optimization (PSO) [22] and the genetic algorithm [23], is employed to optimize a set of fixed parameters of the controller [24,25]. Fuzzy control and neural networks are utilized to obtain adaptive controller parameters [26,27]. However, fuzzy control heavily relies on model information, while neural networks face challenges in making appropriate decisions based on state changes. Therefore, deep reinforcement learning (DRL) algorithms [28] that do not rely on model information and can make autonomous decisions have been promoted. DRL is a kind of algorithm that combines the computational capabilities of neural networks with the decision-making abilities of RL. Its primary objective is to train optimal decision making through continuous interactions between the agent and the environment. Currently, in the field of DRL, several algorithms have been developed, including Deep Q-Networks (DQNs) [29] and Deep Deterministic Policy Gradient (DDPG) [30]. DQNs are well suited to discrete action spaces, whereas DDPG effectively handles continuous action spaces. The Twin Delayed Deep Deterministic Policy Gradient (TD3) algorithm was developed based on DDPG with enhanced stability [31]. Current applications of the TD3 algorithm in motion control can be delineated into two main categories. The first category entails employing the TD3 algorithm directly as a controller to optimize control variables [32,33]. The second category involves integrating the TD3 algorithm with the designed controller to enhance its intelligence and performance [34]. Comparatively, the second approach exhibits noticeable improvements in training efficiency and contributes to the advancement of intelligent control systems.

Motivated by prior research, this paper presents a TD3-optimized LADRC method for the trajectory control of a powered parafoil system. The main contributions of this paper are summarized as follows:

- A guidance law for the trajectory tracking of a powered parafoil is proposed, which effectively addresses the underactuation of the system.
- Based on the guidance law, two LADRC controllers aiming to achieve 3D trajectory tracking control are designed to address challenges stemming from wind disturbances and the coupling between horizontal trajectory and altitude.
- The TD3 algorithm is employed to acquire the controller's real-time parameters by leveraging the powered parafoil's flight states. The TD3-optimized LADRC was compared against the traditional LADRC control method using simulation results, demonstrating the effectiveness of the proposed approach.

This paper is organized as follows: Section 2 establishes the eight-DOF model for the powered parafoil system. Section 3 introduces the guidance law and outlines the design process of the LADRC for horizontal trajectory and altitude control. The design process of the TD3-optimized LADRC is presented in Section 4. Section 5 presents the simulation results, and Section 6 concludes the paper.

2. Dynamic Modeling Introduction of Powered Parafoil

To provide a more precise depiction of the parafoil's motion characteristics, this paper adopts an eight-DOF dynamic model [5]. The model encompasses the parafoil canopy's slew, sway, yaw, heave, pitch, and roll movements, along with the relative pitch and yaw motions between the parafoil canopy and the payload. To facilitate the modeling of the parafoil system, three coordinate systems are introduced: the ground coordinate system, denoted as $O_d x_d y_d z_d$; the parafoil coordinate system, denoted as $O_s x_s y_s z_s$; and the payload coordinate system, denoted as $O_w x_w y_w z_w$. These coordinate systems are illustrated in Figure 1.

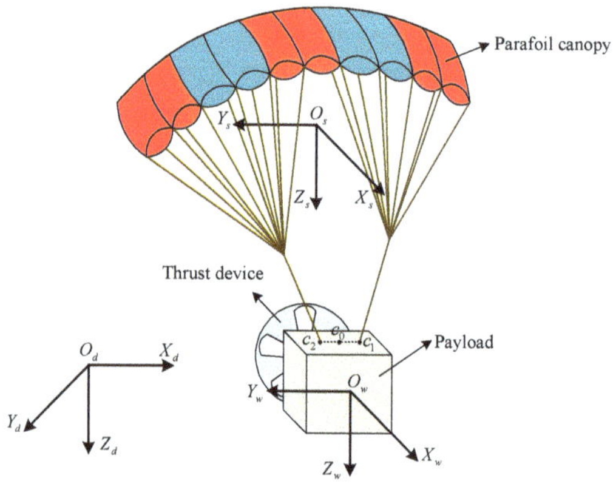

Figure 1. Schematic diagram of parafoil system coordinates.

First of all, based on Figure 1, we can observe that a powered parafoil system comprises a parafoil canopy, a payload, parafoil ropes, and a thrust device. During flight, the paracord can adjust its direction by pulling it either to the left or right. The thrust device, powered by the propeller, generates the necessary upward lift for the parafoil. Hence, compared to the conventional unpowered parafoil, the powered parafoil investigated in this study exhibits enhanced flexibility. Subsequently, we will briefly introduce the dynamic equation of the powered parafoil.

By analyzing the forces acting on the canopy and the payload, the following momentum equation can be obtained,

$$\begin{cases} \dfrac{\partial P_s}{\partial t} + W_s \times P_s = F_s^{aero} + F_s^G + F_s^t \\ \dfrac{\partial P_w}{\partial t} + W_w \times P_w = F_w^{aero} + F_w^G + F_w^t + F_w^{th} \end{cases} \tag{1}$$

where the subscripts s and w refer to the parafoil canopy and the payload, respectively, indicating the variables associated with each component. P_s and P_w represent the momentums, which are calculated as the product of the mass and velocity of the canopy or payload, respectively. In addition, the right side of the equation represents the force exerted on both the canopy and the payload. The canopy experiences the combined effects of aerodynamic force F_s^{aero}, gravity F_s^G, and the tension in the connecting ropes F_s^t. Similarly, the payload undergoes these three forces, but it is further influenced by the propeller's thrust F_w^{th}. The velocity vectors are denoted as $V_s = [u_s, v_s, w_s]^T$ and $V_w = [u_w, v_w, w_w]^T$, respectively. Similarly, the angular velocity vectors are represented by $W_s = [p_s, q_s, r_s]^T$ and $W_w = [p_w, q_w, r_w]^T$. For the specific parameters of the model in this paper, please refer to [5,35]. Equation (2) is the momentum moment equation corresponding to Equation (1),

$$\begin{cases} \dfrac{\partial H_s}{\partial t} + W_s \times H_s + V_s \times P_s = M_s^{aero} + M_s^G + M_s^f + M_s^t \\ \dfrac{\partial H_w}{\partial t} + W_w \times H_w = M_w^{aero} + M_w^f + M_w^t \end{cases} \tag{2}$$

where the moment of momentum H is obtained by multiplying the moment of inertia matrix with the angular velocity.

Indeed, by utilizing Equations (1) and (2), we can derive the dynamic equation of the powered parafoil system. This equation encompasses the state variables V_s, V_w, W_s and W_w, along with the relative yaw angle ψ_r and relative pitch angle θ_r existing between the canopy and the payload. Furthermore, the system comprises two control variables: flap deflection, expressed as $u_1(-10 \le u_1 \le 10\ \text{cm})$, and thrust, expressed as $u_2(0 \le u_2 \le 120\ \text{N})$. u_1 and u_2 represent the variables for flap deflection and thrust, respectively. The acceptable range for these variables is determined by the capabilities of the steering gear and thrust motor. The saturation value is intentionally set to safeguard the equipment. Flap deflection alters the flight direction, while thrust generates lift for the parafoil, enabling climbing. It should be pointed out that $u_1 < 0$ means pulling down the left paracord, and $u_1 > 0$ means pulling down the right paracord.

In general, the dynamic equation of the powered parafoil can be briefly described by Equation (3)

$$\dot{x}_s = f(x_s, u_1, u_2) \tag{3}$$

with $x_s = \left[V_w^T, W_w^T, V_s^T, W_s^T, \dot{\psi}_r, \dot{\theta}_r\right]^T$.

Based on the kinetic equations, the kinematic equation can be further obtained,

$$\begin{bmatrix} \dot{x} \\ \dot{y} \\ \dot{z} \end{bmatrix} = \begin{bmatrix} \cos\theta\cos\psi & \cos\theta\sin\psi & -\sin\theta \\ \sin\phi\sin\theta\cos\psi - \cos\phi\sin\psi & \sin\phi\sin\theta\sin\psi + \cos\phi\cos\psi & \sin\phi\cos\theta \\ \cos\phi\sin\theta\cos\psi + \sin\phi\sin\psi & \cos\phi\sin\theta\sin\psi - \sin\phi\cos\psi & \cos\phi\cos\theta \end{bmatrix}^T V_s \tag{4}$$

where (x, y, z) are the position coordinates of the parafoil in the earth's coordinate system. Additionally, the roll, pitch, and yaw angles are represented by $\phi(\phi \in [-\pi, \pi])$, $\theta(\theta \in [-\frac{\pi}{2}, \frac{\pi}{2}])$, and $\psi(\psi \in [-\pi, \pi])$, respectively. Equation (5) establishes the relationship between these Euler angles and the angular velocity. Furthermore, it should be noted that the pitch angle of the parafoil will not reach ±90° during flight, so there is no need to consider the issue of singular values.

$$\begin{bmatrix} \dot{\phi} \\ \dot{\theta} \\ \dot{\psi} \end{bmatrix} = \begin{bmatrix} 1 & \sin\phi\tan\theta & \cos\phi\tan\theta \\ 0 & \cos\phi & -\sin\phi \\ 0 & \sin\phi/\cos\theta & \cos\phi/\cos\theta \end{bmatrix} W_s \quad (5)$$

The above is an introduction to the model of the powered parafoil system, while the system's flight process is elucidated through dynamic equations. Furthermore, it is noteworthy that the flight state of the parafoil can be dynamically changed by implementing both the steering gear and the thrust device. As a result, this capability enables the parafoil to adeptly accomplish a wide range of predetermined trajectory tasks with remarkable flexibility. However, during the control process, when comparing the built simulation model with the actual system, the simulation model may contain uncertain factors, such as unmodeled dynamics, internal parameter perturbations, and external environmental interferences. Consequently, it becomes imperative for the designed control system to address these challenges effectively.

3. Trajectory Tracking Controller Design Based on LADRC

The trajectory tracking of a powered parafoil system faces an underactuation problem, requiring the utilization of two control variables to facilitate movement along the three coordinate axes, as shown in Figure 2. Hence, it becomes imperative to employ the guidance law before controller design to surmount the challenge posed by underactuation.

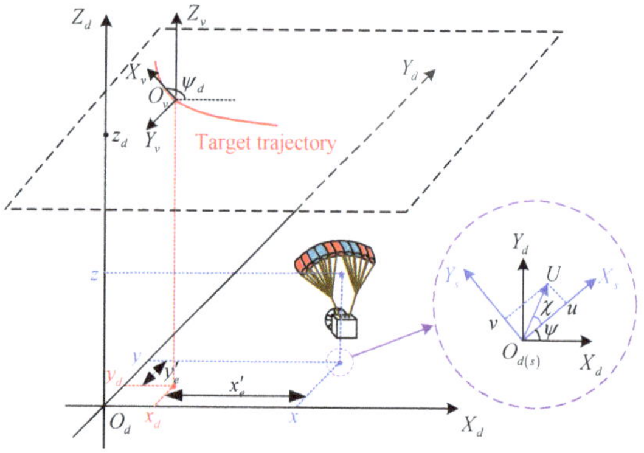

Figure 2. Schematic diagram of trajectory tracking for a powered parafoil system.

3.1. Guidance Law Design for Horizontal Trajectory

In Figure 2, (x, y, z) represents the current position of the parafoil system, while $(x_d(\varpi), y_d(\varpi), z_d(\varpi))$ denotes the target position, where ϖ is the trajectory variable. By considering (x_d, y_d, z_d) as the origin, we establish a target coordinate system denoted as $O_vX_vY_vZ_v$. Then, the horizontal trajectory tracking errors x_e and y_e in $O_vX_vY_vZ_v$ can be expressed as

$$\begin{cases} x_e = (x - x_d)\cos(\psi_d) + (y - y_d)\sin(\psi_d) \\ y_e = -(x - x_d)\sin(\psi_d) + (y - y_d)\cos(\psi_d) \end{cases} \quad (6)$$

where $\psi_d(\varpi) = \arctan(\dot{y}_d(\varpi)/\dot{x}_d(\varpi))$.

In this paper, the guidance law for the horizontal trajectory is designed as

$$\psi_g = \psi_d + \arctan(-\alpha y_e) - \chi \quad (7)$$

where α is a positive constant, ψ_g is the guided yaw angle, and $\chi = arctan(v/u)$ is the sideslip angle. Then, the following theorem arises.

Theorem 1. *Under the premise that the actual yaw angle ψ tracks the guided yaw angle ψ_g very well, the horizontal trajectory tracking error can gradually converge to 0 with the desired forward speed*

$$u_d = U\cos(\psi + \chi - \psi_d) + kx_e \tag{8}$$

where $k > 0$ and $U = \sqrt{u^2 + v^2}$.

Proof of Theorem 1. Construct a Lyapunov function as $V = \frac{1}{2}x_e^2 + \frac{1}{2}y_e^2$; then, its derivative is derived as

$$\dot{V} = x_e\dot{x}_e + y_e\dot{y}_e \tag{9}$$

According to Equation (6), the following expression can be derived,

$$\begin{cases} \dot{x}_e = U\cos(\psi + \chi - \psi_d) - u_d + \dot{\psi}_d y_e \\ \dot{y}_e = U\sin(\psi + \chi - \psi_d) - \dot{\psi}_d x_e \end{cases} \tag{10}$$

where the desired forward speed has the following expression:

$$u_d = \dot{\varpi}\sqrt{\dot{x}_d^2(\varpi) + \dot{y}_d^2(\varpi)} \tag{11}$$

With Equation (10), Equation (9) can be rearranged as

$$\dot{V} = x_e U\cos(\psi + \chi - \psi_d) - x_e u_d + y_e U\sin(\psi + \chi - \psi_d) \tag{12}$$

Further, with $\psi = \psi_g$ and substituting Equation (8) into Equation (12), the following inequality can be obtained

$$\begin{aligned} \dot{V} &= -kx_e^2 + y_e U\sin(\arctan(-\alpha y_e)) \\ &= -kx_e^2 - \alpha y_e^2 \\ &\leq 0 \end{aligned} \tag{13}$$

□

Remark 1. *The guidance law presented in Equation (7) effectively merges the lateral error y_e with the yaw angle ψ to achieve convergence of the lateral error. By altering the flight direction, this approach effectively addresses the issue of underactuation. Furthermore, by combining Equation (8) and Equation (11), we can derive the following rules for $\dot{\varpi}$:*

$$\dot{\varpi} = \frac{U\cos(\psi + \chi - \psi_d) + kx_e}{\sqrt{\dot{x}_d^2(\varpi) + \dot{y}_d^2(\varpi)}} \tag{14}$$

To conclude, when the yaw angle ψ can accurately track the guided yaw angle ψ_g stated in Equation (7), and the parameter ϖ satisfies Equation (14), it is possible to achieve horizontal trajectory tracking.

3.2. LADRC Design Process for Trajectory Tracking

Based on the guidance of the above law, it is necessary to develop a corresponding controller that can effectively regulate the steering gear of the parafoil system. This controller is essential for ensuring accurate tracking of the guidance yaw angle. Additionally, another controller is required to calculate the appropriate thrust, enabling the parafoil system to maintain a stable altitude during flight. In this paper, an LADRC controller is chosen for several reasons. One notable advantage of LADRC is its independence from model information, allowing it to handle unknown disturbances effectively. Moreover, LADRC exhibits inherent decoupling characteristics, effectively addressing the challenge of coupling between horizontal trajectory tracking and altitude tracking. This makes LADRC a suitable choice for the control system design in this study.

3.2.1. Horizontal Trajectory Tracking Controller

LADRC eliminates the need for detailed knowledge about the controlled object, as it solely requires the order relationship between the output and input variables. According to Equation (5), the following expression about ψ can be obtained,

$$\begin{aligned}\ddot{\psi} =& \frac{\sin\phi}{\cos\theta}\dot{q} + \frac{\cos\phi}{\cos\theta}\dot{r} + \frac{\sin\theta\sin 2\phi}{\cos^2\theta}q^2 - \frac{\sin\theta\sin 2\phi}{\cos^2\theta}r^2 + \frac{\cos\phi}{\cos\theta}pq - \frac{\sin\phi}{\cos\theta}pr \\ &+ \frac{2\sin\theta\cos 2\phi}{\cos^2\theta}qr\end{aligned} \tag{15}$$

Then, combining Equations (3) and (15), we obtain the following second-order system,

$$\ddot{\psi} = f_1(\cdot) + f_2(u_1) \tag{16}$$

where, due to the complexity of the model, we use the abbreviated terms f_1 and f_2 to express the system. This does not impact the design of the controller.

Furthermore, let $y = \psi - \psi_g$; then, there is

$$\ddot{y} = f_1(\cdot) + f_2(u_1) - \ddot{\psi}_g \tag{17}$$

To facilitate the design of the controller, Equation (17) is rearranged to

$$\begin{aligned}\ddot{y} &= f_1(\cdot) + f_2(u_1) - \ddot{\psi}_g - b_{01}u_1 + b_{01}u_1 \\ &= f_h + b_{01}u_1\end{aligned} \tag{18}$$

where f_h is the total disturbance and b_{01} is an adjustable parameter.

By defining the state as $x_{11} = y$, $x_{12} = \dot{y}$, and $x_{13} = f_h$, the following state space equation can be obtained,

$$\begin{cases}\dot{x}_{11} = x_{12} \\ \dot{x}_{12} = x_{13} + b_{01}u_1 \\ \dot{x}_{13} = \dot{f}_h \\ y = x_{11}\end{cases} \tag{19}$$

Consequently, a full-order LESO is utilized to estimate the above state,

$$\begin{cases}\dot{\hat{x}}_{11} = \hat{x}_{12} + \beta_{01}(y - \hat{x}_{11}) \\ \dot{\hat{x}}_{12} = \hat{x}_{13} + b_{01}u_1 + \beta_{02}(y - \hat{x}_{11}) \\ \dot{\hat{x}}_{13} = \beta_{03}(y - \hat{x}_{11})\end{cases} \tag{20}$$

where $\hat{x}_{11}$, $\hat{x}_{12}$, and $\hat{x}_{13}$ are the estimated values of x_{11}, x_{12}, and x_{13}, respectively. β_{01}, β_{02}, and β_{03} are observer gains, and these three parameters are related to the accuracy of the estimated values. Usually, the pole configuration method is used to configure the observer gain parameters to the pole $-\omega_{o1}$ ($\omega_{o1} > 0$) that can make the system stable, that is, $\beta_{01} = 3\omega_{o1}$, $\beta_{02} = 3\omega_{o1}^2$, and $\beta_{03} = \omega_{o1}^3$. In this case, only the single parameter ω_o must be adjusted to align the observed values with the actual values.

When the observed states are accurate, we have $\hat{x}_{13} \approx f_h$. Then, we can employ a PD control law to mitigate the disturbance,

$$u_1 = \frac{k_{p1}(y_d - \hat{x}_{11}) - k_{d1}\hat{x}_{12} - \hat{x}_{13}}{b_{01}} \tag{21}$$

where k_{p1} and k_{d1} are controller parameters; y_d is the desired value of y. $y_d = 0$. In addition, by substituting Equation (21) into Equation (18), we observe that the estimated disturbance value effectively compensates for the unknown disturbance within the system. This fundamental concept lies at the core of the LADRC algorithm. In addition, the stability analysis of an LADRC control system is provided in the Appendix A.

3.2.2. Altitude Controller

Altitude control is comparatively more straightforward than horizontal trajectory tracking since it does not require the implementation of guidance laws. Nevertheless, the design process for the altitude controller follows a similar approach to that of the horizontal controller, as both require knowledge of the system order.

According to Equation (4),

$$\dot{z} = -u_s \sin\theta + v_s \sin\phi \cos\theta + w_s \cos\phi \cos\theta \tag{22}$$

In fact, according to ref. [5], there exists a relationship between the parafoil canopy's speed and the thrust u_2, which can be expressed as follows,

$$\begin{cases} \dot{v}_s = \dfrac{\cos\theta_r \sin\psi_r}{m_s + m_{a,11}} u_2 + \ldots \\ \dot{u}_s = \dfrac{\cos\theta_r \cos\psi_r}{m_s + m_{a,22}} u_2 + \ldots \\ \dot{w}_s = \dfrac{-\sin\theta_r}{m_s + m_{a,33}} u_2 + \ldots \end{cases} \tag{23}$$

where the ellipsis represents items not related to u_2.

Then, further deriving Equation (22), it can be deduced that

$$\begin{aligned} \ddot{z} &= -\dot{u}_s \sin\theta + \dot{v}_s \sin\phi \cos\theta + \dot{w}_s \cos\phi \cos\theta - (u_s cos\theta + v_s sin\phi sin\theta + w_s cos\phi sin\theta)\dot{\theta} \\ &\quad -(w_s cos\theta sin\phi - v_s cos\theta cos\phi)\dot{\phi} \\ &= \left(-\frac{\cos\theta_r \cos\psi_r \sin\theta}{m_s + m_{a,22}} + \frac{\sin\phi \cos\theta \cos\theta_r \sin\psi_r}{m_s + m_{a,11}} - \frac{\sin\theta_r \cos\phi \cos\theta}{m_s + m_{a,33}} \right) u_2 + \ldots \end{aligned} \tag{24}$$

As a result, a second-order system can also be obtained:

$$\ddot{z} = f_a + b_{02} u_2 \tag{25}$$

where f_a represents the total unknown disturbance in this system.

Next, we can proceed with the sequential design of the LESO and PD control law based on Equations (19)–(21) mentioned earlier. However, the detailed description of this process is beyond the scope of this discussion.

In summary, the trajectory tracking control of a powered parafoil in this paper depends on two LADRC controllers, each requiring the adjustment of four parameters. Hence, the parameters that necessitate adjustment in the control system are as follows: ω_{o1}, k_{p1}, k_{d1}, b_{01} for the horizontal controller, and ω_{o2}, k_{p12}, k_{d2}, b_{02} for the height controller. These parameters will undoubtedly affect the trajectory tracking accuracy. To explore the parameter adjustment rules within the LADRC controller, interested readers are encouraged to consult ref. [36].

4. Optimized LADRC Approach Using TD3

Parameter tuning is indeed a sequential decision-making problem, and DRL algorithms have been proven as an effective way to solve it. The TD3 algorithm is a deep reinforcement learning algorithm designed to handle problems with a continuous action space. This paper focuses on adaptively varying the parameters, making the TD3 algorithm an ideal choice for optimizing the controller parameters. Additionally, it is worth noting that ref. [37] highlights the significance of ω_o and b_0 in ensuring the stability of the LESO. Therefore, this paper solely focuses on optimizing the parameters within the control law, namely k_p and k_d.

4.1. The Basics of the TD3 Agent

The TD3 algorithm fundamentally derives the optimal strategy by facilitating continuous interaction between the agent and the environment. This paper uses a powered parafoil system with controllers as the environment. At the same time, the agent functions as the algorithm's cognitive component, responsible for decision-making processes, as shown in Figure 3. Specifically, the agent is situated in a specific state, denoted as $s_t \in S$, at each time step. Depending on the state transition probability $P^a_{ss'} = P[s_{t+1} = s' | s_t = s, a_t = a]$ and the action value $a \in A$, the agent undergoes a transition from the current state s_t to the subsequent state s_{t+1} with a certain probability. Simultaneously, the agent receives an immediate reward $r_{t+1} \in R$ associated with this transition. S and A are the state space and action space, respectively.

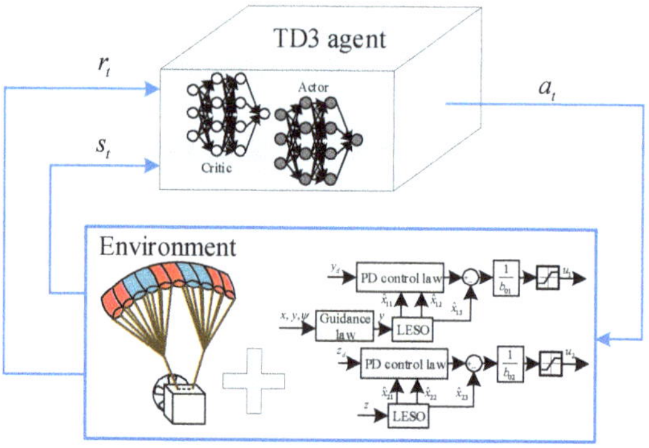

Figure 3. Schematic diagram of the interaction process.

The goal of the TD3 algorithm is to find the optimal strategy. This, of course, necessitates receiving feedback in the form of reward values. Consequently, the optimal strategy is attained by maximizing the expected value of the cumulative reward, which can be expressed as

$$\pi^* = \max_{\pi} E_{\tau \sim \pi}[R_c(\tau)] \tag{26}$$

where $R_c = \sum_{t=0}^{\infty} \gamma^t r_{t+1}$ is the cumulative reward, and the discount factor $\gamma \in (0, 1]$ is employed to represent the importance of future reward values.

The TD3 agent consists of several key components, namely a replay buffer, two critic networks, an actor network, and their respective target critic networks and target actor network, as illustrated in Figure 4. On the one hand, the critic network estimates the Q value expressed in Equation (27) by taking the state and action as inputs and generating the corresponding Q value as output, a common approach in DRL algorithms. On the other hand, the actor network is updated using the policy gradient method, which involves computing the gradient of the expected Q value concerning the actor network parameters. The parameters of the networks are represented by $\theta(\theta')$ for the critic networks and $\phi(\phi')$ for the actor network.

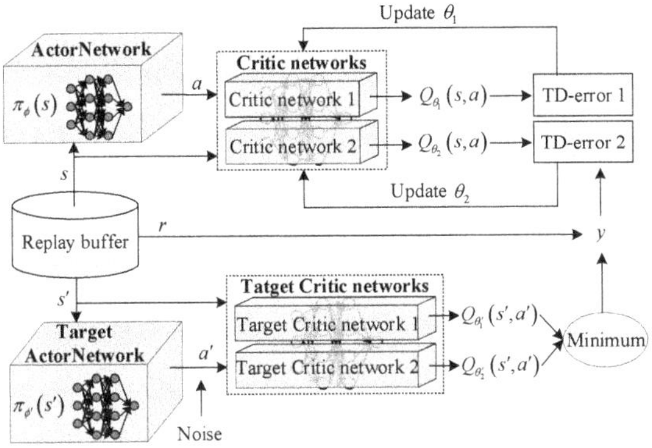

Figure 4. Structure diagram of the TD3 agent.

$$Q_\pi(s,a) = E_\pi[R_c|s_t = s, a_t = a] \tag{27}$$

The training process of the TD3 algorithm is shown in Algorithm 1.

Algorithm 1 TD3 Algorithm

Initialize critic networks $Q_{\theta_1}(s,a)$, $Q_{\theta_2}(s,a)$ and actor network $\pi_\phi(s)$ with random parameters θ_1, θ_2 and ϕ.
Initialize target networks $Q_{\theta_1'}(s,a)$, $Q_{\theta_2'}(s,a)$ and $\pi_{\phi'}(s)$ with weights $\theta_1' \leftarrow \theta_1$, $\theta_2' \leftarrow \theta_2$ and $\phi' \leftarrow \phi$.
Initialize replay buffer $\mathcal{D}$.
if $t \leq T$ **then**
  Select action with exploration noise $a \sim \pi_\phi(s) + \epsilon, \epsilon \sim \mathcal{N}(0,\sigma)$, observe reward r and new states s'.
  Store transition tuple (s,a,r,s') in $\mathcal{D}$.
  Sample mini-batch of m transitions (s,a,r,s') from $\mathcal{D}$.
  $a' \leftarrow \pi_{\phi'}(s') + \epsilon, \epsilon \sim \text{clip}(\mathcal{N}(0,\sigma'), -c, c)$.
  $y \leftarrow r + \gamma \min_{i=1,2} Q_{\theta'_i}(s',a')$.
  Update critics by $\theta_i \leftarrow \arg\min_{\theta_i} \frac{1}{m} \sum (y - Q_{\theta_i}(s,a))^2$.
  if t mod κ **then**
    Update ϕ by the deterministic policy gradient: $\nabla_\phi J(\phi) = \frac{1}{m} \sum \nabla_a Q_{\theta_1}(s,a)\big|_{a=\pi_\phi(s)} \nabla_\phi \pi_\phi(s)$.
    Update target networks by moving average method: $\theta_i' \leftarrow \tau\theta_i + (1-\tau)\theta_i'$, $\phi' \leftarrow \tau\phi + (1-\tau)\phi'$.
  end if
end if

4.2. Agent Design for Powered Parafoil System

Based on the introduction to the TD3 agent mentioned earlier, we will proceed with the design of the state space, action space, and reward function of the agent to address the powered parafoil system's trajectory tracking control problem.

The action variables within the agent are unquestionably parameters that require optimization, namely, k_{p1} and k_{d1} for the horizontal controller and k_{p2} and k_{d2} for the altitude controller. Then, the four-dimensional action space can be expressed as

$$\{a_1, a_2, a_3, a_4 \in A | a_1 = k_{p1}, a_2 = k_{d1}, a_3 = k_{p2}, a_4 = k_{d2}\} \tag{28}$$

State variables are pieces of information that the agent can directly acquire from the environment. For the trajectory tracking problem, the trajectory tracking errors directly indicate the controller's performance. Therefore, the state space is constructed as

$$\{s_1, s_2, s_3, s_4 \in S | s_1 = y, s_2 = \dot{y}, s_3 = z - z_d, s_4 = \dot{s}_3\} \tag{29}$$

In Equation (29), the impact of horizontal trajectory tracking is observed through variable y in Equation (17), with an expected value of 0. Based on the state space, it is necessary to design the reward function. The fundamental principle guiding the design of the reward function is to assign a reward when the state value approximates the desired state, otherwise applying a penalty. In this paper, the reward function is designed as follows:

$$r = -|s_1| - 5|s_3| + a + b \tag{30}$$

where

$$a = \begin{cases} 2\tanh(1/|s_1|), \text{If } \exists \ (s_1 \le 0.5 \& s_2 \le 0.05) \\ 2\tanh(1/|s_3|), \text{If } \exists \ (s_3 \le 5 \& s_4 \le 0.5) \\ 0, \text{Otherwise} \end{cases} \tag{31}$$

$$b = \begin{cases} -2, \text{If } \exists \ s_1 s_2 > 0 || s_3 s_4 > 0 \\ 0, \ \text{Otherwise} \end{cases} \tag{32}$$

In the designed reward function, the terms a and b correspond to the reward and penalty components, respectively. The two terms are employed to encourage minimal trajectory tracking errors.

Once the action space and state space have been established, the number of input and output neurons for both the critic network and actor network of the TD3 agent can be determined. To enhance the visual representation of the network structure, Figure 5 is utilized to present it more intuitively.

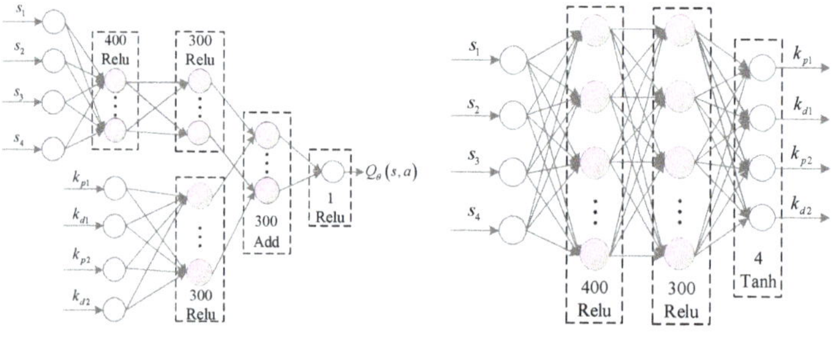

(a) Critic network (b) Actor network

Figure 5. Structure diagram of critic and actor networks.

5. Simulation Results

Table 1 illustrates the dimensions of the powered parafoil investigated in this paper. Numerical simulations were performed in the Matlab environment and executed on a laptop with an i7-10875H CPU. In addition, the hyperparameters involved in the TD3 algorithm were $\gamma = 0.99$ and $\tau = 0.005$. The simulation in this paper was completed on the MATLAB platform. The learning rate of networks was 0.001.

To validate the efficacy of the proposed TD3-LADRC method, simulation verification is performed using the model presented in Section 2. With an initial velocity of the parachute set as $V_0 = [14.9, 0, 2.1]^T$ m/s and $W_0 = [0, 0, 0]^T$ rad/s, the initial position is specified as

$(x_0, y_0, z_0) = (20, 20, 550)$ m. The initial Euler angles are defined as $[\varphi_0, \theta_0, \psi_0] = [0, 0, 0]$. In addition, suppose the following formula expresses the target trajectory:

$$\begin{cases} x_d(\varpi) = 6\varpi \\ y_d(\varpi) = 8\varpi \\ z_d = 500 \end{cases} \tag{33}$$

Table 1. Physical parameters of the powered parafoil system.

Parameter Description	Value
Wing span	4.5 m
Mean aerodynamic chord	1.3 m
Mass of parafoil	1.7 kg
Mass of payload	20 kg
Wing area	6.5 m^2
Rope length	3 m

Subsequently, the TD3-LADRC control method is employed to achieve the desired trajectory, as depicted in Equation (33). In the control system, the parameter values in the guidance law are set as $\alpha = 0.02$ and $k = 50$. For the horizontal trajectory controller, ω_o and b_0 are chosen as 5 and 0.5, respectively. Likewise, for the altitude controller, the values selected are 15 and 2, respectively. Furthermore, the action space is expressed by Equation (34). Moreover, the following four cases are considered:

- Wind-free: there is no wind during the flight;
- Wind-X: a wind of 2 m/s from the west direction is added at 60 s and lasts until the end of the simulation;
- Wind-Y: a wind of 2 m/s from the south direction is added at 60 s and lasts until the end of the simulation;
- Wind-Z: a wind of 2 m/s from the vertical direction is added at 60 s and lasts until the end of the simulation.

$$\begin{cases} k_{p1} \in [0.005, 0.05] \\ k_{d1} \in [0.1, 0.5] \\ k_{p2} \in [0.05, 0.5] \\ k_{d2} \in [1, 2] \end{cases} \tag{34}$$

The simulation results are shown in Figures 6–11. First and foremost, the results of episode rewards are displayed in Figure 6, which indicate that the TD3 agent can achieve stabilization. For the four cases mentioned above, Figure 7 displays the schematic diagrams of both the 3D and 2D trajectories. Additionally, Figure 8 illustrates the progression of the steering gear and thrust obtained by the controller. The corresponding trajectory tracking errors and the reward value change process are depicted in Figure 9. Furthermore, Figure 10 showcases the variations in Euler angles and velocity throughout the flight, while Figure 11 presents the TD3-optimized controller parameters.

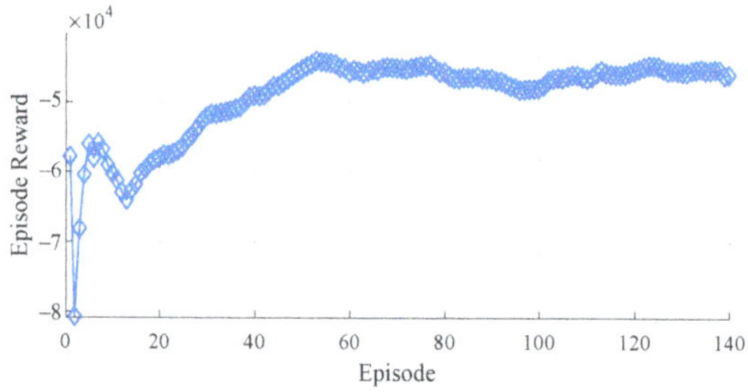

Figure 6. Episode reward for the TD3 agent.

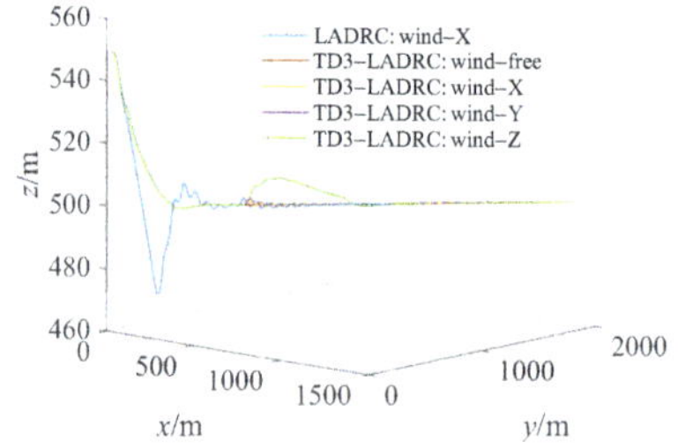

(a) 3D trajectory tracking

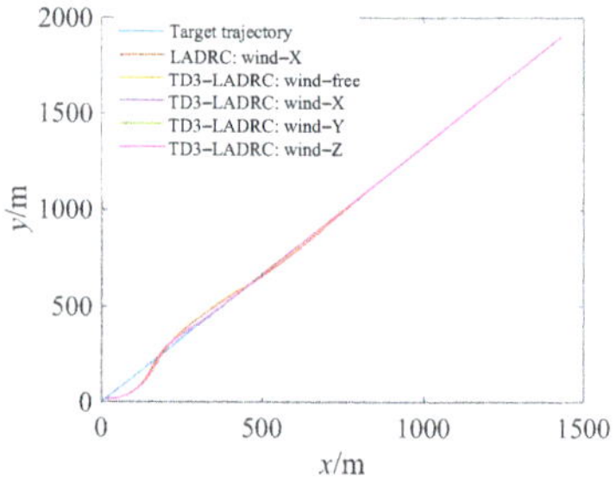

(b) Horizontal trajectory

Figure 7. Trajectory performance in different cases.

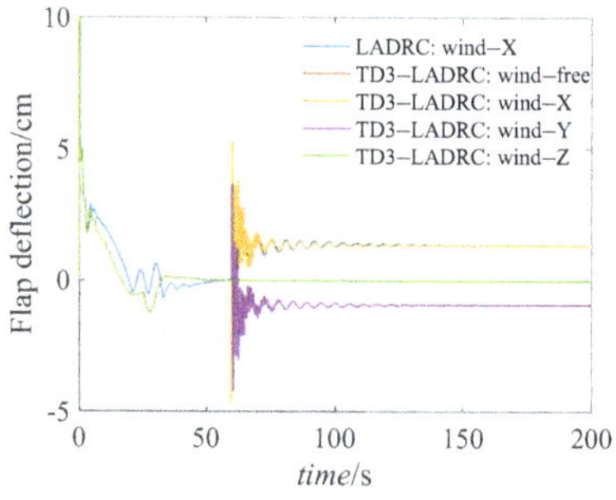

(a) Flap deflection

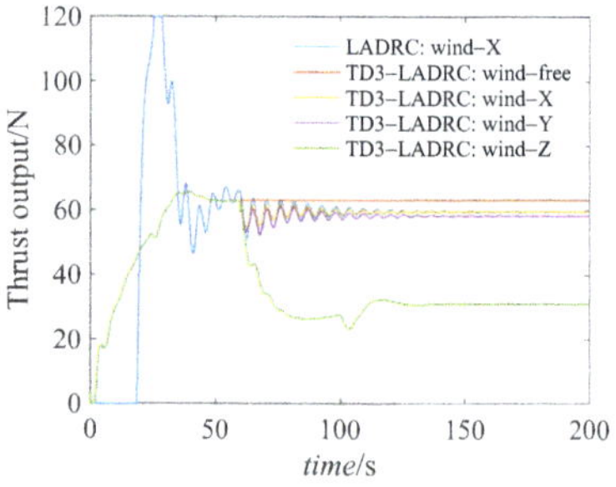

(b) Thrust output

Figure 8. Control variables.

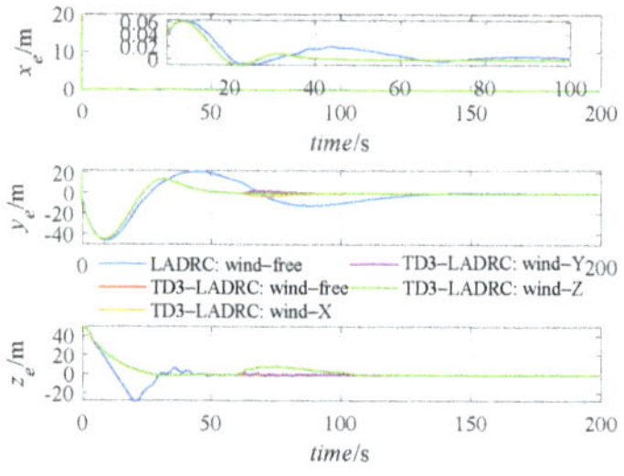

(a) Tracking errors

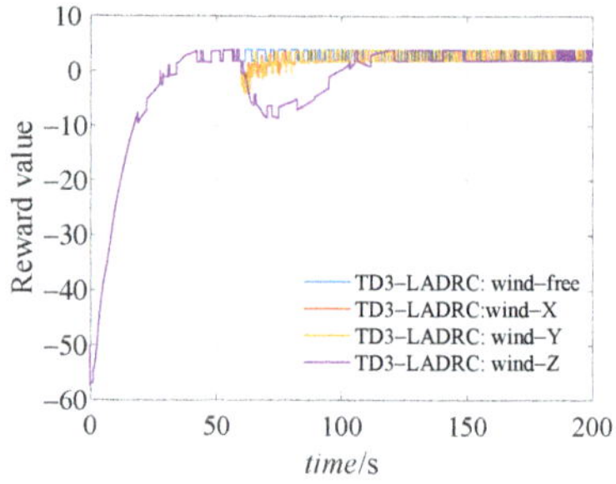

(b) Instant reward value

Figure 9. Trajectory tracking errors and the corresponding reward value.

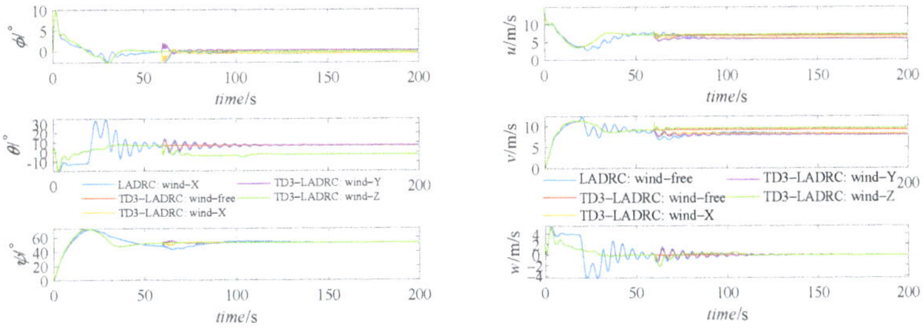

(a) Euler angles (b) Velocity component

Figure 10. Euler angles and speed change process.

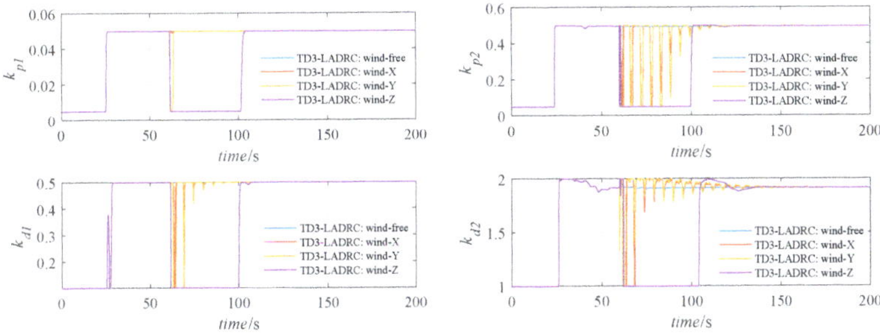

(a) Parameters of the horizontal controller (b) Parameters of the altitude controller

Figure 11. Controller parameters by TD3.

In general, our objective is to test the trajectory tracking effect of the proposed TD3-LADRC in various cases. Additionally, we compared the control effect of the LADRC with fixed parameters in the obtained results. For the fixed parameters, we selected $k_{p1} = 0.005$, $k_{d1} = 0.1$, $k_{p2} = 0.05$, and $k_{d2} = 1$. Overall, the method depicted in the results diagram can successfully accomplish trajectory tracking control. This, to a certain extent, demonstrates the effectiveness of the proposed guidance law and LADRC control method. Specifically, under the same condition of being disturbed by wind in the X direction, it can be found from Figure 7a that the trajectory tracking effect of the yellow curve is better than the blue curve, which shows that the proposed TD3-LADRC method is better than the traditional LADRC method, and this conclusion can also be further verified in Figure 9a. Observing the response of the proposed TD3-LADRC to different disturbances, it can be found that the thrust output and flap deflection will also fluctuate when they are perturbed, and they will eventually stabilize to a constant value, as illustrated in Figure 8. Furthermore, the proposed method can overcome the effects of disturbance and coupling to achieve trajectory tracking control. It can be seen from Figure 10 that the parafoil does not lose control of its attitude during flight and can fly smoothly. The selection of parameters in Figure 11 is determined based on the reward value in Figure 9b. As state changes result in fluctuations in reward values, the controller parameters experience more frequent adjustments in the presence of disturbances compared to disturbance-free scenarios. Furthermore, when subjected to the same disturbance, the trajectory tracking effect optimized by the TD3 algorithm proves superior, as evident from Figure 9a. By examining the change process of the steering gear, thrust output, and controller parameters, as illustrated in Figures 8 and 11, we observe that the system responds differently to various wind disturbances to achieve precise trajectory tracking. This observation further supports the trajectory tracking approach presented in this paper.

6. Conclusions

This paper investigates the trajectory tracking control problem in powered parafoil systems. To address the underactuation, coupling, and wind disturbance challenges during the control process, we propose an intelligent control method based on TD3-optimized LADRC. Initially, an eight-DOF model is established to simulate the actual parafoil system's flight state accurately. Subsequently, we address the underactuation issue by introducing a trajectory tracking guidance law. Moreover, we design two LADRC controllers to achieve decoupling between horizontal trajectory tracking and height control while enabling trajectory tracking control. To further enhance the trajectory tracking process, we employ the TD3 algorithm to obtain real-time parameters for the controller, thereby reducing tracking errors. The proposed method successfully achieves trajectory tracking control under various disturbance conditions, with its effectiveness duly validated.

The proposed method in this paper effectively achieves trajectory tracking control for powered parafoils and is also instructive for the trajectory tracking control of other aircraft. However, during the TD3 optimization process, finding a good balance between the horizontal and height tracking states within the reward function is a significant challenge that warrants further consideration. Assigning excessively high rewards to either state can undermine the feedback loop of the other state during the training process. We intend to continue investigating this issue in our future research. Additionally, in this paper, the configuration of the action space is manually adjusted based on multiple simulations, lacking theoretical solid justification. Addressing this limitation is a crucial aspect that requires dedicated research efforts. Furthermore, this paper did not delve into a theoretical analysis of the actor–critic framework. Some insights on this can be found in refs. [38–40], and we plan to carry out further research in this direction in the future.

Author Contributions: Conceptualization, Y.Z., Z.C. and M.S.; methodology, J.T.; software, Y.Z.; validation, Y.Z., Z.F. and J.T.; formal analysis, Y.Z.; investigation, Q.S.; resources, Q.S.; writing—original draft preparation, Y.Z. and J.T.; writing—review and editing, Q.S. and H.S.; visualization, Y.Z.; supervision, Q.S. and H.S.; funding acquisition, J.T. All authors have read and agreed to the published version of the manuscript.

Funding: This work was supported by the National Natural Science Foundation of China (Grant Nos. 61973172, 61973175, 62003175, 62003177 and 62073177) and Key Technologies Research and Development Program of Tianjin (Grant No. 19JCZDJC32800).

Institutional Review Board Statement: Not applicable.

Informed Consent Statement: Not applicable.

Data Availability Statement: The data presented in this study are available on request from the corresponding author. The data are not publicly available due to copyright issues with co-developers.

Conflicts of Interest: Author Jin Tao was employed by the company Silo AI. The remaining authors declare that the research was conducted in the absence of any commercial or financial relationships that could be construed as a potential conflict of interest.

Appendix A

This section takes the LADRC in Section 3.2.1 as an example to prove the stability of the closed-loop system. Firstly, according to the LESO in Equation (20), the estimation error vector is defined as $\varepsilon = [\varepsilon_1, \varepsilon_2, \varepsilon_3]^T$, with $\varepsilon_i = x_{1i} - \hat{x}_{1i}$. Then, the following Theorem A1 can be obtained.

Theorem A1. *Assuming that $h = \dot{f}_h$ is bounded, that is, $|h| \leq M_1$, $(M_1 > 0)$, then the observer error ε of the LESO is also bounded, that is, $|\varepsilon| \leq M_2$, $M_2 > 0$.*

Proof of Theorem A1. With Equations (19) and (20), the state space equation about ε can be derived as:

$$\dot{\varepsilon} = A_1\varepsilon + Bh \tag{A1}$$

where $A_1 = \begin{bmatrix} -\beta_{01} & 1 & 0 \\ -\beta_{02} & 0 & 1 \\ -\beta_{03} & 0 & 0 \end{bmatrix}, B = \begin{bmatrix} 0 \\ 0 \\ 1 \end{bmatrix}$.

According to Equation (A1), we have

$$\varepsilon(t) = e^{A_1 t}\varepsilon(0) + \int_0^t e^{A_1(t-\tau)} Bh d\tau \tag{A2}$$

Since A_1 is a Hurwitz matrix, there exists an invertible real matrix T that allows the following expression of A_1:

$$A_1 = T diag\{-\lambda_1, -\lambda_2, -\lambda_3\} T^{-1} \tag{A3}$$

where $-\lambda_i(\lambda_i > 0), i = 1,2,3$, represents the eigenvalues.

Then, we have

$$e^{A_1 t} = T diag\left\{e^{-\lambda_1}, e^{-\lambda_2}, e^{-\lambda_3}\right\} T^{-1} \tag{A4}$$

Further, the following inequality can be derived by $m_\infty - norm$:

$$\left\| e^{A_1 t} \right\|_{m_\infty} \leq \beta e^{-\lambda_1 t} \tag{A5}$$

where β is a constant value.

According to Equation (A5), with the assumption of $|h| \leq M_1$, Equation (A2) can have the following inequality derivation process:

$$\begin{aligned} \|\varepsilon(t)\| &= \left\| e^{A_1 t}\varepsilon(0) + \int_0^t e^{A_1(t-\tau)} Bh d\tau \right\| \\ &\leq \left\| e^{A_1 t}\varepsilon(0) \right\| + \left\| \int_0^t e^{A_1(t-\tau)} Bh d\tau \right\| \\ &\leq \left\| e^{A_1 t} \right\|_{m_\infty} \|\varepsilon(0)\| + \int_0^t \left\| e^{A_1(t-\tau)} \right\| \|B\| \|h\| d\tau \\ &\leq \beta e^{-\lambda_1 t} \|\varepsilon(0)\| + \frac{M_1 \beta}{\lambda_1}\left(1 - e^{-\lambda_1 t}\right) \\ &\leq \beta \|\varepsilon(0)\| + \frac{M_1 \beta}{\lambda_1} \\ &= M_2 \end{aligned} \tag{A6}$$

□

Theorem A2. *Assume that the control system tracks a bounded input r and the observer error satisfies*

$$\lim_{t \to \infty} \|\varepsilon(t)\| = 0 \tag{A7}$$

then the tracking errors e can also converge to 0.

Proof of Theorem A2. Let $r_1 = r$, $r_2 = \dot{r}$, $r_3 = {f'}_h$, then the tracking error vector of the controller can be defined as $\xi = [\xi_1, \xi_2]^T$, with $\xi_i = r_i - x_{1i}$. In addition, the PD control law in Equation (21) can have the normal form,

$$u_1 = \frac{k_{p1}(r_1 - \hat{x}_{11}) + k_{d1}(r_2 - \hat{x}_{12}) + (r_3 - \hat{x}_{13})}{b_{01}} \tag{A8}$$

Then, according to Equations (19) and (A8), the following expression can be derived:

$$\begin{cases} \dot{\xi}_1 = \xi_2 \\ \dot{\xi}_2 = -k_{p1}(\xi_1 + \varepsilon_1) - k_{d1}(\xi_2 + \varepsilon_2) - \xi_3 \end{cases} \tag{A9}$$

Furthermore, Equation (A9) can be expressed in another form:

$$\dot{\xi} = A_2\xi + A_3\varepsilon \tag{A10}$$

with $A_2 = \begin{bmatrix} 0 & 1 \\ -k_{p1} & -k_{d1} \end{bmatrix}$, and $A_3 = \begin{bmatrix} 0 & 0 & 0 \\ -k_{p1} & -k_{d1} & -1 \end{bmatrix}$.
Similarly, Equation (A10) has the following solution,

$$\xi(t) = e^{A_2 t}\xi(0) + \int_0^t A_3\varepsilon e^{A_2(t-\tau)}d\tau \tag{A11}$$

A_2 is also a Hurwitz matrix, thus satisfying $\left\|e^{A_2 t}\right\|_{m_\infty} \le \beta e^{-\lambda_1 t}$. As a result, there is the following inequality about $\xi(t)$,

$$\begin{aligned} \|\xi(t)\| &= \left\|\xi^{A_2 t}\xi(0) + \int_0^t A_3\varepsilon e^{A_2(t-\tau)}d\tau\right\| \\ &\le \left\|\xi^{A_2 t}\xi(0)\right\| + \left\|\int_0^t A_3\varepsilon e^{A_2(t-\tau)}d\tau\right\| \\ &\le \beta e^{-\lambda_1 t}\|\xi(0)\| + \|\varepsilon\|\|A_3\|\beta\int_0^t e^{-\lambda_1(t-\tau)}d\tau \\ &\le \beta e^{-\lambda_1 t}\|\xi(0)\| + \frac{M_2\|A_3\|\beta}{\lambda_1}\left(1 - e^{-\lambda_1 t}\right) \end{aligned} \tag{A12}$$

In accordance with the assumption presented in Equation (A7), finding the limit of ξ in Equation (A12) leads to the following result,

$$\lim_{t\to\infty}\|\xi(t)\| = 0 \tag{A13}$$

□

Remark A1. *Theorem A1 proves the stability of the linear extended state observer under the premise that the disturbance is bounded, which shows that the observation errors are bounded.*

Remark A2. *Theorem A2 further establishes that with the utilization of the expanded state observer and PD control law, the tracking error of the closed-loop system is bounded, thus ensuring the stability of the closed-loop system.*

References

1. Li, B.; He, Y.; Han, J.; Xiao, J. A new modeling scheme for powered parafoil unmanned aerial vehicle platforms: Theory and experiments. *Chin. J. Aeronaut.* **2019**, *32*, 2466–2479. [CrossRef]
2. Murali, N.; Dineshkumar, M.; WC, A.K. Parafoil trajectory comparison for optimal control and proportional controller. In Proceedings of the 2013 International Conference on Control Communication and Computing (ICCC), Thiruvananthapuram, India, 13–15 December 2013; pp. 227–232.
3. Yang, H.; Song, L.; Wang, W.; Huang, J. 4-DOF longitudinal dynamic simulation of powered-parafoil. *J. Beijing Univ. Aeronaut. Astronaut.* **2014**, *40*, 1615–1622.
4. Zhang, Z.; Zhao, Z.; Fu, Y. Dynamics analysis and simulation of six DOF parafoil system. *Clust. Comput.* **2018**, *22*, 12669–12680. [CrossRef]
5. Zhu, E.; Sun, Q.; Tan, P.; Chen, Z.; Kang, X.; He, Y. Modeling of powered parafoil based on Kirchhoff motion equation. *Nonlinear Dyn.* **2014**, *79*, 617–629. [CrossRef]
6. Guo, Y.; Yan, J.; Wu, C.; Xiao, B. Modeling and practical fixed-time attitude tracking control of a paraglider recovery system. *ISA Trans.* **2022**, *128*, 391–401. [CrossRef]
7. Hur, G.; Valasek, J. System identification of powered parafoil-vehicle from flight test data. In Proceedings of the AIAA Atmospheric Flight Mechanics Conference and Exhibit, Austin, TX, USA, 11–14 August 2003; p. 5539.
8. Feng, L.; Xing, X.; Gong, Q.; Li, Y.; Guo, Y. Trajectory Control of PFC Recovery under ADRC and Improved LOS Guidance Law. In *International Conference on Guidance, Navigation and Control*; Springer Nature: Singapore, 2022; pp. 5498–5507.
9. Guo, Y.; Yan, J.; Wu, C.; Chen, M.; Xing, X. Autonomous homing design and following for parafoil/rocket system with high-altitude. *J. Intell. Robot. Syst.* **2021**, *101*, 73. [CrossRef]

10. Viswa, S.; Avijit, B.; Sumeet, S.; Roy, S.; Nikolakopoulos, G. Adaptive control for a payload carrying spacecraft with state constraints. *Control Eng. Pract.* **2023**, *135*, 105515.
11. Sun, Q.; Yu, L.; Zheng, Y.; Tao, J.; Sun, H.; Sun, M.; Dehmer, M.; Chen, Z. Trajectory tracking control of powered parafoil system based on sliding mode control in a complex environment. *Aerosp. Sci. Technol.* **2022**, *122*, 107406. [CrossRef]
12. Li, Z.; Nan, Y. Optimal Path Planning and Tracking Control Methods for Parafoil. *Appl. Sci.* **2023**, *13*, 8115. [CrossRef]
13. Guo, Y.; Xing, X.; Wu, X.; Wu, C.; Xiao, B. Adaptive path-following control for parafoil dynamic systems with wind disturbance and rate constraint. *Nonlinear Dyn.* **2023**, *111*, 13039–13051. [CrossRef]
14. Zheng, Y.; Tao, J.; Sun, Q.; Sun, H.; Chen, Z.; Sun, M.; Duan, F. Deep-reinforcement-learning-based active disturbance rejection control for lateral path following of parafoil system. *Sustainability* **2022**, *15*, 435. [CrossRef]
15. Li, Y.; Zhao, M.; Yao, M.; Chen, Q.; Guo, R.; Sun, T.; Jiang, T.; Zhao, Z. 6-DOF modeling and 3D trajectory tracking control of a powered parafoil system. *IEEE Access* **2020**, *8*, 151087–151105. [CrossRef]
16. Zheng, Y.; Tao, J.; Sun, Q.; Sun, H.; Chen, Z.; Sun, M.; Xie, G. Sideslip angle estimation based active disturbance rejection 3D trajectory tracking control for powered parafoil system and hardware-in-the-loop simulation verification. *Aerosp. Sci. Technol.* **2023**, *141*, 108497. [CrossRef]
17. Han, J. From PID to active disturbance rejection control. *IEEE Trans. Ind. Electron.* **2019**, *56*, 900–906. [CrossRef]
18. Gao, Z. On the foundation of active disturbance rejection control. *Control Theory Appl.* **2013**, *30*, 1498–1510.
19. Xia, G.; Chu, H.; Shao, Y.; Xia, B. DSC and LADRC Path Following Control for Dynamic Positioning Ships at High Speed. In Proceedings of the 2019 IEEE International Conference on Mechatronics and Automation (ICMA), Tianjin, China, 4–7 August 2019; pp. 39–44.
20. Kang, N.; Han, Y.; Guan, T.; Wang, S. Improved ADRC-Based Autonomous Vehicle Path-Tracking Control Study Considering Lateral Stability. *Appl. Sci.* **2022**, *12*, 4660. [CrossRef]
21. Li, H.; An, X.; Feng, R.; Chen, Y. Motion Control of Autonomous Underwater Helicopter Based on Linear Active Disturbance Rejection Control with Tracking Differentiator. *Appl. Sci.* **2023**, *13*, 3836. [CrossRef]
22. Marini, F.; Walczak, B. Particle swarm optimization (PSO). A tutorial. *Chemom. Intell. Lab. Syst.* **2015**, *149*, 153–165. [CrossRef]
23. Katoch, S.; Chauhan, S.; Kumar, V. A review on genetic algorithm: Past, present, and future. *Multimed. Tools Appl.* **2021**, *80*, 8091–8126. [CrossRef]
24. Sun, X.; Xiong, Y.; Yao, M.; Tang, X.; Tian, X. A unified control method combined with improved TSF and LADRC for SRMs using modified grey wolf optimization algorithm. *ISA Trans.* **2022**, *131*, 662–671. [CrossRef]
25. Abdul-Kareem, A.I.; Hasan, A.F.; Al-Qassar, A.A.; Humaidi, A.J.; Hassan, R.F.; Ibraheem, I.K.; Azar, A.T. Rejection of wing-rock motion in delta wing aircrafts based on optimal LADRC schemes with butterfly optimization algorithm. *J. Eng. Sci. Technol.* **2022**, *17*, 2476–2495.
26. Sun, C.; Liu, C.; Feng, X.; Jiao, X. Visual servoing of flying robot based on fuzzy adaptive linear active disturbance rejection control. *IEEE Trans. Circuits Syst. II Express Briefs* **2021**, *68*, 2558–2562. [CrossRef]
27. Liu, W.; Zhao, T.; Wu, Z.; Huang, W. Linear active disturbance rejection control for hysteresis compensation based on backpropagation neural networks adaptive control. *Trans. Inst. Meas. Control* **2021**, *43*, 915–924. [CrossRef]
28. Arulkumaran, K.; Deisenroth, M.; Brundage, M.; Bharath, A.A. Deep reinforcement learning: A brief survey. *IEEE Signal Process. Mag.* **2017**, *34*, 26–38. [CrossRef]
29. Osband, I.; Blundell, C.; Pritzel, A.; Van Roy, B. Deep exploration via bootstrapped DQN. In Proceedings of the Advances in Neural Information Processing Systems, Barcelona, Spain, 5–10 December 2016; p. 29.
30. Li, S.; Wu, Y.; Cui, X.; Dong, H.; Fang, F.; Russell, S. Robust multi-agent reinforcement learning via minimax deep deterministic policy gradient. In Proceedings of the AAAI Conference on Artificial Intelligence, Honolulu, HI, USA, 27 January–1 February 2019; Volume 33, pp. 4213–4220. [CrossRef]
31. Dankwa, S.; Zheng, W. Twin-delayed ddpg: A deep reinforcement learning technique to model a continuous movement of an intelligent robot agent. In Proceedings of the 3rd International Conference on Vision, Image and Signal Processing, Vancouver, BC, Canada, 26–28 August 2019; pp. 1–5.
32. Zhang, H.; Yin, C.; Zhang, Y. Motion planning using reinforcement learning method for underactuated ship berthing. In Proceedings of the 2020 IEEE 16th International Conference on Control & Automation (ICCA), Sapporo, Japan, 9–11 October 2020; pp. 354–359.
33. Wang, Y.; Gao, Z.; Zhang, J.; Cao, X.; Zheng, D.; Gao, Y.; Ng, D.W.; Di Renzo, M. Trajectory design for UAV-based Internet of Things data collection: A deep reinforcement learning approach. *IEEE Internet Things J.* **2021**, *9*, 3899–3912. [CrossRef]
34. Chu, Z.; Sun, B.; Zhu, D.; Zhang, M.; Luo, C. Motion control of unmanned underwater vehicles via deep imitation reinforcement learning algorithm. *IET Intell. Transp. Syst.* **2020**, *14*, 764–774. [CrossRef]
35. Zhu, H.; Sun, Q.; Tao, J.; Chen, Z.; Dehmer, M.; Xie, G. Flexible modeling of parafoil delivery system in wind environments. *Commun. Nonlinear Sci. Numer. Simul.* **2022**, *108*, 106210. [CrossRef]
36. Jin, H.; Song, J.; Lan, W.; Gao, Z. On the characteristics of ADRC: A PID interpretation. *Sci. China Inf. Sci.* **2020**, *63*, 1–3. [CrossRef]
37. Qin, H.; Tan, P.; Chen, Z.; Sun, M.; Sun, Q. Deep reinforcement learning based active disturbance rejection control for ship course control. *Neurocomputing* **2022**, *484*, 99–108. [CrossRef]
38. Bu, X.; Xiao, Y.; Lei, H. An adaptive critic design-based fuzzy neural controller for hypersonic vehicles: Predefined behavioral nonaffine control. *IEEE/ASME Trans. Mechatronics* **2019**, *24*, 1871–1881. [CrossRef]

39. Bu, X.; Qi, Q. Fuzzy optimal tracking control of hypersonic flight vehicles via single-network adaptive critic design. *IEEE Trans. Fuzzy Syst.* **2020**, *30*, 270–278. [CrossRef]
40. Qi, Q.; Bu, X. Adaptive dynamic programing design for the neural control of hypersonic flight vehicles. *J. Frankl. Inst.* **2021**, *358*, 8169–8192. [CrossRef]

applied sciences

MDPI

Article

Data-Based Modelling of Chemical Oxygen Demand for Industrial Wastewater Treatment

Henri Pörhö *, Jani Tomperi, Aki Sorsa, Esko Juuso, Jari Ruuska and Mika Ruusunen

Control Engineering Research Group, Environmental and Chemical Engineering Research Unit, University of Oulu, P.O. Box 4300, 90014 Oulu, Finland; jani.tomperi@oulu.fi (J.T.); aki.sorsa@oulu.fi (A.S.); esko.juuso@oulu.fi (E.J.); jari.ruuska@oulu.fi (J.R.); mika.ruusunen@oulu.fi (M.R.)
* Correspondence: henri.porho@oulu.fi

Abstract: The aim of wastewater treatment plants (WWTPs) is to clean wastewater before it is discharged into the environment. Real-time monitoring and control will become more essential as the regulations for effluent discharges are likely to become stricter in the future. Model-based soft sensors provide a promising solution for estimating important process variables such as chemical oxygen demand (COD) and help in predicting the performance of WWTPs. This paper explores the possibility of using interpretable model structures for monitoring the influent and predicting the effluent of paper mill WWTPs by systematically finding the best model parameters using an exhaustive algorithm. Experimentation was conducted with regression models such as multiple linear regression (MLR) and partial least squares regression (PLSR), as well as LASSO regression with a nonlinear scaling function to account for nonlinearities. Some autoregressive time series models were also built. The results showed decent modelling accuracy when tested with test data acquired from a wastewater treatment process. The most notable test results included the autoregressive model with exogenous inputs for influent COD (correlation 0.89, mean absolute percentage error 8.1%) and a PLSR model for effluent COD prediction (correlation 0.77, mean absolute percentage error 7.6%) with 20 h prediction horizon. The results show that these models are accurate enough for real-time monitoring and prediction in an industrial WWTP.

Keywords: soft sensor; wastewater treatment; modelling; resource efficiency; exhaustive search

Citation: Pörhö, H.; Tomperi, J.; Sorsa, A.; Juuso, E.; Ruuska, J.; Ruusunen, M. Data-Based Modelling of Chemical Oxygen Demand for Industrial Wastewater Treatment. *Appl. Sci.* **2023**, *13*, 7848. https://doi.org/10.3390/app13137848

Academic Editor: Dino Musmarra

Received: 30 April 2023
Revised: 22 June 2023
Accepted: 1 July 2023
Published: 4 July 2023

1. Introduction

The purpose of wastewater treatment is to remove suspended solids, organic matter, nutrients and harmful compounds from water so that its quality meets certain limit values before it is discharged back to the environment, typically into the sea or a river. It is very likely that the regulations and limit values for effluent quality set by the authorities will be more stringent in the future. The influent wastewater of an industrial wastewater treatment plant (WWTP) typically contains wastewater from several sources and, therefore, depending on the sourcing process and how it is operated, the quality (e.g., temperature, amount of nutrients and organic matter) and quantity of influent can vary significantly. These changes can be profound and occur quickly, but the heart of the wastewater treatment process, i.e., biomass, adapts slowly to changes. Drastic changes may be challenging for the operation of the treatment process and affect the quality of the effluent. In addition, the treatment process includes varying delays. Hence, there is a need for real-time monitoring of the WWTP process. Real-time monitoring may include online measurements but also soft sensors. In this study, the development of soft sensors for chemical oxygen demand is studied. These soft sensors can help reduce the pollution load and increase the efficiency of the WWTP process.

Chemical oxygen demand (COD) refers to the amount of oxygen consumed by the dissolved and suspended matter in a sample when exposed to a specific oxidising agent under specific conditions [1]. In simple terms, COD provides an estimate of the overall organic pollution or contamination level in water or wastewater. COD is a measure of the wastewater's capacity to consume oxygen in chemical reactions. Typically in WWTPs, the COD is used to quantify the amount of harmful organic matter in the wastewater. The COD is, in many cases, measured in a laboratory offline from a sample or with an expensive online analyser. However, the harsh process conditions in WWTPs can cause deterioration and biofilm formation in analyser sensors that can cause interference, which can lead to reduced measurement precision over time [2]. Therefore, these sensors require constant maintenance, recalibration or replacement to keep them accurate, which is why soft sensors could prove to be a good alternative. A soft sensor can be utilised to indicate the malfunction of a hardware sensor or used instead of a hardware sensor for monitoring a process variable [3–5]. With a real-time estimator, process operators could match the process conditions to the incoming COD more accurately. Combined with a predictive effluent model, with the purpose of predicting the amount of COD discharged into the water basins, the WWTP operation could be optimised to treat the maximum amount of wastewater with minimal effort for both environmental and economic gain.

Regression models such as partial least squares regression (PLSR) and multiple linear regression (MLR) have been used to estimate the COD and other quality parameters in the past [6]. Mujunen et al. [7] utilised PLSR to estimate COD reduction among other parameters to analyse the treatment efficiency of a pulp and paper mill WWTP, using a large number of variables from the WWTP and a forward stepwise procedure to select the variables. One year later, in a similar study, Teppola et al. [8] utilised multiple linear regression, principal component regression and PLSR with a Kalman filter to update regression model coefficients to model COD reduction. Woo et al. [9] applied kernel partial least squares to model the COD, total nitrogen and cyanide of an industrial coke WWTP and compared the results with conventional linear PLSR. They found that the kernel partial least squares method was able to capture the nonlinearities of the WWTP and provide a better estimate for the modelled variables when compared to the linear PLSR. Dürrenmatt and Gujer [10] used generalised least squares regression (along with other modelling methods) to estimate the effluent COD in primary clarifiers and the ammonia concentration in activated sludge tanks. They found that simple linear models could be used accurately as soft sensors in a municipal wastewater treatment setting. Abouzari et al. [11] estimated the COD of a petrochemical wastewater treatment plant using various linear and nonlinear methods. They found that piece-wise regression linear regression provided relatively high accuracy and had better reliability compared to other methods. More recent studies on industrial applications have focused more on either nonlinear model structures or hybrid model structures and have been a popular research topic, as it is believed that these kinds of hybrid models could capture both nonlinear and linear behaviour [12].

Machine learning methods have also been a popular option in studies where soft sensing or prediction of process performance has been the focus [13–16]. Yang et al. [17] used a nonlinear autoregressive network with exogenous inputs (NARX) model to predict effluent COD and total nitrogen and compared the results with artificial neural network (ANN) models. Wang et al. [2] compared nine different machine learning algorithms in total to predict effluent COD. The resulting models demonstrated a high degree of precision. Zhang et al. [18] proposed a novel modelling method using dynamic Bayesian networks with variable importance in projection for soft sensor applications. The study included comparisons of their new modelling method to PLSR, ANN and other Bayesian networks. Many studies focus on nonlinear machine learning models, which provide little knowledge on how a modelled variable could be controlled [19]. These models are also difficult to implement in practice, which is why there is a significant need for models that could be directly derived from process measurements and easily implemented into practice.

In terms of studies where WWTP influent is monitored, municipal WWTPs have been a popular topic of research. This is largely due to rain having a large effect on the operation of municipal WWTPs, as the source of the incoming wastewater naturally greatly affects the characteristics of the wastewater and WWTP operation. Similar modelling methods have been used in studies where influent quality parameters are modelled [20–23]. However, since the main purpose of this research is to study industrial wastewater treatment, these studies are not further explored here.

This research aims to improve the utilisation of online process measurements in the context of industrial wastewater treatment plants. Online COD measurement is difficult and laborious to maintain. If left unmaintained, the measurement reliability is compromised. In addition, the sampling interval for online measurement is four hours, but with a soft sensor, the sampling interval can be reduced. Thus, this study focuses on models that can replace the online measurement device. The aims of this study are to form models for influent and effluent COD using available process data. The first target is to develop an accurate model for the influent, specifically to provide a basis for a soft sensor that estimates COD levels. This model gives online information about the influent COD. The second target is to construct a predictive model for effluent quality. The working principle of this model is similar to the influent model, but the goal is to predict the remaining COD in the wastewater before the wastewater is discharged, assuming the process conditions remain unchanged. The model proposed can be used for online monitoring of the WWTP. Because it predicts future effluent COD values, the information it provides can even be used to prevent undesired changes in the process. It is essential that models developed for both targets possess a high degree of interpretability and are sufficiently straightforward to enable direct implementation using process measurements. For this purpose, this work focuses on straightforward linear model structures.

WWTP process data contain many variables, from which one must be able to select the most important ones for the modelling. The selection of input variables is typically conducted based on available data using either an input variable selection method or process knowledge. The literature reports many techniques for automatic variable selection. This study does not use these, and thus these methods are not described here. An interested reader can find an excellent review of these, for example, by Guyon and Elisseeff [24]. In this study, an exhaustive algorithm is utilised to systematically test various combinations of online process variables from a pool of variables together with delays and model structures. Furthermore, suitable training windows are systematically browsed. By systematically sifting through the data, valuable information for modelling can be found. The key advantage of the whole approach is that it enables a comprehensive exploration of the entire dataset and model structures. In this study, the following model structures are examined: multiple linear regression (MLR), partial least squares regression (PLSR), autoregressive exogenous model (ARX), autoregressive moving average with exogenous input model (ARMAX) and least absolute shrinkage and selection operator (LASSO). Overall, this method offers a thorough approach to variable selection, enabling the extraction of important information from the available data and the creation of straightforward, interpretable models with real-world applicability.

This paper is organised in the following manner: Section 2.1 includes general knowledge about soft sensor development and the challenges related to it. Sections 2.2 and 2.3 includes an introduction to the case WWTP and to the data collected from the plant. They outline the key characteristics and configuration of the WWTP, as well as how the data are used for modelling work. Section 2.4 discusses how these data were pre-processed to be used for modelling purposes. It explores the techniques used to transform the data to ensure their suitability for subsequent modelling purposes. Section 2.5 includes a discussion of the proposed modelling approach. Sections 2.6 and 2.7 includes descriptions of the model structures utilised in this work, as well as the validation procedures used to assess their performance and accuracy. Lastly, Section 3 includes results from the modelling work and discussion.

2. Materials and Methods

2.1. Soft Sensor Development

Soft sensors are mathematical models that combine the outputs of one or more hardware sensors to estimate the targeted variable. A data-based soft sensor uses historical data to predict or estimate the variable of interest, even when direct measurements are not readily available. One of the main advantages of soft sensors is that they enable the estimation of hard-to-measure variables by a created mathematical model that consists of easy-to-measure variables. The mathematical models used in soft sensors are usually derived from data using statistical or machine learning methods. For the soft sensor output to be reliable, there needs to be a large amount of relevant data for soft sensor training [25].

One of the challenges is to find relevant data for model training. The data used for training and validation of the data-derived model should be of high quality to ensure a high-quality soft sensor. There can be various issues related to the data, such as nonlinear behaviour, different process phases and multicollinearity, which make modelling more difficult. Challenges related to information can relate to possible process deviations, sensor faults or over-fitting, or deterioration of the soft sensor model, all of which can make the development of soft sensor models more difficult. Lastly, challenges can be related to the implementation of expert knowledge. Leveraging process knowledge can be valuable in tasks such as pre-selecting relevant process variables or manually detecting outliers in the data, which can enhance the accuracy and reliability of the soft sensor model. Process knowledge can be utilised, for example, in the pre-selection of a process variable or manual detection of outliers [26]. Overall, these challenges in data acquisition, data-related issues, information challenges and utilisation of expert knowledge can pose significant hurdles in the development and successful implementation of high-quality soft sensor models.

2.2. Wastewater Treatment Plant

Data from a certain wastewater treatment plant related to a paper manufacturing plant were utilised in this study. A simplified schematic of the wastewater treatment plant in question is depicted in Figure 1. The wastewater leading to the WWTP originates from multiple sources. These sources include paper machines and the debarking process. The wastewaters from paper machines flow to the wastewater tank as individual streams. This tank also includes the wastewater from debarking. In addition, one wastewater stream (paper machine filtrate) enters the pumping station after primary clarification. The positions where online COD is measured are indicated in Figure 1.

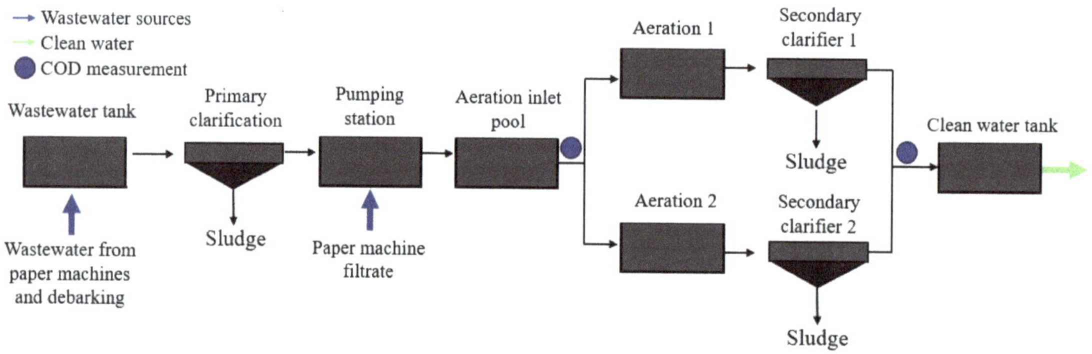

Figure 1. Simplified schematic of the studied wastewater treatment plant and activated sludge process.

The wastewater purification process at the plant consists of primary clarification as a primary treatment method and activated sludge process as a secondary treatment. The primary clarifier plays a crucial role in removing pollutants from the wastewater. It operates by allowing the settling of heavier or more readily separable solids at the bottom of the clarifier, forming a sludge layer, while the clarified water is collected from the top. The primary clarification helps improve the overall efficiency and cost-effectiveness of the process. After the primary clarifier, the paper machine filtrate stream is mixed with the rest of the wastewater. This combined wastewater is then pumped into a tank to wait for aeration. At this point, the wastewater quality measurements that are important for assessing the effectiveness of the treatment process and monitoring the performance of the plant are taken. Parameters such as COD, temperature, pH and other indicators provide valuable information about the overall condition of the wastewater going into aeration. The wastewater is then divided into two streams for the rest of the wastewater treatment. Next, the wastewater streams are sent to biological wastewater treatment, where the wastewater is mixed with air in a tank during the aeration process. The continuous circulation of air promotes the degradation of organic matter present in wastewater through the action of microorganisms. Following the biological treatment (aeration) stage, the wastewater undergoes the final treatment step in a secondary clarifier. In this step, the remaining pollutants and sludge are separated and removed from the wastewater, further improving its quality. The sludge is collected and further processed for disposal or potential reuse. Once the wastewater has undergone all the mentioned treatment steps, it is considered sufficiently treated and ready for discharge into the river. This final step ensures that the purified wastewater meets regulatory requirements and minimises its impact on the receiving water body.

2.3. Data Collection

Three datasets were received from an actual WWTP process, including online measurements from the automation system. Data from the related paper machine were also received. Online data were stored at a one-minute frequency. Table 1 shows the relevant information about the datasets used.

Table 1. Dataset content information and its usage for modelling.

Data	Length	Variables	Variable Info	Dataset Usage
Dataset 1	1 year	44	Wastewater treatment process data	Effluent model development
Dataset 2	4.5 months	31	Wastewater treatment process data	Influent and effluent model development
Dataset 3	6 months	17	Wastewater data from paper machines	Influent and effluent model development

Dataset 1 was the largest of the received datasets, containing one year's worth of data. The initial dataset from the plant included 44 online measurements. From these measurements, 27 were chosen for the next step after the data pre-processing phase. Some variables were neglected because they contained no useful information. The measurements in Dataset 1 included data on temperature, pressure, flow rate, liquid level and various quality measurements from the wastewater process. Dataset 2 included similar data to Dataset 1, i.e., measurements from the wastewater treatment plant, but it covered only the summer period. Dataset 3 included measurements about WWTP influent obtained from the paper machine automation system and covered about the same time period as Dataset 2. These data were crucial for the development of the influent soft sensor. Dataset 2 spanned approximately 4.5 months, while Dataset 3 covered a period of six months. Datasets 2 and 3 were aligned and merged, and thus, about 1.5 month period from Dataset 3 was removed.

Dataset 1 was utilised as training data in developing the predictive effluent model. Dataset 2 served two purposes. Firstly, it was used as validation data for the predictive effluent model. Secondly, it was utilised in conjunction with Dataset 3 for developing an influent soft sensor model.

The device responsible for online COD measurement extracts periodic wastewater samples at a four-hour frequency. These samples undergo thorough analysis giving the online data that are promptly recorded within the automation system. This means that online data for the targeted variables are updated roughly every four hours. This applies to both the influent and effluent COD measurements.

2.4. Data Pre-Processing

The data were pre-processed using MATLAB® software. The purpose of data pre-processing was to process the available data into the most complete form so that it could be used for modelling purposes. This included multiple steps. Firstly, variables that were constant (such as set point values for certain variables) were removed from the datasets. Variables were also removed if they included many Not a Number (NaN) values. Such variables contained no useful information from the modelling perspective.

The NaN values were replaced with interpolated values. Removal of NaN values from the data is important because they can cause issues with mathematical operations and modelling methods later. In this study, linear interpolation was employed to replace NaN values, utilising either the last known value or the next known value. The choice between these options depended on factors such as whether the variable began or ended with a NaN value.

Removal of NaN values was followed by an automatic outlier detection method. Outlier detection is an important step in data analysis and modelling. Firstly, it helps ensure data quality by identifying and addressing data errors, leading to higher data integrity and reliability. It also enables accurate statistical analysis by preventing distortions in data distribution and calculations of statistical measures. The 'quartiles' method was used to identify outlier points automatically [27]. In this method, data elements that are 1.5 interquartile range (IQR) below the lower quartile or above the upper quartile are automatically classified as outliers. The IQR can be calculated as in Equation (1):

$$IQR = Q_3 - Q_1, \tag{1}$$

where Q_3 represents the upper quartile (75 per cent of values from lowest to highest) and Q_1 the lower quartile (25 per cent of values from lowest to highest). After detecting the points that are above or below 1.5 IQR of their respective quartile, the points were marked as outliers and changed to NaN values. This was performed so that the locations of these points would not go missing during deletion, as the removal of values from different parts between datasets would lead to discontinuity with the data timestamps if removed directly.

Usually, during this part of data pre-processing, data timestamps would also have to be fixed. However, the timestamps did not include any errors or multiple values, which is why the timestamps could be ignored during the data pre-processing and modelling as every data point was recorded at steady one-minute intervals.

Next, data points from the dataset, which were clearly outliers (such as negative pH values), were changed to NaN values. Other outlier points were detected by manually inspecting the data for possible outliers. Possible outlier points were left in the dataset if it was unclear whether the point was an outlier or a correct reading. The NaN values were then replaced with interpolated values similarly to before.

Once all outliers and NaN values were removed and interpolated from the data, the data were standardised. Standardisation is performed so that every variable uses the same common scale and can be performed with many different formulas. However, since most of the variables in the datasets were close to normally distributed, the standardisation was performed using the standard score formula (Equation (2)) [28]:

$$Z_i = \frac{x_i - \overline{x}}{S} \tag{2}$$

where $\overline{x}$ is the mean, and S is the standard distribution of the variable being standardised. The standard score Z_i represents how many standard deviations the actual value x_i differs from the variable mean.

The datasets were then sampled utilising a moving median [29], where a median from a certain point window is used to represent all the data points from that window. The data points that were used to calculate the median were removed afterward, and only one point remained to represent all the removed values. Consequently, this means that the number of data points in each variable decreases drastically without losing any critical information. This type of averaging is beneficial as it allows more efficient calculation as well as filtering of the data. The efficient calculation is important later as an algorithm is utilised in the modelling part, which can be considered computationally heavy. The original minute data were reduced to a median of two-hour time intervals between data points.

As the last step of the pre-processing stage, the variables in the datasets were subjected to a nonlinear scaling algorithm with the purpose of making linear methodologies applicable to nonlinear cases. The nonlinear scaling algorithm was developed by Juuso [30]. The purpose of this method is to consider the nonlinear effects of the data. The scaling function transforms the data and scales it to a range of [−2, +2] using two monotonously increasing functions. One function is identified for the range of [−2, 0] and the other for the range of [0, +2]. Nonlinear scaling of variables is mainly utilised in regression modelling. Experiments were also performed without nonlinear scaling.

2.5. Modelling Methodology

Modelling of the influent COD and effluent COD was carried out by testing different model structures on both cases and tuning the optimal model parameters utilising an exhaustive algorithm. Figure 2 shows the overall flow of the modelling methodology steps, including the data pre-processing and analysis steps that were discussed in detail in the earlier section.

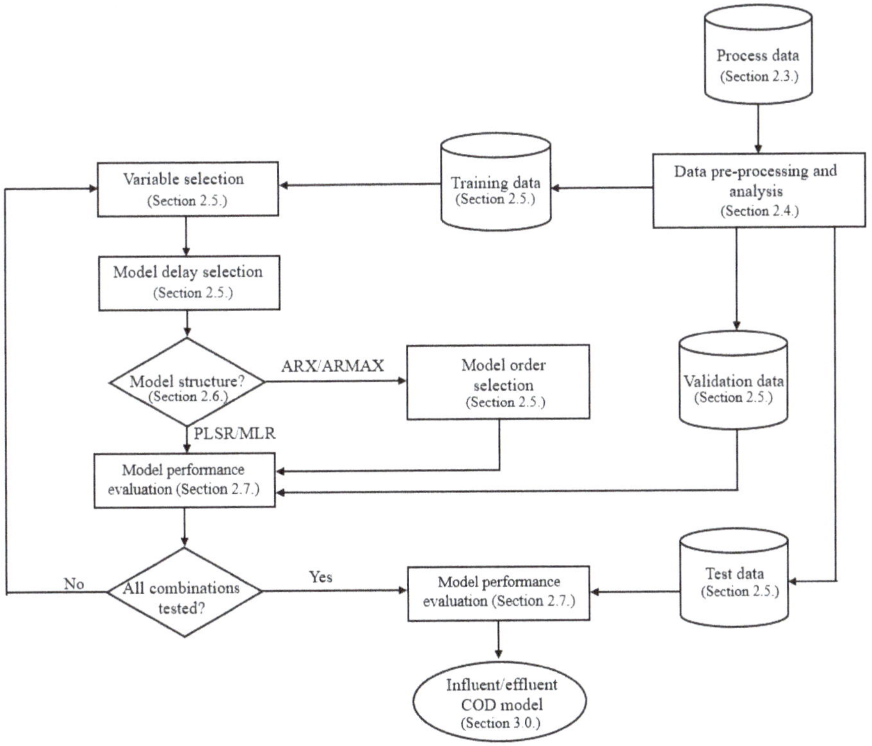

Figure 2. Overall flow of the modelling work as described in Sections 2.3–2.7 and 3.

Since three different datasets were received, the first step was to divide the data into training, test and validation data for both cases. For the influent model, we combined Datasets 2 and 3 into one from the same time period. This was performed because Dataset 3 included data on incoming wastewater from the paper machines that were thought to be important for the estimation of influent COD. The aim was for every measurement that was used in modelling to originate from before or at the aeration inlet pool for the influent model. As discussed above, Dataset 3 fits this criterion perfectly. Variables that fit this criterion were picked from Dataset 2. Dataset 3 had to be trimmed a little due to being slightly longer than the other to make sure that the timestamps would fit correctly and be comparable to each other, as discussed in Section 2.3. It was noticed during the data pre-processing stage that Datasets 2 and 3 both had a section of data that was of poor quality that could not be used for modelling or validation. The majority of the data before the poor-quality section could be used for model training and testing and the later part for model validation.

For the effluent model, it was decided to use Dataset 1 for training and Dataset 2, which included nearly the same variables, for model validation. One deciding factor was that Dataset 1 was the longest of the three datasets and would contain the largest number of variables. However, some of the variables in Dataset 1 could not be utilised because they could not be found in Dataset 2. It was then decided which datasets would be used to model which case; the modelling work for each of the targets could be performed separately.

Both cases were modelled utilising a similar modelling strategy. The modelling work was performed by testing different model structures to see which model structure would fit the data best. Interpretable model structures were prioritised during the selection. The model structures and analysis methods tested included:

- Autoregressive exogenous model (ARX), autoregressive moving average with exogenous input model (ARMAX);
- Multiple linear regression (MLR), partial least squares regression (PLSR);
- Least absolute shrinkage and selection operator (LASSO).

After the model structure was chosen, it was tested on the chosen dataset by systematically testing for different attributes. In general, everything that could be tested systematically was considered. Features that could be tested varied depending on the chosen model structure. Systematic testing included:

- Time delays;
- Training windows;
- Variable combinations;
- Model orders (when needed).

Systematic testing of different attributes was conducted by utilising a design matrix in for-loop in MATLAB® software. The design matrix is based on full factorial design is a statistically valid way to systematically test for different variables, in this case, different attributes [27]. The variables that were chosen for systematic testing were collected into a matrix pool. The numbers in the design matrix represent the indexes of the variables in the pool of variables. For example, with a model using five input variables, experiment 1 would consist of variables 1, 2, 3, 4 and 5; experiment 2 would consist of variables 1, 2, 3, 4 and 6. The design matrix for variables was constructed in the following manner:

1. Choose the total number of variables for the pool of variables.
2. Choose the number of variables for the model.
3. Construct a full factorial design, where the total number of variables in the pool act as levels and the chosen number of variables as factors.
4. Remove rows containing the same variable index.
5. Remove rows that are not unique.

The number of chosen variables for the pool and the number of variables in the model essentially determine how many experiments there will be. However, before the formed design matrix can be used for modelling, some adjustments need to be performed. Rows that contain the same variable indexes (multiple same numbers) need to be removed from the matrix, as it is not beneficial to model cases where the same variable is taken into the model twice. The same applies to cases where the rows are not unique (same numbers, different order). The last two steps are not necessary but make the calculation time faster.

Time delays and model orders could be tested directly by creating a full factorial design of the desired range of time delays and model orders. For the influent models, time delays were tested between data points 1 and 16. With time intervals of two data points in the full factorial design, this meant that there were 32,768 possible time delay combinations to test for each attribute. A similar strategy was utilised when testing for different model orders. However, model orders were limited to the range from 1 to 6. For five variables, this would still mean 7776 different model order combinations. Lastly, different model training windows were tested over the dataset in a sliding window. The training window size also varied from a couple of hundred data points to the whole dataset. Therefore, the whole dataset was examined as thoroughly as possible to find the critical information.

The effluent model was modelled using the same strategy. However, it was found that fewer variables were needed to model the effluent COD, which is why more freedom was given to testing different attributes, as testing for three attributes is computationally significantly lighter compared to five variables. Furthermore, the effluent measurements are located farther away compared to the influent model, which is why it also made sense to increase the range for time delay testing.

In addition, tests with changes to the data pre-processing step were performed. These changes included modelling without the usage of nonlinear scaling. This could especially be performed with dynamic model structures when using more complex model orders. This is because one of the purposes of scaling the data with a nonlinear scaling function is that complex model structures are not needed in the modelling phase. Aside from tests with and without nonlinear scaling, modelling was performed with different values from the moving median window size. We experimented with different sampling rates for a 2, 4 and 8 h moving median value.

The purpose of the following pseudocodes is to provide further explanation of the modelling work. The purpose of these codes is to systematically test all possible variable and parameter combinations and store the results. This section includes pseudocodes for the ARX/ARMAX model structures and one for linear model structures. The pseudocode for the ARX model structure is presented in Figure 3.

```
*variable pool matrix for training- and validation data formation*
for *na coefficients*
   for *number of rows in the nb design matrix*
      nb = *row from nb design matrix*
      for *number of rows in the design matrix for model delays*
      delay = *row from the delay design matrix*
         for *number of rows in the design matrix for variables*
             for *start points of the sliding window*
                for *length of the sliding window*
                   if *sliding window out of bounds*
                      break
                   end
                   *formation of training data based on earlier loops*
                   *ARX model training with na,nb,delay parameters*
                   *formation of validation data*
                   *Model performance evaluation*
                   *Storing important loop data and model performance*
                end
             end
         end
      end
   end
end
```

Figure 3. Pseudocode demonstrating the implementation of ARX modelling. Incorporating nested loops for variable selection, model orders, delays and sliding window parameters that are being systematically tested.

As discussed in Section 2.5, multiple inputs are required for the code to work. Most importantly, the variable pool, design matrixes for the variables, model orders nb and delays. For the ARMAX model, an additional for loop is required for the model orders. The last loops are for determining the lengths and starting points of the varying sliding windows. It is important to consider the length of the data when defining the sliding windows and their starting points so that the whole data can be utilised with varying sliding windows and their starting points without producing an error. Inside the main for loop, the training data should be formed based on the indexes of the variable design matrix and the sliding window. An ARX model should be formed from this training data together with the selected delays and model orders. After the model was trained, validation data were formed based on the selected variables. The length of the validation data is the same every loop, as the model performance must be tested on data from the same period every time. Lastly, the results from the performance evaluation as well as important loop data, must be stored into a variable. This is important so that the results can be accessed afterward to see which variables, model orders, delays and training periods from the available data give the best results. The best model structure is then further tested with independent test data. The code for linear models worked in a similar manner (Figure 4). However, there are some differences. The linear model structures do not include model orders at all. The variables were also manually delayed. Finally, the code for linear models includes cross-validation in the loop.

```
for *number of rows in the design matrix for model delays*
    for *number of rows in the design matrix for variables*
        for *start points of the sliding window*
            for *length of the sliding window*
                if *sliding window out of bounds*
                    break
                end
                *formation of training data based on earlier loops*
                *Manual delay of variables*
                *PLSR/MLR model training and k-fold cross-validation*
                *Formation of validation data*
                *Manual delay of variables to match the model*
                *Model performance evaluation*
                *Storing important loop data and model performance*
            end
        end
    end
end
```

Figure 4. Pseudocode demonstrating the implementation of PLSR/MLR modelling. Incorporating nested loops for variable selection, delays and sliding window parameters that are being systematically tested.

2.6. Model Structures

Different model structures were utilised during this modelling work, including dynamic time series model structures such as the ARX and ARMAX. Aside from dynamic time series models, simple regression models such as PLSR and MLR were used. Lastly, we experimented with LASSO regression.

2.6.1. Dynamic Model Structures

Two dynamic model structures were chosen for this study. The ARX and ARMAX time series models are linear representations of a dynamic system [31]. The ARX model structure can be represented by the following Equation (3):

$$y(t) + a_1 y(t-1) + \ldots + a_{n_a} y(t-n_a) = b_1 u(t-n_k) + \ldots + b_{n_b} u(t-n_b-n_k+1) + e(t), \quad (3)$$

where $y(t)$ represents the model output at time t, and n_a and n_b represent the chosen model orders. The model delays are represented by n_k, which states how many input samples occur before that specific input affects the model output. Finally, $e(t)$ represents the white noise value of the system.

The ARMAX model structure is similar to that of the ARX. The major difference between the model structures is that the ARMAX model includes the moving average (MA) term [32]. The ARMAX model can be represented by the following Equation (4):

$$A(q)y(t) = B(q)u(t - n_k) + C(q)e(t), \tag{4}$$

where, similarly to the ARX model, $y(t)$ represents the model output at time t, n_a, n_b and n_c (included in A, B and C components) are the orders of the ARMAX model, n_k represents the model delays and finally, $e(t)$ is the value of the white noise disturbance.

2.6.2. Static Model Structures

As stated above, of the static modelling methods, PLSR and MLR models were utilised in this study. The advantage of linear regression models is that they are interpretable. However, these model structures may fail to capture nonlinear or dynamic relationships. In this work, nonlinear scaling is utilised in the case of regression models, as stated in the section on nonlinear scaling, which means that nonlinearities are considered this way and should make these model structures perform well without losing their interpretability. Below (Equation (5)), the MLR model structure is given with n amount of input variables [33]:

$$\hat{y} = b_0 + b_1x_1 + b_2x_2 + \ldots + b_nx_n, \tag{5}$$

where $\hat{y}$ represents the predicted values; x_n the predictor variables; b_n represents the slope coefficients for the explanatory variables used in the model; and, finally, b_0 is the y-intercept term. The MATLAB® function 'regress' was utilised to calculate the b coefficient estimates. For PLSR, the MATLAB® function 'plsregress' was utilised [34]. The function follows the SIMPLS algorithm developed and discussed in detail by De Jong [35].

2.6.3. LASSO Regression

Lastly, we experimented with modelling methods that automatically choose variables for the models. LASSO regression does the variable selection and model training simultaneously [36]. It can be a suitable method, especially when there is a situation where data are abundantly available (especially a lot of variables). The LASSO method minimises the sum of squared error, while the model regression coefficients that are not important are given values close to zero [37]. The LASSO model solves the following Equation (6) for different values of λ:

$$\min_{\beta_0,\beta}\left(\frac{1}{2N}\sum_{i=1}^{N}\left(y_i - \beta_0 - x_i^T\beta\right)^2 + \lambda\sum_{j=1}^{p}|\beta_j|\right), \tag{6}$$

where λ represents the regularisation term, N represents the number of observations, y_i represents the response at observation i, x_i represents the input data at observation i, p is the vector length, and β_0 and β are the model parameters (regression coefficients).

2.7. Model Validation

The models were validated with a dataset that was not used during model training. In the case of ARX/ARMAX, a training window was utilised to systematically pick a part of the dataset, train a model and compare the results over the rest of the dataset. In the case of regression models, k-fold cross-validation was used to divide the datasets into training and test data. K-fold cross-validation divides the dataset into k number of folds (or partitions) that are nearly equal in size. After the data were divided, the $k - 1$ number of folds was used for model training, and the remaining data were used for model validation. This procedure was iterated k times, which means that each fold was successively utilised in validation, and the remaining data were used as training data [38]. The value for k was chosen to be 5 because there a large dataset was available and a separate independent validation dataset to test the effluent model on. With this k-value, it was believed that the results would be the most realistic as opposed to biased or optimistic. Monte Carlo repetitions were utilised to repeat this process 2000 times each time model training was performed. Both models were also subsequently tested with independent validation data afterward.

There are many ways to evaluate the performance of an identified model. Commonly utilised measurements include the root mean squared error (RMSE), mean absolute percentage error (MAPE) and the correlation coefficient (r). The following equations were used to calculate these performance metrics for the identified models to evaluate their performance [39]:

$$MSE = \frac{1}{N}\sum\nolimits_{t=1}^{N}(\hat{y}_t - y_t), \tag{7}$$

$$RMSE = \sqrt{MSE}, \tag{8}$$

$$APE_t = \frac{|\hat{y}_t - y_t|}{y_t} \cdot 100\%, \tag{9}$$

$$MAPE = \frac{1}{N}\sum\nolimits_{t=1}^{N} APE_t, \tag{10}$$

$$r_{xy} = \frac{\sum_{i=1}^{n}(x_i - \overline{x})(y_1 - \overline{y})}{(n-1)S_x S_y}, \tag{11}$$

where $\hat{y}_t$ represents the predicted values, y_t is the measured values, N is the number of data points, $\hat{y}$ is the response variables mean and t represents time.

3. Results and Discussion

Modelling work was carried out as described in Section 2.5. In this section, the results are presented and discussed. A summary of the results for influent COD modelling are presented in Table 2. After the best model parameters and structures were identified, a set of measurements were calculated to evaluate the performance of identified models, as discussed in Section 2.7.

The Dynamic model structures (ARX/ARMAX) performed the best when identifying the model for the influent COD. The ARX model demonstrated strong performance on both the training dataset, with a correlation coefficient of 0.82, MAPE of 9.4% and RMSE of 242.7 mg/L. Similarly, on the test dataset, the ARX model exhibited good results, achieving a correlation coefficient of 0.89, a MAPE of 8.1% and an RMSE of 191.1 mg/L. In terms of other models, PLSR and LASSO models also show reasonable performance with moderate r values and acceptable MAPE and RMSE values. The MLR model shows weaker performance compared with the other models (lower r values and higher MAPE and RMSE values). The most effective model (ARX) for the influent soft sensor model is depicted in Figure 5a. In this figure, the measured COD from the aeration inlet pool is represented by the black line, and the modelled COD is represented by the blue line as a function of time. The grey area that is plotted in the figures represents the 95% prediction interval estimated with training data. The ARX/ARMAX models had correlation coefficients of approximately 0.8. In both cases, the same variables were chosen for the model as input variables by the algorithm. The variables included two inflows from the paper machines, the flow from debarking, and pH and temperature from the aeration inlet pool. The addition of the moving average term to the model did not increase the correlation coefficients significantly. Hence, the ARX (orders: n_a: 6, n_b: (2 5 4 5 5)) model can be considered better as the model structure is simpler than the ARMAX model. The best model structures were attained when nonlinear scaling was omitted, and the dynamic model coefficients increased slightly. The identified model structure was then tested with validation data that had not been used in the model training. The results from this testing are presented in Figure 5b.

Table 2. Identified influent COD model structures and their performance metrics.

Inputs								Model Structure	Nonlinear Scaling	Training Data r	Training Data MAPE [%]	Training Data RMSE [mg/L]	Test Data r	Test Data MAPE [%]	Test Data RMSE [mg/L]
X [1]	X [2]	X [3]	X [4]	X [5]	X [6]	X [7]	X [8]								
x	x	x	x	x				ARX	No	0.82	9.4	242.7	0.89	8.1	191.1
x	x	x	x	x				ARMAX	No	0.80	8.8	221.8	0.85	7.5	177.4
	x		x	x	x	x		MLR	Yes	0.46	15.03	399.8	0.4	17.1	371.4
	x		x	x		x	x	PLSR	Yes	0.72	10.87	245.9	0.74	7.8	147.6
x	x	x		x			x	LASSO	Yes	0.55	12.9	284.3	0.70	12.2	208.5

[1] Paper machine wastewater flow (1); [2] paper machine wastewater flow (2); [3] paper machine wastewater flow (3); [4] aeration inlet pool pH; [5] pumping station wastewater temperature; [6] primary clarifier moment; [7] primary clarifier sludge amount; [8] temperature from neutralisation.

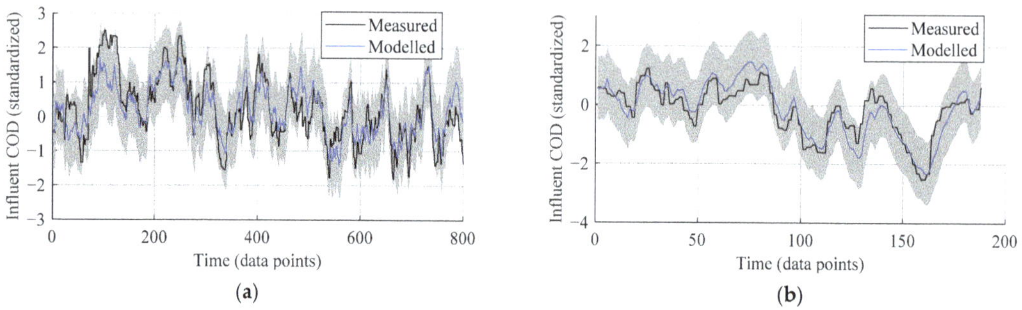

Figure 5. Measured influent COD (black) and soft sensor estimates (blue) as a function of time (1 data point = 2 h), (**a**) training data (correlation 0.82, MAPE 9.4%). (**b**) Model testing on independent test data (correlation 0.89, MAPE 8.1%). Grey area is the estimated 95% prediction interval.

A summary of the results for effluent COD modelling are presented in Table 3. For effluent predictive models, both the chosen dynamic model structures and the linear model, especially the PLSR structure without nonlinear scaling, worked well. The PLSR model without nonlinear scaling demonstrated good performance on both the training dataset, with a correlation coefficient of 0.74, MAPE of 15.7% and RMSE of 42.5 mg/L. On the test dataset, the PLSR model without nonlinear scaling also showed good results, with a correlation coefficient of 0.77, a MAPE of 7.6% and an RMSE of 23 mg/L. The PLSR model with nonlinear scaling also stands out as a well-performing model with high correlation coefficients (r values), low MAPE values and low RMSE values for both the training and test data. The MLR model with nonlinear scaling also performs reasonably well, although it has slightly lower correlation coefficients and higher MAPE and RMSE values compared with PLSR models. The identified ARX/ARMAX models worked best overall for the effluent prediction case based on correlation and MAPE values. However, because one of the goals of this research was model simplicity, more attention was also given to the linear regression model structures as they work for these data.

The identified PLSR model outputs (blue) and measured effluent COD (black) training data are plotted in Figure 6a. The variables chosen for this model were all located at the aeration inlet pool. The variables included the COD, pH and oxygen of the aeration inlet pool. The optimal delays for the identified PLSR model for these variables were 10, 10 and 20 data points, respectively. Since the minimum delay for the model is 10, this would indicate that effluent COD can be predicted 20 h in advance (one data point corresponds to two hours of data), assuming that there are no significant process changes. As discussed in Section 2.4, different moving median values were experimented with, and the 2 h period provided the best results from both the data analysis and modelling perspective. For the training data, the performance metrics show a correlation coefficient of 0.74. Similarly to the influent model, the identified model was tested on independent validation data. The results are presented in Figure 6b.

One explanation for why the correlation is much higher in the validation data when compared to the training data in the case of the effluent model is the number of data points. The training data contained approximately 4000 data points, whereas the validation dataset utilised was only 600 data points long, for the reasons discussed in Section 2.5. The COD measurement does not work as intended between data points 440 and 520 on the test data (Figure 6b), as the measurement output is constant for a long period of time. During this time, the model outputs significantly lower values and provides a much better estimate of the COD than a measurement device that is not working. Such malfunctions occur at constant intervals due to sensor fouling. Zoomed in perspective is presented in Figure 7.

Table 3. Identified effluent COD model structures and their performance metrics.

Inputs															
X [1]	X [2]	X [3]	X [4]	X [5]	X [6]	X [7]	X [8]	Model Structure	Nonlinear Scaling	Training Data r	Training Data MAPE [%]	Training Data RMSE [mg/L]	Test Data r	Test Data MAPE [%]	Test Data RMSE [mg/L]
x	x	x						PLSR	No	0.74	15.7	42.5	0.77	7.6	23.0
x		x	x					PLSR	Yes	0.71	12.5	28.6	0.68	14.5	36.3
x	x			x				MLR	Yes	0.68	12.4	29.9	0.67	25.1	59.4
x				x	x			LASSO	Yes	0.65	13.3	27.5	0.54	21.3	29.4
x						x	x	ARX	No	0.79	14.2	38.6	0.8	10.4	31.7
x						x	x	ARMAX	No	0.80	14.2	38.5	0.78	10.3	31.4

[1] Aeration inlet pool COD 2; [2] aeration pH; [3] aeration oxygen 1; [4] aeration oxygen 2; [5] aeration air pressure; [6] paper machine wastewater flow (4); [7] pumping station flow rate; [8] debarking wastewater flow.

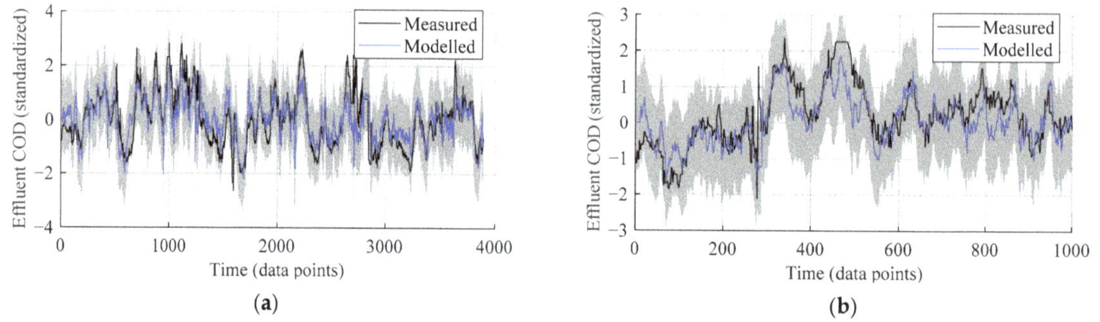

Figure 6. Measured effluent COD (black) and model estimates (blue) as a function of time with a prediction horizon of 20 h (1 data point = 2 h): (**a**) training data (correlation 0.74, MAPE 15.7%); (**b**) model testing with independent test data (correlation 0.77, MAPE 7.6%). Grey area is the estimated 95% prediction interval.

Further model validation was performed by analysing the residuals of the created models. Histograms and normal probability plots were drawn for the training and test sets to evaluate model performance visually. A normal probability plot compares the residual to what would be expected if the data followed a normal distribution. The data are plotted in a way that should result in a straight line. If not, it suggests that the data do not conform to a normal distribution [27]. For the model to be considered good, the model residual should be close to normally distributed. The residuals for the influent COD soft sensor are plotted in Figure 8.

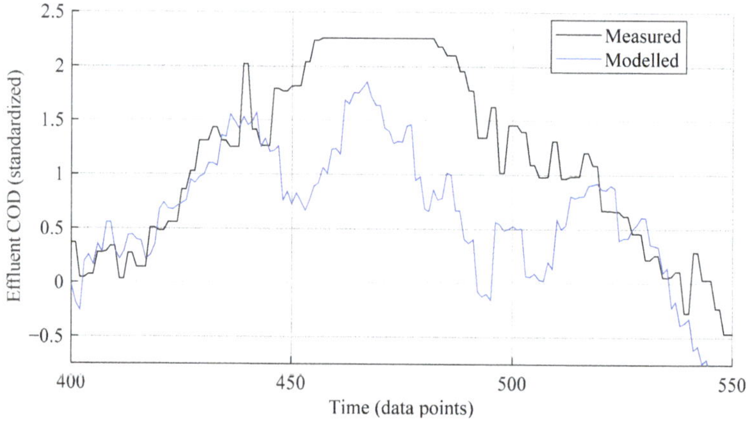

Figure 7. Zoomed view of Figure 6b at time period 400–550 when hardware sensor is malfunctioning (approximately 440–520).

The histogram and the normal probability plot for the soft sensor training data residual in Figure 8a,b suggest that the residual appears to be normally distributed. Minor deviations can be observed at the tails of the distribution. The soft sensor test data residual in Figure 8c,d, on the other hand, shows more deviations at the tails yet shows a relatively straight line in the middle portion of the data. For the effluent COD predictive model, the training data in Figure 9a,b shows significant deviation for residual values that differ from the predicted values by one standard deviation (approx. 10% of values). A similar phenomenon could be observed in the effluent COD test data in Figure 9d, albeit to a lesser degree.

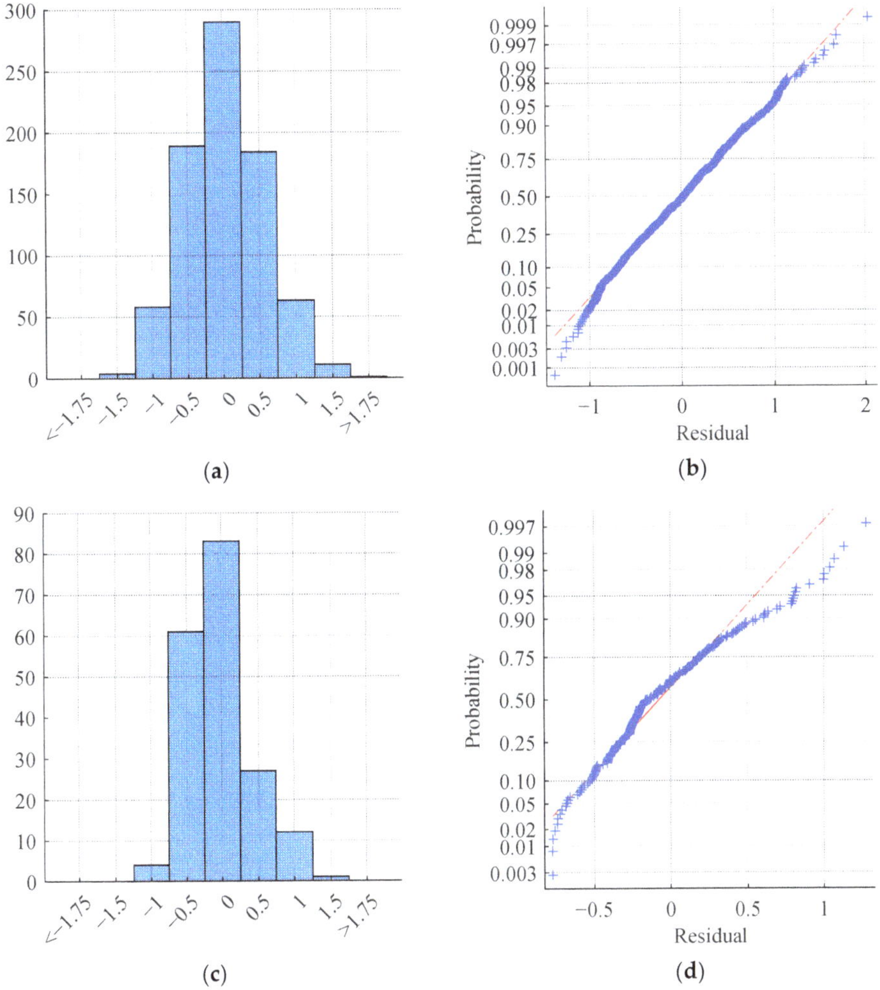

Figure 8. Influent soft sensor model residual for training and test data: (**a**) training data residual histogram; (**b**) training data residual normal probability plot; (**c**) test data residual histogram; (**d**) test data residual normal probability plot.

Lastly, some properties of the residual were calculated (Table 4) to numerically verify the observations. The range indicates the span of residual values, while the standard deviation represents the spread or variability around the model predictions. Skewness and kurtosis reveal the shape and potential outliers in the residual distribution. Monitoring these properties can help identify model deficiencies and guide further improvements.

Table 4. Residual properties.

Residual	Range	Std. Deviation	Skewness	Kurtosis
Influent model training data	[−1.4, 2]	0.54	0.19	2.91
Influent model test data	[−0.8, 1.3]	0.43	0.74	3.3
Effluent model training data	[−2.4, 2.9]	0.67	0.63	4.3
Effluent model test data	[−1.2, 2.87]	0.55	0.34	3.84

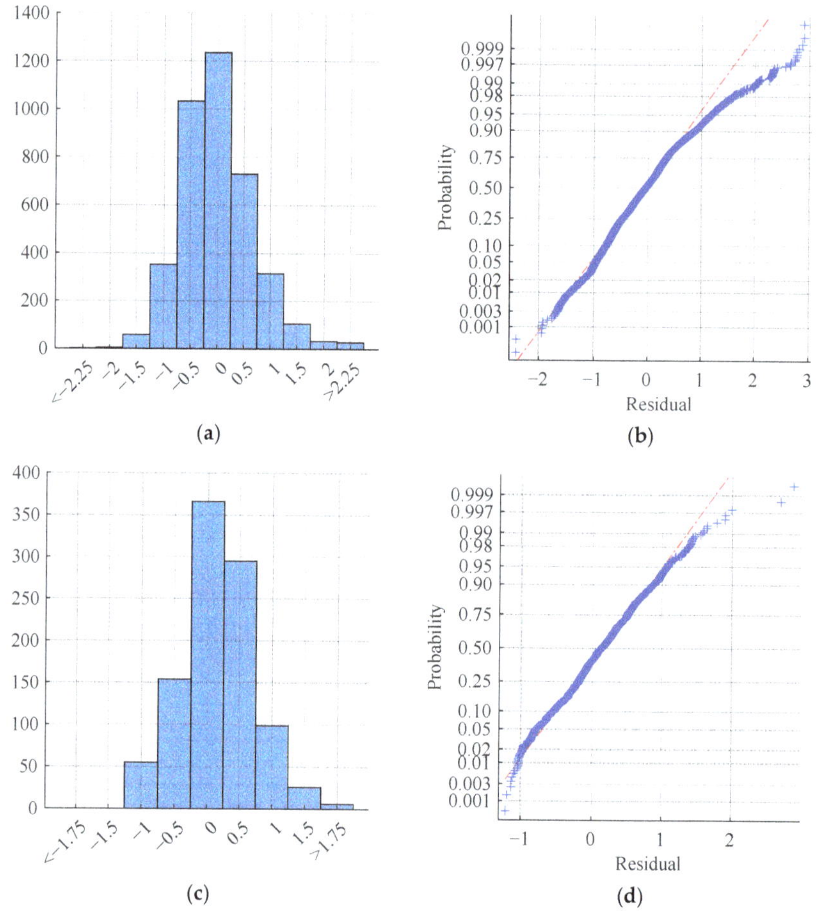

Figure 9. Effluent predictive model residual for training and test data: (**a**) training data residual histogram; (**b**) training data residual normal probability plot; (**c**) test data residual histogram; (**d**) test data residual normal probability plot.

The effluent training data exhibit residual values ranging from −1.4 to 2, with a standard deviation of 0.54. The distribution of residuals is moderately peaked (kurtosis = 2.91) and is slightly skewed (skewness = 0.19) with a longer tail on the right side. This suggests the presence of some outliers or heavy-tailed behaviour. These values are good for a model made with industrial data. The test data for the influent model show residual values ranging from −0.8 to 1.3. The standard deviation decreases slightly to 0.43, indicating a relatively smaller spread of residuals compared to the training data. The distribution remains slightly skewed (skewness = 0.74) and exhibits a higher peak (kurtosis = 3.3), suggesting a higher probability of outliers.

The effluent model's training data exhibit residual values ranging from −2.4 to 2.9. The standard deviation of 0.67 indicates a larger spread of residuals compared to both the influent model's training and test data. The distribution is similarly slightly skewed (skewness = 0.63) with a higher peak and heavier tails (kurtosis = 4.3), also suggesting the presence of extreme values or outliers. The test data for the effluent model show residual values ranging from −1.2 to 2.87. The standard deviation is 0.55, indicating a moderate spread of residuals. The distribution remains slightly skewed (skewness = 0.34) with a lower peak and lighter tails (kurtosis = 3.84) compared to the model's training data. Overall, it seems that both models are a decent fit for their intended purposes, even if the models sometimes exhibit outliers. Considering that the models are a representation of a real wastewater treatment process, modelled with real data where situations and circumstances can vary significantly.

In general, the models perform well, especially when considering the complexity of the wastewater treatment process. Our study yielded results that are similar to previous industrial wastewater studies employing linear model structures. For example, Abouzari et al. [11] reported correlations between 0.68 and 0.835 for various linear models on test data. However, it should be noted that there can be significant differences between different industries on the formation of wastewater. When compared to studies that use machine learning methods for COD modelling, the linear model structures are unable to reach as high accuracies. For example, Güçlü and Dursun [13] were able to reach a correlation of 0.85 on the test data using an artificial network and a somewhat lower MAPE value (approximately 5%). However, as previously mentioned, linear model structures offer significant practical advantages such as interpretability, straightforward model adaptation and computational efficiency.

It is important to consider the specific requirements of the problem and the trade-off between model accuracy and complexity when choosing the most appropriate model, especially since the online hardware data are used mainly for monitoring purposes as laboratory analyses are required to ensure that effluent COD levels are within limits. Thus, the requirement for soft sensor accuracy is not that strict, and an acceptable margin of error ranges between 10 and 20%. This level of deviation is considered reasonable and tolerable, given the nature and objectives of the monitoring tasks at hand.

There are still some limitations and uncertainties in the models and, thus, possibilities for future work. One goal of this work was to develop interpretable models. However, the models developed here do not capture how the changes in manufactured paper grade affect the incoming COD to the WWTP well, for example. One solution could be to create multiple sub-models for each condition. However, this would require additional data fusion concerning the manufactured paper grades.

One of the limiting factors regarding the modelling work is that the data utilised for influent soft sensor modelling were acquired during a summer period. This may mean that the model can accurately estimate COD during similar summer conditions. Therefore, the knowledge of how the modelled solution would behave during winter conditions is still missing. The models have learned how the system behaved during the specific period that the data are from, which means that if the dynamics of the WWTP change over the years, the accuracy of these models may decrease. This is likely to happen when the WWTPs and the paper machine equipment are older, which may change the process dynamics. Therefore, it is important to keep in mind that the models developed here will occasionally require retraining or continuous adaptation for them to remain accurate.

It should also be noted that the dataset used for influent COD modelling only contained useful information regarding the flow rate of the incoming wastewater from the paper machines. With more useful quality data on the incoming wastewater streams, the soft sensor model could be significantly more accurate and simpler. Measurements from both the wastewater and the paper machines themselves could also potentially be utilised in modelling these kinds of model-based soft sensors.

Further research could include studies with more abundant data from process variables at the source of the wastewater. How the wastewater is formed naturally has a large effect on the overall quality of the wastewater, which is why data on the origin of the wastewater are valuable for influent soft sensor modelling. One interesting topic of research could include studies on how the influent soft sensor and the effluent predictive model could be combined.

The effluent predictive model relies on influent COD measurements as an input parameter. This value can be provided by the influent COD soft sensor model, and thus it is possible to predict the effluent COD without the need for physically measuring the influent COD. However, as discussed, for the models to replace the hardware sensor, model adaptation tools need to be developed. This would be a more challenging task if no online COD measurements were available. Instead, other measurements and laboratory data must be utilised to update the model coefficients effectively. This is not studied in this paper and would need more research.

The models developed need to be tested in practice. Implementation of these models is straightforward and only requires changes to the plant's automation system to include the calculation of COD from the existing process measurements. This would give the plant a new monitoring tool, which can be useful as itself or in conjunction with the hardware sensor, especially in determining when the hardware sensor needs replacing and providing an estimate during that time, as depicted in Figure 7. The soft sensors also allow for lowering the sampling frequency of the hardware sensor, which in turn leads to reduced sensor maintenance costs as the measurement instrument is used less frequently. This can be very beneficial because the hardware sensor would be there to generate data for model adaptation but with lower costs.

4. Conclusions

The results indicate that measurements of paper machine wastewater streams can be utilised in estimating the total COD of wastewater incoming to the wastewater treatment plant with reasonable accuracy. The best model structure for the influent model was found to be an autoregressive-exogenous (ARX) model with low model orders. The chosen model structure was able to estimate incoming COD with a correlation coefficient of 0.82 and MAPE of 9.4% on the training data. For independent test data, the correlation and MAPE between the estimated model and measured outputs were 0.89 and 8.1%, respectively.

The results also indicate that measurements of the wastewater treatment plant are sufficient to predict the amount of COD present in the effluent. For the predictive effluent model, the partial least squares regression model was chosen from the results. Dynamic models such as the ARX models give similar results; however, more interpretable models were prioritised for this case as they were also able to obtain acceptable results. The chosen partial least squares regression model was able to estimate the effluent COD with a correlation of 0.74 and a MAPE of 15.7% for the training data. For the test data, the correlation and MAPE were 0.77 and 7.6%, respectively. The results seem reasonable considering the complexity of the wastewater treatment process. The delays indicate that the level of COD can be predicted approximately 20 h before the wastewater leaves the plant.

Author Contributions: Conceptualisation, H.P., A.S. and J.T.; methodology, A.S. and H.P.; software, H.P. and E.J.; validation, H.P.; formal analysis, H.P., A.S. and J.T.; investigation, H.P. and J.T.; resources, J.T., A.S. and E.J.; data curation, H.P.; writing—original draft preparation, H.P.; writing—review and editing, J.T., A.S., E.J., J.R. and M.R.; visualisation, H.P.; supervision, J.T., A.S., E.J., J.R. and M.R.; project administration, J.T. and M.R.; funding acquisition, J.T., J.R., M.R. and E.J. All authors have read and agreed to the published version of the manuscript.

Funding: This research and the APC was funded by Business Finland through the project 'Circular economy of water in industrial processes' (CEIWA) grant number 563/31/2021.

Data Availability Statement: Restrictions apply to the availability of these data. Data was obtained from third party and are available from the authors with the permission of the third party.

Acknowledgments: This research work was carried out as a part of the co-innovation joint project 'Circular economy of water in industrial processes' (CEIWA) funded by Business Finland, which is hereby gratefully acknowledged. The authors would also like to thank the persons involved at UPM and Kemira for their essential help in carrying out this research.

Conflicts of Interest: The authors declare no conflict of interest.

References

1. Geerdink, R.B.; Sebastiaan Van Den Hurk, R.; Epema, O.J. Chemical oxygen demand: Historical perspectives and future challenges. *Anal. Chim. Acta* **2017**, *961*, 1–11. [CrossRef]
2. Wang, R.; Yu, Y.; Chen, Y.; Pan, Z.; Li, X.; Tan, Z.; Zhang, J. Model construction and application for effluent prediction in wastewater treatment plant: Data processing method optimization and process parameters integration. *J. Environ. Manag.* **2022**, *302*, 114020. [CrossRef]
3. Ching, P.M.L.; So, R.H.Y.; Morck, T. Advances in soft sensors for wastewater treatment plants: A systematic review. *J. Water Process Eng.* **2021**, *44*, 102367. [CrossRef]
4. Fernandez de Canete, J.; del Saz-Orozco, P.; Gómez-de-Gabriel, J.; Baratti, R.; Ruano, A.; Rivas-Blanco, I. Control and soft sensing strategies for a wastewater treatment plant using a neuro-genetic approach. *Comput. Chem. Eng.* **2021**, *144*, 107146. [CrossRef]
5. Haimi, H.; Mulas, M.; Corona, F.; Vahala, R. Data-derived soft-sensors for biological wastewater treatment plants: An overview. *Environ. Model. Softw.* **2013**, *47*, 88–107. [CrossRef]
6. Corominas, L.; Garrido-Baserba, M.; Villez, K.; Olsson, G.; Cortés, U.; Poch, M. Transforming data into knowledge for improved wastewater treatment operation: A critical review of techniques. *Environ. Model. Softw.* **2018**, *106*, 89–103. [CrossRef]
7. Mujunen, S.-P.; Minkkinen, P.; Teppola, P.; Wirkkala, R.-S. Modeling of activated sludge plants treatment efficiency with PLSR: A process analytical case study. *Chemom. Intell. Lab. Syst.* **1998**, *41*, 83–94. [CrossRef]
8. Teppola, P.; Mujunen, S.-P.; Minkkinen, P. Kalman filter for updating the coefficients of regression models. A case study from an activated sludge waste-water treatment plant. *Chemom. Intell. Lab. Syst.* **1999**, *45*, 371–384. [CrossRef]
9. Woo, S.H.; Jeon, C.O.; Yun, Y.-S.; Choi, H.; Lee, C.-S.; Lee, D.S. On-line estimation of key process variables based on kernel partial least squares in an industrial cokes wastewater treatment plant. *J. Hazard. Mater.* **2009**, *161*, 538–544. [CrossRef]
10. Dürrenmatt, D.J.; Gujer, W. Data-driven modeling approaches to support wastewater treatment plant operation. *Environ. Model. Softw.* **2011**, *30*, 47–56. [CrossRef]
11. Abouzari, M.; Pahlavani, P.; Izaditame, F.; Bigdeli, B. Estimating the chemical oxygen demand of petrochemical wastewater treatment plants using linear and nonlinear statistical models—A case study. *Chemosphere* **2021**, *270*, 129465. [CrossRef]
12. Newhart, K.B.; Holloway, R.W.; Hering, A.S.; Cath, T.Y. Data-driven performance analyses of wastewater treatment plants: A review. *Water Res.* **2019**, *157*, 498–513. [CrossRef]
13. Güçlü, D.; Dursun, Ş. Artificial neural network modelling of a large-scale wastewater treatment plant operation. *Bioprocess Biosyst. Eng.* **2010**, *33*, 1051–1058. [CrossRef]
14. Ay, M.; Kisi, O. Modelling of chemical oxygen demand by using ANNs, ANFIS and k-means clustering techniques. *J. Hydrol.* **2014**, *511*, 279–289. [CrossRef]
15. Qiu, Y.; Liu, Y.; Huang, D. Date-Driven Soft-Sensor Design for Biological Wastewater Treatment Using Deep Neural Networks and Genetic Algorithms. *J. Chem. Eng. Jpn.* **2016**, *49*, 925–936. [CrossRef]
16. Liu, Y. Adaptive just-in-time and relevant vector machine based soft-sensors with adaptive differential evolution algorithms for parameter optimization. *Chem. Eng. Sci.* **2017**, *172*, 571–584. [CrossRef]
17. Yang, Y.; Kim, K.-R.; Kou, R.; Li, Y.; Fu, J.; Zhao, L.; Liu, H. Prediction of effluent quality in a wastewater treatment plant by dynamic neural network modeling. *Process Saf. Environ. Prot.* **2022**, *158*, 515–524. [CrossRef]
18. Zhang, H.; Yang, C.; Shi, X.; Liu, H. Effluent quality prediction in papermaking wastewater treatment processes using dynamic Bayesian networks. *J. Clean. Prod.* **2021**, *282*, 125396. [CrossRef]
19. Wang, D.; Thunéll, S.; Lindberg, U.; Jiang, L.; Trygg, J.; Tysklind, M.; Souihi, N. A machine learning framework to improve effluent quality control in wastewater treatment plants. *Sci. Total Environ.* **2021**, *784*, 147138. [CrossRef] [PubMed]
20. Yadav, P.; Chandra, M.; Fatima, N.; Sarwar, S.; Chaudhary, A.; Saurabh, K.; Yadav, B.S. Predicting Influent and Effluent Quality Parameters for a UASB-Based Wastewater Treatment Plant in Asia Covering Data Variations during COVID-19: A Machine Learning Approach. *Water* **2023**, *15*, 710. [CrossRef]
21. Wang, X.; Kvaal, K.; Ratnaweera, H. Explicit and interpretable nonlinear soft sensor models for influent surveillance at a full-scale wastewater treatment plant. *J. Process Control* **2019**, *77*, 1–6. [CrossRef]
22. Kim, M.; Kim, Y.; Kim, H.; Piao, W.; Kim, C. Evaluation of the k-nearest neighbor method for forecasting the influent characteristics of wastewater treatment plant. *Front. Environ. Sci. Eng.* **2016**, *10*, 299–310. [CrossRef]
23. Wang, R.; Pan, Z.; Chen, Y.; Tan, Z.; Zhang, J. Influent Quality and Quantity Prediction in Wastewater Treatment Plant: Model Construction and Evaluation. *Pol. J. Environ. Stud.* **2021**, *30*, 4267–4276. [CrossRef]
24. Guyon, I.; Elisseeff, A. An introduction to variable and feature selection. *J. Mach. Learn. Res.* **2003**, *3*, 1157–1182.
25. Alvi, M.; French, T.; Cardell-Oliver, R.; Keymer, P.; Ward, A. Cost Effective Soft Sensing for Wastewater Treatment Facilities. *IEEE Access* **2022**, *10*, 55694–55708. [CrossRef]
26. Brunner, V.; Siegl, M.; Geier, D.; Becker, T. Challenges in the Development of Soft Sensors for Bioprocesses: A Critical Review. *Front. Bioeng. Biotechnol.* **2021**, *9*, 722202. [CrossRef]
27. NIST/SEMATECH e-Handbook of Statistical Methods. 2012. Available online: https://www.itl.nist.gov/div898/handbook/ (accessed on 21 May 2023).
28. Ali, P.J.M.; Faraj, R.H.; Koya, E.; Ali, P.J.M.; Faraj, R.H. Data normalization and standardization: A technical report. *Mach. Learn. Tech. Rep.* **2014**, *1*, 1–6.

29. The MathWorks Inc. Moving Median—MATLAB Movmedian—MathWorks Nordic. 2023. Available online: https://se.mathworks.com/help/matlab/ref/movmedian.html (accessed on 7 June 2023).
30. Juuso, E.; Lahdelma, S. Intelligent scaling of features in fault diagnosis. In Proceedings of the 7th International Conference on Condition Monitoring and Machinery Failure Prevention Technologies, Stratford-upon-Avon, UK, 22–24 June 2010; pp. 1358–1372.
31. The MathWorks Inc. Estimate Parameters of ARX, ARIX, AR, or ARI Model—MATLAB arx—MathWorks Nordic. 2022. Available online: https://se.mathworks.com/help/ident/ref/arx.html (accessed on 7 June 2023).
32. Ljung, L. *System Identification: Theory for the User*, 2nd ed.; Prentice Hall PTR: Upper Saddle River, NJ, USA, 1999. [CrossRef]
33. Chatterjee, S.; Hadi, A.S. Influential Observations, High Leverage Points, and Outliers in Linear Regression. *Stat. Sci.* **1986**, *1*, 379–416.
34. The MathWorks Inc. Partial Least-Squares (PLS) Regression—MATLAB Plsregress—MathWorks Nordic. 2008. Available online: https://se.mathworks.com/help/stats/plsregress.html (accessed on 7 June 2023).
35. De Jong, S. SIMPLS: An alternative approach to partial least squares regression. *Chemom. Intell. Lab. Syst.* **1993**, *18*, 251–263. [CrossRef]
36. Geng, J.; Yang, C.; Li, Y.; Lan, L.; Zhang, F.; Han, J.; Zhou, C. A bidirectional dictionary LASSO regression method for online water quality detection in wastewater treatment plants. *Chemom. Intell. Lab. Syst.* **2023**, *237*, 104817. [CrossRef]
37. Xiao, H.; Bai, B.; Li, X.; Liu, J.; Liu, Y.; Huang, D. Interval multiple-output soft sensors development with capacity control for wastewater treatment applications: A comparative study. *Chemom. Intell. Lab. Syst.* **2019**, *184*, 82–93. [CrossRef]
38. Jung, Y. Multiple predicting K-fold cross-validation for model selection. *J. Nonparametric Stat.* **2018**, *30*, 197–215. [CrossRef]
39. Hietaharju, P. *Predictive Optimization of Heat Demand Utilizing Heat Storage Capacity of Buildings*; University of Oulu: Oulu, Finland, 2021.

applied sciences

MDPI

Article

Analysis and Design of Direct Force Control for Robots in Contact with Uneven Surfaces

Antonio Rosales and Tapio Heikkilä *

VTT Technical Research Centre of Finland Ltd., P.O. Box 1100, FI-90571 Oulu, Finland; antonio.rosales@vtt.fi
* Correspondence: tapio.heikkila@vtt.fi

Abstract: Robots executing contact tasks are essential in a wide range of industrial processes such as polishing, welding, debugging, drilling, etc. Force control is indispensable in these type of tasks since it is required to keep the interaction force (between the robot and the environment/surface) within acceptable values. In this paper, we present a methodology to analyze and to design the force control system needed to regulate the force as close as possible to the desired value. The proposed methods are presented using a widely used generic contact task consisting of exerting a desired force on the normal direction to the surface while a desired velocity/position is tracked on the tangent direction to the surface. The analysis considers environments/surfaces with certain uneven characteristics, i.e., not perfectly flat. The uneven characteristic is studied using ramp or sinusoidal signals disturbing the position on the normal direction to the surface, and we present how the velocity on the tangent direction is related with the slope of the ramp or the frequency of the sinusoidal disturbance. Then, we provide a method to design the force controller that keeps the force error within desired limits and preserves stability, despite the uneven surface. Furthermore, considering the relation between the disturbance (ramp or sinusoidal) and the tangent velocity, we present a method to compute the maximum velocity for which the task can be executed. Simulations exemplifying and verifying the proposed methods are presented.

Keywords: robotics; force control; stability

Citation: Rosales, A.; Heikkilä, T. Analysis and Design of Direct Force Control for Robots in Contact with Uneven Surfaces. *Appl. Sci.* **2023**, *13*, 7233. https://doi.org/10.3390/app13127233

Academic Editors: Seppo Sierla, David Hästbacka and Kai Zenger

Received: 12 May 2023
Revised: 12 June 2023
Accepted: 15 June 2023
Published: 16 June 2023

1. Introduction

Robots executing contact tasks are essential to automate plenty of manufacturing processes. Regulating the force produced during the interaction between the robot and the environment is critical. There are principally two approaches to regulate the force; one is called indirect force control, since the force is regulated through motion control, i.e., changes in the position error at the end-effector, and the second one is called direct force control, since force feedback is directly compared with a desired force to calculate the robot's control input [1].

Direct force control is preferred when the application requires a precise regulation of the force. Additionally, direct force control is capable of accomplishing the contact task without damaging the environment and the robot itself [2]. However, the advantages of direct force control come at a price, since preserving stability is challenging, mainly because of the presence of unavoidable dynamics such as sensor dynamics, filters, and delays [3].

On the other hand, when direct force control techniques are implemented in industrial robots, one should design controllers that generate velocity or position inputs, since these are the standard inputs of industrial robots [4,5]. Admittance controllers are the ones having velocity/position as an output and force as an input [6]. Despite the fact that the implementation of admittance-type controllers has shown efficiency and efficacy [7], there exists a compromise between performance and stability during its design [8,9].

Recent research on force control has been focused in the design of Proportional-Integral-Derivative (PID) controllers that reach quickly the desired force with limited overshoot. For example, the authors in [10] present a force control system based on PID that ensures asymptotic convergence of the force error to zero with small overshoot and short settling time. In [11], a force control system is presented based on PID that keeps the force within the desired value despite uncertainty in the surface's model. In [12], the authors analyze the effect of the surface's stiffness in the force control, and they present a PID controller that reaches the desired force without overshoot. Furthermore, advanced control techniques have been recently applied to regulate force. An application to medical robotics in [13] presents a force controller based on sliding mode control that ensures convergence of the force error to zero in finite time. Data-driven control is used in [14] to present a data-driven force control that ensures global convergence of the error to a steady state. Notwithstanding the prominent results presented in the mentioned references, the velocity of the robot in the tangent direction (along the surface) has not been studied, although this velocity is important since it is related to the velocity at which the task can be executed. Furthermore, a quantitative approach to design the control gains that produces a specified tolerance error is hardly discussed. The mentioned methods (estimation of the velocity of the task and a quantitative design) are relevant to practical applications required to execute the task as fast as possible and to keep the force error within acceptable limits.

In this paper, we propose a methodology to analyze and to design the force control of a robot in contact with an uneven surface. The proposed methods are presented considering the general contact task of maintaining a desired velocity along the surface (in the tangent direction to the surface) while a desired force is applied on the normal direction to the surface. This contact task properly describes applications when the priority is to regulate the force in one direction, such as polishing and assembly tasks, as well as medical applications (see [15]).

We study admittance direct force controllers with Proportional-Integral-Derivative (PID) structure to have methods suitable for industrial robots allowing velocity/position inputs and to fit our methods with the industrially accepted PID controller.

Ramp and sinusoidal signals are used to model the uneven characteristics of the surface, and the relation between the disturbances and the velocity along the surface is presented. Since we are considering only the regulation of the force in the normal direction, the magnitude of the slope (values of frequency) is bounded to avoid steep slopes producing force in a different direction than the normal one.

Then, we propose a method to compute the controller considering the performance in terms of force error and attenuation of disturbances in the normal direction. Additionally, we include the gain margin analysis to estimate how much the control gain/magnitude can be modified without creating instability. In addition, the gain margin is used to predict how much uncertainty in the stiffness the system can tolerate. Furthermore, considering the proportional relation between the velocity along the surface, and the ramp magnitude (or frequency of the sinusoidal), we provide a method to estimate the maximum velocity at which the task can be executed. The proposed methods are validated via simulations. (Preliminary results linked with this paper were presented in [16]).

The structure of the paper is the following. Section 2 presents the problem statement. The methods of analysis and design are presented in Section 3. Section 4 contains the simulations, and the conclusions are presented in Section 5.

2. Problem Statement

Figure 1 presents the robot in contact with the uneven surface. The robot has to execute the following task: to exert a desired force f_d in the normal direction (x direction) to the surface while a desired velocity v_d is maintained along the surface (y direction).

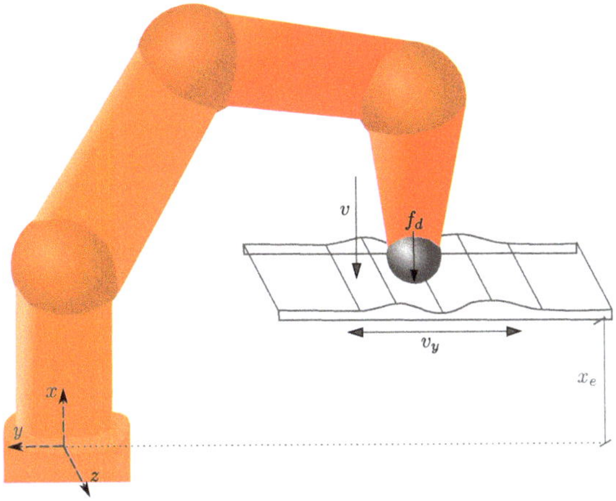

Figure 1. The contact task. v is the velocity in the normal direction, and v_y is the velocity along the surface.

During the execution of the task (see Figure 1), the following assumptions are considered. First, the end-effector of the robot is always in contact with the surface; the methods provided in this paper are not valid when the robot loses contact with the surface. Second, it is assumed that no forces are produced along the z-axis since the end-effector is moving along the y-axis. Third, the end-effector is in compliance with the surface in the x-direction. The compliance in the x-direction helps to direct most of the force produced by the curved surface to the x-direction; hence, the force along the y-axis is minimum and one can consider that the normal force is mainly defined by the force in the x-direction. Then, the interaction force is studied using the one-degree-of-freedom (1DOF) model presented in Figure 2, considering only the movement in the x direction [6].

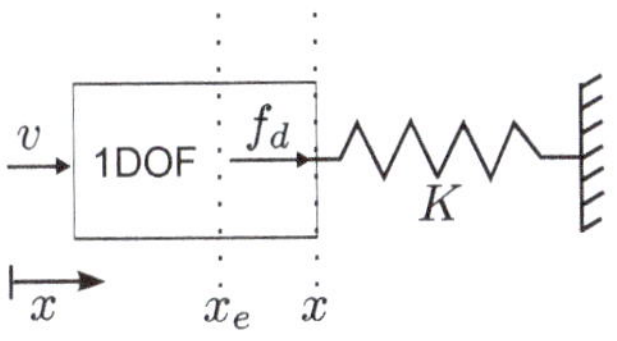

Figure 2. The one-degree-of-freedom interaction force model.

The force exerted by the robot on the surface is described by the following elastic model:

$$f = K(x - x_e) \tag{1}$$

where $K > 0$ is the accumulative stiffness of the tool plus the environment, x is the end-effector position, and the location of the surface in x_e. The control objective is to design the robot's input v that ensures the desired force f_d is applied on the surface.

Considering the models in Figure 2 and Equation (1), the force control system presented in Figure 3 is used to study and to design the control v. The force control system is composed of the following blocks: $G_c(s)$ is the controller, $G_{LP}(s)$ describes the dynamics of a filter used to attenuate noise from force sensor measurements, and $G_T(s)$ corresponds to the delay produced by sensor–hardware communication. The block K corresponds to the stiffness. The block named *Robot* is the single-input single-output model of the robot, and the time-constant τ defines how fast the robot's position x responds to the control input v. The signals f_d, f, $e = f_d - f$, v, and x_d represent the desired force, the measured force, the force error, the control signal, and a disturbance emerging in the position x, respectively.

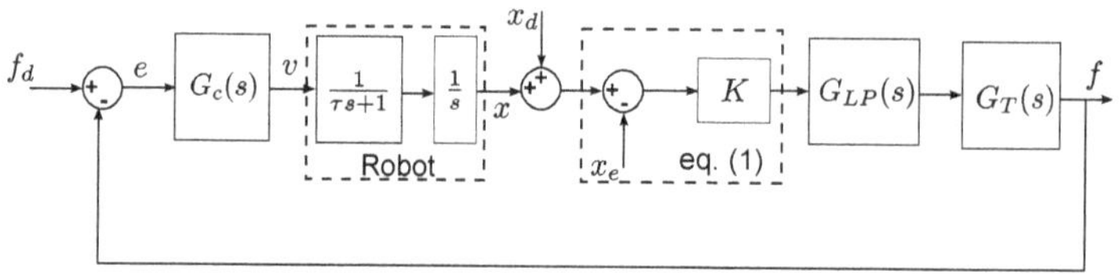

Figure 3. Block diagram of the force control system.

The transfer functions of the force control system in Figure 3 are as follows.

$$G_c(s) = K_p + K_d s + \frac{K_i}{s} \tag{2}$$

$$G_{LP}(s) = \frac{1}{\tau_{LP} s + 1} \tag{3}$$

$$G_T(s) = e^{-Ts} \tag{4}$$

where s is the Laplace variable, $K_p, K_d, K_i > 0$ are control gains, τ_{LP} is the time constant of the filter, and T is the time-delay value. The transfer functions and its parameters were already identified and presented in [17] by our research group. Note that the controller $G_c(s)$ is a direct force control, and it is similar to an admittance control since its input is a force and its output is a velocity.

Direct force control and admittance control have been studied and tested in industrial robots; however, during the adjustment of the gains, there exists an unavoidable compromise between performance and stability [8,9]. Furthermore, when delays and filters are included in the force control system (see Figure 3), these additional dynamics deteriorate the stability of the force control system [3]. Additionally, when disturbances emerge, the design of the gains should consider disturbance rejection as well as the stability of the system.

In this paper, we propose a method for the analysis and design of force control systems, such as the one in Figure 3, considering performance, stability margins, and robustness against disturbances. For the stability analysis, our method estimates how much the control magnitude should be modified before losing stability. Furthermore, using stability margins, we can estimate how much stiffness uncertainty the force control can handle. For the robustness analysis, we considered a disturbance (x_d) on the robot's position, i.e., the x direction. These disturbances represent the uneven nature of the surface, and then the performance of the disturbed system is studied in terms of the force error e, and a method is proposed to compute the control gains that keep the error within given limits and ensure acceptable stability margins.

Ramp and sinusoidal signals are used to disturb the system. The ramp value and the frequency of the sinusoidal signal are used to define the velocity at which the task is executed. Then, from the proposed design method, the maximum velocity at which the task can be executed is estimated.

3. Analysis and Design of the Force Control System

In this section, we present the analysis of the force control system in Figure 3, the design method to keep the force error within acceptable limits, and how to estimate the maximum velocity at which the task can be executed.

3.1. Disturbance Rejection

Consider the uneven characteristics of the surface, a trapezoid with slopes of magnitude M (see Figure 4a). Then, the disturbance x_d is modeled using a ramp signal $X_d(s) = \frac{M}{s^2}$ with magnitude M, and s is the Laplace variable. Note that the ramp magnitude M is proportional to the velocity v_y at which the task is executed. For example, when the robot executes a linear movement from point A to point B, the bigger the velocity v_y, the bigger the magnitude M of the ramp in the x direction.

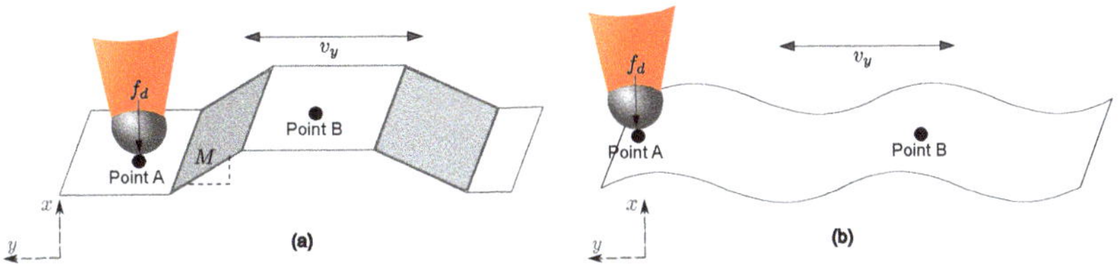

Figure 4. The uneven characteristics of the surface. (**a**) Ramp shape and (**b**) sinusoidal shape.

The performance of the force control system in Figure 3 is analyzed using the steady-state error $e_{ss} = \lim_{s\to 0} sE(s)$, where $E(s)$ is the force error e in the Laplace domain; then

$$e_{ss} = \lim_{s\to 0} s\frac{KG(s)}{1+G_c(s)KG(s)G_{LP}(s)G_T(s)}X_d(s) \quad (5)$$

where $G_c = K_p + K_d s + \frac{K_i}{s}$ is the controller, $G(s) = \frac{1}{s(\tau s+1)}$ is the transfer function of the robot, $G_{LP}(s)$ is the filter, G_T is the transport delay, $X_D(s)$ is the external disturbance, and K is the stiffness.

Considering the ramp disturbance $X_d(s) = \frac{M}{s^2}$, the control $G_c(s) = K_p + K_d s + \frac{K_i}{s}$ ensures zero steady-state error e_{ss} [18]. However, the integral term $\frac{K_i}{s}$ has a drawback since it produces a sluggish and oscillatory response.

On the other hand, when the controller is $G_c(s) = K_p + K_d s$, the steady-state error is $e_{ss} = \frac{M}{K_p}$, but it can be reduced by incrementing the control gain K_p (or the control magnitude $|G_c(s)|$). In Figure 5, the curves for different values of e_{ss} are presented. These curves are obtained from $e_{ss} = \frac{M}{K_p}$ using different ramp values and gains K_p.

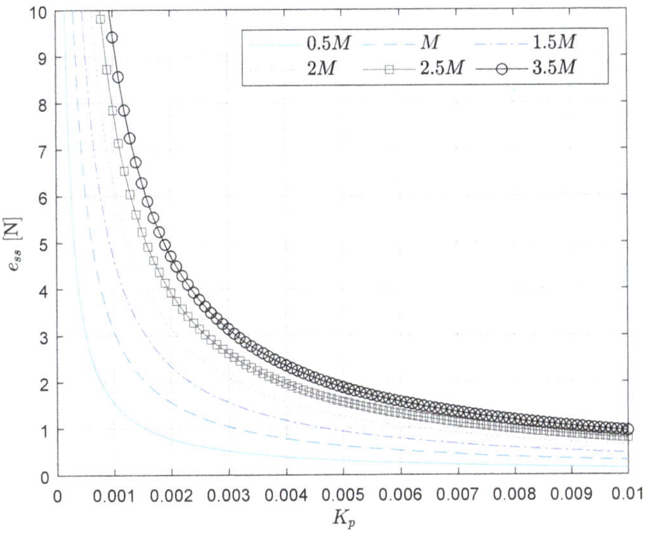

Figure 5. Curves of steady-state error e_{ss} in terms of control gain K_p and ramp value M.

The curves in Figure 5 represent a design tool considering the disturbance ramp magnitude M (proportional to the velocity v_y at which the task is executed) and force error via steady-state error. If the magnitude M is known/estimated, one can obtain the control gain K_p that produces the steady-state error e_{ss} presented in the curves, and vice versa, if a certain steady-state error e_{ss} is desired, one can choose the gain K_p producing this error.

Note than the stiffness value K does not appear in disturbance analysis presented in this section. However, the value of K matters when it is big since the stability of the force control system may be compromised. Furthermore, one should be careful when the gain K_p is selected, since a big K_p value may affect the stability too.

Time-Varying Disturbances

Another way to study the uneven characteristics of the surface is using sinusoidal disturbances $x_d(t) = \sin(\omega t)$ (see Figure 4b). In this case, the velocity v_y at which the task is executed is proportional to the frequency ω of the disturbance in the x direction. For example, the faster the end-effector is moving on the surface from point A to point B, the higher the frequency ω of the sinusoidal disturbance. The proportionality relation depends on the wavelength λ of the sinusoidal, i.e., $v_y = \lambda(\omega/2\pi)$.

When a sinusoidal disturbance appears, the steady-state error e_{ss} cannot be used to analyze the force error, and the analysis presented in Section 3.1 is not valid. However, one can find a relation between the magnitude of the time-varying disturbance and the control gain/magnitude.

Consider the following transfer function,

$$\frac{F(s)}{X_d(s)} = \frac{KG_{LP}(s)G_T(s)}{1 + G_c(s)G(s)KG_{LP}(s)G_T(s)},$$

from the disturbance x_d to f ($f_d = 0$). From [18], this transfer function can be approximated by $\frac{F(s)}{X_d(s)} \approx \frac{1}{G_c(s)G(s)}$. Then, the disturbance $X_d(s)$ can be attenuated by increasing the magnitude of $G_c(s)$, since the goal is to have a magnitude,

$$|F(s)|_{s=j\omega} = \frac{|X_d(s)|_{s=j\omega}}{|G_c(s)|_{s=j\omega}|G(s)|_{s=j\omega}}, \tag{6}$$

as close as possible to zero. Again, one should be aware of stability when the magnitude of the controller increases.

Note that the computation of the magnitude $|F(j\omega)|$ depends on the parameters of the controller G_s, the dynamics of the robot G, and the frequency ω. Whenever the mentioned parameters are available, one can obtain curves similar to those presented in Figure 5; an example of the curves is presented in Section 4.

3.2. *Stability Analysis*

In this section, the relative stability analysis of the force control system in Figure 3 is performed. Then, we find how much the control gain/magnitude K_p (also stiffness K) can be incremented without damaging stability.

3.2.1. Stability in Terms of K

The gain margin is computed using the open-loop transfer function $L(s)$. For the force control system in Figure 3, the transfer function $L(s)$ is as follows (see [18]):

$$L(s) = KG_c(s)G(s)G_f(s)G_d(s). \tag{7}$$

Considering $s = j\omega$, the gain margin is obtained using the magnitude of $L(j\omega)$,

$$|L(j\omega)| = K|G_c(j\omega)||G(j\omega)||G_f(j\omega)||G_d(j\omega)|,$$

where ω is the frequency associated with the frequency response of $L(s)$. Note that the magnitude $|L(j\omega)|$ is directly proportional to the gain K independent of the frequency ω.

From the definition of the gain margin [18], the gain margin is the biggest increment of magnitude $|L(j\omega)|$ that conserves stability. The condition for stability is $|L(j\omega)| < 1$, and this condition can be tested in the following way. First, a multiplicative gain K_{GM} is added to $|L(j\omega)|$, and second, K_{GM} is increased until the stability condition is violated, i.e., $K_{GM}|L(j\omega)| \geq 1$ [19]. The magnitude $|L(j\omega)|_{test}$,

$$|L(j\omega)|_{test} = K_{GM}K|G_c(j\omega)||G(j\omega)||G_f(j\omega)||G_d(j\omega)|,$$

is used to check the gain margin, and the stability is ensured if $|L(j\omega)|_{test} < 1$. Note that the stability condition will be violated for certain $K_{GM} = K_{GM_{max}}$ producing $|L(j\omega)|_{test} = 1$, and the value of the gain margin will be $K_{GM_{max}}$.

One can observe that the term $K_{GM}K$ affects the whole magnitude $|L(j\omega)|_{test}$. Therefore, when the gain margin $K_{GM_{max}}$ is known, one can use $K_{GM_{max}}$ to estimate the maximum increment/change in stiffness K that maintains the stability.

3.2.2. Stability in Terms of K_p

For the computation of the gain margin in terms of K_p, the stiffness K is considered constant and the frequency response $G_c(j\omega)$ is divided in real and imaginary parts, $G_c(j\omega) = K_p + \left(\frac{K_d\omega^2 - K_i}{\omega}\right)j$. Adding the multiplicative gain K_{GM} to $G_c(j\omega)$, the magnitude $|G_c(j\omega)|_{K_{GM}}$ is defined as

$$\begin{aligned} |G_c(j\omega)|_{K_{GM}} &= K_{GM}|G_c(j\omega)| = \left|K_{GM}K_p + \left(\frac{K_{GM}K_d\omega^2 - K_{GM}K_i}{\omega}\right)j\right|, \\ &= K_{GM}\left|K_p + \left(\frac{K_d\omega^2 - K_i}{\omega}\right)j\right|. \end{aligned}$$

Note that the gain K_{GM} is directly proportional to the control magnitude $|G_c(j\omega)|_{K_{GM}}$ or directly proportional to each control gain K_p,K_d, and K_i.

Using $|G_c(j\omega)|_{K_{GM}}$, the transfer function to test and compute the gain margin is

$$|L(j\omega)|_{test} = K_{GM}|G_c(j\omega)|K|G(j\omega)||G_f(j\omega)||G_d(j\omega)|,$$

where K_{GM} represents an increment/change in the magnitude $|G_c(j\omega)|$. Since the stability condition is $|L(j\omega)|_{test} < 1$, the gain margin is the gain $K_{GM} = K_{GM_{max}}$ that produces $|L(j\omega)|_{test} = 1$. Therefore, the gain margin computation gives an estimate of how much one can modify the control gain/magnitude without producing instability.

3.3. Design Method

Considering the stability analysis presented in the preceding section and the design curve in Figure 5, one can observe a compromise between stability and error attenuation. Selecting a big value of control magnitude $|G_c(j\omega)|$ might result in an acceptable force error but this magnitude may deteriorate the stability.

The proposed design method for the controller $G_c = K_p + K_d s$ is obtained, when one includes in the curves of Figure 5 the maximum value of magnitude/gain K_{GMmax} that preserves stability (see Figure 6). The set of gains K_p presented in Figure 6 is selective since it considers only the gains K_p that guarantee stability. The values of e_{ss} corresponding to the gain $K_{GMmax}K_p$ are the minimum values one can have in the force error considering the disturbance magnitude M and the stability margin. Therefore, the curves in Figure 6 provide a better design method for the controller $G_c(s)$ compared with the curves in Figure 5.

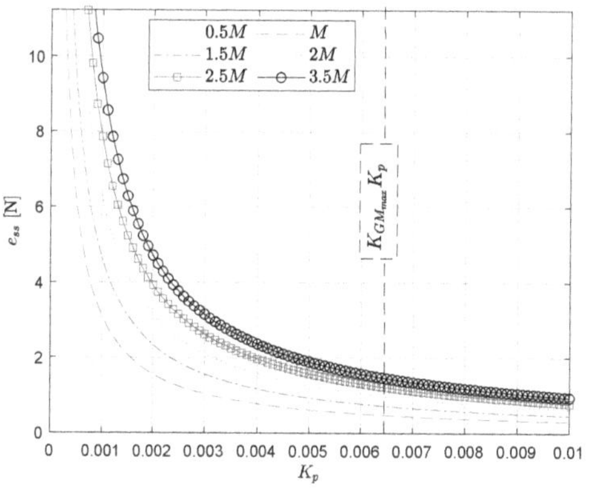

Figure 6. Design method: steady-state error e_{ss} in terms of control gain K_p and ramp value M K_p considering gain margin.

Selecting Gains of G_c Considering Stiffness K

From Equation (7), one can observe how the product of K and $|G_c(j\omega)|$ affects the gain margin. Therefore, when the control gains in Equation (2) are selected/adjusted, one should consider the value of stiffness K in order to preserve the relative stability of the system.

Assume the stiffness K can be modified/adjusted (adding elasticity to the end-effector using a spring). Then, from Equation (7), the magnitude $|L(j\omega)|$ contains two adjustable terms (its parameters are at hand); the first one is the controller G_c and the second one is the stiffness K.

If the goal is to preserve a desired gain margin, one should keep the magnitude $|L(j\omega)|$ as close as possible to its value associated with the desired gain margin. Therefore, when the control gains are adjusted (or the stiffness is adjusted), one should keep a balance between the magnitude of the controller G_c and the value of stiffness K. For example, if the magnitude of G_c increases, one should balance/compensate this change with a decrease in K to preserve the desired magnitude $|L(j\omega)|$ associated with the desired gain margin.

Therefore, in order to preserve a stable contact force, the following relations between the stiffness and the controller exist:

- For a rigid surface/environment, a compliant controller is needed, i.e., $K >> |G_c|$.
- For a compliant surface/environment, a rigid controller is needed, i.e., $K << |G_c|$.

3.4. Estimation of the Maximum Velocity at Which the Task Is Executed

Assume e_{max} is the maximum tolerable force error in the force control system in Figure 3. Then, all the errors $e_{ss} < e_{max}$ are acceptable.

On the other hand, when one selects the maximum gain $K_{GMmax}K_p$ from Figure 6, this gain is the critical gain since it corresponds to the case $|L(j\omega)|_{test} = 1$. In practice, one should avoid having a critical gain, since the system may have an oscillatory response, and a small disturbance may cause instability. Therefore, the selection of the controller gain should be $K_p < K_{GMmax}K_p$.

Considering the maximum error e_{max} and the recommended selection of the gain $K_p < K_{GMmax}K_p$, it is possible to obtain a more selective set of gains K_p from Figure 6. In Figure 7, certain values for e_{max} and $K_p < K_{GMmax}K_p$ are presented. One can observe a selective set of gains K_p defined by the limits e_{max} and $K_p < K_{GMmax}K_p$. The mentioned region contains the set of gains that ensure an acceptable force error and a safer response, since K_p is far from the critical gain. Additionally, there are curves corresponding to different values of M, and a maximum value M_{max} can be obtained from the region. In Figure 7, $M_{max} = 1.5M$. Since M is proportional to the velocity at which the task is executed (see Section 3.1), the maximum velocity can be estimated from M_{max}.

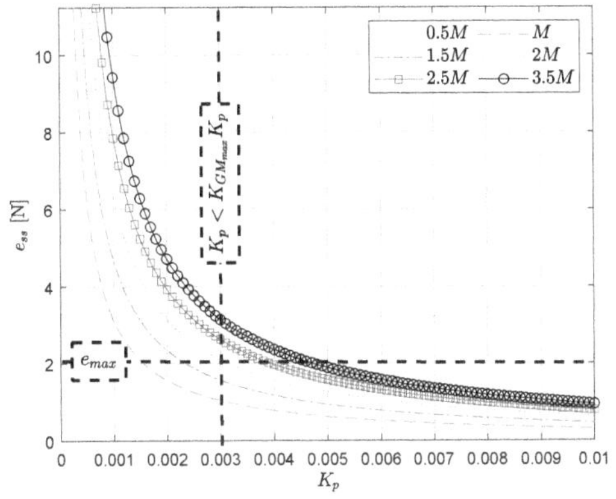

Figure 7. Curves including maximum tolerable error e_{max} and recommended $K_p < K_{GMmax} K_p$.

4. Simulations

Firstly, using the *pidTuner* of Matlab, we tuned three controllers $G_c(s)$, a Proportional (P), Proportional-Derivative (PD), and Proportional-Integral-Derivative (PID) to havethe same settling time $t_s \approx 0.8$ seconds and overshoot of 15%. The gains of the mentioned controllers are presented in Table 1.

Table 1. Control gains.

	K_p	K_d	K_i	t_s	**Overshoot**
P	0.002229	0	0	0.88 s	14.8% (7.4 N)
PD	0.004211	0.001111	0	0.71 s	14.4% (7.2 N)
PID	0.0053947	0.0005154	0.01411	0.88 s	15.4% (7.7 N)

For the simulation, the force control system in Figure 3 is built in Simulink, and the simulation is executed using the solver ode1(euler) with a fixed sampling time of 1 millisecond. The parameters of the force control system used in the simulation are $\tau = 0.05$, $T = 0.008$, $K = 3000$, and $\tau_{LP} = 0.05$. We test a step input of 50 N at 30 s. Figure 8 shows the time response; one can see that the settling time and overshoot are similar but the PD controller is faster than P and PID.

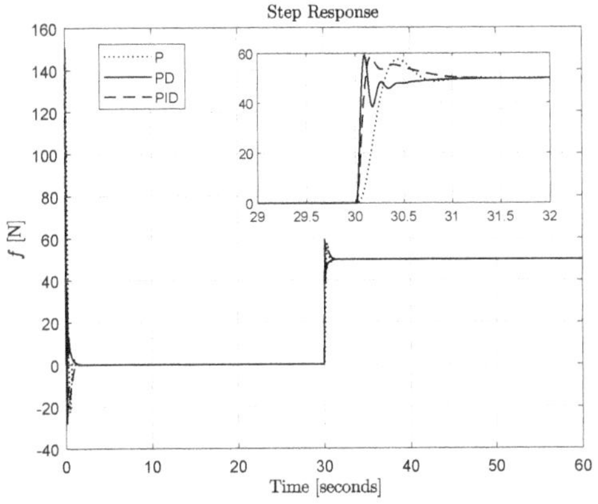

Figure 8. Simulation results: force f with P, PD, and PID.

4.1. Disturbance Rejection

Consider the controller $G_c = K_p + K_d s$ with the parameters of Table 1, and a ramp disturbance of magnitude $M = 3.14 \times 10^{-3}$ emerging at $t = 20$ s. Then, the simulation is performed, and Figure 9 presents the disturbance $x_d(t)$ and the force error e from the simulation. Note that the disturbance $x_d(t)$ produces a force error of $e_{ss} \approx 0.74$ [N]. This error corresponds with that estimated theoretically using $M = 0.00314$ and $K_p = 0.004211$, i.e., $e_{ss} \approx \frac{0.00314}{0.004211} \approx 0.74$.

Considering the design curves of Figure 6, if we want to reduce the error $e_s s$, we need to increment the gain K_p. Then, increasing the gain K_p to $K_{p_a} = K_p + 0.002$ and $K_{p_b} = K_p + 0.004$, the simulation of the force control system using these gains is performed, and the resulting error is shown in Figure 9. One can observe that e_{ss} is reduced when the value of K_p is increased.

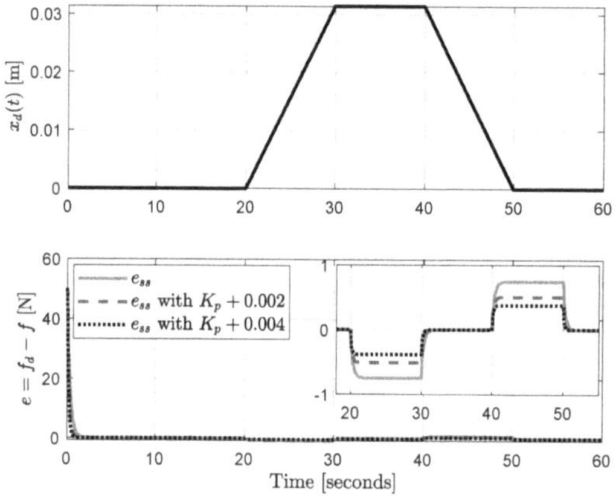

Figure 9. Force error e_{ss} in presence of ramp disturbance and disturbance $x_d(t)$.

Time-Varying Disturbances

Considering a sinusoidal disturbance $x_d(t) = 0.01\sin(0.628t)$ emerging at $t = 20$ s, and the controller $G_c = K_p + K_d s + \frac{K_i}{s}$ with the gains in Table 1, the simulation of the force control system is performed. The resulting force error e is presented in Figure 10 for different values of control magnitude. One can observe that the error decreases when the gains of magnitude of $G_c(s)$ increase, as expected from Equation (6).

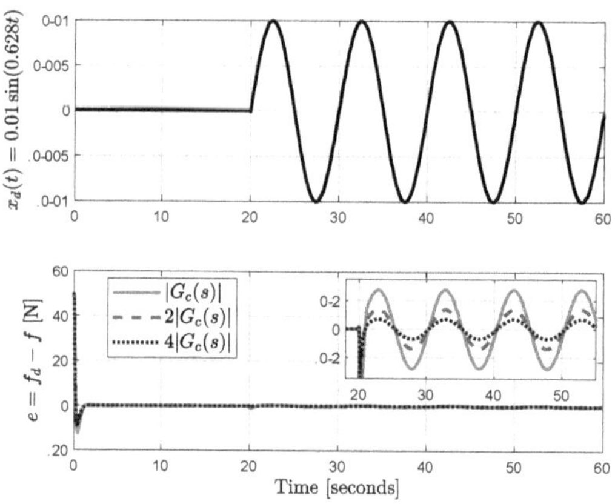

Figure 10. Force error e_{ss} in presence of sinusoidal disturbance $x_d(t) = 0.01\sin(0.628t)$ and disturbance $x_d\ (t)$.

4.2. Stability

In this subsection, we compute the gain margin of the force control system in Figure 3. Figure 11 presents the Bode plot of the system with controller $G_c = K_p + K_d s$ and $G_c = K_p + K_d s + \frac{K_i}{s}$. The gain margin is computed in the crossing of the magnitude Bode plot with zero decibels (see [18]); this intersection is indicated with an arrow in Figure 11. For the PD controller, the gain margin is equal to 11.1 dB, which is equivalent to 3.6 ($10^{(11.1/20)}$) in magnitude. For the PID controller, the gain margin is equal to 16 dB, which is equivalent to 6.3 ($10^{(16/20)}$) in magnitude. This gain margin represents the maximum value of the control gain (magnitude) that one can use without compromising the stability of the system. From the analysis presented in Section 3.3, the gain for the system with the PD controller is $K_{GM_{max}} = 3.6$, and for PID, the magnitude is $K_{GM_{max}} = 6.3$. From the design curves in Figure 5, the control gain K_p can be increased until 3.6 times without losing stability when the PD controller is used.

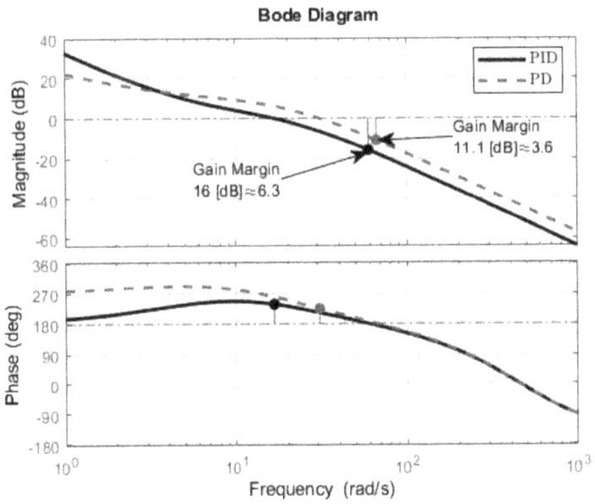

Figure 11. Bode plot and stability margins.

Now, the simulation is executed with $G_c = K_p + K_d s$, and two values of K_p, i.e., $K_{p_1} = 3K_p$ and $K_{p_2} = 3.45K_p$. The resulting force error $e = f_d - f$ is presented in Figure 12a,b. One can observe that the higher the gain, the more oscillations in the force error e. Furthermore, a gain of $K_{p_3} = 3.6K_p$ was tested, but these results are not presented in Figure 12, since this gain produces instability. Note that the simulation results correspond with the gain margin presented in Figure 11, since oscillations appear when the control gains are closer to the gain margin.

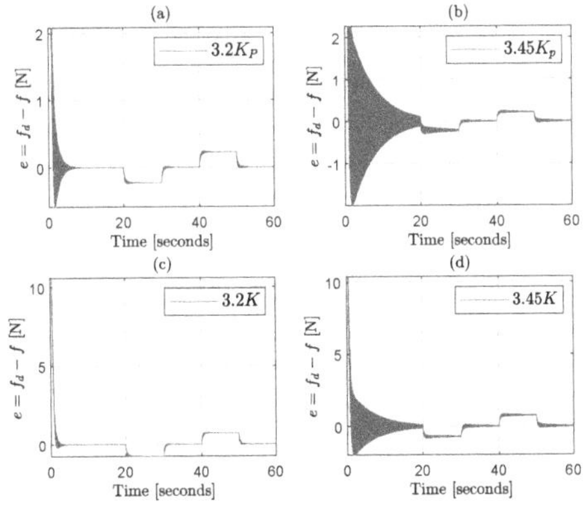

Figure 12. Force error $e = f_d - f$ with PD controller. (**a**,**b**) The control gain K_p increases. (**c**,**d**) The stiffness K increases.

In accordance with Section 3.3, one can relate the gain margin shown in Figure 11 with the maximum value of stiffness that preserves stability. This value is $K_{max} \approx K_{GM_{max}} K \approx 3.6\ K$. Figure 12c,d present the simulation of the force control system with two different values of stiffness, $K_a = 3.2\ K$ and $K_b = 3.45\ K$, where $K = 3000$. The resulting force error e presents oscillations when K increases. For stiffness values higher than 3.5 K, the system lost stability. This unstable case is not presented in Figure 12 for visibility purposes. The simulation matches with the estimated gain margin, since oscillations/instability appear when the value of stiffness K approaches/reaches the gain margin.

4.3. Design Method

In Section 4.2, a gain margin of 3.6 was obtained. Considering a constant stiffness K, the maximum gain K_{pmax} that preserves stability is $K_{p_{max}} \approx 3.6K_p$. Then, adding this maximum gain $K_{p_{max}} \approx 3.6K_p$ into the design curves in Figure 6, one can obtain the gain that keeps the error within desired values while preserving stability. Figure 13 shows the design curves, including the stability margin bound $K_{p_{max}} \approx 3.6(0.004211) \approx 0.0152$. The curves are obtained considering a value of $M = 0.00314$.

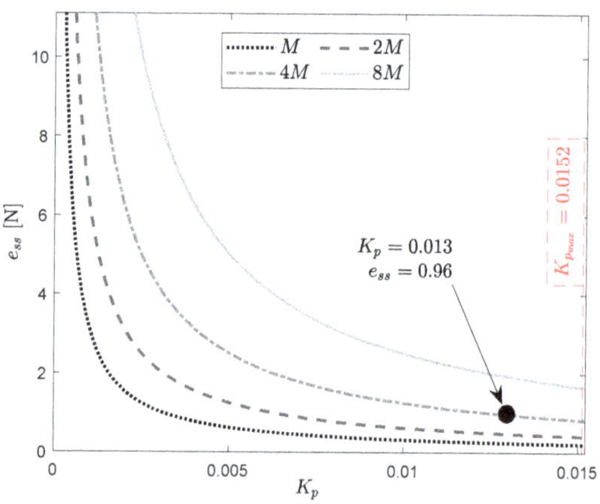

Figure 13. Design method: steady-state error e_{ss} in terms of control gain K_p and ramp value M, considering gain margin.

The curves in Figure 13 can be used to find the control gain K_p that gives a desired force error. Assume the magnitude of the disturbance is provided, for example, $4M$. Then, if one selects a control gain of $K_p = 0.013$, the expected steady-state error is $e_{ss} \approx 0.96$ N (see the curve $4M$ in Figure 13).

Considering the disturbance of magnitude $4M$ and the controller $G_c = K_p + K_d s$ with $K_p = 0.013$, the force control system is simulated. Figure 14 presents the disturbance and the resulting force error e. Note that the force error e in Figure 14, when $K_p = 0.013$, corresponds to the value of $e \approx 1$ in the curves of Figure 13.

Since $K_p = 0.013$ is close to $K_{p_{max}}$, a small increase in K_p can cause oscillations and instability in the system. The presented technique can be combined with root-locus analysis to make an adjustment of K_p to have a desired damping. Figure 15 presents the root-locus of the force control system, computed from the open-loop transfer function $L(s)$ in Equation (7) with $G_c = K_p + K_d s$ and using a second-order Padé approximation of $G_T(s)$, i.e., $G_T(s) =\approx \frac{N_r(sL)}{D_r(sL)}$, where $N_r(sL) = \sum_{k=0}^{r} \frac{(2r-K)!}{k!(r-k)!}(-sT)^k$, $D_r(sL) = \sum_{k=0}^{r} \frac{(2r-K)!}{k!(r-k)!}(sT)^k$, T is the value of the delay, and r is the order of the approximation (see [18]). Figure 15 contains three markers showing the critical gain value 6.3 (similar to the gain margin), the gain 3.08 corresponding to $K_p = 0.013$, and the gain value 0.231 corresponding to a damping factor of 0.7.

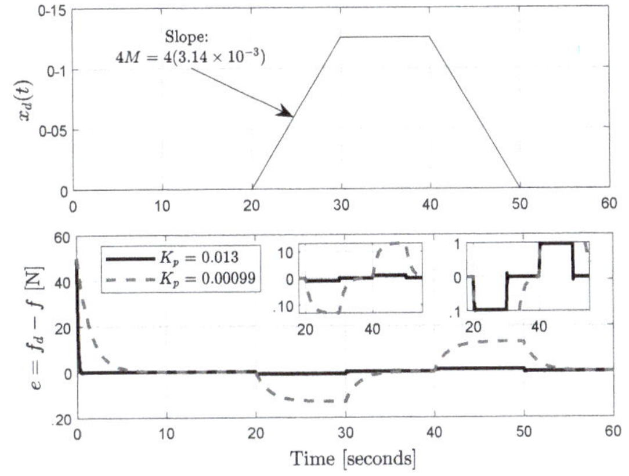

Figure 14. Force error e_{ss} in presence of ramp disturbance and disturbance $x_d(t)$.

Figure 14 presents the simulation when K_p is adjusted by the gain value 0.231, i.e., $K_p = 0.231 \times 0.004422 = 9.9 \times 10^{-4}$. One can see that the force error e has a damped response when $K_p = 9.9 \times 10^{-4}$ but the value of e is bigger than the case when K_P is close to the gain margin value. Therefore, one can observe the compromise between force regulation and stability.

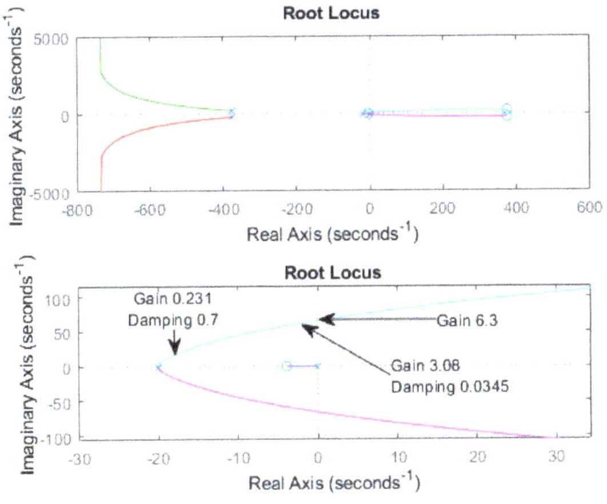

Figure 15. Root-locus analysis computed with $L(s)$ in Equation (7). Bottom part: zoom-in around the origin.

Time-Varying Disturbances

The design curves, such as those in Figure 5, for the case of time-varying disturbance are computed as follows. Considering the disturbance $x_d(t) = 0.01\sin(0.628t)$ and the controller $G_c = K_p + K_d s + \frac{K_i}{s}$ with the gains presented in Table 1, Equation (6) can be used to obtained the curves presented in Figure 16. These curves are computed for a fixed frequency of 0.628 and different sinusoidal amplitudes (from 0.005 to 0.08). The horizontal axis represents the controller magnitude, and the vertical axis represents the deviation of the force from its desired value.

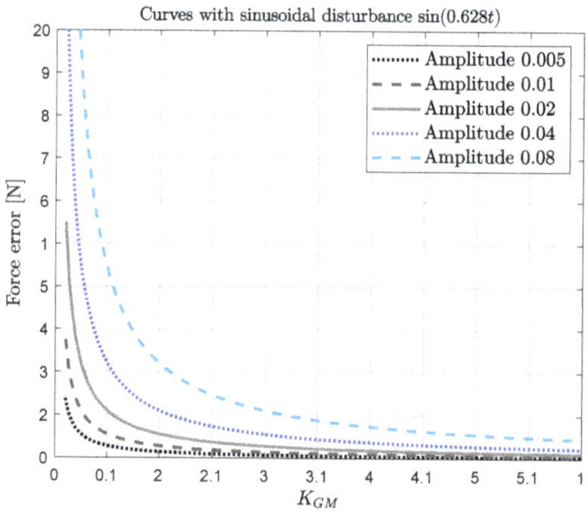

Figure 16. Curves of steady-state error e_{ss} in terms of control gain K_p and sinusoidal amplitude.

The simulation of the force control system with disturbance $x_d(t) = \sin(0.628t)$ for different amplitudes (0.01, 0.02, 0.04, and 0.08) is performed, and the results are presented in Figure 17. Note that the deviation of the force f with respect to the reference $f_d = 50$ N corresponds with the deviation predicted by the curves in Figure 16 for the case $K_{GM} = 1$, since the control magnitude was not changed. Specifically, Figure 16 predicts an approximated deviation of 0.25, 0.5, 1, and 2, when a sinusoidal disturbance with magnitude 0.01, 0.02, 0.04, and 0.08, respectively, appears in the system. This prediction matched with the simulation results presented in Figure 17; see the zoom-in of the figure.

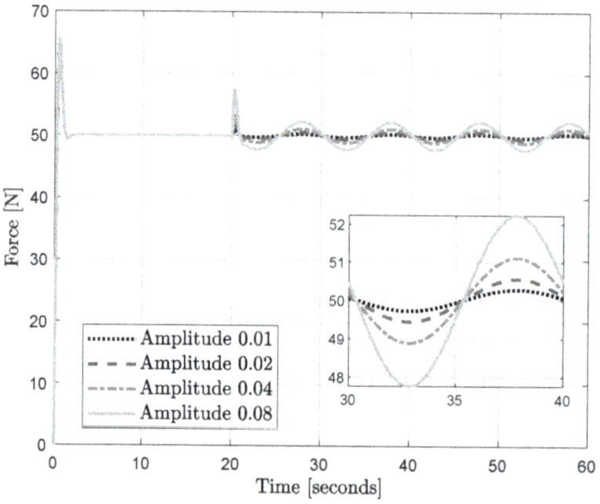

Figure 17. Simulation of the force control system: sinusoidal disturbance with variable amplitude.

When the amplitude of the sinusoidal disturbance is fixed, one can obtain curves similar to those presented in Figure 16 for several frequency values. Figure 18 presents the mentioned curves, when the sinusoidal disturbance has an amplitude of 0.01 and different frequency values. Then, whenever the amplitude and frequency are known, the curves in Figure 18 can be used to tune the control magnitude in accordance with the desired force error.

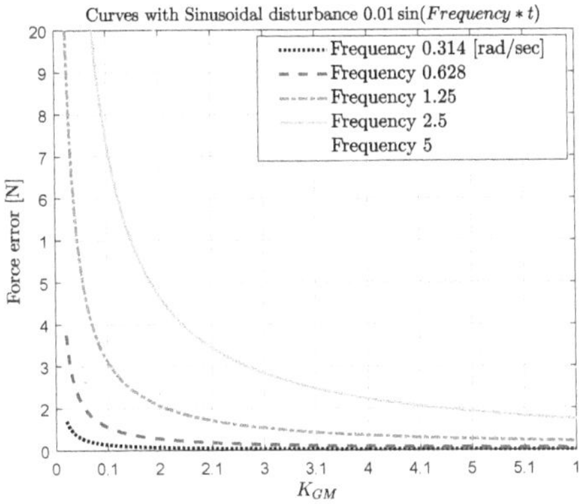

Figure 18. Curves of steady-state error e_{ss} in terms of control magnitude K_{GM} and sinusoidal frequency.

Figure 19 presents the results of the simulation of the force control system with the sinusoidal disturbance of amplitude of 0.01 and different values of frequency. One can see that the simulation results matched with the predicted force error of the design curves in Figure 18. For a control magnitude of one, i.e., $K_{GM} = 1$, the predicted force errors are 0.5, 1, 3.5, and 10 [N], when a disturbance with frequency 0.628, 1.25, 2.5, and 5 rad/s, respectively, emerges. These force errors are similar to the ones obtained in the simulation presented in Figure 19; see the zoom-in. Note that the gain margin of 6.3 (see Figure 11) must be considered during the selection of the control magnitude K_{GM} in the curves presented in Figures 16 and 18.

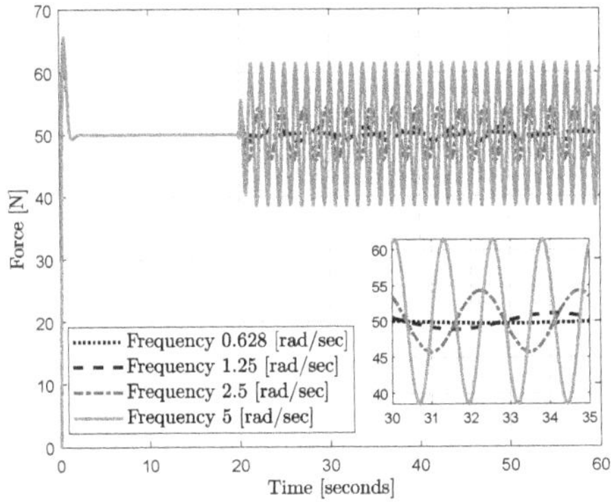

Figure 19. Simulation of the force control system: sinusoidal disturbance with variable frequency.

4.4. Maximum Speed along the Surface

The maximum speed at which the task can be executed is computed as follows. Consider that the maximum force error tolerated by the system is $e_{max} = 3$ N, and controller gain $K_p = 0.005$ (close to the one in Table 1). Then, locating these values in the design curves of Figure 13, one obtains a region containing the possible values of disturbance magnitude M that can be compensated (see Figure 20). The maximum value of M is the one located in the upper right corner of the rectangular region delimited by $e_{max} = 3$ N and $K_p = 0.005$. Note that the maximum value is $4M$. Then, the maximum speed at which the task can be executed is computed as $4M = 4 \times 0.00314 = 0.0126$ m/s.

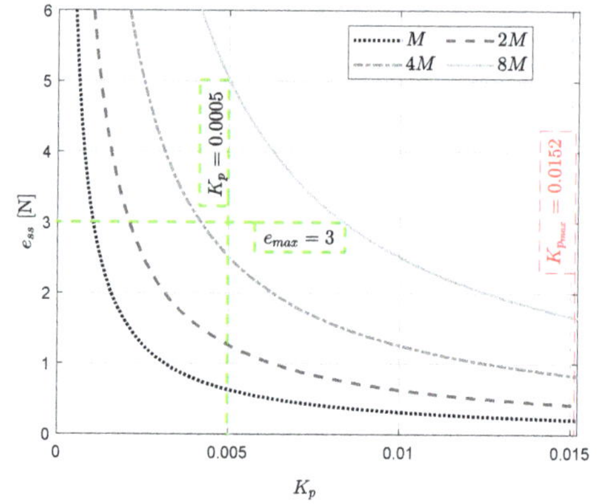

Figure 20. Computing the maximum speed using the curves of steady-state error e_{ss} in terms of control gain K_p and ramp value M.

For the case of time-varying disturbances, the maximum speed at which the task can be executed is computed using the curves presented in Figure 18. Considering a maximum error of $e_{max} = 3$ N and a selection of control magnitude $K_{GM} = 1.5$, the maximum velocity can be estimated with the frequency value associated with the closest curve to the upper right corner of the rectangular region delimited by $e_{max} = 3$ N and $K_{GM} = 1.5$. In Figure 21, this frequency value is 2.5 rad/s. Then, assuming a wavelength $\lambda = 0.1$ m and considering the maximum frequency of 2.5 rad/s, the maximum velocity is $0.1 \times (2.5/2\pi) = 0.0199$ m/s.

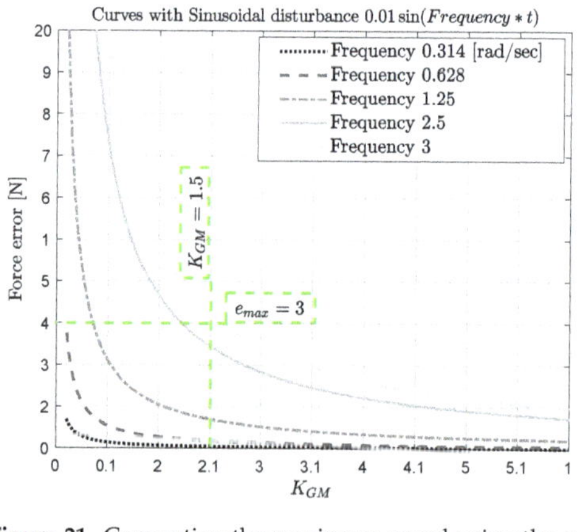

Figure 21. Computing the maximum speed using the curves of steady-state error e_{ss} in terms of control magnitude K_{GM} and disturbance frequency.

5. Conclusions

The methods of analysis and design presented in this paper are useful to keep the force error within desired limits while guaranteeing stability. Furthermore, the presented design curves can be used to estimate the maximum velocity at which the task can be executed. Since this method is model-based, its application requires certain knowledge about the disturbances acting on the system, such as maximum magnitude and frequency. However, these parameters might be available in practical applications or not difficult to estimate. The simulations presented in the paper verify the effectiveness of the proposed methods.

Author Contributions: A.R. and T.H. contributed equally to this paper. All authors have read and agreed to the published version of the manuscript.

Funding: This research was funded by Business Finland and VTT Technical Research Centre of Finland Ltd.

Institutional Review Board Statement: Not applicable.

Informed Consent Statement: Not applicable.

Data Availability Statement: No new data were created or analyzed in this study. Data sharing is not applicable to this article.

Conflicts of Interest: The authors declare no conflict of interest.

References

1. Siciliano, B.; Sciavicco, L.; Villani, L.; Oriolo, G. *Robotics: Modelling, Planning and Control*; Springer: London, UK, 2009.
2. Suomalainen, M.; Karayiannidis, Y.; Kyrki, V. A survey of robot manipulation in contact. *Robot. Auton. Syst.* **2022**, *156*, 104224. [CrossRef]
3. Balachandran, R.; Jorda, M.; Artigas, J.; Ryu, J.H.; Khatib, O. Passivity-based stability in explicit force control of robots. In Proceedings of the 2017 IEEE International Conference on Robotics and Automation (ICRA), Singapore, 29 May–3 June 2017; pp. 386–393. [CrossRef]
4. Mariotti, E.; Magrini, E.; Luca, A.D. Admittance Control for Human-Robot Interaction Using an Industrial Robot Equipped with a F/T Sensor. In Proceedings of the 2019 International Conference on Robotics and Automation (ICRA), Montreal, QC, Canada, 20–24 May 2019; pp. 6130–6136. [CrossRef]
5. Gutierrez-Giles, A.; Evangelista-Hernandez, L.U.; Arteaga, M.A.; Cruz-Villar, C.A.; Rodriguez–Angeles, A. A Force/Motion Control Approach Based on Trajectory Planning for Industrial Robots With Closed Control Architecture. *IEEE Access* **2021**, *9*, 80728–80740. [CrossRef]
6. Keemink, A.Q.; van der Kooij, H.; Stienen, A.H. Admittance control for physical human–robot interaction. *Int. J. Robot. Res.* **2018**, *37*, 1421–1444. [CrossRef]
7. Park, J.H. Compliance/Impedance Control Strategy for Humanoids. In *Humanoid Robotics: A Reference*; Goswami, A., Vadakkepat, P., Eds.; Springer: Dordrecht, The Netherlands, 2016; pp. 1–20. [CrossRef]
8. Zou, W.; Chen, X.; Li, S.; Duan, P.; Yu, N.; Shi, L. Robust Admittance Control for Human Arm Strength Augmentation with Guaranteed Passivity: A Complementary Design. *IEEE/ASME Trans. Mechatron.* **2022**, *27*, 5936–5947. [CrossRef]
9. Griffiths, P.G.; Gillespie, R.B.; Freudenberg, J.S. A Fundamental Linear Systems Conflict Between Performance and Passivity in Haptic Rendering. *IEEE Trans. Robot.* **2011**, *27*, 75–88. [CrossRef]
10. Li, J.; Guan, Y.; Chen, H.; Wang, B.; Zhang, T.; Liu, X.; Hong, J.; Wang, D.; Zhang, H. A High-Bandwidth End-Effector with Active Force Control for Robotic Polishing. *IEEE Access* **2020**, *8*, 169122–169135. [CrossRef]
11. Li, J.; Guan, Y.; Chen, H.; Wang, B.; Zhang, T. Robotic Polishing of Unknown-Model Workpieces With Constant Normal Contact Force Control. *IEEE/ASME Trans. Mechatron.* **2023**, *28*, 1093–1103. [CrossRef]
12. Pérez-Ubeda, R.; Zotovic-Stanisic, R.; Gutiérrez, S.C. Force Control Improvement in Collaborative Robots through Theory Analysis and Experimental Endorsement. *Appl. Sci.* **2020**, *10*, 4329. [CrossRef]
13. Feng, Z.; Liang, W.; Ling, J.; Xiao, X.; Tan, K.K.; Lee, T.H. Precision Force Tracking Control of a Surgical Device Interacting with a Deformable Membrane. *IEEE/ASME Trans. Mechatron.* **2022**, *27*, 5327–5338. [CrossRef]
14. Fan, J.; Jin, L.; Xie, Z.; Li, S.; Zheng, Y. Data-Driven Motion-Force Control Scheme for Redundant Manipulators: A Kinematic Perspective. *IEEE Trans. Ind. Inform.* **2022**, *18*, 5338–5347. [CrossRef]
15. Li, H.; Nie, X.; Duan, D.; Li, Y.; Zhang, J.; Zhou, M.; Magid, E. An admittance-controlled amplified force tracking scheme for collaborative lumbar puncture surgical robot system. *Int. J. Med. Robot. Comput. Assist. Surg.* **2022**, *18*, e2428. [CrossRef] [PubMed]
16. Rosales, A.; Heikkilä, T. On Force Control for Robot Manipulators in Contact with Uneven Planar Surfaces. In Proceedings of the 2022 18th IEEE/ASME International Conference on Mechatronic and Embedded Systems and Applications (MESA), Taipei, Taiwan, 28–30 November 2022; pp. 1–6. [CrossRef]
17. Ahola, J.M.; Koskinen, J.; Seppälä, T.; Heikkilä, T. Development of Impedance Control for Human/Robot Interactive Handling of Heavy Parts and Loads. In Proceedings of the 2015 ASME/IEEE International Conference on Mechatronic and Embedded Systems and Applications, Boston, MA, USA, 2–5 August 2015 [CrossRef]

18. Dorf, R.; Bishop, R. *Modern Control Systems*, 12th ed.; Prentice Hall: Hoboken, NJ, USA, 2011.
19. Rosales, J.A.; Shtessel, Y.; Fridman, L. Phase and Gain Margins in Systems with SMC/HOSM. In Proceedings of the American Control Conference 2012, Montreal, QC, Canada, 27–29 June 2012.

applied sciences

MDPI

Article

Digital Twin of Food Supply Chain for Cyber Exercises

Tuomo Sipola *, Tero Kokkonen, Markku Puura, Kalle-Eemeli Riuttanen, Kari Pitkäniemi, Elina Juutilainen and Teemu Kontio

Institute of Information Technology, Jamk University of Applied Sciences, 40100 Jyväskylä, Finland; tero.kokkonen@jamk.fi (T.K.)
* Correspondence: tuomo.sipola@jamk.fi; Tel.: +358-50-310-3339

Abstract: The food supply chain is a critical part of modern societies. As with other facets of life, it is thoroughly digitalized, and uses network connections. Consequently, the cyber security of the supply chain becomes a major concern as new threats emerge. Cyber ranges can be used to prepare for such cyber security threats by creating realistic scenarios mimicking real-world systems and setups. Organizations can participate in cyber security training and exercises that present them with these scenarios. Cyber ranges can also be used efficiently for research and development activities, because cyber ranges are realistic environments and can be used for the generation of realistic data. The aim of this study is to describe a digital twin of the food supply chain built for cyber range-based cyber security exercises. The digital twin mirrors the real-world situation with sufficient detail, as required by the cyber exercise. This research uses the design science methodology, which describes the construction and evaluation of the proposed system. The study explains the general capabilities of the food supply chain digital twin and its use in the cyber range environment. Different parts of the supply chain are implemented as Node.js services that run on the Realistic Global Cyber Environment (RGCE) platform. The flow of ingredients and products is simulated using an apparatus model and message queues. The digital twin was demonstrated in a real live cyber exercise. The results indicate that the apparatus approach was a scalable and realistic enough way to implement the digital twin. The main limitations of the implemented system are the implementation on one specific platform, and the need for more feedback from multiple exercises. Creation of a digital twin enables the use of cyber ranges to train organizations related to the food supply chain.

Keywords: cyber security; cyber exercise; digital twin; critical systems; food supply chain

Citation: Sipola, T.; Kokkonen, T.; Puura, M.; Riuttanen, K.-E.; Pitkäniemi, K.; Juutilainen, E.; Kontio, T. Digital Twin of Food Supply Chain for Cyber Exercises. *Appl. Sci.* **2023**, *13*, 7138. https://doi.org/10.3390/app13127138

Academic Editor: Jose Machado

Received: 28 April 2023
Revised: 5 June 2023
Accepted: 13 June 2023
Published: 14 June 2023

1. Introduction

The food supply chain represents the interlinked flow of raw materials to food products. It consists of food production, processing, distribution, and retail [1]. Such systems include traditional and modern Internet of Things (IoT) devices. As a critical system, the resilience of the supply chain against any disturbances is important [2], including environmental [3] and pandemic [4] reasons. Cyber threats against supply chains have been identified earlier, e.g., using target IT systems to facilitate weapons trafficking, pharma sabotage, or cargo theft [5]. Similar threats could target any supply chain, taking into account their characteristics. The concept of the supply chain covers all aspects of society, including the use of subsidy schemes, which can be modeled mathematically [6]. Demand disruptions are possible, and the effects of such events can be modeled in a simplified setup of one manufacturer and one retailer [7]. Figure 1 illustrates the basic schematic structure of the food supply chain, adapted from [1,8].

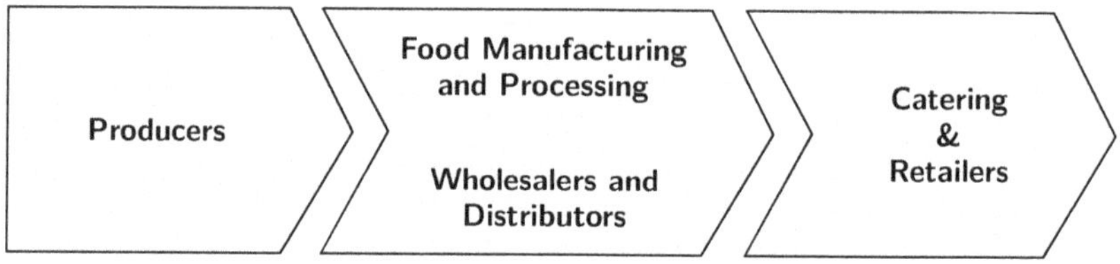

Figure 1. Food supply chain.

1.1. Cyber Exercises

Like all IT systems, the food supply chain is vulnerable to cyber security threats, e.g., in the areas of smart farming and cyber–physical systems [9]. Cyber attacks against food supply chains can be devastating. Therefore, preparing for such scenarios in a safe environment is important. An effective solution to enhance the knowledge and skills of staff members against cyber threats is the cyber security exercise, where the learning audience participates in a realistic scenario using a technical infrastructure that mirrors the systems and networks in the real world [10]. Such technical infrastructure is called cyber range and/or cyber arena, especially when an expansive environment is considered. Karjalainen and Kokkonen introduce the requirements for cyber arena environments [11]: (i) realism, (ii) isolated and controlled environment, (iii) internet simulation, (iv) user and network traffic generation, (v) attack execution and simulation, (vi) organizations' infrastructures, (vii) collaboration, and (viii) planning, executing, monitoring, and analyzing. When creating new target domains for cyber arenas, the requirements of realism, user and network traffic generation, and organizations' infrastructures in particular become essential.

Cyber arenas need services that replicate the real-world environments where the staff members would face realistic cyber attacks. One way of replicating the food supply chain is to create a digital twin, which mirrors the production cycle and factory setups of the domain. Digital models such as digital twins have their roots in life-cycle management, with a focus on computational modeling; they are virtual representations mirroring physical systems [12]. These models are, naturally, software programs that copy the behavior of their real-world counterparts. The exact definition of a digital twin is an elusive concept that is perhaps not enough distinguished from computing models and simulations [13].

Figure 2 illustrates a typical cyber exercise conducted in a cyber arena. Domain expertise defines the scenario, which can be realized with digital twins and models. The white team (WT), also known as exercise control, controls the planning and execution of the exercise. The blue team (BT) is the learning audience of the exercise defending their systems: by implementing required incident response and forensics maneuvers, for example. The BT is usually modeled in accordance with real organizational structures, and there can be one or several BTs in the exercise. The red team (RT) acts as the threat actor by executing real cyber attacks against the exercise assets of the BTs [14,15]. There is also a green team (GT); they act as system administrations for the whole exercise environment. Basically, the GT enable the technical exercise and assist the other teams if there are out-of-scenario technical issues during the exercise. In this paper, the domain is the food supply chain, the organizations are companies in that domain, and the Realistic Global Cyber Environment (RGCE) [16] serves as the cyber arena.

The cyber arena models the whole networked information security infrastructure required for the cyber exercise. Consequently, it can be realized using digital twins, which meet the requirements set by cyber security exercises. Themes related to digital twins, such as physical and virtual processes and virtual environments [17], are relevant in the cyber arena.

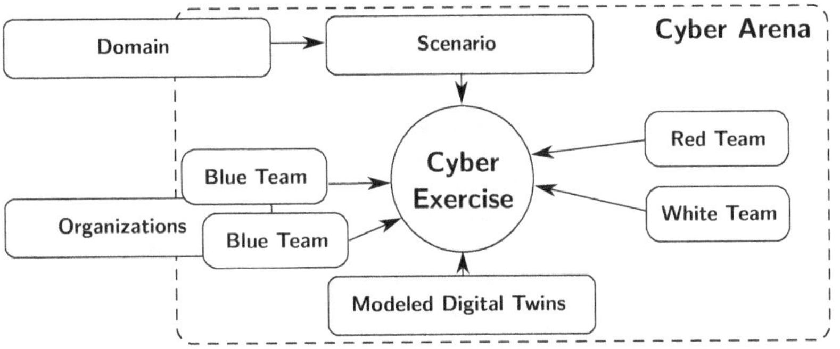

Figure 2. Elements of a cyber exercise.

1.2. Digital Twins and Supply Chain

Digital twins include a physical and a virtual entity, which should have a similar state in the end of the realized twinning. The physical entity is measured or observed, and then realized as a virtual entity. The flow of information is similar: back from the virtual entity back to the real world [17]. The concept of the digital model might be more appropriate for our research, i.e., a system where data flow is not automatic [13]. However, the supply chain itself is not a single distinct entity, but a network of actors. Calling a digital representation of such an entity a digital twin is meaningful, as the concept itself is not well-defined.

The data flows in mirroring or twinning are presented in Figure 3, as suggested by Jones et al. [17]. Such real-time approaches are not quite feasible for cyber security situations, not least because of the often sensitive nature of the domain data. We discuss the actual solution in the result section of this paper.

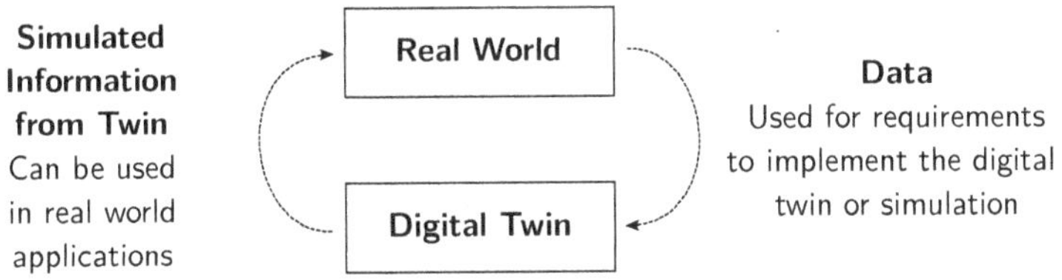

Figure 3. Theoretical dependencies between a real-world system and a digital twin.

The use of digital twins is somewhat implicit in cyber exercises. The concept for a supply chain digital twin has been discussed elsewhere, e.g., by Barykin et al. [18]. They conclude that such twins differ from twins of other—mainly physical—concepts, and that simulation, optimization, and data analytics are the main technologies needed for implementation, although there is no clarity about this in the literature they reviewed. Wang et al. propose a smart supply chain driven by digital twins and highlight a real-use case involving a retailer [19]. Marmolejo-Saucedo describes the design and development of digital twins for supply chains. The presented case study focuses on a pharmaceutical company, and includes simulations related to the supply chain [20]. In their review, Abideen et al. [21] emphasize the use of data analytics as the next step for digital twins in the supply chain and logistics.An review articleby Eckhart and Ekelhart [22] concludes that the concept of digital twins has possibilities beyond the few present uses. They also present a definition of the digital twin for cyber–physical systems, where real-time or historical data is used to build a replica with sufficient fidelity. Studies such as Alim et al. [23] have implemented digital twins with physical testbeds to mirror farmland canal systems. Enns and Suwanruji have created a simulation testbed that was used for supply chain modeling. The solution was based on network flows and featured a user interface [24]. The mentioned studies illustrate the usefulness of digital twins in testbeds for various domains. However, little literature exists about actual implementations of such systems in the context of supply chains and cyber security.

1.3. Aims and Motivation

We aim to show that the digital twin can also be built to support cyber security concerns. Consequently, a digital twin of relevant parts of the food supply chain is described. This study aims to describe the implementation of the food production cyber arena, which meets the eight high-level requirements mentioned above. This digital representation facilitates the creation of a simulated supply chain for a cyber exercise aimed at organizations working in the domain of food production and processing. For example, food production companies could exercise their response to cyber attacks targeted at critical points in their processes. A cyber exercise in the food supply domain could include participants from a food processing factory. Staff members from departments such as management, communications, and operations could participate. The scenario includes a cyber attack to the factory, to which the participants should react. The resolution of the problem will provide resilience information to the departments. In this article, we describe the design of the digital twin for this purpose.

The following key questions in this study can be identified:

- RQ1: How can we develop a digital twin of the food supply chain for cyber exercises?
- RQ2: What kind of simulation concept fulfills the requirements of the food supplychain digital twin?

This article is structured in the following manner. After the introduction, the cyber range used in this study, the Realistic Global Cyber Environment (RGCE), is described in Section 2. Section 3 describes the proposed design, the design science approach used in this study, the requirements of the system, architecture, implementation, and simulation concerns. The results are discussed in Section 4, describing the use of digital twins in RGCE, and evaluating how the system fulfilled the requirements. Finally, Section 5 concludes the article.

2. Realistic Global Cyber Environment

The most recognized term for a technical cyber exercise environment is the cyber range. To understand the term cyber range, it can be associated with a shooting range where one can improve one's skills with firearms [25], or a driving range, where players can improve their golf swings. In a cyber range, one can train and improve their cyber security-related skills and tactics. There are, globally, a multitude of cyber ranges developed by governmental organizations, industries, universities, and research centers. The inaccuracy of the term cyber range is that it is used from the one-server testbed to enormous infrastructure mimicking global internet in organization environments.Because of this heterogeneity, Karjalainen and Kokkonen introduced the term cyber arena to describe those massive cyber environments which are implemented for the simulation of a total and complex cyber–physical system of systems [11].

One of the most valuable and critical assets of cyber security is the knowledge and skills (know-how) of the individuals. At the organizational level, the cyber know-how of the staff members forms the cyber resilience of the organization. Cyber exercise is an effective way to improve skills facing the stressful situation of a cyber attack. Cyber exercise is beneficial to the skills of individual people but also to the cyber security capability of the organization. During the exercise, organization's internal processes and co-operation interfaces with other organizations are trained during realistic scenarios in a realistic environment. To demonstrate the need for such environments, we refer to Finland's cyber security strategy, where measures to promote cyber security competence include, for example [26], *"Training programmes related to cyber and information security"*. The strategy also emphasizes the support provided *"by both national and international training and exercises"* [26]. Nationally, exercises are encouraged as well as *"digital security training in the public administration"* to develop the personnel's skills, including those of businesses, stakeholders, and citizens [26].

The cyber arena used for this study is the RGCE, which is a fully functional live cyber arena. It performs in an isolated private cloud, a realistic digital globe with realistic organization environments, by combining virtualization techniques, physical devices, and business-specific systems. As a digital twin of that global entity, it offers possibilities not only for realistic trainings and exercises but also for research and development activities [16].

RGCE is isolated and fully controlled, so it allows usage of vulnerabilities and real attack vectors, which is a specific feature to be considered when implementing a digital twin for cyber exercises: how can we realistically mimic the systems that can be compromised during the cyber exercise?RGCE has been implemented since 2011 by various research and development projects. In the ongoing project *Food Chain Cyber Resilience*, critical food-production infrastructure is mimicked as a digital twin for cyber security exercises for food-production organizations [27]. The environment is implemented and hosted by the JYVSECTEC (Jyväskylä Security Technology) center for cyber security, artificial intelligence, and data analytics-focused research. The development and training center is hosted by the Institute of Information Technology at Jamk University of Applied Sciences.

3. Proposed Design

3.1. Design Science Approach

This study takes the design science approach. The approach focuses on the processes and especially the artifacts created in the processes. The two main tasks are to build and evaluate the artifact during the research. Consequently, the approach is suitable for information science research [28]. Design science closely resembles constructive research, where the goal is also to produce an artifact [29]. The presentation of such research varies, although some efforts have been made when considering software engineering and design science [30]. The process elements of design science can be summarized as follows [31]:

- Problem identification and motivation,
- Objectives of a solution,
- Design and development,
- Demonstration,
- Evaluation,
- Communication.

The goal of the design science process is to create a new artifact, which in this study is the digital twin model of the food supply chain. The objectives and design are described further in this section. The demonstration and evaluation of the system take place during the cyber exercises that use the digital twin, which are discussed in Section 4 of this article.

3.2. Requirements

The requirements were discovered from domain experts via interviews and group work. Both domain requirements and cyber exercise requirements need to be taken into account when creating a system for the cyber arena. The requirements considered the following categories: (i) Realistic enough to represent farms and factories. (ii) Factory system simulation at the level that cyber attacks could be used against the simulated machines. (iii) Scalable and flexible so that multiple copies of the target, e.g., farms, could be created effortlessly. (iv) Possibility to represent food shipments and storage. (v) Dynamic possibility to create recipes for food products.

3.3. Architecture and Implementation

Figure 4 illustrates the setup of the food supply chain simulation. The basis for the simulation was mainly implemented using the Node.js runtime environment. Each service is simulated using the Node.js application that provided the needed interfaces. The various services run on virtual machines in containers on the virtual machine platform of the cyber arena. The services communicate via the (virtual) network, sending the simulated control messages and simulated material flow using TCP/IP. Messages are passed using REST APIs or mock-ups of protocols such as Modbus. Such messages are usually formatted as JSON using schemas specific to the scenario. Storage is presented with a simple PostgreSQL database solution, which can increase and decrease the amount of material as needed by the scenario or as requested by the simulation. The raw materials and products passed from apparatus to another are simulated using the Bull queue system for the Redis in-memory cache. Figure 5 also shows the relation of the technologies to the simulation.

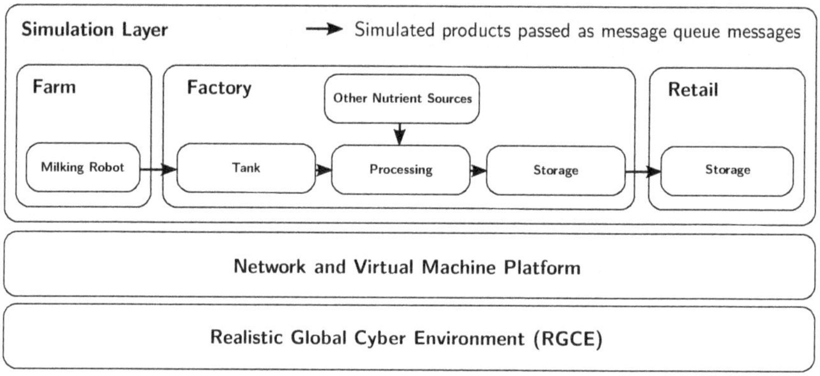

Figure 4. Food supply chain simulation building blocks.

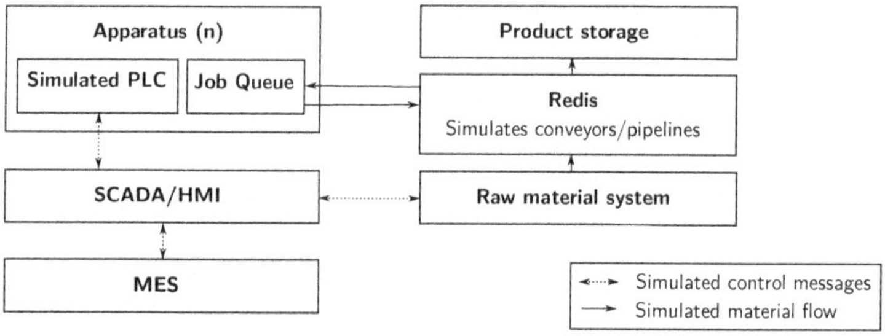

Figure 5. Apparatus schematic.

3.4. Simulation

The simulated factory in the cyber exercise is created so that malicious actors can use cyber attacks against the factory. Each of the parts described below can be targeted as required by the exercise scenario.

The supply chain itself is modeled using two basic elements: apparatus and messages. The apparatus represents the various machines and storage in the supply chain. Apparatus can represent, for example, milking robots, food-processing machines, and packaging machines. The messages are passed from one apparatus to another. These messages contain the relevant domain information (e.g., a message could contain the amount of milk in liters), and metadata (such as the measurement unit).

The simulated factory has the following parts created as Node.js services. As with many industrial applications, a supervisory control and data acquisition (SCADA) unit controls the programmable logic controllers (PLC). Both SCADA and PLCs are built for the exercise scenario. The SCADA system is used via a human machine interface (HMI), which enables humans to give commands via, for example, a web interface. While SCADA controls the machinery's PLCs, the manufacturing execution system (MES) controls the production process itself. Therefore, the production plan dictated by MES will be followed by SCADA, which commands the individual apparatuses. For exercise purposes, each of these can have bespoke user interfaces created for the exercise scenario.

The apparatus are the various machines in the factory. There can be many apparatus, since a food-production process could require multiple sequential or parallel steps. A simulated apparatus contains a PLC, which runs programs as instructed by SCADA, and a job queue, which requests raw materials from conveyors and sends products to conveyors.

The raw material system (RMS) contains various tanks, from which the SCADA system can make requests. There could be a tank for each type of ingredient which can be arbitrarily created for the exercise scenario. The virtual raw material is then conveyed to the apparatuses, which require ingredients to create the products. Redis simulates the conveyors and pipelines in the factory. Product storage is the end point for the products.

The apparatus schematic is shown in Figure 5. Here, all simulated control messages and simulated material flow are passed via TCP/IP at the exercise infrastructure level.

4. Results and Discussion

4.1. Digital Twins in RGCE

The RGCE can be considered as one comprehensive digital twin of the global internet, consisting of several interconnected digital twins. As a basis, there is the RGCE's internet, consisting of several realistic functions and services: for example, BGP routing and realistic structure with public IP addresses, or global PKI infrastructure for certificates. The RGCE includes a wide range of internet public services, such as news sites, social media, and discussion forums. The other layer of the digital twins in the RGCE are the specific organization environments. There is a wide range of organization environments implemented for the RGCE: financial organization, electricity companies, and healthcare-related organizations, to name a few examples. As in the real world, there are interrelated connections between those different elements and, for example, a cyber attack against an electricity company may cause cascade effects to other elements. Similarly, attacks against some crucial software may cause effects on another organization, or if the other organization offers services to another, those might be interrupted because of the cyber attack, which allows training for co-operation between organizations [16].

In this study, the digital twin of the food-production value chain is modeled. It consists of several organizational elements connected digitally which are dependent on those previously implemented services. These parts of the food production value chain are, for example, smart farming, food-production companies, and retail chains. For example, if there is a cyber attack against a refrigeration unit of the food-production organization, it affects other elements, and that same unit with the same vulnerability can also be used in retail.

During the implementation of those digital twins, there is a lot of co-operation between the real actors of the industry sectors. By that co-operation, the requirements for the implementation can be gathered to ensure that the implemented digital twins are, from the cyber security training and exercise point of view, as realistic as possible.

The schematic idea behind every digital twin in the RGCE is presented in Figure 6. The requirements describing processes and structures related to the domain are passed from the real world. The feedback to the real world after an exercise concerns organizational practices and processes.

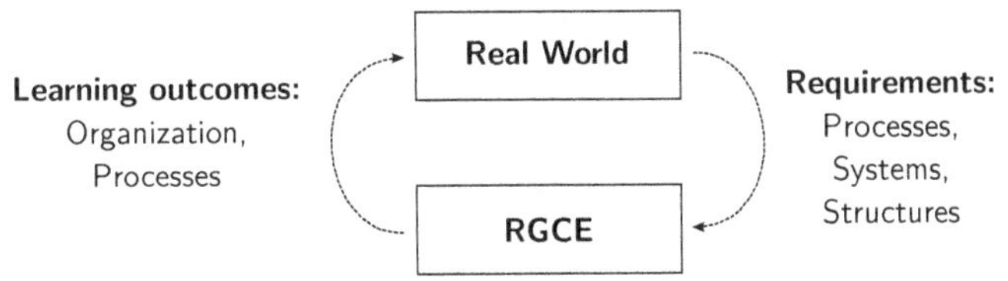

Figure 6. Digital representations in RGCE.

4.2. Evaluation

The implemented digital twin of the food production value chain was tested during the pilot cyber security exercise on 28–29 March 2023. Participants of the exercise varied from governmental organizations to the private sector, including direct participants of food production (for example, smart farming, food production, and retail chains) but also companies that offer services for food production (for example, internet service operators or manufacturers of special hardware) [27,32].

The requirements for the system are presented in the previous Section 3.2. Table 1 compares the requirements with the implemented solution. In the following sections, the requirements are evaluated individually, based on the cyber exercise where the system was used as part of the cyber arena.

Table 1. Solutions that were implemented to satisfy the requirements.

Requirement	Solution
Realism of the environment	Realistic products and descriptions, realistic supply chain components
Factory system as cyber attack target	Open to vulnerabilities, identifiable inconsistencies
Scalability	Each apparatus running on dedicated virtual instance
Representation of food shipments and storage	JSON descriptions and Redis pipeline
Dynamic food recipes	Versatile JSON descriptions

4.2.1. Realism of the Environment

The realism of the environment was achieved with the use of realistic products and product descriptions. The sufficient representation of the food supply chain was achieved so that the participants could recognize and understand the simulated supply chain. The visual presentation of the various views was also a concern. The ultimate evaluation for this is how well the system was received by the participants of the cyber exercise.

After the exercise, feedback was collected from the participants in order to further develop the cyber arena and the exercise concept. As a motivation for this goal, it seemed that nearly all of the BT and WT members would participate in an exercise again.Feedback also included ideas and requirements for future development. In general, it can be said that the pilot exercise was a success, and the participants were satisfied with the technical implementation. Furthermore, the pilot exercise was arranged to identify possible deficiencies and future implementation topics. After a thorough analysis of the feedback and the next version of the implementation, there will be the first full version of the food production cyber range as a digital twin for training and exercise usage.

Figure 7 shows the view in the SCADA/HMI (see also Figure 5) This view indicates the production status of three production lines. The name of the line and the current product are mentioned on the left. The completion percentage of the production line for the batch is indicated on the right.

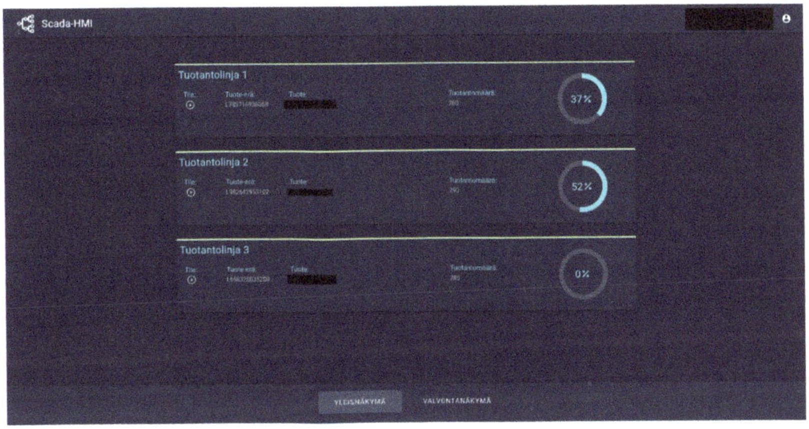

Figure 7. Production-line view in the user interface.

4.2.2. Factory System as Cyber Attack Target

The system was used during a cyber exercise. This demonstrates that it was at a mature enough level to provide cyber attack targets for the exercise scenario. The use of the system also shows that its functioning could be disturbed in a meaningful way, so that the participants could detect the attack, react, and defend the critical infrastructure. By leaving the system open to simulated cyber attacks, the red team could create threat scenarios during the exercise. The participants were able to detect the consequences and inconsistencies in the information. Figure 8 shows an interface to follow the production process. Interruptions in the graphs and logs could indicate cyber attacks. Either the organizing white team or the defending blue team could use such an interface to monitor the processes.

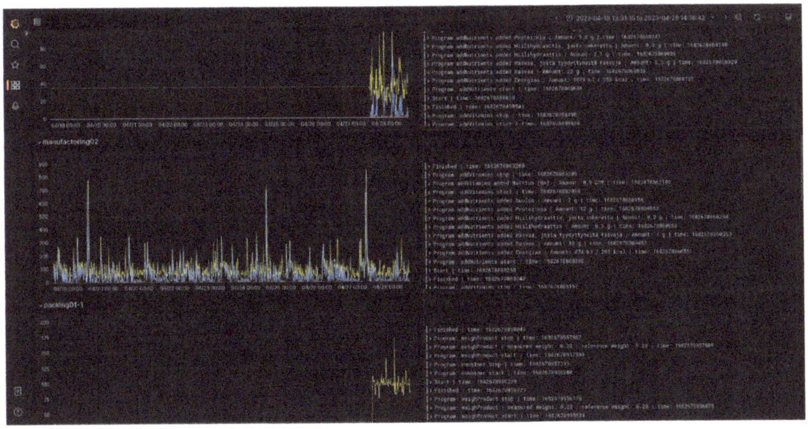

Figure 8. Apparatus monitoring.

4.2.3. Scalability

Running all apparatuses on one virtual machine was not feasible because a realistic representation of the food supply chain contains many production lines and many machines. Consequently, each apparatus runs on its own virtual instance, so that new apparatus can be spawned and killed from the simulation as needed by the exercise scenario. This way, only the capacity of the virtual machine platform limits the size of the simulated manufacturing plants. Figure 9 shows the user interface to inspect a certain production line, where each block is one apparatus in the line and there are seven in total in this line. This illustrates how crucial it is to have a scalable number of apparatus. A full supply chain simulation includes several production lines.

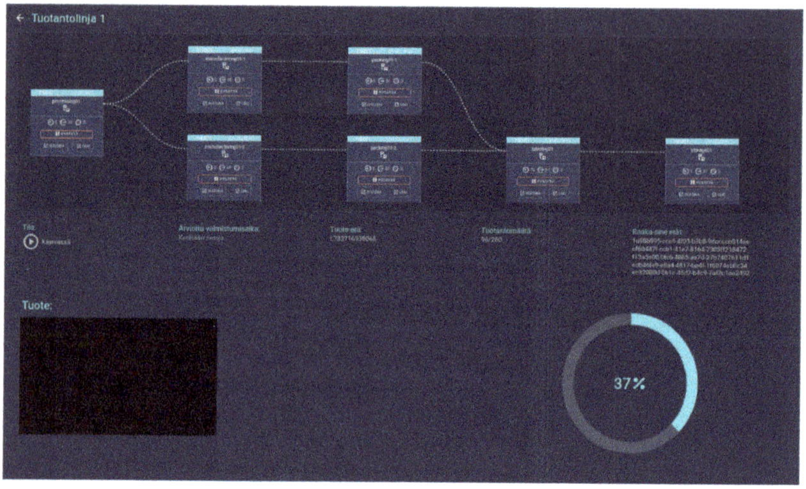

Figure 9. Apparatus in a production line.

4.2.4. Representation of Food Shipments and Storage

Representing food shipments was one of the core features for demonstrating the food supply chain. As described in Section 3.4, the raw material system and product storage services represent the storage. Food shipments were simulated, and the representations of raw material and food product shipments were handled internally as JSON messages. The relevant information was included in the shipment messages. Listing 1 provides an example of the representations of the raw materials in the system. Each shipment has an ID number and metrics describing its properties relevant to the food supply chain use case.

Listing 1. JSON representation of raw material.


```
{
        "id": "283d61bf-fafd-465a-a525-ca43b27c4cbe",
        "amount": 359,
        "batchId": "7552b60a-6413-4d2d-82b5-e3d2255ae4b6",
        "metrics": {
             "temperature": 5,
             "acidValue": 2.2132,
             "somaticCells": 344558
        },
        "type": "milk"
}
```


4.2.5. Dynamic Food Recipes

There was also a need to represent the products in detail, so that cyber attacks in the production line could cause changes in the composition of the products. The label and content descriptions of the products were sufficient to enable the tracking of product contents during the cyber exercise. In a cyber attack scenario, the description on the label could be erroneous due to manufacturing deficiency. A shortened example of the basic structure of food product representations is shown in Listing 2.

Listing 2. A shortened example of JSON representation of food products.

```
{
      "label": {
         "ean": "1234567890",
         "name": "Rye bread product X",
         "lotId": "L077007126630",
         "price": {
           "vat": {
                 "rate": 12,
                 "class": 3
            },
            "value": 1.50,
            "currency": "\euro",
            "priceUnit": ""
          },
      },
      "content": {
          "properties": {
             "nutrients": [
                {
                   "name": "Energy",
                   "value": "1213 kJ / 290 kcal"
                },
                {
                    "name": "Carbohydrate",
                    "value": "50 g"
                },
             ]
          },
          "batchAmount": 0.200
      }
   }
}
```

5. Conclusions

This article presented a way to design a digital twin to represent supply chains for cyber exercises. The development of a digital twin of a food supply chain for cyber exercises (RQ1) could be achieved with standard web technologies. The design of a food supply chain digital twin uses generic apparatus services to simulate various production machines. In addition, the raw material system and the end storage can be simulated with databases and queues. Standard web technologies are sufficient to build the services required by a digital twin for cyber exercises. Accordingly, the developed simulation concept for the food supply chain (RQ2) followed a web service architecture. The use of simulated parts of the food supply chain actors, such as MES and SCADA, facilitates the immersiveness of the exercise. In addition, the scalable apparatus architecture makes it feasible to create new scenarios and extend the existing ones, depending on the domain needs.

Digital modeling and twinning can be seen as valuable tools for exercises. When building digital twins, a restricted domain and application area, e.g., cyber security, serve to constrain the complexity of the system. However, the evaluation of such constructs could be difficult because of the specifics of the domain. The realistic nature of the scenario is essential to cyber exercises. The simulated products were dynamically created as a process which enabled unusual events during the exercise. Cyber attacks against such targets are sensible for the attackers (RT) and for the exercise, because the consequences affect a realistic process.

The main limitation of this study is that the system was built for one specific cyber range, the RGCE. The solutions used in this cyber range could be idiosyncratic to it, and adaptability to other environments might be inconvenient. Secondly, as this is the first iteration of this kind of digital twin approach, the design and development process of future digital twins might reveal better technical practices in the implementation.

The use of digital twins of domain systems as part of cyber exercises improves the immersiveness by simulating real supply chains. This way, the participants can exercise in a realistic environment which mirrors the systems and processes in their ordinary work. Implementing the digital twin requires a modular design with appropriate messaging simulating the real-world counterparts. Further research includes detailed validation by analyzing the conducted cyber exercises. The generalizability of the solution could also be studied.

Author Contributions: Conceptualization, M.P., K.-E.R., K.P., E.J. and T.K. (Teemu Kontio); methodology, M.P., K.-E.R., K.P., E.J. and T.K. (Teemu Kontio); software, M.P., K.-E.R., K.P., E.J. and T.K. (Teemu Kontio); investigation, T.S. and T.K. (Tero Kokkonen); resources, T.K. (Tero Kokkonen); writing—original draft preparation, T.S. and T.K. (Tero Kokkonen); writing—review and editing, T.S., T.K. (Tero Kokkonen) and M.P.; visualization, M.P. and T.S.; supervision, T.K. (Tero Kokkonen); project administration, T.K. (Teemu Kontio) and T.S.; funding acquisition, T.K. (Tero Kokkonen). All authors have read and agreed to the published version of the manuscript.

Funding: This research and the APC were funded by the Regional Council of Central Finland/Council of Tampere Region with fund of Leverage from the EU, European Regional Development Fund (ERDF) and Recovery Assistance for Cohesion and the Territories of Europe (REACT-EU) Instrument as part of the European Union's response to the COVID-19 pandemic, as part of the Food Chain Cyber Resilience project of Jamk University of Applied Sciences Institute of Information Technology (grant number A77620).

Institutional Review Board Statement: Not applicable.

Informed Consent Statement: Not applicable.

Data Availability Statement: Data sharing not applicable.

Acknowledgments: The authors would like to thank project manager Elina Suni for assistance with project data and Tuula Kotikoski for proofreading the manuscript.

Conflicts of Interest: The authors declare no conflict of interest.

References

1. Bourlakis, M.A.; Weightman, P.W.H. Introduction to the UK Food Supply Chain. In *Food Supply Chain Management*; Bourlakis, M.A., Weightman, P.W.H., Eds.; Blackwell: Oxford, UK, 2004; Chapter 1, pp. 1–10.
2. Manning, L.; Soon, J.M. Building strategic resilience in the food supply chain. *Br. Food J.* **2016**, *118*, 1477–1493. [CrossRef]
3. Davis, K.F.; Downs, S.; Gephart, J.A. Towards food supply chain resilience to environmental shocks. *Nat. Food* **2021**, *2*, 54–65. [CrossRef] [PubMed]
4. Hobbs, J.E. Food supply chain resilience and the COVID-19 pandemic: What have we learned? *Can. J. Agric. Econ. Can. D'Agroecon.* **2021**, *69*, 189–196. [CrossRef]
5. Urciuoli, L.; Männistö, T.; Hintsa, J.; Khan, T. Supply chain cyber security — Potential threats. *Inf. Secur. Int. J.* **2013**, *29*, 51–68. [CrossRef]
6. Li, C.; Liu, Q.; Zhou, P.; Huang, H. Optimal innovation investment: The role of subsidy schemes and supply chain channel power structure. *Comput. Ind. Eng.* **2021**, *157*, 107291. [CrossRef]
7. Zhai, Y.; Bu, C.; Zhou, P. Effects of channel power structures on pricing and service provision decisions in a supply chain: A perspective of demand disruptions. *Comput. Ind. Eng.* **2022**, *173*, 108715. [CrossRef]
8. Stock, J.R. The US Food Supply Chain. In *Food Supply Chain Management*; Bourlakis, M.A., Weightman, P.W.H., Eds.; Blackwell: Oxford, UK, 2004; Chapter 14, pp. 211–220.
9. Alatalo, J.; Sipola, T.; Kokkonen, T. Food Supply Chain Cyber Threats: A Scoping Review. In Proceedings of the WorldCist'23—11th World Conference on Information Systems and Technologies, Pisa, Italy, 4–6 April 2023; *in press*.
10. Kokkonen, T.; Päijänen, J.; Sipola, T. Multi-National Cyber Security Exercise, Case Flagship 2. In Proceedings of the 14th International Conference on Education Technology and Computers (ICETC 2022), Barcelona, Spain, 28–30 October 2022; p. 7. [CrossRef]
11. Karjalainen, M.; Kokkonen, T. Comprehensive Cyber Arena; The Next Generation Cyber Range. In Proceedings of the 2020 IEEE European Symposium on Security and Privacy Workshops (EuroS&PW), Genoa, Italy, 7–11 September 2020; pp. 11–16. [CrossRef]
12. VanDerHorn, E.; Mahadevan, S. Digital Twin: Generalization, characterization and implementation. *Decis. Support Syst.* **2021**, *145*, 113524. [CrossRef]
13. Fuller, A.; Fan, Z.; Day, C.; Barlow, C. Digital Twin: Enabling Technologies, Challenges and Open Research. *IEEE Access* **2020**, *8*, 108952–108971. [CrossRef]

14. Kokkonen, T.; Puuska, S. Blue Team Communication and Reporting for Enhancing Situational Awareness from White Team Perspective in Cyber Security Exercises. In *Internet of Things, Smart Spaces, and Next Generation Networks and Systems*; Galinina, O., Andreev, S., Balandin, S., Koucheryavy, Y., Eds.; Springer International Publishing: Cham, Switzerland, 2018; pp. 277–288.
15. Seker, E.; Ozbenli, H.H. The Concept of Cyber Defence Exercises (CDX): Planning, Execution, Evaluation. In Proceedings of the 2018 International Conference on Cyber Security and Protection of Digital Services (Cyber Security), Glasgow, UK, 11–12 June 2018; pp. 1–9. [CrossRef]
16. Jamk University of Applied Sciences, Institute of Information Technology/JYVSECTEC. Realistic Global Cyber Environment (RGCE). Available online: https://www.jyvsectec.fi/rgce (accessed on 21 March 2023).
17. Jones, D.; Snider, C.; Nassehi, A.; Yon, J.; Hicks, B. Characterising the Digital Twin: A systematic literature review. *CIRP J. Manuf. Sci. Technol.* **2020**, *29*, 36–52. [CrossRef]
18. Barykin, S.Y.; Bochkarev, A.A.; Kalinina, O.V.; Yadykin, V.K. Concept for a Supply Chain Digital Twin. *Int. J. Math. Eng. Manag. Sci.* **2020**, *5*, 1498–1515. [CrossRef]
19. Wang, L.; Deng, T.; Shen, Z.J.M.; Hu, H.; Qi, Y. Digital twin-driven smart supply chain. *Front. Eng. Manag.* **2022**, *9*, 56–70. [CrossRef]
20. Marmolejo-Saucedo, J.A. Design and Development of Digital Twins: A Case Study in Supply Chains. *Mob. Networks Appl.* **2020**, *25*, 2141–2160. [CrossRef]
21. Abideen, A.Z.; Sundram, V.P.K.; Pyeman, J.; Othman, A.K.; Sorooshian, S. Digital Twin Integrated Reinforced Learning in Supply Chain and Logistics. *Logistics* **2021**, *5*, 84. [CrossRef]
22. Eckhart, M.; Ekelhart, A., Digital twins for cyber-physical systems security: State of the art and outlook. In *Security and Quality in Cyber-Physical Systems Engineering*; Biffl, S., Eckhart, M., Lüder, A., Weippl, E., Eds.; Springer: Cham, Switzerland, 2019; pp. 383–412. [CrossRef]
23. Alim, M.E.; Wright, S.R.; Morris, T.H. A Laboratory-Scale Canal SCADA System Testbed for Cybersecurity Research. In Proceedings of the 2021 Third IEEE International Conference on Trust, Privacy and Security in Intelligent Systems and Applications (TPS-ISA), Atlanta, GA, USA, 13–15 December 2021; pp. 348–354. [CrossRef]
24. Enns, S.T.; Suwanruji, P. A simulation test bed for production and supply chain modeling. In Proceedings of the 2003 Winter Simulation Conference, New Orleans, LA, USA, 7–10 December 2003; Volume 2, pp. 1174–1182. [CrossRef]
25. Tian, Z.; Cui, Y.; An, L.; Su, S.; Yin, X.; Yin, L.; Cui, X. A Real-Time Correlation of Host-Level Events in Cyber Range Service for Smart Campus. *IEEE Access* **2018**, *6*, 35355–35364. [CrossRef]
26. Secretariat of the Security Committee. *Finland's Cyber Security Strategy, Government Resolution 3.10.2019*; Secretariat of the Security Committee: Helsinki, Finland, 2019, ISBN 978-951-663-055-0. Available online: https://turvallisuuskomitea.fi/wp-content/uploads/2019/10/Kyberturvallisuusstrategia_A4_ENG_WEB_031019.pdf (accessed on 14 June 2023).
27. Jamk University of Applied Sciences, Institute of Information Technology/JYVSECTEC. Food Chain Cyber Resilience. Available online: https://jyvsectec.fi/2021/09/food-chain-cyber-resilience/ (accessed on 21 March 2023).
28. Hevner, A.R.; March, S.T.; Park, J.; Ram, S. Design Science in Information Systems Research. *MIS Q.* **2004**, *28*, 75–105. [CrossRef]
29. Piirainen, K.A.; Gonzalez, R.A. Constructive Synergy in Design Science Research: A Comparative Analysis of Design Science Research and the Constructive Research Approach. *Liiketal. Aikakauskirja* **2013**, *62*, 206–234.
30. Engström, E.; Storey, M.A.; Runeson, P.; Höst, M.; Baldassarre, M.T. How software engineering research aligns with design science: A review. *Empir. Softw. Eng.* **2020**, *25*, 2630–2660. [CrossRef]
31. Peffers, K.; Tuunanen, T.; Gengler, C.E.; Rossi, M.; Hui, W.; Virtanen, V.; Bragge, J. The Design Science Research Process: A Model for Producing and Presenting Information Systems Research. In *Proceedings of the First International Conference on Design Science Research in Information Systems and Technology*; Claremont Graduate University: Claremont, CA, USA, 2006; pp. 83–106.
32. Jamk University of Applied Sciences, Institute of Information Technology/JYVSECTEC. Elintarvikeketjun Kyberturvallisuuden Pilottiharjoitus-Pilot Cyber Exercise for Food Production Value Chain. Available online: https://www.jamk.fi/fi/tapahtuma/elintarvikeketjun-kyberturvallisuuden-pilottiharjoitus (accessed on 21 April 2023).

applied sciences

MDPI

Article

Comparison of Single Control Loop Performance Monitoring Methods

Teemu Pätsi [1,*], Markku Ohenoja [1], Harri Kukkasniemi [2], Tero Vuolio [1,3], Petri Österberg [1], Seppo Merikoski [2], Henry Joutsijoki [2] and Mika Ruusunen [1]

1 Environmental and Chemical Engineering Research Unit, Control Engineering Group, University of Oulu, P.O. Box 4300, 90014 Oulu, Finland; markku.ohenoja@oulu.fi (M.O.); tero.vuolio@oulu.fi (T.V.); petri.osterberg@oulu.fi (P.Ö.); mika.ruusunen@oulu.fi (M.R.)

2 Insta Advance Oy, Sarankulmankatu 20, 33900 Tampere, Finland; harri.kukkasniemi@insta.fi (H.K.); seppo.merikoski@insta.fi (S.M.); henry.joutsijoki@insta.fi (H.J.)

3 Process Metallurgy Research Unit, Faculty of Technology, University of Oulu, P.O. Box 4300, 90014 Oulu, Finland

* Correspondence: teemu.patsi@oulu.fi

Abstract: Well-performing control loops have an integral role in efficient and sustainable industrial production. Control performance monitoring (CPM) tools are necessary to establish further process optimization and preventive maintenance. Data-driven, model-free control performance monitoring approaches are studied in this research by comparing the performance of nine CPM methods in an industrially relevant process simulation. The robustness of some of the methods is considered with varying fault intensities. The methods are demonstrated on a simulator which represents a validated state-space model of a supercritical carbon dioxide fluid extraction process. The simulator is constructed with a single-input single-output unit controller for part of the process and a combination of relevant faults in the industry are introduced into the simulation. Of the demonstrated methods, Kullback–Leibler divergence, Euclidean distance, histogram intersection, and Overall Controller Efficiency performed the best in the first simulation case and could identify all the simulated fault scenarios. In the second case, integral-based methods Integral Squared Error and Integral of Time-weighted Absolute Error had the most robust performance with different fault intensities. The results highlight the applicability and robustness of some model-free methods and construct a solid foundation in the application of CPM in industrial processes.

Keywords: performance; control loop; monitoring; overall controller efficiency; single-input single-output

Citation: Pätsi, T.; Ohenoja, M.; Kukkasniemi, H.; Vuolio, T.; Österberg, P.; Merikoski, S.; Joutsijoki, H.; Ruusunen, M. Comparison of Single Control Loop Performance Monitoring Methods. *Appl. Sci.* **2023**, *13*, 6945. https://doi.org/10.3390/app13126945

Academic Editors: Seppo Sierla, Kai Zenger and David Hästbacka

Received: 30 April 2023
Revised: 1 June 2023
Accepted: 6 June 2023
Published: 8 June 2023

1. Introduction

In industrial applications, processes are automatically controlled for the purposes of increasing production efficiency and reducing wasted resources. Many processes also require continuous control to stay within the operational limits. Well-performing control loops have an integral role in these tasks. However, the control loops require regular maintenance for keeping up with disturbances and decay present in industrial applications. Thus, the effectiveness of each control loop should be monitored to identify the maintenance needs.

The primary objective of control loop monitoring is to identify the control loops with inadequate performance. For this aim, a plethora of performance estimation methods is available in the current literature [1–3]. A well-performing control loop creates a solid foundation for further process optimization and preventive maintenance.

Poorly performing control loops may be caused by normal process deterioration over time or by disturbances and failures in sensors, controllers, actuators, and the process itself. In a performed analysis [4], some of the most common issues for control, process, and signal processing include manually overridden loops, control element out of range, and step out or quantization. In [5], the most common faults according to control engineers in the industry comprised controller saturation, oscillations, manual control, sluggish behavior, and quantization.

The most applied automatic control strategy is the proportional, integral, and derivative controller (PID controller). PID control loops are usually tuned at the time of installation but could receive less attention in the continuous maintenance work. This could result in poor control and consequently declining process performance over time.

Control loop performance monitoring tools are widely used in industry. In a survey [5], it was found that approximately two-thirds of control engineers use control performance monitoring (CPM) tools or packages. The use of CPM tools has been on the rise and automation companies provide solutions for use in industrial plants. Some companies may develop their own internal solutions for control performance monitoring. For example, ABB developed a control loop performance monitoring application, ServicePort, which allows for the monitoring of plant-wide control loop performance and provides an automated procedure for disturbance analysis [4].

Control performance measurement methods can be categorized based on the method's required a priori knowledge [1]; model-based methods require modeling of the monitored process and utilize the model as a reference to assess the current control loop performance. Model-free methods require no initial knowledge of the process but are instead based on the data collected during process operation.

In this paper, data-driven, model-free approaches are prioritized for the purpose of obtaining easily adaptable methodologies. Generally, the methods should be applicable to an industrial plant, where the modeling of countless numbers of sub-processes would require immense effort. Some commercial products are founded on similar aims. Non-invasiveness, utilization of existing sensors, minimal process knowledge, and simple algorithms are demanded from control loop performance monitoring tools [6]. Many of the demonstrated methods have been widely used in control loop tuning applications, and this work further utilizes these methods in a dynamic performance monitoring application. Machine learning and deep learning methods may also be used for control performance monitoring purposes [7,8]; however, the training and validation of these methods may prove impractical in industrial applications with countless numbers of control loops. Thus, this work focuses on easily applicable model-free methods.

This work evaluates the applicability of several conventional and machine learning, model-free CPM methods on a simulated dynamic process. In addition, a method for control performance monitoring is presented, namely, adopting the ideas from the framework of Overall Equipment Efficiency (OEE) to this new context, the OCE (Overall Controller Efficiency) method. OEE is one well-known utilization-based metric to measure productivity and efficiency. Other acknowledged metrics include total preventive maintenance, lean, 5S, and the virtual factory [9]. In monitoring, OEE can be efficiently used to identify the underlying production losses to systemically establish process performance improvements [10]. It has also been applied as one possible indicator for measuring the impact of maintenance practices on sustainability performance (overall sustainability score) in [11].

The comparative study in this paper is conducted with a validated simulator representing a sub-process in a supercritical fluid extraction system. A single control loop is isolated and single-input single-output control performance is evaluated dynamically with the demonstrated methods. Several simulation scenarios are created to deteriorate the system behavior from the nominal control performance and thus illustrate the performance of the CPM methods. With the simulated process data, a comparison of the ability to identify faults and the robustness of the CPM methods is performed.

The structure of this article is as follows: Section 2 describes the considered CPM methods, the simulated process, and the simulation scenarios of the faulty control. Section 3 presents the obtained results from the CPM methods' application on the simulated dataset. In Section 4, the results are further discussed. Finally, Section 5 concludes this study.

2. Materials and Methods

Control performance monitoring is performed utilizing data from processes to estimate the state of control. Several methods have been adapted for these purposes, with different requirements and restrictions. Some methods utilize modeling of the process to obtain accurate estimation. Unlike these model-based methods, model-free methods require no process model.

Model-free control performance measurement methods can be further divided into sub-categories such as statistical factors, integral time measures, correlation measures, and alternative indices. The CPM method classification according to [1] is shown in Figure 1.

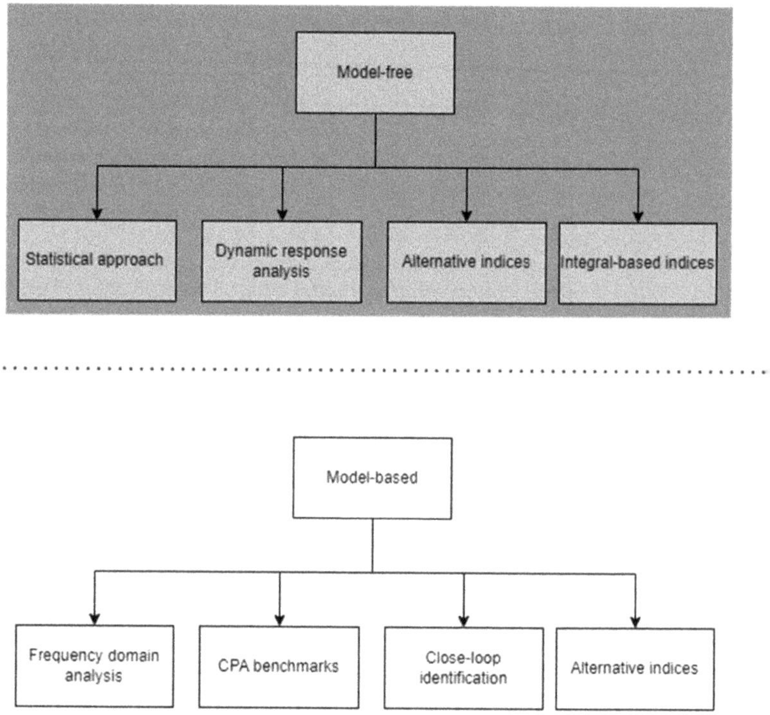

Figure 1. CPM method classification (adapted from [1]). The methods focused on in this work are highlighted in grey.

Among the model-free CPM methods, the statistical approaches have shown benefits for the cases of processes with non-linear properties. In [12], higher-order statistics-based methods are used to identify oscillatory behavior and diagnose the possible cause for the disturbance. Gaussianity and linearity are tested for in the process and possible identified oscillatory behavior can be characterized by visual analysis of the process output vs. the controller output plot. For example, valve stiction is generally identified by elliptical cycles and sharp corners in the plot [12]. Statistical approaches also include methods such as cross-correlation-based oscillation detection [13] and autocorrelation-based control performance monitoring implementation [14].

Integral-based indices are a set of widely used performance indices such as Mean Square Error (MSE), Integral Absolute Error (IAE), Integral Squared Error (ISE), and Integral of Time-weighted Absolute Error (ITAE). Further adaptations of integral time measures have been developed, some of which are described in Section 2.1. Integral-based indices have been widely utilized in the field of tuning control loops [15–18]. This work considers application of these methods in dynamic control performance monitoring.

Alternative indices utilize other methods such as wavelets and entropy. The applicability of dynamic response analysis is often limited in on-line control performance monitoring, as it might require repeated process experiments and excitation.

2.1. Implemented CPM Indices

CPM methods for demonstration were chosen based on the criteria previously mentioned. The methods should perform without the need for modeling of the process. A priori knowledge of the process should not be needed for estimating the control performance. As such, the methods described in the following section were chosen.

Integrated Squared Error (*ISE*, Equation (1)) is calculated as a function of time and in a sliding window. Here, a sliding window of one day is selected as:

$$ISE = \int_{n-x}^{n} e(t)^2 dt, \tag{1}$$

where *ISE* is comprised of the sum of squared errors ($e(t)$) between the current time (n) and the duration of the sliding window (x).

For the performed step changes, the Integral of Time-weighted Absolute Error (*ITAE*, Equation (2)) is monitored for identifying longer period faults in the process. The longer a fault is present, the larger the time weight grows and directly increases the metric. The time weight used is the time since the last setpoint change:

$$ITAE = \int_{1}^{w} t|e(t)|dt, \tag{2}$$

where *ITAE* is the sum of the absolute values of errors ($e(t)$) multiplied by the time since the last setpoint change (w). Additionally, Amplitude Index (*AMP*, Equation (3)) is used to measure the ratio between the maximum amplitude of process error and the size of the performed step change. The value is obtained from the minimum and maximum values after the rise time period, as in [3]:

$$AMP = \frac{y_{max} - y_{min}}{\Delta y_{sp}}, \tag{3}$$

where y_{max} and y_{min} are the maximum and minimum values, respectively, of the process value after the rise time and Δy_{sp} is the magnitude of the performed step change.

The difference from normal operation in the process can be identified by utilizing the measurement error residuals and comparing the distribution to a selected time period from normal operation. Kullback–Leibler divergence (*KL*, Equation (4)) [19] provides a measurement for difference between the two datasets. In real processes, obtaining data from the normal operation may prove difficult, especially if the process has been in operation for a while and unknown disturbances may have occurred. Kullback–Leibler divergence has been previously adapted to an index in MIMO controller performance monitoring [20]:

$$KL = \int h_1 \log \frac{h_1}{h_2} dx, \tag{4}$$

where h_1 is the reference dataset and h_2 is the dataset in the chosen sliding window. Additionally, histogram intersection (*HI*, Equation (5)) [21] and Euclidean distance (*ED*, Equation (6)) [22] are used here to estimate the difference between the reference data and the sliding window testing datasets:

$$HI = \frac{\sum_{j=1}^{m} min(h_{1,m}, h_{2,m})}{\sum_{j=1}^{m} h_{2,m}}, \tag{5}$$

$$ED = \sqrt{\sum_{j=1}^{m} (h_{1,m} - h_{2,m})^2}, \quad (6)$$

where the datasets h_1 and h_2 are divided into m histogram bins.

In addition, a commercial CPM tool was applied to the studied process. Overall Controller Efficiency (OCE) is a method developed by Insta Advance. The idea of OCE was inspired from a more general framework called OEE and is an adaptation of it in the context of PID controller performance. OCE defines one number that describes one PID controller's history, present, and future ability to function in a specified task. The main point in OCE is to follow the trend of the OCE value, and a continuous decrease in the OCE value may indicate the need for action. On the contrary, an increase in the OCE value can show the recovery or improvement of PID controller efficiency. OCE was first developed for detecting long-term phenomena (e.g., crawling due to wearing), but in this paper, OCE's suitability to detect short-term phenomena has been examined in detail in the experimental part.

In general, OCE_{total} is a product of three separate factors, as indicated in Equation (7):

$$OCE_{total} = OCE_a \times OCE_p \times OCE_q. \quad (7)$$

In Equation (7), OCE_a is the availability, or the portion of time the controller autonomously produces good-quality data. OCE_p is the performance, or the accuracy to follow the setpoint value without oscillation, and OCE_q is the quality, or the ability to continue as part of the production process in the future.

In this application, availability is calculated based on the proportion of automatic and manual control of the studied control loop, while performance is related to the setpoint tracking error. Quality is related to several indices describing the control loop performance in long-term trends. The details of the quality factors are omitted due to company confidentiality reasons. Overall, the calculation of the OCE_{total} value relies on a statistical algorithm. The OCE method includes parameters to finetune the process, and in this paper, the two parameters that describe the number of days in the buffer and evaluation are considered. In both cases, a value of 10 was used.

Since OCE_{total} represents a product of the three aforementioned factors, it is sensitive to variability in any of the indices. An extreme example is that if any of the factors are zero, the whole OCE_{total} value becomes zero. Moreover, in the case of asymmetric indices, OCE may become less appropriate.

2.2. Simulated Process

A supercritical fluid extraction (SFE) process utilizes properties of a supercritical fluid to extract product from a raw material. Carbon dioxide (CO_2) is commonly used as the supercritical fluid due to the properties of CO_2, with it being sufficiently easy to achieve pressure (73.8 bar) and temperature (32.1 °C) for the critical point. The process consists of six parts, namely, the extraction reactor, extract separator, condenser, CO_2 storage, CO_2 flow pre-heater, and pump, as shown in Figure 2. A set of central composite design experimental test runs were performed and state-space models for the process components were identified in [23,24]. Thus, the simulator used represents a validated model of the physical process.

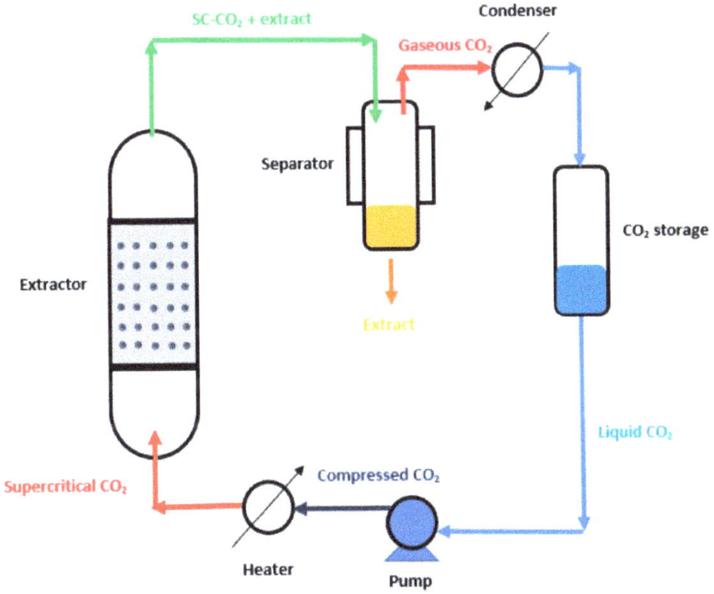

Figure 2. Flow chart of the supercritical CO_2 fluid extraction process [23].

One control loop from the previously identified simulator was isolated for this work. The selected discrete-time, state-space model (see Equations (8) and (9)), namely, the CO_2 flow, was identified from open-loop measurements of the original work [17,18], while other portions of the simulator were identified with the existing PID control in the process. The CO_2 flow is the controlled variable, $y(n)$, and valve position is the manipulated variable, $u(n)$. The second input is the external variable, ΔP. In this study, the external variable is utilized as a disturbance, with a value of 0 in normal operation.

$$x(n+1) = \begin{bmatrix} 0.9895 & 0.03677 \\ -0.01237 & 0.9649 \end{bmatrix} x(n) + \begin{bmatrix} -2.520e-05 & -1.673e-06 \\ -2.199e-04 & -5.346e-06 \end{bmatrix} u(n), \tag{8}$$

$$y(n) = \begin{bmatrix} -10.22 \\ -0.1235 \end{bmatrix} x(n) \left(+ \begin{bmatrix} 0 \\ 0 \end{bmatrix} u(n) \right), \tag{9}$$

The state-space model for the supercritical fluid extraction process was implemented to MATLAB® and Simulink® software (Version R2020b Update 2). PI control, with parameters 8 for proportional gain and 0.2 for integral gain, was added to the simulator, and the parameters were kept constant for the simulations. As the simulator models the CO_2 flow into the reactor, the lower limit for the output was limited to 0. The closed-loop process settling time after a step change is approximately 400 s. Therefore, the simulation scenario involved setpoint changes every 1200 s. The setpoint values were selected randomly from an even distribution between 0 and 0.8, with an interval of 0.1. With these chosen step changes, a representative dataset for the process was obtained for the whole area of operation of the process. Additionally, having frequent step changes in the process, the overall size of the dataset could be reduced, decreasing computing time in the later stages of the demonstration. The obtained measurement data were then sampled every 10 s to further reduce the size of the data matrix.

2.3. Simulated Faults

In Case 1, the performance of the CPM methods for different kinds of faults was studied in a long simulation period. The faults were added to the simulated process, first occurring individually and later simultaneously. From the common faults presented in [5], the following faults were used in this work:

- Valve stiction, where a certain difference between the previous and new controller output is required in order to have an effect on the actuator position. Nominally, the valve stiction in a faulty situation was set to 0.002.
- Valve change rate limit—simulating a scenario where the motor controlling the valve has a sudden fault limiting the speed of the valve change. In this case, the speed is limited to 0.04 valve rotations/s.
- Sin-wave with a constant amplitude of 75 bar, a frequency of 0.00002 Hz, and a rising amplitude (from 0 to 141.6 bar), with a frequency of 0.0001 Hz representing an external disturbance to the process. This disturbance acts as the second input variable in the state-space model (pressure error), as described in Section 2.2.
- Quantization, where the measured process value fed back for the controller is quantized within an accuracy of 0.08 L/min instead of a floating number. This value was selected to produce a noticeable effect on the process control behavior.
- PID controller tuning error, where the value of the P-parameter is changed from 8 to 0.8 for the duration of the fault.

The simulator with the implemented control and faults is displayed in Figure 3.

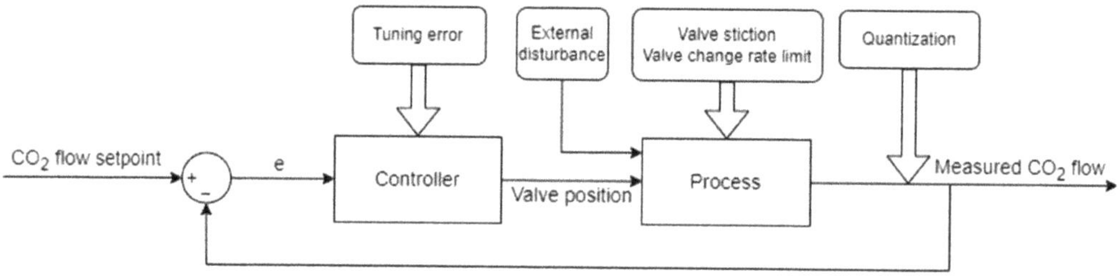

Figure 3. Control and fault implementation for the simulated process. The rounded boxes at the top represent the common faults in this work.

The faults are enabled one by one as follows. The first 15 days of the simulation are fault-free. The following 2.3 days of the simulation have only one fault activated. The remaining faults are then enabled one by one, every 1.2 days, until each fault is enabled. The faults are then disabled one by one every 1.2 days, following the order of activation for the faults. Thus, during the period from 20.8 to 22.0 days, all faults are present. Afterwards, a rising sin-wave external fault is enabled during the time period of 26.6 to 30.1 days. The final 9.9 days of the simulation are without faults, where restoration to the normal state can be observed.

Figure 4 depicts the simulation of 40 days containing the setpoint changes mentioned in Section 2.3 and the faults described above for the case with PID *p*-value disturbance. Simulations were repeated with different fault scenarios for a comparison of different measurement metrics with each fault case.

In Case 2, the robustness of the methods was tested. A simulation dataset with different values for fault intensities was obtained, focusing on the valve stiction fault. First, a simulation with no faults was performed to obtain a reference dataset. A total of 500 different simulations were performed with different fault intensities for valve stiction, chosen randomly for each simulation from an even distribution. For the valve stiction intensity, a required difference from 0 to 0.0036 between new and old actuator values was chosen. To speed up the simulation, 800 s between setpoint changes was used instead of the 1200 s used in Case 1. With the reduction of the simulation time, the OCE method does not perform adequately and is left out for this case.

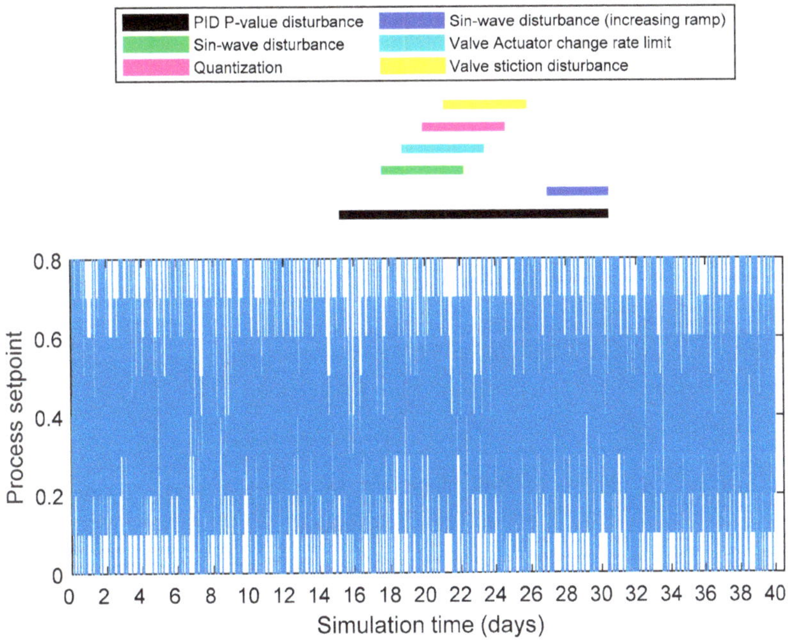

Figure 4. Faults and setpoints during a simulation run of 40 days.

3. Results

3.1. Case 1. Identification of Faults with Different CPM Methods

Kullback–Leibler divergence, histogram intersection, and Euclidean distance are used in this case to compare the selected reference dataset to a testing set selected from a sliding window of one day (8640 data points). The training data are selected from the beginning of the simulation with a size of 50,000 data points. The start of the dataset is known to represent the normal behavior of the process and can thus provide an accurate reference for the methods. Additionally, the number of bins for the histograms used is set to 8.

In practice, identifying normal behavior of the process is a challenge for accurate monitoring in industrial processes. For this purpose, the utilized simulator allows for a fault-free scenario when identifying the normal process behavior and provides means for estimating the performance of the chosen CPM indices.

In Figure 5, the differences between the reference data (first 50,000 data points) and a testing set selected with a sliding window of size 8640 (1 day) can be seen for the histogram intersection method. For the *HI* method, the high index values indicate good performance as the statistical properties of the test set are close to the reference data obtained during a normal control loop performance. Slight changes in the metrics occur even in normal operation (days 6–15), due to the randomly chosen setpoints. During the periods with faults, the index clearly deviates from the values in normal operation. After the simulated faults have ceased, the index returns to nominal value range, indicating a good performance of the CPM method. Similar performance was observed for the Kullback–Leibler divergence and Euclidean distance metrics.

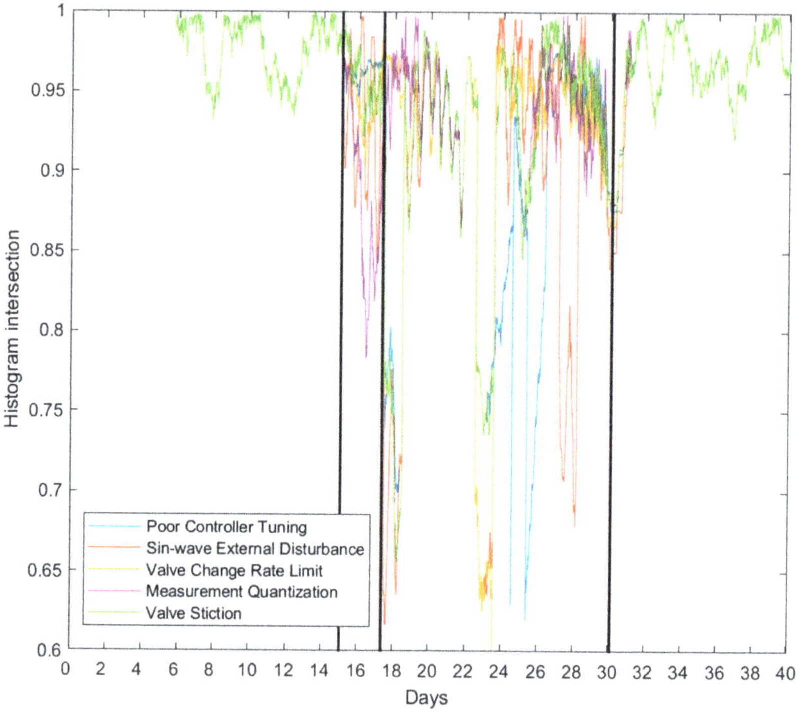

Figure 5. Histogram intersection between reference data and a sliding window of 1 day. Individual faults enabled between the first two vertical lines. Faults disabled after the last vertical line. The lines overlap on days 6–15 and 32–40.

However, with these methods, properties of the training data can affect the resulting metrics. Deviations from the training data have a significant effect and retraining may be necessary to adapt to an evolving process environment. Moreover, selection of the size of the sliding window for the metrics affects the resolution of the results. With a larger window size, the observation of a fault might be delayed as a lower proportion of the window is from faulty data. Determining alarm limits is dependent on the process as tolerances can vary.

Identification of an individual fault was considered by comparing a period of the simulation where one fault was present with an equal-sized duration from the fault-free period. In Figure 6a, this comparison for the OCE method was performed and presented as a boxplot for normal, fault-free data, and separately for the five fault scenarios. A high OCE_{total} value corresponds to good control, whereas lower values indicate decreased control loop performance. It can be seen that the OCE method can separate all of the faulty situations from the normal operation, as the notches of the plot (95% confidence) do not overlap. The process was repeated for all metrics (boxplots presented in Appendix A, Figures A1–A7) and qualitatively compiled in Table 1. The fault was considered to be identified when the index significantly differed from the normal behavior in the expected direction. As indicated in Figure 6b, *ISE* shows a lower index value for the fault scenarios' quantization and valve stiction, although it is expected that the integrated error value would increase in the presence of fault. According to Table 1, among the tested CPM methods, *KL*, *HI*, *ED*, OCE_p, and OCE_{total} could detect the decreased control loop performance simulated in Case 1.

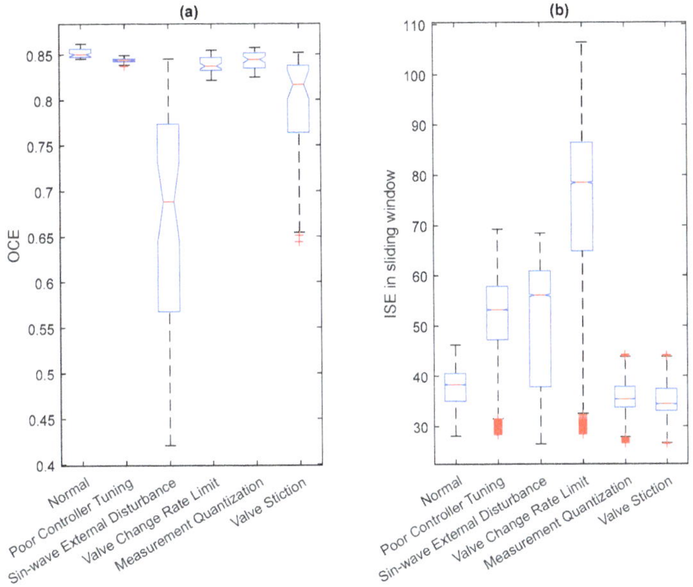

Figure 6. (**a**) Boxplot of OCE_{total} during a single fault, (**b**) Boxplot of *ISE* in sliding window during a single fault.

Table 1. Qualitative performance of CPM indices. The fault situations marked with X showed statistically significant difference in the monitored index between normal and faulty operation.

CPM Index	Cont. Tuning	Ext. Dist.	Rate Limit	Quant.	Valve Stiction
ISE	X	X	X	-	-
ITAE	X	-	-	X	X
AMP	X	-	X	-	-
KL	X	X	X	X	X
ED	X	X	X	X	X
HI	X	X	X	X	X
OCE_p	X	X	X	X	X
OCE_q	-	X	X	-	X
OCE_{total}	X	X	X	X	X

3.2. Case 2. Robustness of the Methods with Varying Fault Intensities

The robustness of the demonstrated methods was considered with the second simulation case, where the fault intensity for valve stiction was changed randomly for 500 different simulations. The resulting index values for the histogram intersection are shown in Figure 7.

It can be seen in Figure 7 that some of the intensities for valve stiction can be identified, as the index value clearly decreases below the normal operation (dashed horizontal line). However, most of the index values are near normal operation limits, suggesting a limited performance of the CPM index in this case. To improve the identification of the fault, the CPM method parameters need to be adjusted. After testing a different number of bins for the histogram intersection method, the best results in terms of the method's robustness to different fault intensities was achieved with a parameter value of 15 bins. Figure 8 depicts the result. It is notable that the resolution (absolute values of the index) of the method was now considerably lower in comparison to the results in Figure 7.

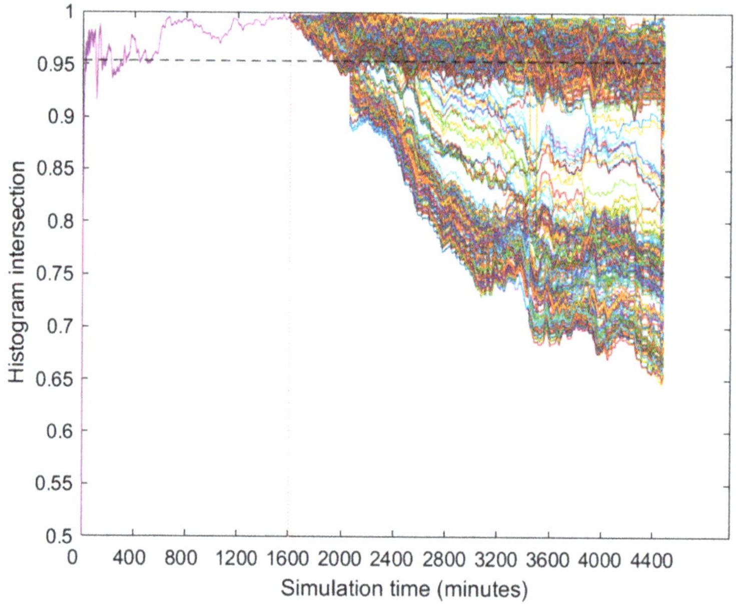

Figure 7. Histogram intersection for 500 different amplitudes for valve stiction. The vertical dotted line marks the time where the fault starts. The horizontal dashed line is the lower quartile of histogram intersection in the fault-free simulation.

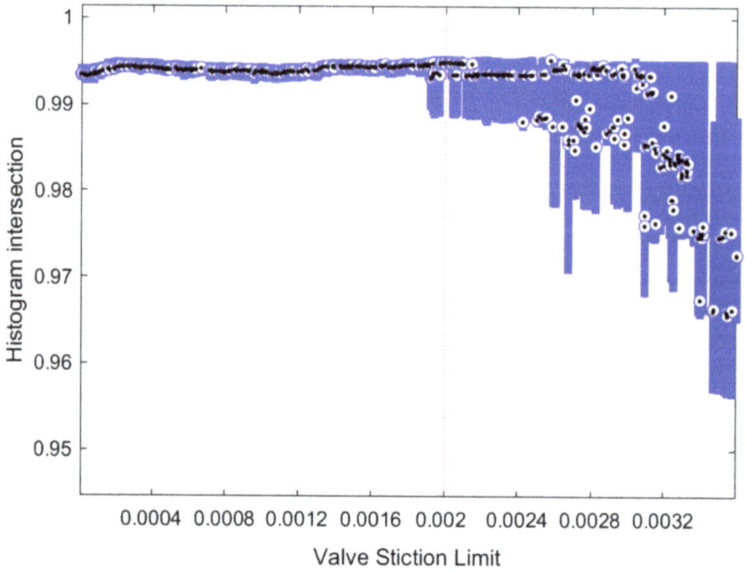

Figure 8. Boxplot (median and IQR) for adjusted histogram intersection with 500 different valve stiction intensities. The red vertical line shows the value of valve stiction in Case 1.

Valve stiction was identified for different methods with varying degrees of intensity for the fault required. In Figures 8 and 9, the metrics are drawn as a boxplot (median, and lower and upper quartiles) as a function of the fault intensity. *HI* (Figure 8), *ED*, and *KL* (Figure 9a) can identify the fault well, as the intensity of the fault increases above 0.002. *AMP* performed poorly with all chosen intensities, due to the nature of the valve stiction fault. Among the studied CPM methods, *ITAE* showed the most robust behavior for different intensities of the valve stiction, shifting from the normal operation with even small disturbance values, as shown in Figure 9b. *ISE* also performed well, as shown in Figure 9c.

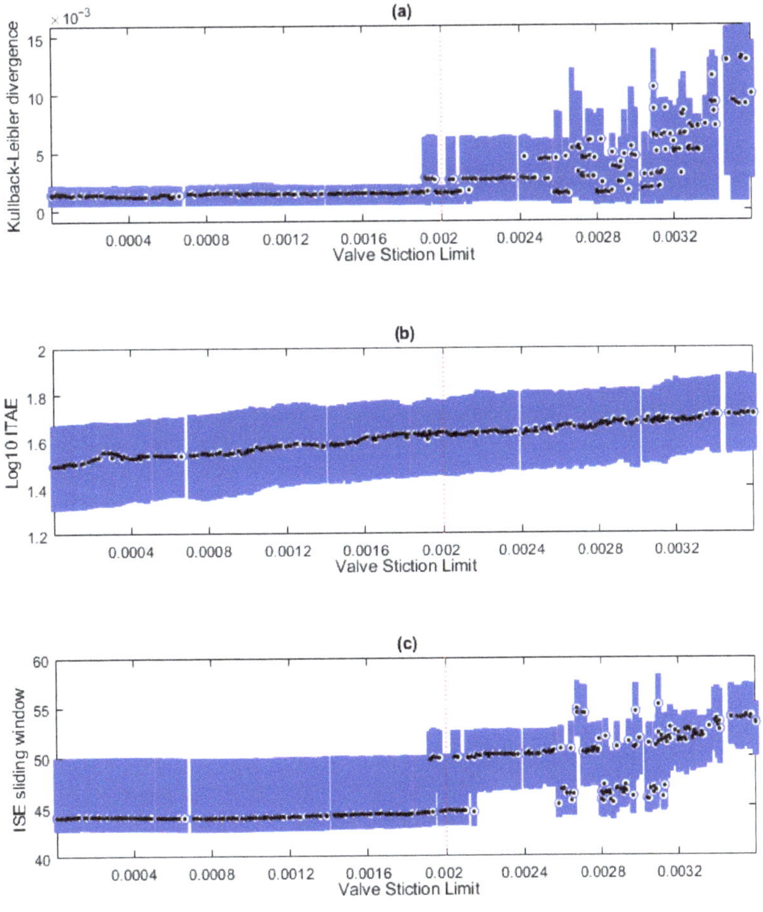

Figure 9. (**a**) Boxplot (median and IQR) for adjusted Kullback–Leibler divergence with 500 different valve stiction intensities. (**b**) Boxplot (median and IQR) for *ITAE* with 500 different valve stiction intensities. (**c**) Boxplot (median and IQR) for *ISE* in sliding window with 500 different valve stiction intensities. For comparison, the red vertical line shows the value of valve stiction used in simulations in Case 1 (Section 3.1).

The sensitivity of the demonstrated indices was compiled in Table 2, where statistically significant difference (95% confidence) for the medians in the fault-free simulation and the simulations with different fault intensities were compared.

The results suggest that *KL*, *HI*, and *ED* can identify small fault intensities with some accuracy, but only reach accurate identification with the highest intensities. Additionally, the absolute values of these metrics were low, and the performance may vary in more non-ideal conditions. *AMP* could not identify any of the implemented fault intensities. Integrating methods *ISE* and *ITAE* performed well and had only a small range between the lowest identified and highest non-identified fault intensities.

Table 2. Index performance with different fault intensities.

CPM Index	Lowest Identified Fault Intensity	Highest Non-Identified Fault Intensity	Identified Fault Intensities	Identification Percentage
ISE	1.4×10^{-3}	0.0015	307/500	61.4%
AMP	-	-	0/500	0%
ITAE	1.1×10^{-3}	0.0014	345/500	69%
KL	6.9×10^{-6}	0.0026	447/500	89.4%
HI	2.5×10^{-5}	0.0031	194/500	38.8%
ED	2.5×10^{-5}	0.0031	194/500	38.8%

4. Discussion

The current state of control performance monitoring methods was explored, and different model-free CPM methods were chosen for a demonstration case with the aim of providing easily adaptable methodologies for control loop performance monitoring in industrial applications. Some of these methods are widely used in control loop design and tuning, and this work further adapts these methods in a dynamic control performance monitoring application. A simulated environment was used to obtain a representative dataset for testing, with the possibility of including different faults in different time periods in the simulation.

Among the studied methods, histogram intersection well identified the control error residual difference from the reference data. Increased error from poor control results in an abnormal distribution. However, the metric is heavily dependent on the conditions from which reference data were obtained. Naturally causing drift and other changes in the process can cause the metric to shift from an optimal area, even though the process may perform adequately. As such, multiple metrics should be monitored for verifying the results of other metrics and observing the actual state of the process. One option to facilitate this is to take the approach used in the OCE method, which uses a product of several indices to assess the overall controller performance. For example, the histogram intersection is naturally scaled to values between 0 and 1, thus being an appropriate candidate for such a combined CPM index.

With respect to the second case with varying fault intensities, the *KL*, *HI*, and *ED* methods performed rather poorly. The metrics mostly stayed at levels of normal operation with the original method parameters. Adjusting the parameters for these methods allowed accurate identification of the fault with the valve stiction values above 0.0031, as seen in Table 2. However, robustness was compromised, with the methods only falling slightly below the normal operation levels (for example, the median stayed above 0.96 for histogram intersection in the highest valve stiction cases). The metrics could identify some of the lowest fault intensities with decent accuracy but missed the identification of some of the highest intensities. Amplitude Index performed poorly in the second case; however, the metric has utilization potential in different fault cases. The integral methods *ITAE* and *ISE* performed well, with *ISE* identifying 61.4% and *ITAE* 69% of the varying fault intensities. This can be explained by the nature of the implemented fault, which caused residual setpoint error that integrating methods can identify well. Additionally, due to the nature of the simulation, the chosen sliding window has a large and very homogenous number of step changes. In practice, setpoint changes can happen infrequently and at random time intervals. As such, applicability of the methods should be considered when implementing CPM tools.

This paper focused on a single control loop case to build on a solid foundation for further research. Multiple-input multiple-output control could prove an interesting topic in the future. The setpoint changes utilized in the demonstrations were chosen to be rather short, while industrial applications may run in the same state for weeks at a time. Additionally, only one process was utilized for the simulations. Differences in process dynamics may cause differences in the behavior of the control performance monitoring metrics. Thus, the performance of the methods should also be studied for different types of data to ensure industrial applicability. Further, the demonstration presented was based on simulated, noise-free data. Stability and tuning of the methods will require more attention with real data, where noise is present or partially filtered.

5. Conclusions

In this work, it was found that the Kullback–Leibler divergence, Euclidean distance, histogram intersection, and OCE method could identify all the simulated fault scenarios in the first simulation case. In the second case, the robustness and sensitivity of the metrics were further analyzed in the presence of valve stiction fault, where the integral-based ISE and ITAE metrics demonstrated robust performance.

Control performance may suffer due to different sources of faults and different CPM methods' performance varies depending on the nature of the fault. Thus, a combination of methods should be considered as a monitoring solution. As noted in this work, the OCE method consisted of several factors and responded well to different fault scenarios.

Author Contributions: Conceptualization, T.P., H.J., M.O. and M.R.; Methodology, T.P. and M.O.; Software, H.K. and T.V.; Data curation, T.P., H.K., S.M. and H.J.; Writing—original draft, T.P.; Writing—review & editing, M.O., P.Ö., H.J. and M.R.; Visualization, T.P.; Supervision, M.O., P.Ö. and M.R.; Project administration, P.Ö., M.O. and M.R.; Funding acquisition, M.O. and M.R. All authors have read and agreed to the published version of the manuscript.

Funding: This research was funded by Business Finland grant numbers 5586/31/2019 and 5812/31/2019.

Institutional Review Board Statement: Not applicable.

Informed Consent Statement: Not applicable.

Data Availability Statement: Data sharing not applicable.

Conflicts of Interest: The authors declare no conflict of interest.

Appendix A

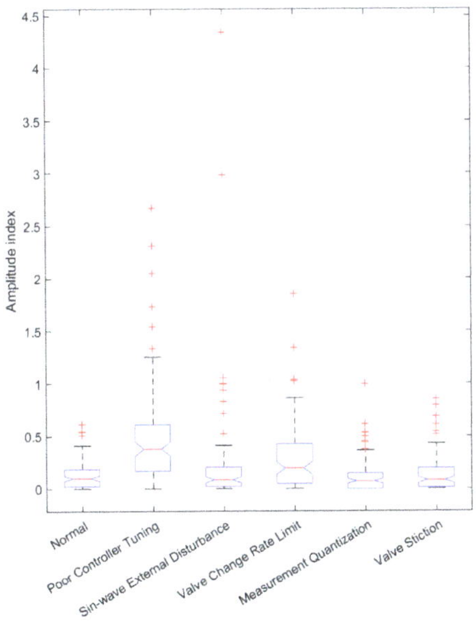

Figure A1. Boxplot of Amplitude Index during a single fault.

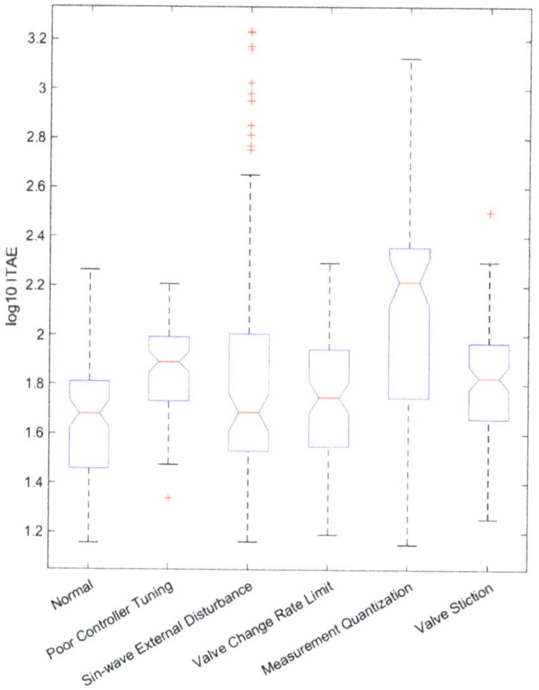

Figure A2. Boxplot of ITAE during a single fault.

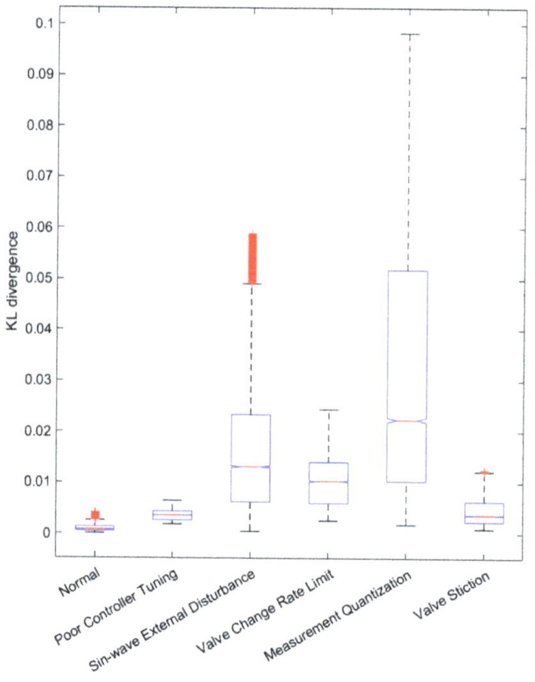

Figure A3. Boxplot of Kullback–Leibler divergence during a single fault.

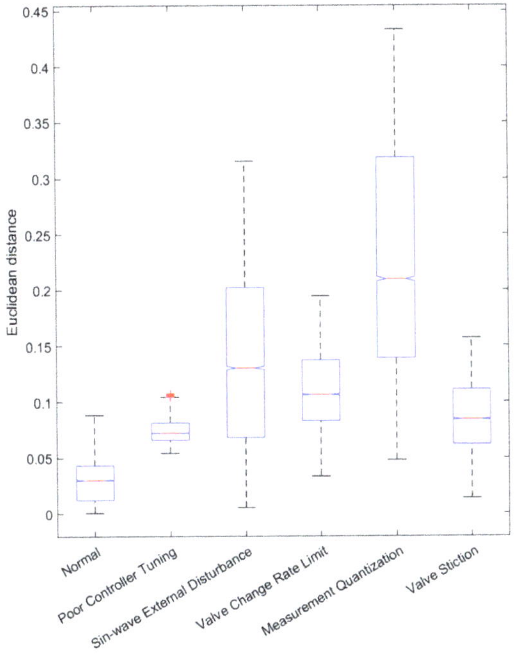

Figure A4. Boxplot of Euclidean distance during a single fault.

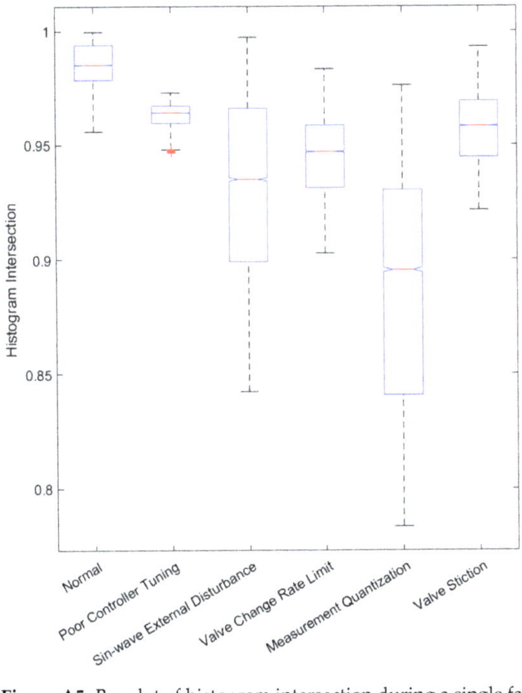

Figure A5. Boxplot of histogram intersection during a single fault.

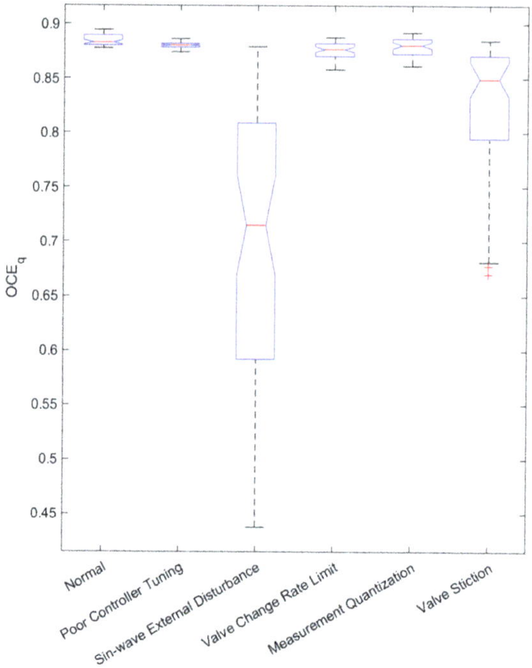

Figure A6. Boxplot of OCE method quality factor during a single fault.

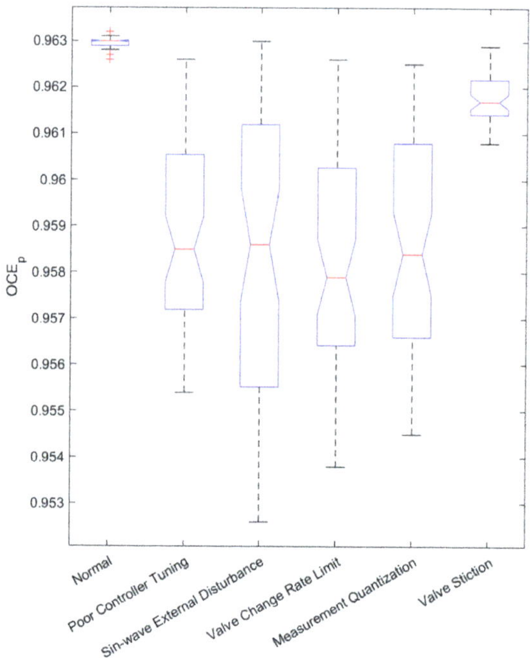

Figure A7. Boxplot of OCE method performance factor during a single fault.

References

1. Domański, P.D. Performance Assessment of Predictive Control—A Survey. *Algorithms* **2020**, *13*, 97. [CrossRef]
2. Al Soraihi, H.G. Control Loop Performance Monitoring in an Industrial Setting. Master's Thesis, RMIT University, Melbourne, VIC, Australia, 2006.
3. Jamsa-Jounela, S.-L.; Poikonen, R.; Georgiev, Z.; Zuehlke, U.; Halmevaara, K. Evaluation of control performance: Methods and applications. In Proceedings of the International Conference on Control Applications, Glasgow, UK, 18–20 September 2002; Volume 2, pp. 681–686. [CrossRef]
4. Starr, K.D.; Petersen, H.; Bauer, M. Control loop performance monitoring—ABB's experience over two decades. *IFAC-PapersOnLine* **2016**, *49*, 526–532. [CrossRef]
5. Bauer, M.; Horch, A.; Xie, L.; Jelali, M.; Thornhill, N. The current state of control loop performance monitoring—A survey of application in industry. *J. Process Control* **2016**, *38*, 1–10. [CrossRef]
6. Holstein, F. Control Loop Performance Monitor. Lund Institute of Technology. 2004. Available online: https://lup.lub.lu.se/luur/download?func=downloadFile&recordOId=8848037&fileOId=8859439 (accessed on 16 June 2022).
7. Múnera, J.G.; Jiménez-Cabas, J.; Díaz-Charris, L. User Interface-Based in Machine Learning as Tool in the Analysis of Control Loops Performance and Robustness. In *Computer Information Systems and Industrial Management*; Saeed, K., Dvorský, J., Eds.; In Lecture Notes in Computer Science; Springer International Publishing: Cham, Switzerland, 2022; pp. 214–230. [CrossRef]
8. Grelewicz, P.; Khuat, T.T.; Czeczot, J.; Nowak, P.; Klopot, T.; Gabrys, B. Application of Machine Learning to Performance Assessment for a Class of PID-Based Control Systems. *IEEE Trans. Syst. Man Cybern. Syst.* **2023**, *2023*, 1–13. [CrossRef]
9. Stamatis, D.H. *The OEE Primer: Understanding Overall Equipment Effectiveness, Reliability, and Maintainability*; Productivity Press: New York, NY, USA, 2011. [CrossRef]
10. Vorne Industries, Inc. What Is OEE (Overall Equipment Effectiveness)? | OEE. 2022. Available online: https://www.oee.com/ (accessed on 4 November 2022).
11. Ghaleb, M.; Taghipour, S. Assessing the impact of maintenance practices on asset's sustainability. *Reliab. Eng. Syst. Saf.* **2022**, *228*, 108810. [CrossRef]
12. Choudhury, M.A.A.S.; Shah, S.L.; Thornhill, N.F. Diagnosis of poor control-loop performance using higher-order statistics. *Automatica* **2004**, *40*, 1719–1728. [CrossRef]
13. Horch, A. A simple method for detection of stiction in control valves. *Control Eng. Pract.* **1999**, *7*, 1221–1231. [CrossRef]
14. Howard, R.; Cooper, D. A novel pattern-based approach for diagnostic controller performance monitoring. *Control Eng. Pract.* **2010**, *18*, 279–288. [CrossRef]
15. Mok, R.; Ahmad, M.A. Fast and optimal tuning of fractional order PID controller for AVR system based on memorizable-smoothed functional algorithm. *Eng. Sci. Technol. Int. J.* **2022**, *35*, 101264. [CrossRef]
16. Ekinci, S.; Hekimoğlu, B. Improved Kidney-Inspired Algorithm Approach for Tuning of PID Controller in AVR System. *IEEE Access* **2019**, *7*, 39935–39947. [CrossRef]
17. Ziane, M.A.; Pera, M.C.; Join, C.; Benne, M.; Chabriat, J.P.; Steiner, N.Y.; Damour, C. On-line implementation of model free controller for oxygen stoichiometry and pressure difference control of polymer electrolyte fuel cell. *Int. J. Hydrogen Energy* **2022**, *47*, 38311–38326. [CrossRef]
18. Yang, Y.; Chen, C.; Lu, J. Parameter Self-Tuning of SISO Compact-Form Model-Free Adaptive Controller Based on Long Short-Term Memory Neural Network. *IEEE Access* **2020**, *8*, 151926–151937. [CrossRef]
19. Kullback, S.; Leibler, R.A. On Information and Sufficiency. *Ann. Math. Stat.* **1951**, *22*, 79–86. [CrossRef]
20. Wu, P. Performance monitoring of MIMO control system using Kullback-Leibler divergence. *Can. J. Chem. Eng.* **2018**, *96*, 1559–1565. [CrossRef]
21. Patacchiola, M. The Simplest Classifier: Histogram Comparison. Mpatacchiola's Blog. 12 November 2016. Available online: https://mpatacchiola.github.io/blog/2016/11/12/the-simplest-classifier-histogram-intersection.html (accessed on 1 July 2021).
22. Cha, S.-H. Taxonomy of Nominal Type Histogram Distance Measures. In Proceedings of the MATH '08, Harvard, MA, USA, 24–26 March 2008; p. 6.
23. Hämäläinen, H. Identification and Energy Optimization of Supercritical Carbon Dioxide Batch Extraction. Ph.D. Thesis, University of Oulu, Oulu, Finland, 2020.
24. Hämäläinen, H.; Ruusunen, M. Identification of a supercritical fluid extraction process for modelling the energy consumption. *Energy* **2022**, *252*, 124033. [CrossRef]

applied sciences

MDPI

Article

From DevOps to MLOps: Overview and Application to Electricity Market Forecasting

Rakshith Subramanya [1,*], Seppo Sierla [1] and Valeriy Vyatkin [1,2]

[1] Department of Electrical Engineering and Automation, School of Electrical Engineering, Aalto University, 02150 Espoo, Finland
[2] Department of Computer Science, Electrical and Space Engineering, Luleå Tekniska Universitet, 97187 Luleå, Sweden
* Correspondence: rakshith.subramanya@aalto.fi

Abstract: In the Software Development Life Cycle (SDLC), Development and Operations (DevOps) has been proven to deliver reliable, scalable software within a shorter time. Due to the explosion of Machine Learning (ML) applications, the term Machine Learning Operations (MLOps) has gained significant interest among ML practitioners. This paper explains the DevOps and MLOps processes relevant to the implementation of MLOps. The contribution of this paper towards the MLOps framework is threefold: First, we review the state of the art in MLOps by analyzing the related work in MLOps. Second, we present an overview of the leading DevOps principles relevant to MLOps. Third, we derive an MLOps framework from the MLOps theory and apply it to a time-series forecasting application in the hourly day-ahead electricity market. The paper concludes with how MLOps could be generalized and applied to two more use cases with minor changes.

Keywords: continuous software engineering; DevOps; electricity market; Machine Learning; MLOps; time-series analysis

Citation: Subramanya, R.; Sierla, S.; Vyatkin, V. From DevOps to MLOps: Overview and Application to Electricity Market Forecasting. *Appl. Sci.* **2022**, *12*, 9851. https://doi.org/10.3390/app12199851

Academic Editor: Emanuele Carpanzano

Received: 26 August 2022
Accepted: 27 September 2022
Published: 30 September 2022

1. Introduction

Sufficient motivation for the DevOps process emerged around 2009 [1]. At this time, Development and Operations teams struggled to achieve smooth rollouts of software products. The main reason for this struggle was that the software developers were not concerned about deployments and the operation teams were not concerned about the development processes. DevOps is a set of processes that utilizes cross-functional teams to build, test, and release software faster, in a reliable and repeatable manner, through automation [1–3]. Recently, investment in Machine Learning (ML) applications has enabled stakeholders to solve complex business use cases that were difficult to solve. However, in most cases, ML applications are only a tiny part of a more extensive software system, and this small fraction of ML code is surrounded by a variety of software, libraries, and configuration files [4]. Hence, the main challenge in ML applications is to build continuous software engineering practices [5,6], such as DevOps [7], which can promise stakeholders the seamless integration and deployment known as MLOps [8,9]. MLOps refers to DevOps principles applied to ML applications. This paper introduces both DevOps and MLOps, provides a detailed explanation of both, and explains how to implement MLOps from the perspective of DevOps. Before diving deep into these technologies, it is helpful to understand some history behind DevOps and how MLOps has evolved from DevOps. This paper makes three contributions:

1. The literature on the motivations and the state of the art of MLOps is reviewed.
2. An overview of MLOps theory and DevOps theory relevant to the implementation of MLOps is presented, and an MLOps framework is proposed.
3. The proposed framework is applied to a time-series forecasting application as a case study. The case study is implemented with MLOps pipelines.

Most importantly, this paper systematically presents the concept of MLOps from DevOps and explores how to implement and extend the generic MLOps pipeline to multiple use cases. These two aspects are the motivation and significance of this paper. The remainder of the article is organized as follows: Section 2 reviews related works from the context of MLOps. Section 3 provides an overview of DevOps principles that lead to the development of MLOps, along with our generic MLOps framework. Section 4 presents the application of the proposed generic MLOps use case for forecasting an hourly day-ahead electricity market price.

2. Related Work

2.1. Software Development Life Cycle

The Software Development Life Cycle (SDLC) is a methodology with defined processes for creating high-quality software [10]. SDLC processes include different phases, such as planning, analysis, design, and implementation. The Waterfall model, Spiral model, Iterative model, Prototype model, V-model, Rapid Development model (RAD), and Agile model are some of the major SDLC models [10,11]. For successful project implementation, it is crucial to select a proper SDLC model depending on different parameters, such as software complexity and type [12,13]. Dayal Chauhan et al. [14] analyzed the impacts of various SDLC methods on the cost and risk of projects. Several authors have classified all of the available SDLC models into two types of methodology: heavyweight and lightweight methodologies [10,11,15]. Heavyweight methodologies are mainly process-oriented, might not entertain requirement changes, and emphasize documentation. The Waterfall, Spiral, and Incremental models are a few examples of heavyweight methodologies [15,16]. Lightweight methodologies are mainly people-oriented, entertain frequent requirement changes, have short development life cycles, and involve the customer. The Prototyping, RAD, and Agile models are a few examples of lightweight methodologies [15,16].

Several authors have compared lightweight and heavyweight methodologies and provided more insights on the SDLC selection process. For instance, Ben-Zahia and Jaluta [11] discussed the criteria for selecting proper SDLC models based on people, process, or plan orientations. A few authors have defined a third methodology called the hybrid development methodology, which uses both heavyweight and lightweight methods [17]. Khan et al. [10] used the analytic hierarchy process to select the best SDLC model from all three methodologies. Among the lightweight, heavyweight, and hybrid SDLC methodologies, Waterfall and Agile are the most used SDLC methods, based on different parameters such as usability [18,19], cost [20,21], safety [22,23], and customer involvement [24]. Several authors have shown that customers are transitioning to Agile from the traditional Waterfall SDLC due to the advantages of Agile, including short development life cycle, frequent changes, customer involvement, and usability [19,22]. However, Agile SDLC methods have also been criticized by some practitioners in cases where the requirements do not often change [25] or where there are human-related challenges related to a lack of emotional intelligence. Various authors [26,27] have analyzed issues such as quality and productivity with traditional software development strategies such as Waterfall and compared them to the Agile methodology, where clear advantages can be seen in Agile.

2.2. Agile and DevOps

Agile methodologies are the most widely implemented project management approaches in modern software systems. The 12 principles of the Agile Manifesto [28,29] characterize the process integrity and methods of Agile project management, which are applied to different Agile methodologies. Scrum, extreme programming, lean software development, and crystal methodologies are some of the Agile methodologies [14,30,31]. Ever-changing business needs demand a continuous process in software development, delivery, and system operations [32]. Implementing these continuous software practices in Agile has enabled fast delivery of software [33]. Martin Fowler introduced the idea of Continuous Integration (CI) and, later, J. Humble and D. Farley extended these ideas into

Continuous Delivery (CD) as a concept of the deployment pipeline [34]. Several authors, including Arachchi et al. [34] and Süß et al. [35], conducted research on automating CI and CD for Agile. With Agile, faster software development, quality improvement, frequent requirement changes, and customer involvement are achieved throughout the project. Nevertheless, the structural gap between the Development and Operations teams remains with the Agile methodologies. Development and Operations (DevOps) practices close this gap [36].

The working nature of software developers and operational professionals is different, and they work in isolation. This isolation might cause some conflicts between them [3]. The Development and Operations teams work under different departments and leadership [37]. Working in isolation leads to different Key Performance Indices (KPIs) [38], which are important in most organizations as they are used to define the performance of an individual or a team [39]. Not only do KPIs define the performance alone, they are also a function of several metrics [40]. An example of a developer KPI could be the time needed to roll out a feature with minor or no bugs. For the operations team, one KPI could be the time taken to roll out a feature with less or no downtime. To improve the KPIs, each team should concentrate on the task at hand. As the size of the software grows, maintainability and scalability become increasingly serious concerns [41,42]. For instance:

- An error might occur when the operations team tries to deploy a new feature to the production environment [43,44]. However, the same code might work on the developer's machine and the Quality Assurance (QA) instance.
- The new codebase might break old features.
- It is difficult to track what has changed.
- The software might not serve its core purpose at all.

These are only a subset of the issues that can arise due to the Development and Operations teams working in isolation and chasing their own KPIs. None of the product owners [45], developers [46], or team leaders from either team are responsible for addressing the issues mentioned above. Even though these issues can be solved, this requires more discussions and code exchanges between the Development and Operations teams. Various studies [47–49] have been performed to understand the effects of such impacts. Any software project has one more key stakeholder—the customer [50,51]. The customer plays a significant role in the software life cycle [13], as the customer's tolerance to risk and ability to support collaborative routines influences key parameters such as project cost and implementation time.

These issues are the driving factors that led to the formulation of the Agile and DevOps methodologies [52–54]. Agile focuses on formal requirement gathering, on small–medium but rapid releases and, finally, on continuous customer feedback. It enforces collaboration between various teams to ensure rapid reaction times to ever-changing consumer needs [55,56]. This collaboration contrasts with the traditional project management approach, which concentrates on long timelines and schedules. DevOps is the extension of the Agile methodology [57,58], and the two can work in tandem [37,51], as shown in Figure 1.

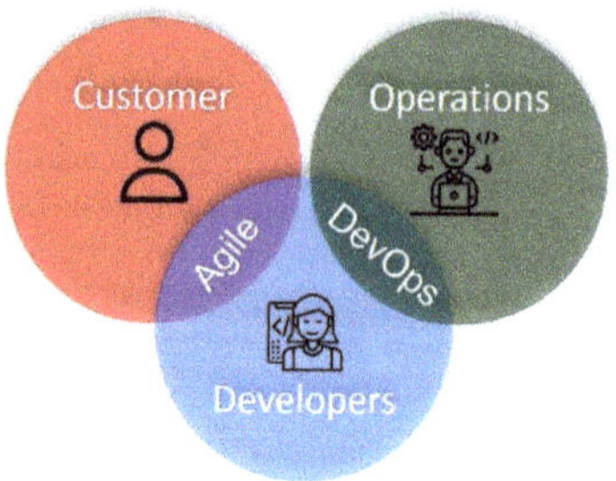

Figure 1. Agile and DevOps.

The Agile workflow assumes that the software development process is divided into multiple sprints [59,60] and the customer is notified about the changes. A sprint is the smallest duration of Agile, where a team works on an assigned task [60]. The main goal for the Development and Operations teams in a sprint is to produce a stable software release in every sprint cycle [61]. Combining Agile activities with the DevOps framework is reasonable considering the software development and delivery aspects. One such example is integrating Agile tools with DevOps tools.

2.3. MLOps from DevOps

With the successful adoption of DevOps, various organizations are trying to incorporate continuous practices in ML system development [62]. ML developers and operations teams are trying to adopt DevOps concepts to ML systems for end-to-end life-cycle automation. Containerized microservices and cloud-based DevOps have seen good stability and a reasonable success rate in production deployments [63]. For example, Kubeflow [64,65] is an ML toolkit for Kubernetes, available for almost all major cloud providers. Such toolkits aim to create ML workflows in which containers are already present. Karamitsos et al. [66] discussed such concepts and issues of applying DevOps practices to ML applications, while John et al. [62] discusses DevOps applications in ML systems. Data play an influential role in any ML application. Unlike conventional software development practices, the SDLC of an ML application revolves around data. In most cases, the core ML code is minimal, but it must integrate with some significant components of a bigger system. Sculley et al. [4] analyzed such systems and explored the hidden technical debt. The complexity increases when ML applications are deployed on the cloud or interfaced with web APIs. Banerjee et al. [67] proposed operationalizing ML applications for such an environment, and MLOps could be implemented for such hybrid cloud deployments.

Several authors have investigated MLOps. Makinen et al. [9] studied the state of ML to understand the extent of MLOps required and to analyze the issues with data; however, the authors did not consider deployment. Some research has been performed on the trends and challenges in MLOps. Tamburri et al. [68] recapped trends in terms of properties such as the fairness and accountability of sustainable ML operations of a software system. Several works propose the MLOps framework for applications [62,69] such as the automotive industry, supply chain management, and IoT. Granlund et al. [70] presented issues related to the MLOps pipeline when multiple organizations are involved, highlighting factors such as scalability. Different cloud providers offer MLOps solutions as a service so that the whole ML product life cycle can be managed on the cloud. Azure MLOps [71] and AWS SageMaker for MLOps [72] are some examples of such cloud services. A few cloud providers have published a detailed guide on the MLOps life cycle for the purpose of building ML applications and MLOps pipelines on the cloud or on-premises servers [73].

2.4. Summary of MLOps from DevOps

This section presents state-of-the-art MLOps articles mentioned in Section 2.3 in terms of methodology, novelty, and results. Table 1 provides the summary.

Table 1. Summary of state-of-the-art MLOps articles.

Paper	Methodology	Novelty	Result
[62]	Systematic literature review along with a grey literature review to derive a framework	MLOps framework that describes the activities involved in the continuous development of the ML model	Framework validation in three embedded systems case companies
[65]	Verified the feasibility of creating an ML pipeline with CI/CD capabilities on various appliances with specific hardware configuration	Performance evaluation of ML pipeline platforms characterized by Kubeflow on different models according to various metrics.	Consumption of time and resources concerning the ML platform and computational models.

Table 1. *Cont.*

Paper	Methodology	Novelty	Result
[66]	Review of the two DevOps components CI and CD, in the ML context	ML manual and automated pipeline design with CI/CD components	Scaling ML models
[67]	Five issues in ML-based solutions for performance diagnostics	MLOps pipeline to resolve the five challenges in the performance diagnostics	Fully automated pipeline for continuously training the new models upon the arrival of new data
[9]	Surveyed and compiled responses from ML professionals to investigate the role of MLOps in their daily activities	Survey with questions and goals	Based on survey, presented data on challenges based on survey data, ML problem types, and future plans with ML
[68]	A brief overview of the state-of-the-art MLOps and an overview of the organizational and educational structures around AI software operations	Challenges and trends in AI software operations	Challenges in educating AI operations and properties to be supported by software for the domain it was designed for
[69]	Multiple IoT experimental setups. Each setup is equipped with an IoT device and an edge device	An automated framework for MLOps at the edge, i.e., edge MLOps	Deployed and monitored IoT data and edge node operations in real time
[70]	Study integration between two organizations in detail for a multi-organization setup	Addressed scaling of ML to a multi-organization context	Integrated challenges of the ML pipeline, datasets, models, and monitoring.

3. An Overview of DevOps and MLOps

3.1. DevOps

DevOps is a set of practices or fault-tolerant workflows built to increase software quality by providing continuous development and delivery through end-to-end automation [35,53,74]. DevOps practices bring together the development, testing, and operational software development teams through automation [2]. DevOps enables a shorter code–build–deploy loop with a better end product [4,75]. A typical DevOps workflow is shown in Figure 2.

3.1.1. DevOps Workflow and Components

The main focus of DevOps is to automate the software delivery process throughout, thereby ensuring continuous delivery and the feedback loop of the software [76]. Continuous delivery combines the development, testing, and deployment processes into one streamlined operation. The primary goal is to quicken the whole process through automation. If both Development and Operations teams are practicing DevOps, they can quickly deploy code improvements, improving the transparency between two teams and allowing the end user to see changes quickly [53,74,77]. Due to continuous deployment and the involvement of customers in the DevOps workflow, the customers do not have to wait for a monthly/quarterly/yearly software release cycle [53,78] to test or provide feedback about the software.

The DevOps workflow shown in Figure 2 helps the teams to build, test, and deploy software quickly and efficiently through a combination of tools and practices, from development to maintenance. DevOps reduces Time to Market (TTM) and enables Agile software development processes [79,80]. These DevOps components are closely related to Agile. DevOps is the next step in the evolution of Agile methodologies [53,79]. The following subsections discuss the components—or phases [53]—within the DevOps workflow [58,79,81].

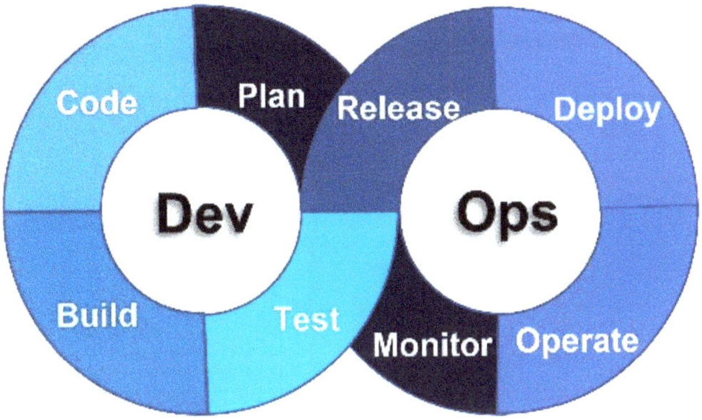

Figure 2. Typical DevOps workflow adapted from [66,79].

Plan

In this phase, requirements are defined, and the initial execution plan is created. The tools used for DevOps help the user and the developers to be constantly in sync. In this phase, if Agile is used as the SDLC, the user stories and tech stories should be defined with the teams [82]. Various issue-tracking and project-management tools, such as Jira [83], are used in this phase to help with the planning.

Code

Coding is the first step in DevOps automation, and all of the team members should adhere to the agreed coding standards and best practices [2,84]. Test-Driven Development (TDD), Acceptance Test-Driven Development (ATDD), and Behavior-Driven Development (BDD) are a few of the best practices [84]. One of the significant areas in coding that is still highly neglected is versioning of the software via source control. Versioning not only helps to maintain the software, but also helps to automate the DevOps workflow properly [85,86]. It is essential to implement good practices within the source control, such as pull requests, proper branching, and commit messages [87–89]. Several authors [90,91] have shown that artifact traceability can be achieved if performed adequately with good practices.

A branching strategy is used to share and collaborate the code changes among development teams. Feature-branching-based versioning and trunk-based versioning are the two most widely used branching strategies. Some versioning tools include Git, Subversion (SVN), and Team Foundation Server (TFS). Figure 3 shows a feature branching strategy with different types of branches [92,93], while Figure 4 shows typical trunk-based versioning [94,95].

Build

The software build usually refers to the whole software package, consisting of the business logic, the software dependencies, and the environment [96]. A few authors refer to the build phase as the verify phase [81]. In either case, the main aim of DevOps build systems is to evaluate the correctness of software artifacts [81,97]. Typically, three standard deployment instances are used while developing an application—development, Quality Assurance (QA), and production instances [98,99]. The build systems in DevOps make sure that code integrity is maintained. Software build systems are highly dependent on software configuration management systems, and multiple builds are possible among these environments [97,100], including private system builds. Several authors, including Leite et al. [101], mention various build tools for DevOps.

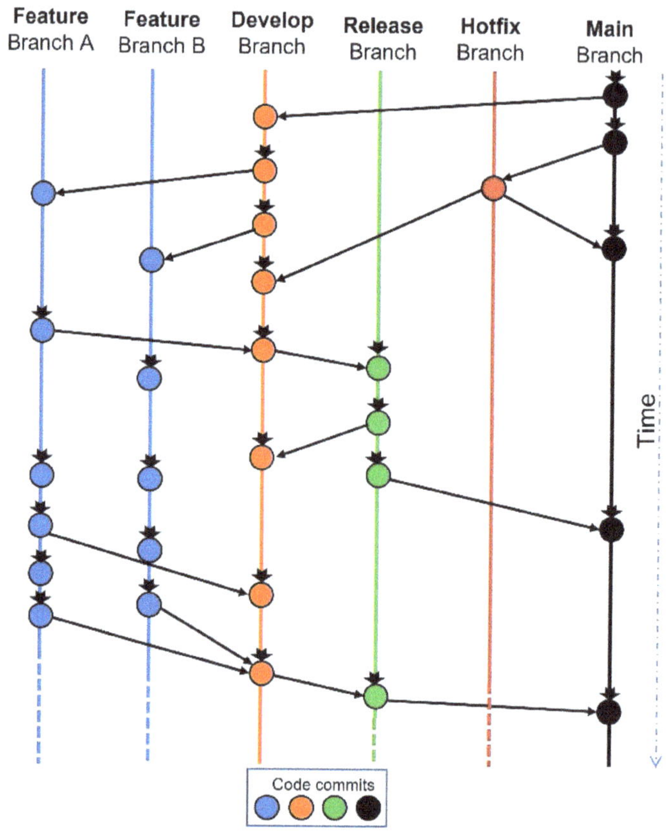

Figure 3. Feature branching strategy adapted from [92,93].

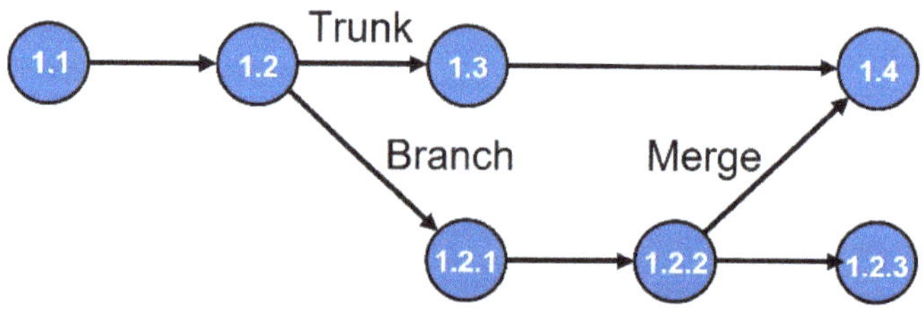

Figure 4. Typical trunk-based versioning adapted from [94,95].

Test

In the test phase of DevOps, automated testing is performed continuously to ensure the quality of the software artifact [84,102]. There are different ways to include test cases such as units and integration while the software is being written. One such method is to use Test-Driven Development (TDD) [103]. In this case, the developer writes the test cases first, and then the actual functionality. There is another approach called Behavior-Driven Development (BDD), which is an extension of TDD [104]. Some good practices, such as code coverage [105], are part of the DevOps pipeline, and some cloud DevOps services, such as Azure DevOps [106], provide this within the service.

Release

Once all test cases are passed, the software is ready for deployment. By this phase, a code change has already passed a series of manual and automated tests [107]. Regular feature releases can be carried out according to a regular schedule or once milestones are met. A manual approval process could be added at the release stage, allowing only a few people within an organization to authorize a release for production [74,78].

Deploy

In the deployment stage, the focus is on continuously deploying or redeploying the software. The deployment varies depending on the type and nature of the application. The deployment process can be automated easily for the production environment, using virtualization or containerization as the orchestration technology. Jenkins is one of the most widely used deployment tools in the industry [53,87].

Operate

The operate phase involves maintaining and troubleshooting applications in a production environment. Teams ensure system reliability and high availability. They aim for zero downtime while reinforcing security [108]. Selecting the proper hardware size for scaling or implementing the scaling methods on the cloud is crucial for the application's uptime and ability to handle high loads [109,110]. This configuration is performed in the operate phase.

Monitor

After the application is deployed and configured to handle the ever-changing load, it is essential to monitor the application to ensure that it is stable enough to handle the promised uptime [111]. The monitor phase helps perform operations such as application health tracking and incident management. "New Relic" is one such tool to monitor the application.

3.1.2. DevOps Pipeline

In practice, some of the DevOps components mentioned above are combined to form a sequence of operations called a pipeline. There is no single generalized pipeline structure [80,112]. Every pipeline is unique, and the pipeline structure depends on the nature of the application and the implementation technology. In DevOps, the following common pipeline components can be found [53,54,58,77,84]:

- Continuous Integration (CI);
- Continuous Delivery (CD);
- Continuous Deployment;
- Continuous Monitoring.

These pipelines include DevOps components mentioned in the previous section. Most of the DevOps implementations consider CI and CD as the core components.

Continuous Integration

Continuous integration is the practice of integrating code changes from multiple developers into a single source via automation [77]. The important practice of CI is that all developers commit the code frequently to the main or trunk branch [113] mentioned in Section 3.1, subsection 'Plan' After the commitment, the code building is performed as explained in Section 3.1, subsection 'Build'. As soon as the build succeeds, the unit test cases are run as explained in Section 3.1, subsection 'Test'. Primarily, CI uses SCM (Software Configuration Management) tools such as Git, as explained in Section 3.1, subsection 'Code', to merge the code changes into SCM for code versioning. CI also performs automated code quality tests, syntax style reviews, and code validation [114]. Since many developers integrate the code, the following issues may occur:

- **Code or merge conflicts:** This is the state when SCM is unable to resolve the difference in code between two commits automatically. Until the merge conflict is resolved, the SCM will usually not allow the code to be merged. Usually, merge conflicts happen if the changes are inconsistent when merging changes from two branches [115].
- **Dead code:** Dead code is a block of code never reached by the execution flow [116]. Dead code can be introduced at any step in the programming as part of a code merge. For instance, consider two feature branches: Feature A and Feature B. Feature A's developers might have considered some exceptions from Feature B and created code blocks to handle that. However, if this exception never happens or some logic in the Feature B branch changes, this exception block will never be executed [117,118].
- **Code overwrites:** As the software evolves, there is a high possibility that the old code needs to be updated to meet the ever-changing requirements. Nevertheless, this might also affect the old features, resulting in code breaks after merging.

One of the primary benefits of CI is that it saves time during the development cycle by identifying and addressing conflicts early [119]. The first step in avoiding the abovementioned issues is to set up an automated testing pipeline [80,120].

In a CI testing pipeline, the code should be built successfully with no code conflicts before the tests are run. The CI pipeline tests vary depending on the nature of the application. To get an early warning of the possible issues, it is suggested to run this CI pipeline for every branch of the SCM and not only on the main or trunk branches. The basic CI pipeline is ready once the SCM and an automated unit testing framework are ready. The following are some of the critical points to keep in mind while implementing CI:

- Unit tests are fast and cost less in terms of code execution time as they check a smaller block of code [121].
- UI tests are slower and more complex to run, more complex to set up, and might also have high costs in terms of execution time and resource usage. Furthermore, a mobile development environment with multiple emulators and environments might add more complexity. Hence, UI tests should be selected more carefully and run less frequently than the unit tests [103,122].
- Running these tests automatically for every code commit is preferred, but doing this on a development or feature branch might be costlier than manual testing [123].
- To meet the code coverage criteria [105], both white-box and black-box testing could be part of CI. However, white-box testing can be time-consuming, depending on the codebase [124].
- Combining code coverage metrics with a test pipeline is the most effective way to know how much code the test suite covers [105]. This coverage report can help in eliminating dead code [125].

The following two practices help to avoid or detect early merge conflicts [115]:

- Pushing of local changes to the SCM should be performed early and often.
- Changes should be pulled from the SCM before pushing. This frequent code pulling will reveal any merge conflicts early.

Various software builds such as Integration builds should be rebuilt and retested after every change [119]. In a CI tool, if every test case runs smoothly without issues, and if there are no merge conflicts, the CI tool shows the current build status as "Pass". If anything goes wrong, this will be changed to "Fail". The priority of the whole development team is to keep the builds "Passing" [126].

Continuous Delivery and Continuous Deployment

Continuous Delivery (CD) and Continuous Deployment are implemented in the DevOps pipeline after CI. In Continuous Delivery, the aim is to keep the application ready for production deployment. At the least, unit test cases, a few optional quality checks, and other tests should have been completed before continuous delivery [54,127]. Continuous Delivery/Deployment is a process of deploying the application to various deployment instances, such as testing or production. The key differences between Continuous Delivery and Continuous Deployment are as follows: The Continuous Delivery process is the frequent code shipping to production or test instances manually, whereas Continuous Deployment is the automated deployment of code to the instances. In both cases, the code is kept ready for deployment at any point [53,58,120].

Continuous Delivery (CD) is an extension of the previously discussed CI. CD automatically deploys all code changes to the testing and/or production environment after the code-building stage. It is possible to deploy the application manually from the CD pipeline utilizing a manual trigger. CD is mainly used for automated deployments as soon as the build artifacts are ready. In this paper, a build artifact is defined as a binary such as a container or a web portal build after this binary has passed all of the tests and the build stage [128,129]. CD is beneficial when the build artifacts are deployed to production as soon as possible. This frequent deployment ensures that the software release contains small batches, which are easy to debug in case of any issues in the post-production deployment. Figure 5 shows the sample CI/CD pipeline.

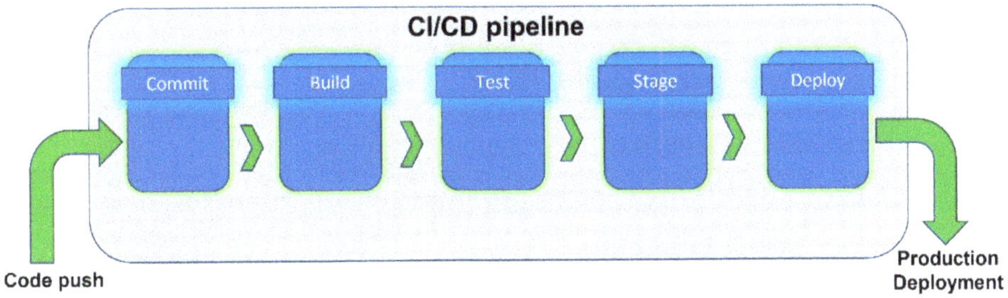

Figure 5. A typical CI/CD pipeline adapted from [54,77,80,127].

Continuous Monitoring

Continuous Monitoring (CM) is an automated DevOps pipeline to monitor the vitals of the deployed application on the production instance. CM comes at the end of the DevOps pipeline and provides real-time data from the monitoring instance. CM helps to avoid and track system downtimes and evaluate application performance, security threats, and compliance concerns [130].

3.2. *MLOps*

Machine Learning Operations (MLOps) is a set of practices that aims to maintain and deploy Machine Learning code and models with high reliability and efficiency. MLOps is primarily based on DevOps practices such as CI and CD to manage the ML life cycle [131,132]. The main target of MLOps is to achieve faster development and deployment of the ML models with high quality, reproducibility, and end-to-end tracking. Like DevOps, MLOps also enables a shorter code–build–deploy loop and aims to automate and monitor all steps of ML [9,68,69].

3.2.1. MLOps Workflow and Components

Like DevOps, the focus of MLOps is to automate the software delivery process throughout, ensuring continuous delivery and a feedback loop of the software. However, in most cases, the ML application must work with the other software assets in a DevOps-based CI/CD environment. In such cases, additional steps are introduced to the existing DevOps process because existing DevOps tools and pipelines cannot be applied to ML applications [9]. The adaptation of MLOps practices is still in its initial stages, as there is little research on MLOps compared with DevOps [62]. For the ML systems, data scientists and operations teams are trying to automate the end-to-end life cycle of ML by utilizing DevOps concepts [66]. Due to the variations in ML methodologies, it is challenging to generalize MLOps components.

To date, numerous designs with different components have been proposed, such as Iterative/Incremental processes [132] and Continuous Delivery for Machine Learning (CD4ML) [133]. In 2015, Sculley et al. [4] highlighted that in most real-world ML applications, the quantity of actual ML code is significantly smaller than the surrounding infrastructure, and a vast infrastructure supports this small ML code. The authors also discussed technical issues and challenges in ML systems, such as model complexity, reproducibility of the results, testing, and monitoring. Most of these are also relevant for DevOps components. Hence, it is vital to include the data, infrastructure, and core ML code in the MLOps life cycle. Numerous ML life-cycle processes such as CRISP-ML(Q) [134] have been proposed to establish a standard process model for ML development. John et al. [62] presented a maturity model outlining various stages by which companies evolve their MLOps approaches.

A generic MLOps workflow is shown in Figure 6. As mentioned, the concerns cited by Sculley et al. [4]—such as code maintenance problems and system-level issues—are also present in traditional software development, and DevOps solves most of them via CI/CD. This CI/CD process creates reliable pipelines with assured quality to release the software into production. A cross-functional team is a way of involving expertise from different functional areas [78,135], such as data scientists and ML engineers [131]. In MLOps, a cross-functional team produces ML applications in small increments based on three parameters: code, data, and models. These can be released and reproduced at any time, using a constant seed value for random sample initialization to set the weights of the trainable layers, if applicable [136]. The following subsections define the generic MLOps process model illustrated in Figure 6.

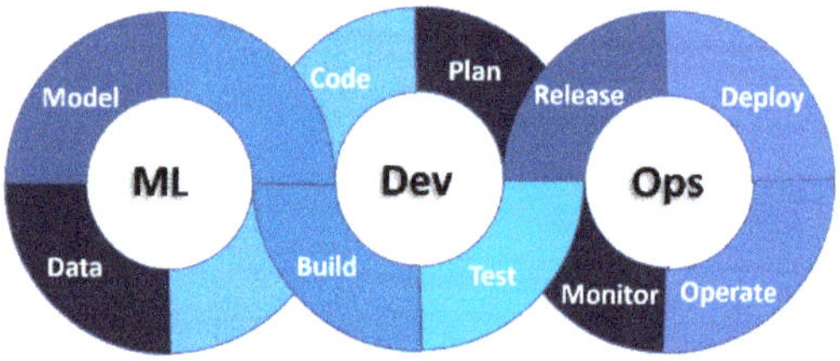

Figure 6. Typical MLOps workflow adapted from [68,131].

The MLOPs workflow in Figure 6 is similar to the DevOps workflow in Figure 2 but introduces two new components: data and model. Furthermore, the MLOps components testing, deployment, and monitoring are slightly different from their DevOps counterparts. Along with data and model, these differences are explained in the following sections.

Data

ML is driven by data; hence, data analysis and operations are vital to MLOps. [137,138]. Unlike DevOps, ML operations are experimental, which is true in almost all of the steps of MLOps. For instance, hyperparameter optimization is varied during implementation. The same is true for data, and the following operations are involved in data analysis [139,140]:

- Data extraction;
- Data validation;
- Data analysis;
- Data preparation.

The sequence and usage of these components depend on the type of ML and the nature of the application.

Data extraction is mainly concerned with the gathering of data from different sources. The data sources—such as online APIs, cloud-based data lakes, CSV files, or a combination of these—can be diverse. Extra precautions should be taken while extracting the data for some ML tasks. For instance, for a classification issue, the data must be balanced after they are extracted. Failing to do so might degrade the classifier's performance [141]. The data extraction component in the MLOps pipeline is usually the first step, in which data from one or more sources are integrated for further processing [139].

To detect inaccurate data early and avoid training ML models with flawed data, the suggested technique is to incorporate a **data validation** process [140]. Common data quality issues include the following [140,142]:

- Incomplete data; for instance, the presence of null values.
- Inconsistent data, such as issues with the data type.
- Inaccurate data; for example, data collection with the wrong measurements.

Data analysis is a crucial step in the creation of a model. In this step, Exploratory Data Analysis (EDA) is performed to understand the characteristics of the data [138]. Depending on this knowledge, feature engineering is performed in the following steps, and a suitable model is designed.

In **data preparation**, the validated data are split into three standard datasets: training, test, and validation [143]. Features are selected from the data, data-cleaning operations are performed, and some extra features are added after EDA. EDA shows the trends and patterns in the data, and we can add more features from new data sources to support the existing data [144]. In data preparation, common data quality issues can be fixed. If required, data transformations such as date–time format matches from different data sources [145] are performed on the data and, finally, the three sets of data are sent to the model.

Model

The ML model is the heart of any ML application. Neural networks are the most common type of ML model, and the rest of this paper assumes that the ML model is a neural network. Once the model structure is defined, model training, model evaluation, and model validation operations are performed.

Model training trains one or several models with the prepared data. Hyperparameter optimization is performed, where model variables such as the number of layers and nodes in each layer are optimized in different iterations. After this optimization, the model is trained or well-fitted [146,147].

Once the model is trained, it is evaluated in **model evaluation** of the validation data. The trained model is evaluated using the held-out validation datasets to measure the model's quality. Model validation gives the measure of performance of the model [148]. Metrics such as absolute error and mean absolute error are used to define the model quality. These metrics are helpful in testing and comparing different models [149,150].

Testing

As in DevOps, unit and integration tests should be performed. Testing of ML models is mostly limited to checks related to the convergence of models, shapes of passed tensors/vectors, and other model-related variables. However, there is a lot of code surrounding an ML model, which should also be tested [151]. However, white-box testing for ML-based systems could entail high test efforts due to the large test input space [152]. In MLOps, test cases should check the proper input and output data format.

Deployment

Unlike DevOps, deploying ML applications is not straightforward, especially if the ML application is a part of a DevOps application such as a web API. In ML applications, the arrival of new data triggers the retraining and redeployment of models. An automated pipeline must be created to perform these actions [153].

Monitoring

It is crucial to monitor the performance of the deployed ML model. Continuous monitoring helps to understand the model performance and trigger retraining if required [154]. In DevOps, the main concern is ensuring that the application is healthy and able to handle the load. If the ML is part of an application such as a web API, the monitoring component should check for ML parameters such as data drift and model performance [131,155].

As in DevOps, some of these steps are combined to form a pipeline. Usually, these are combined with DevOps pipelines. As in DevOps, there is no single generalized pipeline structure. Every pipeline is unique, and the pipeline structure depends on the nature of the application, the type of ML, and the implementation technology.

3.2.2. MLOps Pipeline

In MLOps, the following standard pipeline components are implemented [62,69,131]:

- Continuous Integration (CI);
- Continuous Deployment (CD);
- Continuous Training (CT).

Continuous Integration

As in DevOps, the CI pipeline is about the testing and validation of code components. For ML applications, data and model validations are added along with classical unit and integration tests [65]. Unit tests are written to cover the changes in feature engineering, and different methods used to implement the models. Moreover, tests should be written to check the convergence of the model training. During training, a machine learning model reaches a convergence state when the model loss value settles within an error range, after which any additional training might not improve the model's accuracy [156].

Continuous Deployment

There are considerable changes in the Continuous Deployment pipeline compared to DevOps. As the ML models evolve continuously, verifying the models' compatibility with the target deployment environments with respect to computing power and any changes in the deployment environments is essential. The process changes depending on the use case and whether the ML prediction is online or batch processing [157].

Continuous Training

This new pipeline component is unique to MLOps., The Continuous Training (CT) pipeline automatically retrains the model [158]. Different ML components explained in Section 3.2.1 are automated to work in a sequence to achieve this. Retraining the model is essential, as the data keep changing or updating in any ML application. To cope with the new incoming data, the model needs retraining. This retraining includes automating several model retraining, data validation, and model validation processes. To initiate such processes, triggers are included in the pipeline.

Some additional components, such as feature storage and metadata management, are used along with these pipelines in MLOps. They help in managing data and reproducibility aspects. These are discussed below.

3.2.3. Feature Store

Due to many variations, such as the components involved in the ML applications, feature stores are used. This feature store acts as a central repository for standardizing the definition, access, and storage of a feature set. A feature store helps to achieve the following [159]:

- Store commonly used features;
- Build feature sets from the available raw data;
- Reuse custom feature sets;

- Model monitoring and data drift detection;
- Transform and store the data for training or inference purposes.

3.2.4. Metadata Management

The fundamental nature of ML is experimentation. It would not be easy to track the steps that lead to an ideal model or the best-performing dataset with many experiments in all of the different components. With the help of metadata management, almost all of the metadata for the whole ML process can be tracked and used to repeat the desired result. The most significant metadata include [160]:

- Experiments and training metadata—Metadata such as environment configuration, hardware metrics, code versions, and hyperparameters.
- Artifact metadata—Metadata such as dataset paths, model hashes, dataset previews, and artifact descriptions.
- Model metadata—Model-related metadata such as model versions, data and performance drifts, and hardware usage.
- Pipeline metadata—Pipeline metadata such as node information and completion reports of each pipeline.

MLOps pipelines might look highly automated. Nevertheless, not all of the pipelines or pipeline components are necessary to implement. The pipeline and its components can be selected depending on the implementation and use case. Sculley et al. [4] mentioned that only a minority of the application is ML code, since most of the system is composed of data collection and verification components, model analysis and building, resource and metadata management, automation, and configuration. Google Cloud [161] proposes three MLOps process levels for implementing the CI/CD pipeline for different needs based on the work of Sculley et al. [4]; these define the different levels of maturity of the MLOps processes:

- MLOps level 0: Manual process;
- MLOps level 1: ML pipeline automation;
- MLOps level 2: CI/CD pipeline automation.

3.3. Research Gap

In the next section, MLOps is applied for a time-series forecasting application, which predicts the price of a day-ahead hourly electricity market. The MLOps level 2 automated CI/CD pipeline is implemented. CI and CD services are utilized for reliable delivery of the ML results.

This use case fills the following research gap observed in Sections 2 and 3:

- Even though the core ML is a tiny part of the whole software ecosystem, the ML application needs various new tools for the MLOps implementation.
- MLOps tools might not be compatible with the DevOps tools, burdening the complete system.
- Creating an MLOps pipeline with traditional software—such as a web application where DevOps is already implemented—is an issue.
- Additionally, to explain the generalization of the created MLOps pipeline and the tools, Case Study 1 is extended to two more case studies. In the last two case studies, the price forecast solution (Case Study 1) is adapted with minimal work.

4. Case Study 1: Forecasting an Hourly Day-Ahead Electricity Market Using an MLOps Pipeline

The reliable operation of the electric power grid relies on a complex system of markets, which ensures that electric power consumption and generation are matched at every point in time. This matching is crucial for the stability of the grid, since the grid cannot store electric energy. From an MLOps perspective, forecasting the price of any electricity market depends on the market schedule, and the ML experts do not need to understand how the market contributes to stabilizing the grid. The timing characteristics of the market represent important knowledge for the developers of time-series forecasting solutions. In particular, two characteristics are crucial:

- Does the price change weekly, daily, hourly, or at some other interval?
- When does the market participation occur and, thus, how far into the future should forecasts be available?

There are numerous markets in a single country, and significant differences can exist between different countries. Thus, an ML team working on electricity price forecasting would do well to avoid hardcoding assumptions related to the questions above, and should instead parameterize them. A common market structure in Europe and elsewhere is the hourly day-ahead market [162,163], which used as a concrete example in this paper. Such markets have the following characteristics:

- The market interval is one hour; in other words, there is a separate price for each hour.
- The market participants need to place their bids on the previous day; for example, before the market deadline today, separate bids should be placed for each hour of the next day.

In our case study, we look at a specific hourly day-ahead market—the Finnish Frequency Containment Reserves for Normal Operations (FCR-N) market. The FCR markets compensate participants for maintaining a reserve that can be activated to generate or consume energy in case such an activation is required due to a momentary imbalance in the power grid. An offline neural-network-based forecasting solution for this market is presented in [164].

4.1. The Frequency Containment Reserves Market

With the advent of smart grids and Virtual Power Plants (VPPs), various Distributed Energy Resources (DERs)—such as smart loads, batteries, photovoltaics (PVs), and wind power—are being exploited on various electricity markets, including frequency reserves [165–168]. Frequency reserves with a fast response time for frequency deviations are generally called Primary Frequency Reserves (PFRs), and traditionally they consist of fossil-fuel-burning spinning reserves. These reserves are now being replaced with DERs in the push towards reducing carbon emissions [169]; due to this, under the current allowed delays for PFRs, the reduced grid inertia is becoming a threat to the stability of power systems [170]. The FCR-N market was selected among other ancillary services for this case study, as the FCR-N does not have hard real-time constraints and a minimum power bid for market participation. The FCR-N is a day-ahead market, and bidders must submit all of the bids for the hours of the next day before 6 p.m. of the current day [171,172].

If the day-ahead reserve market prices can be predicted, then the DER owners can anticipate variations in price peaks and low or zero prices. Thus, this case study presents a solution based on artificial neural networks, which are deployed online, so that the predictions are automatically updated and available before the bidding deadline of the day-ahead market. A transformer-based ANN model is exploited to predict the day-ahead ancillary energy market prices. The MLOps pipelines are configured to ingest the data at 1 p.m. on the current day, so the forecasts are available, e.g., at 2 p.m., so that the person or system doing the bidding has the forecast a few hours before submitting the bid.

4.2. Prediction Model

For the energy price predictions in ML, ANNs are widely used. For instance, based on the architecture defined in [173], Recurrent Neural Networks (RNNs) and feed-forward neural networks are the two major ANN categories. RNNs can predict the high energy spikes better, whereas feed-forward networks can predict the spot market prices for day-ahead prediction [174]. An ANN was employed to predict ancillary market prices by considering different data sources where the results outperformed Support-Vector Regression (SVR) and Autoregressive Integrated Moving Average (ARIMA) [164]. For implementing the FCR-N market price forecasting using the MLOps pipeline, this case study uses the Temporal Fusion Transformer (TFT) model structure defined in [175]. Energy price prediction datasets have a time component, and forecasting the future price values can provide significant value for multi-horizon forecasting, i.e., predicting variables of interest at multiple future time steps. Deep Neural Networks (DNNs) have been used in multi-horizon forecasting, showing substantial performance improvements over traditional time-series models. However, most existing RNN models often do not consider the different inputs commonly present in multi-horizon forecasting, and either assume that all exogenous inputs are known in the future or do not consider static covariates. Conventional time-series models are influenced by complex nonlinear interactions between many parameters, making it difficult to explain how such models arrive at their predictions. Attention-based models are proposed for sequential data such as energy price prediction datasets. However, multi-horizon forecasting has many different types of inputs, and attention-based models can provide an understanding of appropriate time steps, but they cannot contrast the importance of different features at a given time step, and TFT solves these issues in terms of accuracy and interpretability.

TFT is an attention-based architecture that combines multi-horizon forecasting with interpretable insights into temporal dynamics. TFT utilizes recurrent layers for local processing and interpretable self-attention layers for learning long-term dependencies with the knowledge of temporal relationships at diverse scales [175]. The major components of TFT are summarized below.

- *Gating mechanisms* skip any unused components of the model.
- *Variable selection networks* choose relevant input variables at each time step.
- Static features can have a meaningful impact on forecasts, and *static covariate encoders* integrate such features based on which temporal dynamics are modeled.
- A sequence-to-sequence *temporal processing* layer to learn long-term and short-term temporal relationships.

Table 2 provides additional information on TFT hyperparameters for practitioners who may wish to reproduce the results.

Table 2. TFT hyperparameters.

Temporal Fusion Transformer	
hidden_size	32
attention_head_size	1
dropout	0.1
hidden_continuous_size	16
learning_rate	0.03
loss	QuantileLoss()
log_interval	2
reduce_on_plateau_patience	4
Trainer	
gpus	1
max_epochs	10
gradient_clip_val	0.1

4.3. MLOps Pipeline for FCR-N Market Price Forecasting

The main scope of this example is to define an MLOps pipeline for such applications and determine how the whole process could be automated. First, the data are ingested via Fingrid and the Finnish Meteorological Institute's (FMI) REST API into raw data storage. The data from Fingrid and FMI are available online via the REST API, but not as a manual download via files; hence, it is possible to automate this pipeline. Next, the data are prepared for further processing by selecting the essential features from the raw data storage, and this feature selection is based on past experimentation. Data are then validated for missing values or the presence of *NaN* values and stored in a feature store for data reusability. Additionally, EDA is performed on the data to understand any data drifts. The next step is to build the model through model training and evaluation. Once the model is evaluated, the prediction is performed on the new dataset. The performance of the model is evaluated for monitoring purposes. The resulting pipeline architecture is shown in Figure 7.

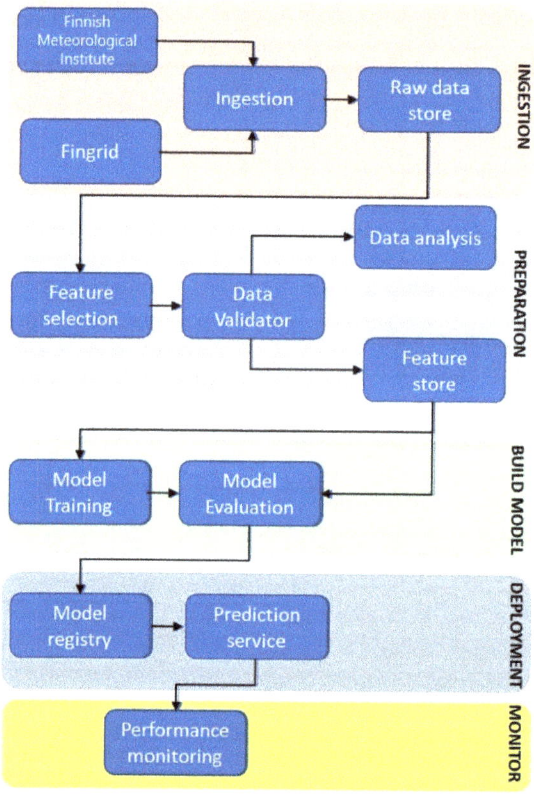

Figure 7. Proposed MLOps pipeline.

4.4. MLOps Runtime Environment

As mentioned in Section 3.1, subsection 'Code', the first step is to ensure that the code is appropriately versioned. GIT was selected as the version control for this implementation, and GIT feature branching was followed. Figure 8 shows the commits and GIT branches.

Two feature branches were created for the development of the solution, namely, "feature/build-model" and "feature/ingest-data". Additionally, one "develop" branch and one "release" branch were created. The develop branch was branched out from the main branch, and the feature branches were branched out of the develop branch. The feature branches were frequently merged back to the development branch, and all the feature branches were updated with the recent changes. Once the final code was merged back to the develop branch, the code was planned for release from the release branch. The code was versioned correctly, and a stable version of the code was always kept in the main branch after tagging correctly.

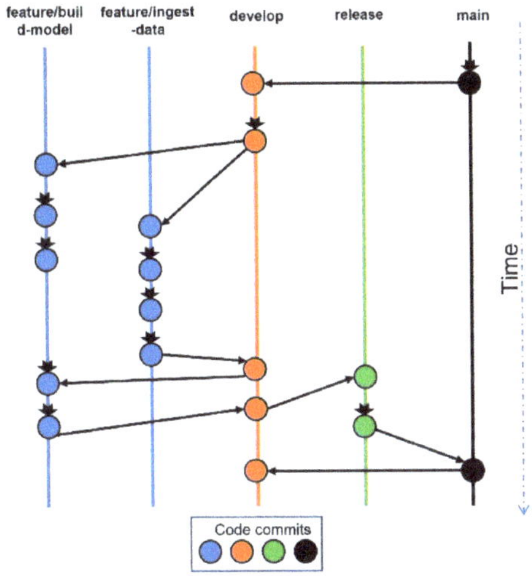

Figure 8. Commits in GIT showing branches, merging, and tags.

In this use case—MLOps level 2—CI/CD implementation was followed as explained at the end of Section 3. Hence the CI/CD should include source control, ML pipelines, test services, model services, feature storage, and deployment services. The first step in the CI/CD process is to create pipelines. These pipelines run in a sequence to implement the price forecast task. Moreover, the pipelines should provide a supportive environment, including runtimes and libraries. We selected PyTorch as the ML library and Python as the scripting language. Python libraries such as NumPy and Pandas were installed in a virtual environment and loaded by the pipeline at the beginning to prepare the environment for the forecasting job. For this implementation, 10 pipelines were selected, and the modular code was created to run in each component. The required unit tests were also implemented and included along with data validation. The trigger was set to any commit changes in the SCM main branch; the pipelines would be triggered upon such changes, and the code would be deployed to generate the forecasting results. There is a variety of software available for creating CI/CD pipelines. Jenkins was selected as the CI/CD server because it is the most commonly used CI/CD server for DevOps. MLOps pipelines were incorporated using Jenkinsfile and Python. In this use case, we also used the DevOps process for implementing a web UI using Django, where the Django web framework was used for viewing the predicted result. All of the required software—including GIT, Jenkins, Python, Anaconda, and Docker—was installed on the CSC cloud.

Figure 9 shows the pipelines created for the FCR-N market price forecaster. A new SCM commit change at the main branch would trigger the pipeline. The following pipelines were created in this example implementation:

- Data ingestion;
- Data preparation;
- EDA;
- Model building;
- Deployment and monitoring pipelines with a few sub-pipelines.

"Data Ingestion—Data Fetch" fetches the data from the Fingrid and FMI API. "Data Ingestion—Store Raw Data" pipeline stores these data in an SQL database, and PostgreSQL is used as the database, which stores the raw data. "Data Preparation—Feature Selection" performs the feature selection from the raw data. Different experiments have been performed in the past, based which this pipeline selects the features. "Data Preparation—Data Validator" validates the data and checks against different validation rules and data consistency, including null values, the presence of NaN, and data types. Along with this code level, unit test cases are also executed to ensure code integrity. These data are then stored in a feature store for future use and analysis using the "Data Preparation—Feature Store" pipeline.

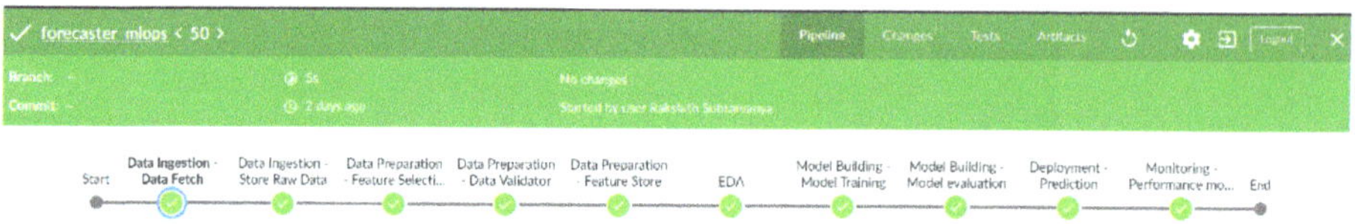

Figure 9. MLOps pipeline for FCR-N market price forecasting.

Data analysis is performed automatically with the "EDA" pipeline to avoid data drift and other issues with data quality. The next step is to normalize the data and build the model, and this is done via the "Model Building—Model Training" and "Model Building—Model evaluation" pipelines. It is then necessary to create a docker container of the prediction model. "Deployment—Prediction" pipeline does that, and then forecasts the FCR-N market price for the next 24 h. The forecasted result is stored in the PostgreSQL database. The model's accuracy and performance are monitored via the "Monitoring—Performance monitor" pipeline. The EDA and performance monitoring results are monitored regularly, and the pipelines are updated if the performance has gone down.

Due to the modular nature of the CI/CD pipeline design, it is easy to plug in/out a module. If a build fails—for instance, at the "Data Ingestion—Data Fetch"—the CI/CD system shows a detailed log on the CI/CD UI, as shown in Figure 10.

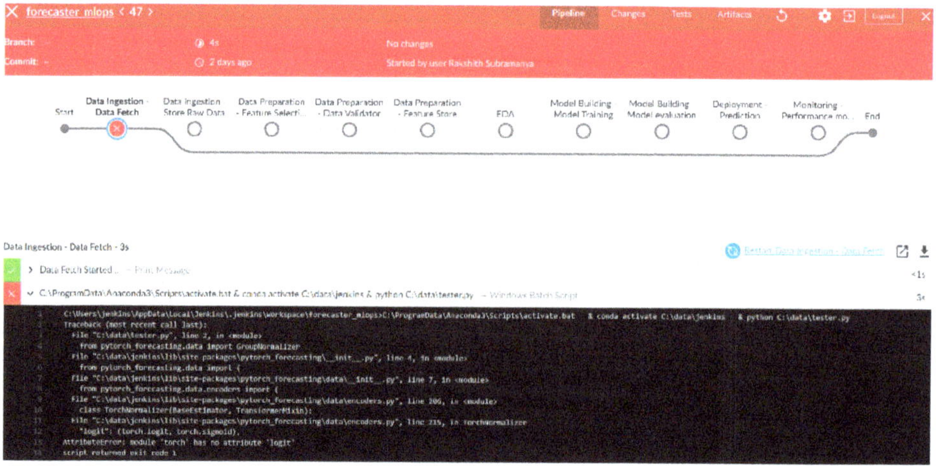

Figure 10. Build fail notification.

These logs are maintained in the CI/CD system so that it is easy to debug and replicate the errors in the developer's machine using the local build discussed in Section 3.1, subsection 'Build'. Figure 10 shows the failure pipeline. Once the pipeline finishes the job execution, depending on the build's status, an email is triggered from the CI/CD system to the configured emails notifying about the new build job. This notification system is created while building the pipelines.

MLflow was selected as the ML application life-cycle management tool. MLflow was integrated with the ML model operations to track the model parameters and performance metrics. Figure 11 shows the MLflow UI hosted on an SaaS service.

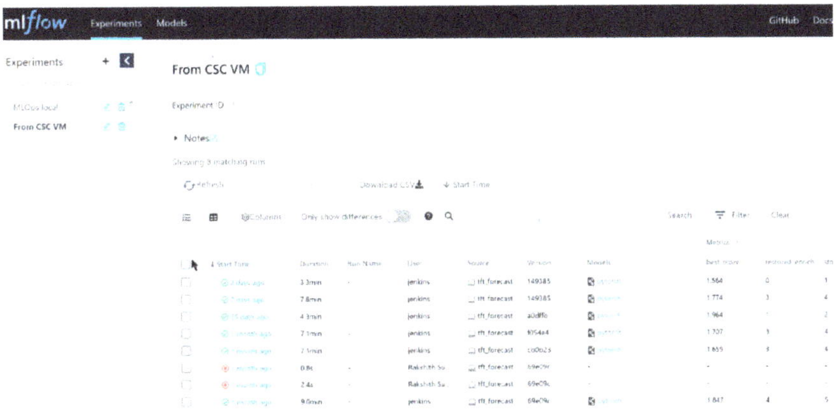

Figure 11. ML life-cycle management with MLflow.

MLflow includes experimentation tracking and reproducibility. This is achieved by logging the metrics and the parameters of each experiment. As shown in Figure 11, several experiments' results can be logged and compared. MLflow stores the artifacts such as configuration files that save information about the model input and the model under training. These artifacts can be stored in a cloud object store such as MinIO for future reproducibility, as shown in Figure 12.

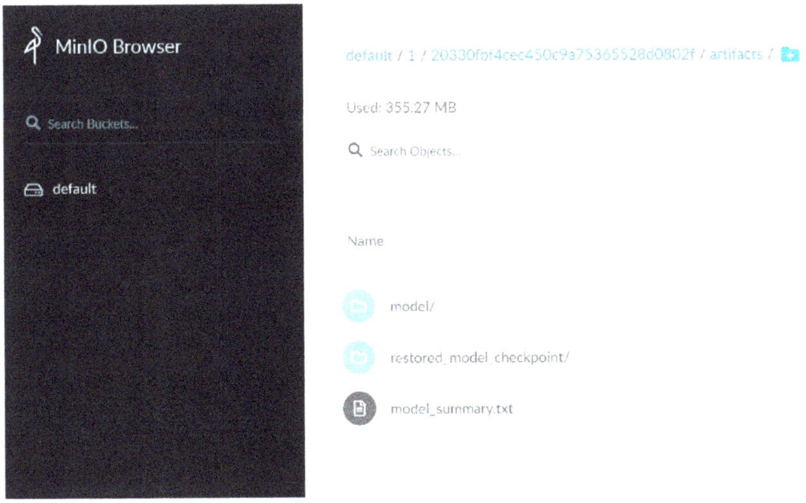

Figure 12. ML artifact storage using the MinIO object store.

4.5. FCR-N Forecasting Results

Figure 13 shows the one-day predicted vs. actual price prediction for the FCR-N market price. The ML model runs daily, and the predicted values are stored in the database. A Django-based web UI was designed for viewing these values and hosted in the CSC cloud as an SaaS, as shown in Figure 14. This SaaS service can also act as a REST API to expose the predicted data to a third-party system.

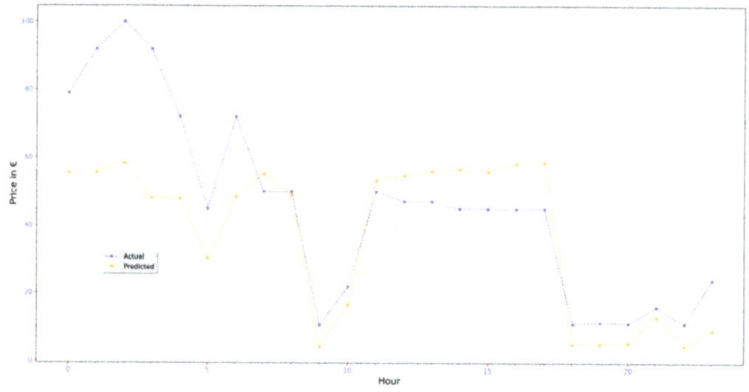

Figure 13. Predicted vs. actual price for 16 April 2020.

Figure 14. Web UI for exploring the model prediction values.

5. Case Study 2: National Electricity Consumption Forecast Adapted from the Price Forecast MLOps Pipeline

In the above use case, the MLOps pipeline was defined and implemented as shown in Figure 7, while in this use case, the same MLOps pipeline was adapted with minimal changes to forecast the Finnish national electricity consumption. The data were collected from the Finnish Transmission System Operator (TSO) via an online API. The TSO defines the electricity consumption as follows:

$$\text{Consumption} = \text{Production} + \text{Import} - \text{Export} \tag{1}$$

This use case was implemented with all of the pipeline components defined in Figure 7. However, the following changes were made to the previous MLOps source code:

- In the TFT, *the FCR_N price* variable was replaced with *electricity_consumption* as the prediction variable.
- In the GIT, a new feature branch was created.
- A new experiment name was created for tracking the ML model parameters using MLflow.
- A new Jenkins project as created, and MLOps pipelines were incorporated using the same Jenkinsfile.
- Unit test cases are updated.
- To explore the predicted values via web UI, as shown in Figure 14, the corresponding legend and variable names were changed.

Except for the test cases, most of the abovementioned changes were in the configuration files and, most importantly, the same MLOps pipeline and tools were reused on the same cloud platform. Figure 15 shows the one-day predicted vs. actual electricity consumption forecasts for Finland.

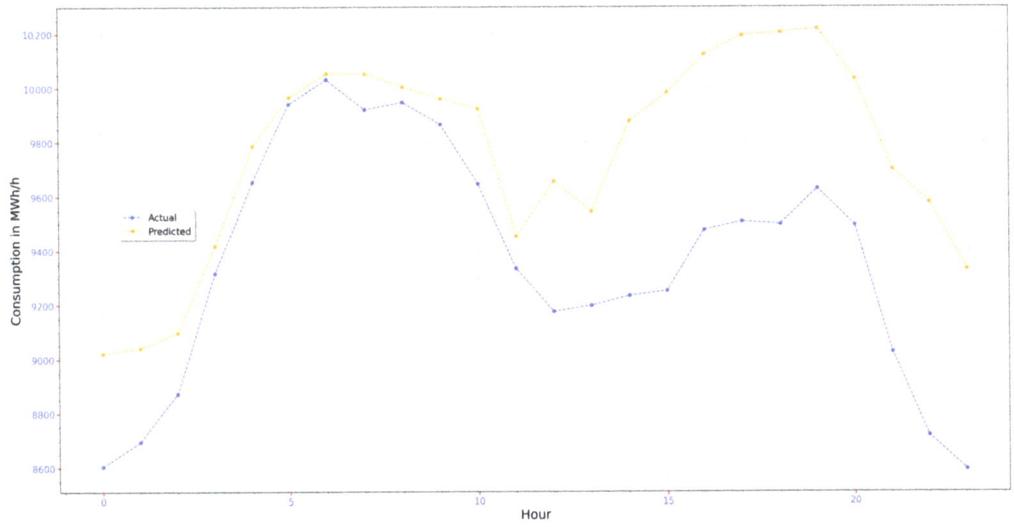

Figure 15. Predicted vs. actual electricity consumption for 16 April 2020.

6. Case Study 3: National Electricity Generation Forecast Adapted from the Price Forecast MLOps Pipeline

In the previous use case, electricity consumption was forecasted by adapting to the MLOps pipelines created for FCR-N market price forecasting. In this example, electricity production was forecasted, and the MLOps pipeline changes made for the previous use case were used here. As in the electricity consumption forecasting, the data were collected from the Finnish TSO via an online API.

However, the following changes were made to the previous MLOps source code:

- In the TFT, the *electricity_consumption* variable was replaced with *electricity_production* as the prediction variable.
- In the GIT, a new feature branch was created.
- A new experiment name was created for tracking the ML model parameters using MLflow. Creating a new experiment name is helpful in grouping the new experiments within a project or use case.
- A new Jenkins project was created, and MLOps pipelines were incorporated using the Jenkinsfile used for the above use case.
- Unit test cases were updated.
- To explore the predicted values via web UI, as shown in Figure 14, corresponding legend and variable names were changed.

Figure 16 shows the one-day predicted vs. actual electricity production forecasts for Finland.

Case Studies 2 and 3 were implemented with minimal work by adapting to the implementation of Case Study 1. Case Studies 1 and 2 both used the same MLOps pipeline structure and the same set of tools. This generalization is applicable while forecasting similar variables—for instance, wind power forecasting or photovoltaic power generation forecasting—with 1 h as the sampling interval. However, if the sampling interval changes—for example, to 15 min—considerable work must be performed in the MLOps pipeline, such as "Data ingestion" and "Prediction service".

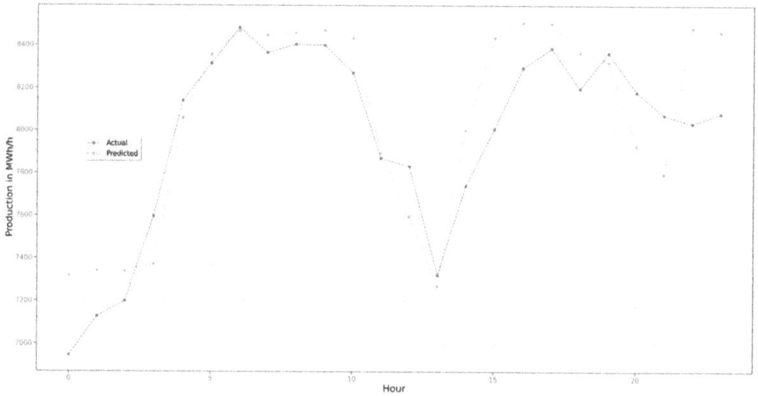

Figure 16. Predicted vs. actual electricity production for 16 April 2020.

7. Conclusions

The main aim of MLOps is to introduce ML products to production by avoiding Development and Operations bottlenecks and automating the workflows. The MLOps system and workflow design need to be modular to accommodate such a system. Such a modular design cannot be generalized and must be specific to the application. This would ensure a system with reduced development, deployment, and monitoring issues. The end-to-end life-cycle management of MLOps is easy. This paper presents a use case where we built modular pipelines for an ML time-series forecasting system. There are several ways to implement MLOps, but the principles of DevOps and modularity should be considered as the primary key factors. Even though it is hard to generalize the pipeline structure, in this paper we explain the things to consider when creating the MLOps design architecture.

The case study is generalizable with minor changes to other hourly day-ahead electricity markets. The main changes are related to identifying the relevant features. The case study is further generalizable to other electricity markets operating on a similar timescale. For example, the market interval in some countries is 30 min or 15 min instead of an hour. For a day-ahead market, the market interval will impact the size of the input layer as well as the output layer of the ANN. For electricity markets that are not day-ahead—for example, intraday markets—the bidding deadlines are different, which needs to be taken into account in scheduling the execution of the deployed containers. All of these generalizations require minor efforts in the form of manual work. A topic for further research would be the development of a generic MLOps solution for day-ahead or intraday electricity markets, which would further reduce this manual work. The current case studies are only integrated with the web application to explore the forecasted values. This MLOps work could be extended for Virtual Power Plants, which use the predicted data for managing the assets using the REST API, where concurrency and response time matter. Currently, the REST API implements a basic authentication for exposing the predicted values, and this basic authentication could be further improved.

Author Contributions: Conceptualization, R.S. and S.S.; methodology, R.S. and S.S.; software, R.S.; validation, R.S. and S.S.; formal analysis, R.S. and S.S.; investigation, R.S.; resources, R.S. and S.S.; data curation, R.S.; writing—original draft preparation, R.S. and S.S.; writing—review and editing, R.S. and S.S.; visualization, R.S.; supervision, S.S. and V.V.; project administration, S.S.; funding acquisition, S.S. All authors have read and agreed to the published version of the manuscript.

Funding: This work was supported in part by Business Finland under grant 7439/31/2018.

Institutional Review Board Statement: Not applicable.

Informed Consent Statement: Not applicable.

Data Availability Statement: Not applicable.

Acknowledgments: The calculations presented above were performed using computer resources within the Aalto University School of Science's "Science-IT" project and the CSC—IT Center for Science, Finland, for computational resources.

Conflicts of Interest: The authors declare no conflict of interest.

References

1. Pang, C.; Hindle, A.; Barbosa, D. Understanding DevOps education with Grounded theory. In Proceedings of the ACM/IEEE 42nd International Conference on Software Engineering: Companion Proceedings, Seul, Korea, 5–11 October 2020; ACM: New York, NY, USA, 2020; pp. 260–261.
2. Macarthy, R.W.; Bass, J.M. An Empirical Taxonomy of DevOps in Practice. In Proceedings of the 2020 46th Euromicro Conference on Software Engineering and Advanced Applications (SEAA), Portorož, Slovenia, 26–28 August 2020; IEEE: Piscataway, NJ, USA, 2020; pp. 221–228.
3. Wahaballa, A.; Wahballa, O.; Abdellatief, M.; Xiong, H.; Qin, Z. Toward unified DevOps model. In Proceedings of the 2015 6th IEEE International Conference on Software Engineering and Service Science (ICSESS), Beijing, China, 23–25 September 2015; IEEE: Piscataway, NJ, USA, 2015; pp. 211–214.
4. Sculley, D.; Holt, G.; Golovin, D.; Davydov, E.; Phillips, T.; Ebner, D.; Chaudhary, V.; Young, M.; Crespo, J.F.; Dennison, D. Hidden technical debt in machine learning systems. In Proceedings of the Advances in Neural Information Processing Systems, Montreal, QC, Canada, 7–12 December 2015.
5. Fitzgerald, B.; Stol, K.-J. Continuous software engineering: A roadmap and agenda. *J. Syst. Softw.* **2017**, *123*, 176–189. [CrossRef]
6. Haindl, P.; Plosch, R. Towards Continuous Quality: Measuring and Evaluating Feature-Dependent Non-Functional Requirements in DevOps. In Proceedings of the 2019 IEEE International Conference on Software Architecture Companion (ICSA-C), Hamburg, Germany, 25–29 March 2019; IEEE: Piscataway, NJ, USA, 2019; pp. 91–94.
7. Steffens, A.; Lichter, H.; Döring, J.S. Designing a next-generation continuous software delivery system. In Proceedings of the 4th International Workshop on Rapid Continuous Software Engineering, Gothenburg, Sweden, 29 May 2018; ACM: New York, NY, USA, 2018; pp. 1–7.
8. Liu, Y.; Ling, Z.; Huo, B.; Wang, B.; Chen, T.; Mouine, E. Building A Platform for Machine Learning Operations from Open Source Frameworks. *IFAC-PapersOnLine* **2020**, *53*, 704–709. [CrossRef]
9. Makinen, S.; Skogstrom, H.; Laaksonen, E.; Mikkonen, T. Who needs MLOps: What data scientists seek to accomplish and how can MLOps help? In Proceedings of the 2021 IEEE/ACM 1st Workshop on AI Engineering—Software Engineering for AI, WAIN, Madrid, Spain, 30–31 May 2021.
10. Khan, M.A.; Parveen, A.; Sadiq, M. A method for the selection of software development life cycle models using analytic hierarchy process. In Proceedings of the 2014 International Conference on Issues and Challenges in Intelligent Computing Techniques (ICICT), Ghaziabad, India, 7–8 February 2014; IEEE: Piscataway, NJ, USA, 2014; pp. 534–540.
11. Ben-Zahia, M.A.; Jaluta, I. Criteria for selecting software development models. In Proceedings of the 2014 Global Summit on Computer & Information Technology (GSCIT), Sousse, Tunisia, 14-16 June 2014; IEEE: Piscataway, NJ, USA, 2014; pp. 1–6.
12. Öztürk, V. Selection of appropriate software development life cycle using fuzzy logic. *J. Intell. Fuzzy Syst.* **2013**, *25*, 797–810. [CrossRef]
13. Lekh, R. Pooja Exhaustive study of SDLC phases and their best praxctices to create CDP model for process improvement. In Proceedings of the 2015 International Conference on Advances in Computer Engineering and Applications, Ghaziabad, India, 19–20 March 2015; IEEE: Piscataway, NJ, USA, 2015; pp. 997–1003.
14. Dayal Chauhan, B.; Rana, A.; Sharma, N.K. Impact of development methodology on cost & risk for development projects. In Proceedings of the 2017 6th International Conference on Reliability, Infocom Technologies and Optimization (Trends and Future Directions) (ICRITO), Noida, India, 20–22 September 2017; IEEE: Piscataway, NJ, USA, 2017; pp. 267–272.
15. Akbar, M.A.; Sang, J.; Khan, A.A.; Shafiq, M.; Hussain, S.; Hu, H.; Elahi, M.; Xiang, H. Improving the Quality of Software Development Process by Introducing a New Methodology–AZ-Model. *IEEE Access* **2018**, *6*, 4811–4823. [CrossRef]
16. Akbar, M.A.; Sang, J.; Khan, A.A.; Amin, F.-E.; Hussain, S.; Sohail, M.K.; Xiang, H.; Cai, B. Statistical Analysis of the Effects of Heavyweight and Lightweight Methodologies on the Six-Pointed Star Model. *IEEE Access* **2018**, *6*, 8066–8079. [CrossRef]
17. Cho, J. A Hybrid Software Development Method For Large-Scale Projects: Rational Unified Process With Scrum. *Issues Inf. Syst.* **2009**, *10*, 340–348. [CrossRef]
18. Velmourougan, S.; Dhavachelvan, P.; Baskaran, R.; Ravikumar, B. Software development Life cycle model to build software applications with usability. In Proceedings of the 2014 International Conference on Advances in Computing, Communications and Informatics (ICACCI), Delhi, India, 24–27 September 2014; IEEE: Piscataway, NJ, USA, 2014; pp. 271–276.
19. Fisher, K.G.; Bankston, A. From Cradle to Sprint: Creating a Full-Lifecycle Request Pipeline at Nationwide Insurance. In Proceedings of the 2009 Agile Conference, Chicago, IL, USA, 24–28 August 2009; IEEE: Piscataway, NJ, USA, 2009; pp. 223–228.
20. Poort, E.R. Driving Agile Architecting with Cost and Risk. *IEEE Softw.* **2014**, *31*, 20–23. [CrossRef]

21. Owais, M.; Ramakishore, R. Effort, duration and cost estimation in agile software development. In Proceedings of the 2016 Ninth International Conference on Contemporary Computing (IC3), Noida, India, 11–13 August 2016; IEEE: Piscataway, NJ, USA, 2016; pp. 1–5.
22. Webster, C.; Shi, N.; Smith, I.S. Delivering software into NASA's Mission Control Center using agile development techniques. In Proceedings of the 2012 IEEE Aerospace Conference, Big Sky, MT, USA, 3–10 March 2012; IEEE: Piscataway, NJ, USA, 2012; pp. 1–7.
23. Cleland-Huang, J. Safety Stories in Agile Development. *IEEE Softw.* **2017**, *34*, 16–19. [CrossRef]
24. Alyahya, S.; Bin-Hezam, R.; Maddeh, M. Supporting Remote Customer Involvement in Distributed Agile Development: A Coordination Approach. *IEEE Trans. Eng. Manag.* **2022**, 1–14. [CrossRef]
25. Kumar, G.; Bhatia, P.K. Comparative Analysis of Software Engineering Models from Traditional to Modern Methodologies. In Proceedings of the 2014 Fourth International Conference on Advanced Computing & Communication Technologies, Rohtak, India, 8–9 February 2014; IEEE: Piscataway, NJ, USA, 2014; pp. 189–196.
26. Sinha, A.; Das, P. Agile Methodology Vs. Traditional Waterfall SDLC: A case study on Quality Assurance process in Software Industry. In Proceedings of the 2021 5th International Conference on Electronics, Materials Engineering & Nano-Technology (IEMENTech), Kolkata, India, 4–5 May 2018; IEEE: Piscataway, NJ, USA, 2021; pp. 1–4.
27. Ahmed, A.; Ahmad, S.; Ehsan, N.; Mirza, E.; Sarwar, S.Z. Agile software development: Impact on productivity and quality. In Proceedings of the 2010 IEEE International Conference on Management of Innovation & Technology, Singapore, 2–5 June 2010; IEEE: Piscataway, NJ, USA, 2010; pp. 287–291.
28. Tommy, R.; Mhaisekar, M.; Kallepally, S.; Varghese, L.; Ahmed, S.; Somaraju, M.D. Dynamic quality control in agile methodology for improving the quality. In Proceedings of the 2015 IEEE International Conference on Computer Graphics, Vision and Information Security (CGVIS), Bhubaneshwar, India, 2–3 November 2015; IEEE: Piscataway, NJ, USA, 2015; pp. 233–236.
29. Darrin, M.A.G.; Devereux, W.S. The Agile Manifesto, design thinking and systems engineering. In Proceedings of the 2017 Annual IEEE International Systems Conference (SysCon), Montreal, QC, Canada, 24–27 April 2017; IEEE: Piscataway, NJ, USA, 2017; pp. 1–5.
30. Boehm, B. Get ready for agile methods, with care. *Computer* **2002**, *35*, 64–69. [CrossRef]
31. Dybå, T.; Dingsøyr, T. Empirical studies of agile software development: A systematic review. *Inf. Softw. Technol.* **2008**, *50*, 833–859. [CrossRef]
32. Samarawickrama, S.S.; Perera, I. Continuous scrum: A framework to enhance scrum with DevOps. In Proceedings of the 2017 Seventeenth International Conference on Advances in ICT for Emerging Regions (ICTer), Colombo, Sri Lanka, 6–9 September 2017; IEEE: Piscataway, NJ, USA, 2017; pp. 1–7.
33. Miller, A. A hundred days of continuous integration. In Proceedings of the Agile 2008 Conference, Toronto, ON, Canada, 4–8 August 2008; Microsoft Corporation: Albuquerque, NM, USA, 2008; pp. 289–293.
34. Arachchi, S.A.I.B.S.; Perera, I. Continuous Integration and Continuous Delivery Pipeline Automation for Agile Software Project Management. In Proceedings of the 2018 Moratuwa Engineering Research Conference (MERCon), Moratuwa, Sri Lanka, 28–30 July 2020; IEEE: Piscataway, NJ, USA, 2018; pp. 156–161.
35. Süß, J.G.; Swift, S.; Escott, E. Using DevOps toolchains in Agile model-driven engineering. *Softw. Syst. Model.* **2022**, 1–16. [CrossRef]
36. Nagarajan, A.D.; Overbeek, S.J. A DevOps Implementation Framework for Large Agile-Based Financial Organizations. In *OTM Confederated International Conferences On the Move to Meaningful Internet Systems*; Springer International Publishing: Cham, Switzerland, 2018; pp. 172–188.
37. Hemon, A.; Lyonnet, B.; Rowe, F.; Fitzgerald, B. From Agile to DevOps: Smart Skills and Collaborations. *Inf. Syst. Front.* **2020**, *22*, 927–945. [CrossRef]
38. Marrero, L.; Astudillo, H. DevOps-RAF: An assessment framework to measure DevOps readiness in software organizations. In Proceedings of the 2021 40th International Conference of the Chilean Computer Science Society (SCCC), La Serena, Chile, 15–19 November 2021; IEEE: Piscataway, NJ, USA, 2021; pp. 1–8.
39. Pan, W.; Wei, H. Research on Key Performance Indicator (KPI) of Business Process. In Proceedings of the 2012 Second International Conference on Business Computing and Global Informatization, Shanghai, China, 12–14 October 2012; IEEE: Piscataway, NJ, USA, 2012; pp. 151–154.
40. Durga Prasad, N.V.P.R.; Radhakrishna, C. New Key Performance Indicators (KPI) For Substation Maintenance Performance. In Proceedings of the 2019 International Conference on Computing, Power and Communication Technologies (GUCON), New Delhi, India, 27–28 September 2019; IEEE: Piscataway, NJ, USA, 2019. ISBN 9789353510985.
41. Zhu, H.; Bayley, I. If Docker is the Answer, What is the Question? In Proceedings of the 2018 IEEE Symposium on Service-Oriented System Engineering (SOSE), Bamberg, Germany, 26–29 March 2018; IEEE: Piscataway, NJ, USA, 2018; pp. 152–163.
42. Weyuker, E.J.; Avritzer, A. A metric to predict software scalability. In Proceedings of the Eighth IEEE Symposium on Software Metrics, Ottawa, ON, Canada, 4–7 June 2002; IEEE Computer Society: Washington, DC, USA; pp. 152–158.
43. Dearle, A. Software Deployment, Past, Present and Future. In Proceedings of the Future of Software Engineering (FOSE '07), Minneapolis, MN, USA, 23–25 May 2007; IEEE: Piscataway, NJ, USA, 2007; pp. 269–284.

44. Shahin, M.; Babar, M.A.; Zahedi, M.; Zhu, L. Beyond Continuous Delivery: An Empirical Investigation of Continuous Deployment Challenges. In Proceedings of the 2017 ACM/IEEE International Symposium on Empirical Software Engineering and Measurement (ESEM), Oulu, Finland, 11–12 October 2018; IEEE: Piscataway, NJ, USA, 2017; pp. 111–120.
45. Unger-Windeler, C.; Klunder, J.; Schneider, K. A Mapping Study on Product Owners in Industry: Identifying Future Research Directions. In Proceedings of the 2019 IEEE/ACM International Conference on Software and System Processes (ICSSP), Montreal, QC, Canada, 25 May 2019; IEEE: Piscataway, NJ, USA, 2019; pp. 135–144.
46. Tsunoda, M.; Matsumura, T.; Matsumoto, K. Modeling Software Project Monitoring with Stakeholders. In Proceedings of the 2010 IEEE/ACIS 9th International Conference on Computer and Information Science, Kaminoyama, Japan, 18–20 August 2010; IEEE: Piscataway, NJ, USA, 2010; pp. 723–728.
47. Riungu-Kalliosaari, L.; Mäkinen, S.; Lwakatare, L.E.; Tiihonen, J.; Männistö, T. DevOps adoption benefits and challenges in practice: A case study. In *Lecture Notes in Computer Science (Including Subseries Lecture Notes in Artificial Intelligence and Lecture Notes in Bioinformatics)*; Springer: Cham, Switzerland, 2016; Volume 10027 LNCS.
48. Iden, J.; Tessem, B.; Päivärinta, T. Problems in the interplay of development and IT operations in system development projects: A Delphi study of Norwegian IT experts. *Inf. Softw. Technol.* **2011**, *53*, 394–406. [CrossRef]
49. Tessem, B.; Iden, J. Cooperation between developers and operations in software engineering projects. In Proceedings of the 2008 International Workshop on Cooperative and Human Aspects of Software Engineering, Leipzig, Germany, 13 May 2008; ACM: New York, NY, USA, 2008; pp. 105–108.
50. Woods, E. Aligning Architecture Work with Agile Teams. *IEEE Softw.* **2015**, *32*, 24–26. [CrossRef]
51. Govil, N.; Saurakhia, M.; Agnihotri, P.; Shukla, S.; Agarwal, S. Analyzing the Behaviour of Applying Agile Methodologies & DevOps Culture in e-Commerce Web Application. In Proceedings of the 2020 4th International Conference on Trends in Electronics and Informatics (ICOEI) (48184), Tirunelveli, India, 15–17 June 2020; IEEE: Piscataway, NJ, USA, 2020; pp. 899–902.
52. Khmelevsky, Y.; Li, X.; Madnick, S. Software development using agile and scrum in distributed teams. In Proceedings of the 2017 Annual IEEE International Systems Conference (SysCon), Montreal, QC, Canada, 24–27 April 2017; IEEE: Piscataway, NJ, USA, 2017; pp. 1–4.
53. Ebert, C.; Gallardo, G.; Hernantes, J.; Serrano, N. DevOps. *IEEE Softw.* **2016**, *33*, 94–100. [CrossRef]
54. Agrawal, P.; Rawat, N. Devops, A New Approach To Cloud Development & Testing. In Proceedings of the 2019 International Conference on Issues and Challenges in Intelligent Computing Techniques (ICICT), Ghaziabad, India, 27–28 September 2019; IEEE: Piscataway, NJ, USA, 2019; pp. 1–4.
55. Choudhary, B.; Rakesh, S.K. An approach using agile method for software development. In Proceedings of the 2016 International Conference on Innovation and Challenges in Cyber Security (ICICCS-INBUSH), Greater Noida, India, 3–5 February 2016; IEEE: Piscataway, NJ, USA, 2016; pp. 155–158.
56. Dyba, T.; Dingsoyr, T. What Do We Know about Agile Software Development? *IEEE Softw.* **2009**, *26*, 6–9. [CrossRef]
57. Jabbari, R.; Bin Ali, N.; Petersen, K.; Tanveer, B. What is DevOps? In Proceedings of the Scientific Workshop Proceedings of XP2016, Edinburgh, UK, 24 May 2016; ACM: New York, NY, USA, 2016; pp. 1–11.
58. Gokarna, M.; Singh, R. DevOps: A Historical Review and Future Works. In Proceedings of the 2021 International Conference on Computing, Communication, and Intelligent Systems (ICCCIS), Greater Noida, India, 19–20 February 2021; IEEE: Piscataway, NJ, USA, 2021; pp. 366–371.
59. Sharma, S.; Kumar, D.; Fayad, M.E. An Impact Assessment of Agile Ceremonies on Sprint Velocity Under Agile Software Development. In Proceedings of the 2021 9th International Conference on Reliability, Infocom Technologies and Optimization (Trends and Future Directions) (ICRITO), Noida, India, 4–5 June 2020; IEEE: Piscataway, NJ, USA, 2021; pp. 1–5.
60. Srivastava, A.; Bhardwaj, S.; Saraswat, S. SCRUM model for agile methodology. In Proceedings of the 2017 International Conference on Computing, Communication and Automation (ICCCA), Greater Noida, India, 5–6 May 2017; IEEE: Piscataway, NJ, USA, 2017; pp. 864–869.
61. Paasivaara, M.; Durasiewicz, S.; Lassenius, C. Distributed Agile Development: Using Scrum in a Large Project. In Proceedings of the 2008 IEEE International Conference on Global Software Engineering, Bangalore, India, 17–20 August 2008; IEEE: Piscataway, NJ, USA, 2008; pp. 87–95.
62. John, M.M.; Olsson, H.H.; Bosch, J. Towards MLOps: A Framework and Maturity Model. In Proceedings of the 2021 47th Euromicro Conference on Software Engineering and Advanced Applications (SEAA), Palermo, Italy, 1–3 September 2021; IEEE: Piscataway, NJ, USA, 2021; pp. 334–341. [CrossRef]
63. Kang, H.; Le, M.; Tao, S. Container and microservice driven design for cloud infrastructure DevOps. In Proceedings of the 2016 IEEE International Conference on Cloud Engineering, IC2E 2016: Co-located with the 1st IEEE International Conference on Internet-of-Things Design and Implementation, Berlin, Germany, 4–8 April 2016.
64. Kubeflow–ML Toolkit. Available online: https://www.kubeflow.org/ (accessed on 26 August 2022).
65. Zhou, Y.; Yu, Y.; Ding, B. Towards MLOps: A Case Study of ML Pipeline Platform. In Proceedings of the 2020 International Conference on Artificial Intelligence and Computer Engineering (ICAICE), Beijing, China, 23–25 October 2020; IEEE: Piscataway, NJ, USA, 2020; pp. 494–500.
66. Karamitsos, I.; Albarhami, S.; Apostolopoulos, C. Applying DevOps Practices of Continuous Automation for Machine Learning. *Information* **2020**, *11*, 363. [CrossRef]

67. Banerjee, A.; Chen, C.C.; Hung, C.C.; Huang, X.; Wang, Y.; Chevesaran, R. Challenges and experiences with MLOps for performance diagnostics in hybrid-cloud enterprise software deployments. In Proceedings of the OpML 2020—2020 USENIX Conference on Operational Machine Learning, Online, 28 July–7 August 2020.
68. Tamburri, D.A. Sustainable MLOps: Trends and Challenges. In Proceedings of the 22nd International Symposium on Symbolic and Numeric Algorithms for Scientific Computing, SYNASC, Timisoara, Romania, 1–4 September 2020.
69. Raj, E.; Buffoni, D.; Westerlund, M.; Ahola, K. Edge MLOps: An Automation Framework for AIoT Applications. In Proceedings of the 2021 IEEE International Conference on Cloud Engineering (IC2E), San Francisco, CA, USA, 4–8 October 2021; pp. 191–200. [CrossRef]
70. Granlund, T.; Kopponen, A.; Stirbu, V.; Myllyaho, L.; Mikkonen, T. MLOps challenges in multi-organization setup: Experiences from two real-world cases. In Proceedings of the 2021 IEEE/ACM 1st Workshop on AI Engineering—Software Engineering for AI, WAIN 2021, Madrid, Spain, 22–30 May 2021.
71. Azure MLOps. Available online: https://azure.microsoft.com/en-us/services/machine-learning/mlops/ (accessed on 26 August 2022).
72. AWS MLOps—Sagemaker. Available online: https://aws.amazon.com/sagemaker/mlops/ (accessed on 26 August 2022).
73. Practitioners Guide to MLOps—Google Cloud. Available online: https://services.google.com/fh/files/misc/practitioners_guide_to_mlops_whitepaper.pdf (accessed on 26 August 2022).
74. Dyck, A.; Penners, R.; Lichter, H. Towards Definitions for Release Engineering and DevOps. In Proceedings of the 2015 IEEE/ACM 3rd International Workshop on Release Engineering, Florence, Italy, 19 May 2015; IEEE: Piscataway, NJ, USA, 2015; p. 3.
75. What is Devops. Available online: https://www.atlassian.com/devops (accessed on 26 August 2022).
76. Cois, C.A.; Yankel, J.; Connell, A. Modern DevOps: Optimizing software development through effective system interactions. In Proceedings of the 2014 IEEE International Professional Communication Conference (IPCC), Pittsburgh, PA, USA, 13–15 October 2014; IEEE: Piscataway, NJ, USA, 2014; pp. 1–7.
77. Virmani, M. Understanding DevOps & bridging the gap from continuous integration to continuous delivery. In Proceedings of the Fifth International Conference on the Innovative Computing Technology (INTECH 2015), Galicia, Spain, 20–22 May 2015; IEEE: Piscataway, NJ, USA, 2015; pp. 78–82.
78. Kerzazi, N.; Adams MCIS, B.; Montreal, P. Who Needs Release and DevOps Engineers, and Why? In Proceedings of the International Workshop on Continuous Software Evolution and Delivery, Austin, TX, USA, 14–15 May 2016. [CrossRef]
79. Bankar, S.; Shah, D. Blockchain based framework for Software Development using DevOps. In Proceedings of the 2021 4th Biennial International Conference on Nascent Technologies in Engineering (ICNTE), Navi Mumbai, India, 15–16 January 2021; IEEE: Piscataway, NJ, USA, 2021; pp. 1–6.
80. Soni, M. End to End Automation on Cloud with Build Pipeline: The Case for DevOps in Insurance Industry, Continuous Integration, Continuous Testing, and Continuous Delivery. In Proceedings of the 2015 IEEE International Conference on Cloud Computing in Emerging Markets (CCEM), Bangalore, India, 25–27 November 2015; IEEE: Piscataway, NJ, USA, 2015; pp. 85–89.
81. Alnafessah, A.; Gias, A.U.; Wang, R.; Zhu, L.; Casale, G.; Filieri, A. Quality-Aware DevOps Research: Where Do We Stand? *IEEE Access* **2021**, *9*, 44476–44489. [CrossRef]
82. Dalpiaz, F.; Brinkkemper, S. Agile Requirements Engineering with User Stories. In Proceedings of the 2018 IEEE 26th International Requirements Engineering Conference (RE), Banff, AL, Canada, 20–24 August 2018; IEEE: Piscataway, NJ, USA, 2018; pp. 506–507.
83. Sarkan, H.M.; Ahmad, T.P.S.; Bakar, A.A. Using JIRA and Redmine in requirement development for agile methodology. In Proceedings of the 2011 Malaysian Conference in Software Engineering, Kuantan, Malaysia, 27–29 June 2011; IEEE: Piscataway, NJ, USA, 2011; pp. 408–413.
84. Perera, P.; Silva, R.; Perera, I. Improve software quality through practicing DevOps. In Proceedings of the 2017 Seventeenth International Conference on Advances in ICT for Emerging Regions (ICTer), Colombo, Sri Lanka, 6–9 September 2017; IEEE: Piscataway, NJ, USA, 2017; pp. 1–6.
85. Majumdar, R.; Jain, R.; Barthwal, S.; Choudhary, C. Source code management using version control system. In Proceedings of the 2017 6th International Conference on Reliability, Infocom Technologies and Optimization (Trends and Future Directions) (ICRITO), Noida, India, 20–22 September 2017; IEEE: Piscataway, NJ, USA, 2017; pp. 278–281.
86. Ren, Y.; Xing, T.; Quan, Q.; Zhao, Y. Software Configuration Management of Version Control Study Based on Baseline. In Proceedings of the 2010 3rd International Conference on Information Management, Innovation Management and Industrial Engineering, Kunming, China, 26–28 November 2010; IEEE: Piscataway, NJ, USA, 2010; pp. 118–121.
87. Shah, J.; Dubaria, D.; Widhalm, J. A Survey of DevOps tools for Networking. In Proceedings of the 2018 9th IEEE Annual Ubiquitous Computing, Electronics & Mobile Communication Conference (UEMCON), New York, NY, USA, 8–10 November 2018; IEEE: Piscataway, NJ, USA, 2018; pp. 185–188.
88. Spinellis, D. Git. *IEEE Softw.* **2012**, *29*, 100–101. [CrossRef]
89. Hinsen, K.; Läufer, K.; Thiruvathukal, G.K. Essential Tools: Version Control Systems. *Comput. Sci. Eng.* **2009**, *11*, 84–91. [CrossRef]
90. Paez, N. Versioning Strategy for DevOps Implementations. In Proceedings of the 2018 Congreso Argentino de Ciencias de la Informática y Desarrollos de Investigación (CACIDI), Buenos Aires, Argentina, 28–30 November 2018; IEEE: Piscataway, NJ, USA, 2018; pp. 1–6.

91. Palihawadana, S.; Wijeweera, C.H.; Sanjitha, M.G.T.N.; Liyanage, V.K.; Perera, I.; Meedeniya, D.A. Tool support for traceability management of software artefacts with DevOps practices. In Proceedings of the 2017 Moratuwa Engineering Research Conference (MERCon), Moratuwa, Sri Lanka, 29–31 May 2017; IEEE: Piscataway, NJ, USA, 2017; pp. 129–134.
92. Git branching Model. Available online: https://nvie.com/posts/a-successful-git-branching-model/ (accessed on 26 August 2022).
93. Chang, C.-Y.; Ou, P.-P.; Deng, D.-J. Cross-Site Large-Scale Software Delivery with Enhanced Git Branch Model. In Proceedings of the 2019 IEEE 10th International Conference on Software Engineering and Service Science (ICSESS), Beijing, China, 18–20 October 2019; IEEE: Piscataway, NJ, USA, 2019; pp. 153–156.
94. Louridas, P. Version control. *IEEE Softw.* **2006**, *23*, 104–107. [CrossRef]
95. Branching vs Trunk Based Development. Available online: https://launchdarkly.com/blog/git-branching-strategies-vs-trunk-based-development/ (accessed on 26 August 2022).
96. Spinellis, D. Package Management Systems. *IEEE Softw.* **2012**, *29*, 84–86. [CrossRef]
97. Sadowski, C.; Aftandilian, E.; Eagle, A.; Miller-Cushon, L.; Jaspan, C. Lessons from building static analysis tools at Google. *Commun. ACM* **2018**, *61*, 58–66. [CrossRef]
98. Jebbar, O.; Saied, M.A.; Khendek, F.; Toeroe, M. Poster: Re-Testing Configured Instances in the Production Environment—A Method for Reducing the Test Suite. In Proceedings of the 2019 12th IEEE Conference on Software Testing, Validation and Verification (ICST), Xi'an, China, 22–27 April 2019; IEEE: Piscataway, NJ, USA, 2019; pp. 367–370.
99. Chen, W.; Ye, K.; Wang, Y.; Xu, G.; Xu, C.-Z. How Does the Workload Look Like in Production Cloud? Analysis and Clustering of Workloads on Alibaba Cluster Trace. In Proceedings of the 2018 IEEE 24th International Conference on Parallel and Distributed Systems (ICPADS), Singapore, 11–13 December 2018; IEEE: Piscataway, NJ, USA, 2018; pp. 102–109.
100. Neitsch, A.; Wong, K.; Godfrey, M.W. Build system issues in multilanguage software. In Proceedings of the 2012 28th IEEE International Conference on Software Maintenance (ICSM), Trento, Italy, 23–28 September 2012; IEEE: Piscataway, NJ, USA, 2012; pp. 140–149.
101. Leite, L.; Rocha, C.; Kon, F.; Milojicic, D.; Meirelles, P. A Survey of DevOps Concepts and Challenges. *ACM Comput. Surv.* **2020**, *52*, 1–35. [CrossRef]
102. Pietrantuono, R.; Bertolino, A.; De Angelis, G.; Miranda, B.; Russo, S. Towards Continuous Software Reliability Testing in DevOps. In Proceedings of the 2019 IEEE/ACM 14th International Workshop on Automation of Software Test (AST), Montreal, QC, Canada, 27 May 2019; IEEE: Piscataway, NJ, USA, 2019; pp. 21–27.
103. Hellmann, T.D.; Hosseini-Khayat, A.; Maurer, F. Supporting Test-Driven Development of Graphical User Interfaces Using Agile Interaction Design. In Proceedings of the 2010 Third International Conference on Software Testing, Verification, and Validation Workshops, Paris, France, 7–9 April 2010; IEEE: Piscataway, NJ, USA, 2010; pp. 444–447.
104. Gohil, K.; Alapati, N.; Joglekar, S. Towards behavior driven operations (BDOps). In Proceedings of the 3rd International Conference on Advances in Recent Technologies in Communication and Computing (ARTCom 2011), Bangalore, India, 14–15 September 2011; IET: London, UK, 2011; pp. 262–264.
105. Chen, B.; Song, J.; Xu, P.; Hu, X.; Jiang, Z.M. An automated approach to estimating code coverage measures via execution logs. In Proceedings of the 33rd ACM/IEEE International Conference on Automated Software Engineering, Montpellier, France, 3–7 September 2018; ACM: New York, NY, USA, 2018; pp. 305–316.
106. Azure DevOps Code Coverage. Available online: https://docs.microsoft.com/fi-fi/azure/devops/pipelines/test/review-code-coverage-results?view=azure-devops (accessed on 26 August 2022).
107. Callanan, M.; Spillane, A. DevOps: Making It Easy to Do the Right Thing. *IEEE Softw.* **2016**, *33*, 53–59. [CrossRef]
108. Humble, J.; Read, C.; North, D. The Deployment Production Line. In Proceedings of the AGILE 2006 (AGILE'06), Minneapolis, MN, USA, 23–28 July 2006; IEEE: Piscataway, NJ, USA; pp. 113–118.
109. Lin, C.-C.; Wu, J.-J.; Lin, J.-A.; Song, L.-C.; Liu, P. Automatic Resource Scaling Based on Application Service Requirements. In Proceedings of the 2012 IEEE Fifth International Conference on Cloud Computing, Honolulu, HI, USA, 24–29 June 2012; IEEE: Piscataway, NJ, USA, 2012; pp. 941–942.
110. Netto, M.A.S.; Cardonha, C.; Cunha, R.L.F.; Assuncao, M.D. Evaluating Auto-scaling Strategies for Cloud Computing Environments. In Proceedings of the 2014 IEEE 22nd International Symposium on Modelling, Analysis & Simulation of Computer and Telecommunication Systems, Paris, France, 9–12 September 2014; IEEE: Piscataway, NJ, USA, 2014; pp. 187–196.
111. Anand, M. Cloud Monitor: Monitoring Applications in Cloud. In Proceedings of the 2012 IEEE International Conference on Cloud Computing in Emerging Markets (CCEM), Bangalore, India, 11–12 October 2012; IEEE: Piscataway, NJ, USA, 2012; pp. 1–4.
112. Düllmann, T.F.; Paule, C.; van Hoorn, A. Exploiting DevOps Practices for Dependable and Secure Continuous Delivery Pipelines. In Proceedings of the 2018 IEEE/ACM 4th International Workshop on Rapid Continuous Software Engineering (RCoSE), Gothenburg, Sweden, 29 May 2018. [CrossRef]
113. Meyer, M. Continuous Integration and Its Tools. *IEEE Softw.* **2014**, *31*, 14–16. [CrossRef]
114. Vassallo, C.; Palomba, F.; Bacchelli, A.; Gall, H.C. Continuous code quality: Are we (really) doing that? In Proceedings of the 33rd ACM/IEEE International Conference on Automated Software Engineering, Montpellier, France, 3–7 September 2018; ACM: New York, NY, USA, 2018; pp. 790–795.
115. Owhadi-Kareshk, M.; Nadi, S.; Rubin, J. Predicting Merge Conflicts in Collaborative Software Development. In Proceedings of the 2019 ACM/IEEE International Symposium on Empirical Software Engineering and Measurement (ESEM), Recife, Brazil, 19–20 September 2019; IEEE: Piscataway, NJ, USA, 2019; pp. 1–11.

116. AlAbwaini, N.; Aldaaje, A.; Jaber, T.; Abdallah, M.; Tamimi, A. Using Program Slicing to Detect the Dead Code. In Proceedings of the 2018 8th International Conference on Computer Science and Information Technology (CSIT), Amman, Jordan, 11–12 July 2018; IEEE: Piscataway, NJ, USA, 2018; pp. 230–233.
117. Wang, X.; Zhang, Y.; Zhao, L.; Chen, X. Dead Code Detection Method Based on Program Slicing. In Proceedings of the 2017 International Conference on Cyber-Enabled Distributed Computing and Knowledge Discovery (CyberC), Nanjing, China, 12–14 October 2017; IEEE: Piscataway, NJ, USA, 2017; pp. 155–158.
118. Romano, S. Dead Code. In Proceedings of the 2018 IEEE International Conference on Software Maintenance and Evolution (ICSME), Madrid, Spain, 23–29 September 2018; IEEE: Piscataway, NJ, USA, 2018; pp. 737–742.
119. Abbass, M.K.A.; Osman, R.I.E.; Mohammed, A.M.H.; Alshaikh, M.W.A. Adopting Continuous Integeration and Continuous Delivery for Small Teams. In Proceedings of the 2019 International Conference on Computer, Control, Electrical, and Electronics Engineering (ICCCEEE), Khartoum, Sudan, 21–23 September 2019; IEEE: Piscataway, NJ, USA, 2019; pp. 1–4.
120. Agarwal, A.; Gupta, S.; Choudhury, T. Continuous and Integrated Software Development using DevOps. In Proceedings of the 2018 International Conference on Advances in Computing and Communication Engineering (ICACCE), Paris, France, 22–23 June 2018; IEEE: Piscataway, NJ, USA, 2018; pp. 290–293.
121. Runeson, P. A survey of unit testing practices. *IEEE Softw.* **2006**, *23*, 22–29. [CrossRef]
122. Grechanik, M.; Xie, Q.; Fu, C. Maintaining and evolving GUI-directed test scripts. In Proceedings of the 2009 IEEE 31st International Conference on Software Engineering, Vancouver, BC, Canada, 16–24 May 2009; IEEE: Piscataway, NJ, USA, 2009; pp. 408–418.
123. Misra, R.B. On determining the software testing cost to assure desired field reliability. In Proceedings of the IEEE INDICON 2004, First India Annual Conference, Kharagpur, India, 20–22 December 2004; IEEE: Piscataway, NJ, USA, 2004; pp. 517–520.
124. Komargodski, I.; Naor, M.; Yogev, E. White-Box vs. Black-Box Complexity of Search Problems: Ramsey and Graph Property Testing. In Proceedings of the 2017 IEEE 58th Annual Symposium on Foundations of Computer Science (FOCS), Berkeley, CA, USA, 15–17 October 2017; IEEE: Piscataway, NJ, USA, 2017; pp. 622–632.
125. Horváth, F.; Bognár, S.; Gergely, T.; Rácz, R.; Beszédes, Á.; Marinković, V. Code Coverage Measurement Framework for Android Devices. *Acta Cybern.* **2014**, *21*, 439–458. [CrossRef]
126. Adams, B.; McIntosh, S. Modern Release Engineering in a Nutshell—Why Researchers Should Care. In Proceedings of the 2016 IEEE 23rd International Conference on Software Analysis, Evolution, and Reengineering (SANER), Osaka, Japan, 14–18 March 2016; IEEE: Piscataway, NJ, USA, 2016; pp. 78–90.
127. Shahin, M.; Ali Babar, M.; Zhu, L. Continuous Integration, Delivery and Deployment: A Systematic Review on Approaches, Tools, Challenges and Practices. *IEEE Access* **2017**, *5*, 3909–3943. [CrossRef]
128. Build Artifact. Available online: https://www.jetbrains.com/help/teamcity/build-artifact.html (accessed on 26 August 2022).
129. Storing Build Artifact. Available online: https://circleci.com/docs/2.0/artifacts/ (accessed on 26 August 2022).
130. Rufino, J.; Alam, M.; Ferreira, J. Monitoring V2X applications using DevOps and docker. In Proceedings of the 2017 International Smart Cities Conference (ISC2), Wuxi, China, 14–17 September 2017; IEEE: Piscataway, NJ, USA, 2017; pp. 1–5.
131. Symeonidis, G.; Nerantzis, E.; Kazakis, A.; Papakostas, G.A. MLOps-Definitions, Tools and Challenges. In Proceedings of the 2022 IEEE 12th Annual Computing and Communication Workshop and Conference (CCWC), Las Vegas, NV, USA, 26–29 January 2022.
132. Iterative Incremental Process. Available online: https://ml-ops.org/content/mlops-principles (accessed on 26 August 2022).
133. CD4ML—Continuous Delivery for Machine Learning. Available online: https://martinfowler.com/articles/cd4ml.html (accessed on 14 December 2021).
134. Studer, S.; Bui, T.B.; Drescher, C.; Hanuschkin, A.; Winkler, L.; Peters, S.; Mueller, K.-R. Towards CRISP-ML(Q): A Machine Learning Process Model with Quality Assurance Methodology. *Mach. Learn. Knowl. Extr.* **2021**, *3*, 392–413. [CrossRef]
135. Santa, R.; Bretherton, P.; Ferrer, M.; Soosa, C.; Hyland, P. The role of cross-functional teams on the alignment between technology innovation effectiveness and operational effectiveness. *Int. J. Technol. Manag.* **2011**, *55*, 122–137. [CrossRef]
136. Alahmari, S.S.; Goldgof, D.B.; Mouton, P.R.; Hall, L.O. Challenges for the Repeatability of Deep Learning Models. *IEEE Access* **2020**, *8*, 211860–211868. [CrossRef]
137. Victor, K.F.; Michael, I.Z. Intelligent data analysis and machine learning: Are they really equivalent Concepts? In Proceedings of the 2017 Second Russia and Pacific Conference on Computer Technology and Applications (RPC), Vladivostok, Russia, 25–29 September 2017; IEEE: Piscataway, NJ, USA, 2017; pp. 59–63.
138. Hafen, R.; Critchlow, T. EDA and ML—A Perfect Pair for Large-Scale Data Analysis. In Proceedings of the 2013 IEEE International Symposium on Parallel & Distributed Processing, Workshops and Phd Forum, Cambridge, MA, USA, 20 May 2013; IEEE: Piscataway, NJ, USA, 2013; pp. 1894–1898.
139. Guruvayur, S.R.; Suchithra, R. A detailed study on machine learning techniques for data mining. In Proceedings of the 2017 International Conference on Trends in Electronics and Informatics (ICEI), Tirunelveli, India, 11–12 May 2017; IEEE: Piscataway, NJ, USA, 2017; pp. 1187–1192.
140. Schelter, S.; Lange, D.; Schmidt, P.; Celikel, M.; Biessmann, F.; Grafberger, A. Automating large-scale data quality verification. *Proc. VLDB Endow.* **2018**, *11*, 1781–1794. [CrossRef]
141. Wang, L.; Han, M.; Li, X.; Zhang, N.; Cheng, H. Review of Classification Methods on Unbalanced Data Sets. *IEEE Access* **2021**, *9*, 64606–64628. [CrossRef]

142. Lwakatare, L.E.; Range, E.; Crnkovic, I.; Bosch, J. On the Experiences of Adopting Automated Data Validation in an Industrial Machine Learning Project. In Proceedings of the 2021 IEEE/ACM 43rd International Conference on Software Engineering: Software Engineering in Practice (ICSE-SEIP), Madrid, Spain, 25–28 May 2021; IEEE: Piscataway, NJ, USA, 2021; pp. 248–257.
143. Subramanya, R.; Yli-Ojanperä, M.; Sierla, S.; Hölttä, T.; Valtakari, J.; Vyatkin, V. A Virtual Power Plant Solution for Aggregating Photovoltaic Systems and Other Distributed Energy Resources for Northern European Primary Frequency Reserves. *Energies* **2021**, *14*, 1242. [CrossRef]
144. Galhotra, S.; Khurana, U.; Hassanzadeh, O.; Srinivas, K.; Samulowitz, H.; Qi, M. Automated Feature Enhancement for Predictive Modeling using External Knowledge. In Proceedings of the 2019 International Conference on Data Mining Workshops (ICDMW), Beijing, China, 8–11 November 2019; IEEE: Piscataway, NJ, USA, 2019; pp. 1094–1097.
145. Pham, M.; Knoblock, C.A.; Pujara, J. Learning Data Transformations with Minimal User Effort. In Proceedings of the 2019 International Conference on Big Data (Big Data), Los Angeles, CA, USA, 9–12 December 2019; IEEE: Piscataway, NJ, USA, 2019; pp. 657–664.
146. Marculescu, D.; Stamoulis, D.; Cai, E. Hardware-aware machine learning. In Proceedings of the International Conference on Computer-Aided Design, San Diego, CA, USA, 5–8 November 2018; ACM: New York, NY, USA, 2018; pp. 1–8.
147. Gada, M.; Haria, Z.; Mankad, A.; Damania, K.; Sankhe, S. Automated Feature Engineering and Hyperparameter optimization for Machine Learning. In Proceedings of the 2021 7th International Conference on Advanced Computing and Communication Systems (ICACCS), Coimbatore, India, 19–20 March 2021; IEEE: Piscataway, NJ, USA, 2021; pp. 981–986.
148. Kahloot, K.M.; Ekler, P. Algorithmic Splitting: A Method for Dataset Preparation. *IEEE Access* **2021**, *9*, 125229–125237. [CrossRef]
149. Medar, R.; Rajpurohit, V.S.; Rashmi, B. Impact of Training and Testing Data Splits on Accuracy of Time Series Forecasting in Machine Learning. In Proceedings of the 2017 International Conference on Computing, Communication, Control and Automation (ICCUBEA), Pune, India, 17–18 August 2017; IEEE: Piscataway, NJ, USA, 2017; pp. 1–6.
150. Li, S.; Hu, W.; Cao, D.; Dragičević, T.; Huang, Q.; Chen, Z.; Blaabjerg, F. Electric Vehicle Charging Management Based on Deep Reinforcement Learning. *J. Mod. Power Syst. Clean Energy* **2021**, *10*, 719–730. [CrossRef]
151. Posoldova, A. Machine Learning Pipelines: From Research to Production. *IEEE Potentials* **2020**, *39*, 38–42. [CrossRef]
152. Marijan, D.; Gotlieb, A.; Kumar Ahuja, M. Challenges of Testing Machine Learning Based Systems. In Proceedings of the 2019 International Conference On Artificial Intelligence Testing (AITest), Newark, CA, USA, 4–9 April 2019; IEEE: Piscataway, NJ, USA, 2019; pp. 101–102.
153. Gisselaire, L.; Cario, F.; Guerre-berthelot, Q.; Zigmann, B.; du Bousquet, L.; Nakamura, M. Toward Evaluation of Deployment Architecture of ML-Based Cyber-Physical Systems. In Proceedings of the 2019 34th IEEE/ACM International Conference on Automated Software Engineering Workshop (ASEW), San Diego, CA, USA, 11–15 November 2019; IEEE: Piscataway, NJ, USA, 2019; pp. 90–93.
154. Barque, M.; Martin, S.; Vianin, J.E.N.; Genoud, D.; Wannier, D. Improving wind power prediction with retraining machine learning algorithms. In Proceedings of the 2018 International Workshop on Big Data and Information Security (IWBIS), Jakarta, Indonesia, 12–13 May 2018; IEEE: Piscataway, NJ, USA, 2018; pp. 43–48.
155. Fields, T.; Hsieh, G.; Chenou, J. Mitigating Drift in Time Series Data with Noise Augmentation. In Proceedings of the 2019 International Conference on Computational Science and Computational Intelligence (CSCI), Las Vegas, NV, USA, 5–7 December 2019; IEEE: Piscataway, NJ, USA, 2019; pp. 227–230.
156. Bock, S.; Weis, M. A Proof of Local Convergence for the Adam Optimizer. In Proceedings of the 2019 International Joint Conference on Neural Networks (IJCNN), Budapest, Hungary, 14–19 July 2019; IEEE: Piscataway, NJ, USA, 2019; pp. 1–8.
157. Wang, K.; Gopaluni, R.B.; Chen, J.; Song, Z. Deep Learning of Complex Batch Process Data and Its Application on Quality Prediction. *IEEE Trans. Ind. Inform.* **2020**, *16*, 7233–7242. [CrossRef]
158. Qian, C.; Yu, W.; Liu, X.; Griffith, D.; Golmie, N. Towards Online Continuous Reinforcement Learning on Industrial Internet of Things. In Proceedings of the 2021 SmartWorld, Ubiquitous Intelligence & Computing, Advanced & Trusted Computing, Scalable Computing & Communications, Internet of People and Smart City Innovation (SmartWorld/SCALCOM/UIC/ATC/IOP/SCI), Atlanta, GA, USA, 18–21 October 2021; IEEE: Piscataway, NJ, USA, 2021; pp. 280–287.
159. Feature Store Comparision. Available online: https://mlops.community/learn/feature-store/ (accessed on 26 August 2022).
160. Metadata Management MLOps. Available online: https://mlops.community/learn/metadata-storage-and-management/ (accessed on 26 August 2022).
161. MLOps Pipelines in ML. Available online: https://cloud.google.com/architecture/mlops-continuous-delivery-and-automation-pipelines-in-machine-learning (accessed on 26 August 2022).
162. de la Nieta, A.A.S.; Gibescu, M. Day-ahead Scheduling in a Local Electricity Market. In Proceedings of the 2019 International Conference on Smart Energy Systems and Technologies (SEST), Porto, Portugal, 9–11 September 2019; IEEE: Piscataway, NJ, USA, 2019; pp. 1–6.
163. Zhao, Q.; Shen, Y.; Li, M. Control and Bidding Strategy for Virtual Power Plants With Renewable Generation and Inelastic Demand in Electricity Markets. *IEEE USA Trans. Sustain. Energy* **2016**, *7*, 562–575. [CrossRef]
164. Giovanelli, C.; Sierla, S.; Ichise, R.; Vyatkin, V. Exploiting artificial neural networks for the prediction of ancillary energy market prices. *Energies* **2018**, *11*, 1906. [CrossRef]
165. Sierla, S.; Pourakbari-Kasmaei, M.; Vyatkin, V. A taxonomy of machine learning applications for virtual power plants and home/building energy management systems. *Autom. Constr.* **2022**, *136*, 104174. [CrossRef]

166. Alanne, K.; Sierla, S. An overview of machine learning applications for smart buildings. *Sustain. Cities Soc.* **2022**, *76*, 103445. [CrossRef]
167. Sierla, S.; Ihasalo, H.; Vyatkin, V. A Review of Reinforcement Learning Applications to Control of Heating, Ventilation and Air Conditioning Systems. *Energies* **2022**, *15*, 3526. [CrossRef]
168. Subramanya, R.; Sierla, S.A.; Vyatkin, V. Exploiting Battery Storages With Reinforcement Learning: A Review for Energy Professionals. *IEEE Access* **2022**, *10*, 54484–54506. [CrossRef]
169. Chouhan, B.S.; Rao, K.V.S.; Kumar Saxena, B. Reduction in carbon dioxide emissions due to wind power generation in India. In Proceedings of the 2017 International Conference On Smart Technologies For Smart Nation (SmartTechCon), Bengaluru, India, 17–19 August 2017; IEEE: Piscataway, NJ, USA, 2017; pp. 257–264.
170. Takano, H.; Zhang, P.; Murata, J.; Hashiguchi, T.; Goda, T.; Iizaka, T.; Nakanishi, Y. A Determination Method for the Optimal Operation of Controllable Generators in Micro Grids That Copes with Unstable Outputs of Renewable Energy Generation. *Electr. Eng. Jpn.* **2015**, *190*, 56–65. [CrossRef]
171. Karhula, N.; Sierla, S.; Vyatkin, V. Validating the Real-Time Performance of Distributed Energy Resources Participating on Primary Frequency Reserves. *Energies* **2021**, *14*, 6914. [CrossRef]
172. Aaltonen, H.; Sierla, S.; Subramanya, R.; Vyatkin, V. A Simulation Environment for Training a Reinforcement Learning Agent Trading a Battery Storage. *Energies* **2021**, *14*, 5587. [CrossRef]
173. Weron, R. Electricity price forecasting: A review of the state-of-the-art with a look into the future. *Int. J. Forecast.* **2014**, *30*, 1030–1081. [CrossRef]
174. Saâdaoui, F. A seasonal feedforward neural network to forecast electricity prices. *Neural Comput. Appl.* **2017**, *28*, 835–847. [CrossRef]
175. Lim, B.; Arik, S.O.; Loeff, N.; Pfister, T. Temporal Fusion Transformers for Interpretable Multi-horizon Time Series Forecasting. *Int. J. Forecast.* **2019**, *37*, 1748–1764. [CrossRef]

applied sciences

MDPI

Article

Whitening CNN-Based Rotor System Fault Diagnosis Model Features

Jesse Miettinen [1,*], Riku-Pekka Nikula [2], Joni Keski-Rahkonen [3], Fredrik Fagerholm [3], Tuomas Tiainen [1], Seppo Sierla [4] and Raine Viitala [1]

1 Department of Mechanical Engineering, Aalto University, 02150 Espoo, Finland; tuomas.tiainen@aalto.fi (T.T.); raine.viitala@aalto.fi (R.V.)
2 Control Engineering, Environmental and Chemical Engineering, University of Oulu, 90014 Oulu, Finland; riku-pekka.nikula@oulu.fi
3 Kongsberg Maritime Finland Oy, 26101 Rauma, Finland; joni.keski-rahkonen@km.kongsberg.com (J.K.-R.); fredrik.anton.fagerholm@km.kongsberg.com (F.F.)
4 Department of Electrical Engineering and Automation, Aalto University, 02150 Espoo, Finland; seppo.sierla@aalto.fi
* Correspondence: jesse.miettinen@aalto.fi; Tel.: +358-40-822-9580

Abstract: Intelligent fault diagnosis (IFD) models have the potential to increase the level of automation and the diagnosis accuracy of machine condition monitoring systems. Many of the latest IFD models rely on convolutional layers for feature extraction from vibration data. The majority of these models employ batch normalisation (BN) for centring and scaling the input for each neuron. This study includes a novel examination of a competitive approach for layer input normalisation in the scope of fault diagnosis. Network deconvolution (ND) is a technique that further decorrelates the layer inputs reducing redundancy among the learned features. Both normalisation techniques are implemented on three common 1D-CNN-based fault diagnosis models. The models with ND mostly outperform the baseline models with BN in three experiments concerning fault datasets from two different rotor systems. Furthermore, the models with ND significantly outperform the baseline models with BN in the common CWRU bearing fault tests with load domain shifts, if the data from drive-end and fan-end sensors are employed. The results show that whitened features can improve the performance of CNN-based fault diagnosis models.

Keywords: CNN architecture; normalization techniques; intelligent fault diagnosis; vibration

Citation: Miettinen, J.; Nikula, R.P.; Keski-Rahkonen, J.; Fagerholm, F.; Tiainen, T.; Sierla, S.; Viitala, R. Whitening CNN-Based Rotor System Fault Diagnosis Model Features. *Appl. Sci.* **2022**, *12*, 4411. https://doi.org/10.3390/app12094411

Academic Editor: Valentin L. Popov

Received: 5 April 2022
Accepted: 25 April 2022
Published: 27 April 2022

1. Introduction

A malfunctioning rotating system is a common concern across a multitude of industries in the modern world. A malfunction in a rotating system can be caused by a number of reasons such as faulty bearings, broken shafts or worn gears. Typically, these faults increase the harmful vibration of the system by exciting the rotating parts on a per revolution basis. Often these excitations that alter the vibration profile of the system can be observed from measurements conducted with vibration sensors such as accelerometers.

Vibration based fault diagnosis for rotating systems has been developed for decades [1]. Most developed methods can be described as two step processes of feature extraction and fault recognition [2]. Features can be extracted from vibration data with a set of signal processing techniques in the time domain, the frequency domain and the time-frequency domain [3]. Typically, the features most sensitive to various faults are then exploited in fault recognition. Some of the studied fault recognition models employing traditional machine learning rely on, for example, random forests [4], support vector machines [5] and shallow neural networks [6]. Despite the successful results related to these techniques, they still suffer from a few disadvantages. Designing the signal processing techniques for feature extraction requires manual labour and often task-specific feature selection. Furthermore, the learning capacity of the models limits their performance if many non-linear relations between the input space and the fault label space are required.

Currently, deep learning (DL) seems like a promising solution for the challenges related to the other machine learning (ML) related fault diagnosis techniques. Deep learning requires no manual feature extraction nor sophisticated signal processing techniques, for it can be utilized to process the raw vibration data directly. The advantage of DL algorithms originates from their capacity to learn hierarchical and non-linear features autonomously between the raw data and the fault label space [7]. This implies that both steps, the feature extraction and the fault recognition can be simultaneously optimised and combined under one deep learning model. Furthermore, some studies have indicated that features acquired with deep learning increase the machine fault classification accuracy and noise tolerance when compared to features acquired with signal processing tools [8,9].

These advantages have attracted a growing amount of research interest toward deep learning based fault diagnosis [1,10,11]. Many deep learning architectures, such as deep-belief networks (DBN) [12], autoencoders (AE) [9] and recurrent neural networks (RNN) [13] have been proposed for anomaly detection and fault diagnosis tasks. Despite these impressive results, learning the rich features required for fault recognition is difficult. Fortunately, many works have shown that convolutional neural networks (CNN) are effective in extracting features from vibration data [1,10,14]. For example, a number of studies have shown that 1D-CNNs can diagnose faults from time-series data [15–18]. Furthermore, a number of studies have also demonstrated that CNNs can effectively diagnose faults from the vibration frequency spectrum [19–21]. In addition, some studies have demonstrated the efficiency of 2D-CNNs for diagnosing the faults from time-frequency spectrograms [19,22]. Furthermore, CNN-based fault diagnosis models seem to be at the core of the most recent research branch of fault diagnosis concerning transfer learning [23–25]. Although deep learning based fault diagnosis models have been extensively studied and the focus seems to be shifting towards transfer learning, the techniques improving the feature extraction of the current models are still relevant.

Many of the recent CNN-based state-of-the-art deep learning algorithms for fault diagnosis rely on batch-normalisation (BN) [15–17]. BN efficiently accelerates the model convergence and improves model generalisation [26,27]. In essence, this standardisation method centres and scales the layer activations based on the mini-batch statistics [26]. Centring and scaling each layer activation per mini-batch effectively stabilises the gradient distribution for each corresponding weight [27]. Stabilised gradient distribution increases the consistency of the gradient descent. However, BN can be considered an incomplete normalisation method, since its design includes a compromise that separates it from whitening [26]. In addition to centering and scaling, whitening includes decorrelation, which has been argued to simplify the optimisation of the model weights by making the adjacent weights independent [28]. Decorrelation has been excluded from BN due to the heavy toll it introduces to the computation [26]. Fortunately, recent studies have shown how to implement full whitening of the activations without excessive computational cost. These studies have also shown that whitening improves the learning results over BN [29–31].

Despite the promising results regarding feature whitening techniques, CNN-based fault diagnosis models still mostly rely on BN. This study shows how whitening the layer activations improves the current state-of-the-art 1D-CNN-based algorithms for machine fault diagnosis. The novel experiments employ three previously published fault diagnosis models. These commonly known models are Ince's model [32], WDCNN [15] and SRD-CNN [18]. The experiments reveal the fault diagnosis accuracies of these baseline models in parallel with corresponding models employing a whitening normalisation technique instead of BN. The whitening technique is adapted from an earlier study showing that decorrelating layer inputs channel-wise and pixel-wise consistently improved 2D-CNN-based model performance and training convergence on image data [31]. This "network deconvolution" (ND) operation, developed in [31], is further adjusted and integrated with the three 1D-CNN-based fault diagnosis models for time series data in this study. The experiments of this work complement the previously reported results with ND performance in 1D-CNN-based models. The three experiments in this study employ two vibration datasets acquired from different rotor systems. The first dataset is the thoroughly studied bearing fault dataset produced by Case Western Reserve University [33]. The second dataset consists of vibration data from three azimuth thrusters before and after bearing and gear related faults were noticed. Each experiment shows that models with whitened features achieve high performance. More specifically, the models with whitened features achieve mostly better or significantly better diagnosis accuracies compared to the baseline models in the three experiments.

2. CNNs and Normalization Layers

Convolutional neural networks (CNNs) typically consist of convolutional layers, pooling layers, normalisation layers and a few fully connected layers. In vibration-based fault classification, the final fully-connected layer can be considered as the classifier in the fault recognition step. The other fully-connected layers, convolutional layers, normalisation, and pooling layers are used for the feature extraction step.

2.1. 1D Convolutional Layer

1D convolutional layers consist of filters computing cross-correlations over local areas of the input. Each filter consisting of N kernels with M weights computes an output value for a local area that consists of $N \times M$ values, where N denotes the number of channels e.g., different vibration sensors at the first layer and M denotes the length of the local area e.g., time steps. The filters process the local areas subsequently along the length axis with the same set of weights. Equation (1) shows this cross-correlation computation for a given local area:

$$y_j^{l,i} = \sum_{n=0}^{N} \mathbf{k}_{j,n}^{l} * \mathbf{x}_n^{l,i} + b_{j,n}^{l} \quad (1)$$

where $y_j^{l,i}$ denotes the i-th local area output value of j-th filter on the layer l, $\mathbf{k}_{j,n}^{l}$ is the kernel for n-th channel of j-th filter on the layer l, $\mathbf{x}_n^{l,i}$ is the n-th channel of the i-th local area, $*$ denotes the dot product and $b_{j,n}^{l}$ is the bias term of the kernel n of filter j on layer l. To conclude, the output value $y_j^{l,i}$ is the sum of the dot-products between the kernels and the local areas computed at each corresponding input channel n. This computation is commonly referred to as the depth-wise convolution.

The computation at a given convolutional layer can be formulated as matrix multiplication $\mathbf{X}\mathbf{w}$. With one dimensional data and a single input channel, for example, time series data from a single sensor at the first layer, the rows in matrix $\mathbf{X}$ would correspond to each local area $\mathbf{x}_1^{1,i}$ and $\mathbf{w}$ corresponds to a column vector of the weights in the only kernel $\mathbf{k}_{j,1}^{1}$ of the filter j. Typically, there are multiple input channels to each convolutional layer, and the number of kernels in a convolutional layer filter equals the number of input channels to that layer. The local areas $\mathbf{x}_n^{l,i}$ of the latter input channels are concatenated to the transformed data matrix $\mathbf{X}$, so that each local area $\mathbf{x}_n^{i}$, corresponding to the i-th convolution, are on the same row. Similarly, the weights of each kernel $\mathbf{k}_n$ for all channels n are vertically concatenated to the column vector $\mathbf{w}$. This transformation of input data to matrix $\mathbf{X}$ is similar to the commonly known im2col transformation with the difference that time series data is one-dimensional. The transformation is visualised in Figure 1.

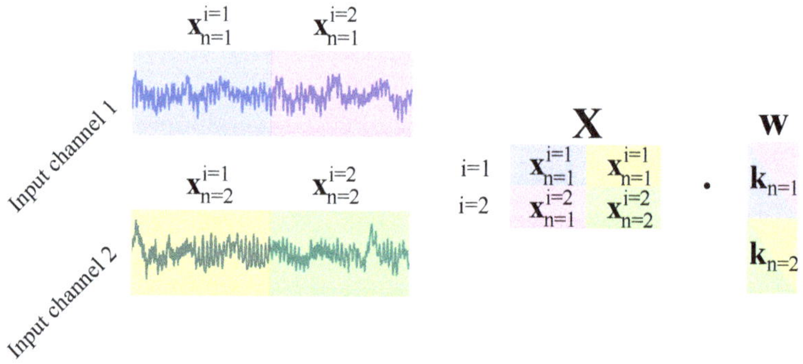

Figure 1. Convolutional layer computation composed in the matrix multiplication form visualised over two non-overlapping local areas and two channels.

2.2. Pooling Layer and ReLU Activation

Pooling layers efficiently reduce the model complexity and redundant information passed between the layers in CNNs. Each pooling layer consists of kernels that slide through the input array similar to the convolution layer kernels. Pooling layers rely on sub-sampling each local area under the kernels' receptive field. The most common pooling layers are the max-pooling and the average-pooling layer. Max-pooling has been shown to consistently outperform average pooling [34]. A max-pooling layer compresses the signals between layers by concatenating the maximum values of each local area for every channel separately. Equation (2) demonstrates the max-pooling operation:

$$\hat{y}_j^{l,k} = max(\mathbf{y}_j^{l,k}) \tag{2}$$

where $\mathbf{y}_j^{l,k}$ denotes the values under the max-pooling kernel receptive field from the k-th local area of the j-th channel between convolutional layers l and $l+1$, and $\hat{y}_j^{l,k}$ is the corresponding maximum value.

Typically between consequent cross-correlation computations, the output values are processed with a non-linear activation function, such as the rectified linear unit (ReLU) shown in Equation (3). The processed output values $x_j^{l+1,i}$ can then be passed forward to the next layer $l+1$.

$$x_j^{l+1,i} = ReLU(y_j^{l,i}) = max(0, y_j^{l,i}) \tag{3}$$

2.3. Batch Normalisation

Batch normalisation (BN) layers are additional layers that fix the activation distributions. This technique reduces the effect of internal covariate shift, a phenomenon hindering stochastic gradient descent optimisation [26]. Internal covariate shift can be described as a drastic change in the activation distributions due to the changed network parameters. BN normalises each activation separately with activation mean μ_b and variance σ_b^2 estimated from the mini-batch statistics. Furthermore, BN learns an additional set of scale γ and shifts β parameters by backpropagation. The computations related to BN are shown in Formulas (4)–(7).

$$\mu_b \leftarrow \frac{1}{m}\sum_{i=1}^{m} x_i \tag{4}$$

$$\sigma_b^2 \leftarrow \frac{1}{m}\sum_{i=1}^{m} (x_i - \mu_b)^2 \tag{5}$$

$$\hat{x}_i \leftarrow \frac{x_i - \mu_b}{\sqrt{\sigma_b^2 + \epsilon}} \tag{6}$$

$$y_i \leftarrow \gamma \widehat{x}_i + \beta \tag{7}$$

In Formulas (4)–(6), x_i denotes the i-th convolution layer output values in a batch, i.e., $x_i = y_j^{l,i}$ as in Equation (1). More explicitly, $x_i \in X = [x_{1...m}]$, where X is the batch with m convolution layer activations $y_j^{l,i}$. Alternatively, BN can operate on the activation values given by the ReLU-activation function in Equation (3). In Formulas (4) and (5), the mean μ_b and the variance σ_b^2 are computed from the distribution of the corresponding output values in the batch. Formula (6) shows the normalisation computation, where $\widehat{x}_i$ is the normalised output, and ϵ is a small constant introduced for numerical stability. In Formula (7), y_i is the BN layer output and γ and β are weights for scaling and shifting activations, optimised with backpropagation. Furthermore, during training the moving averages of μ_b and σ_b^2 are collected and utilised during testing.

2.4. From BN to Whitening Features

Image data may contain correlating data between nearby pixels and channels. For example, the pixels nearby a blurry object in an image correlate spatially. In addition, a grey object in an RGB image results in channel-wise correlation, since the RGB values are close to equal in the grey pixels. Machine vibration data may contain a similar correlation. For example, nearby sensors likely collect similar vibration patterns. Such data can hamper the optimisation process by inducing a correlation between the features learned by the neural network. Moreover, correlated features have been deemed problematic for neural network optimisation in the past [28].

Although BN has been shown to be effective in numerous state-of-the-art works [35–38], it merely scales and shifts the activations. BN was not designed to decorrelate the features due to the expense of computing the inverse square root of the activation covariance matrix and the corresponding derivatives. Nevertheless, several normalisation techniques that also decorrelate features have been proposed. These techniques typically seek better optimisation results by whitening the activations directly. Activations can be whitened for example according to the population statistics [39,40]. However, the estimation of the population statistics is hindered by the computational constraints and the changes to the activation distributions caused by the weight updates during optimisation [27]. Fortunately, these problems can be avoided by whitening the activations based on the mini-batch statistics. Such techniques are, for example, decorrelated batch normalisation (DBN) [30], IterNorm [41] and network deconvolution [31]. These three techniques first estimate the covariance matrix of the activations in the batch, as shown in Equation (8). In Equation (8), $\mathbf{X} \in \mathbb{R}^{C \times N}$ is the activation matrix with C channels and N samples, and $\boldsymbol{\mu} \in \mathbb{R}^C$ is the mean of the N activations in the batch. The batch of activations is then whitened with the inverse square root of the covariance matrix, i.e., the whitening matrix, and the batch mean, as shown in Equation (9). DBN has a slight disadvantage since it computes the whitening matrix with eigenvalue decomposition. IterNorm was proposed to solve the computational problems of DBN. IterNorm approximates the inverse square root of the whitening matrix with Newton's iteration. Network Deconvolution is similar to IterNorm. However, it employs coupled Newton-Schulz iteration, which was shown both a quick and stable approximation technique for the whitening matrix [31].

$$\mathbf{Cov} = \frac{1}{N}(\mathbf{X} - \boldsymbol{\mu})^T(\mathbf{X} - \boldsymbol{\mu}) \tag{8}$$

$$\tilde{\mathbf{X}} = (\mathbf{X} - \boldsymbol{\mu})\mathbf{Cov}^{-\frac{1}{2}} \tag{9}$$

3. Proposed Improvement for Fault Diagnosis Models

This study seeks to improve the current state-of-the-art CNN-based techniques for diagnosing faults from raw vibration data. The experiments in this study adapt three reportedly highly performing 1D-CNN models, remove all BN functions and normalise the layer inputs with ND instead. The study then evaluates the original models employing BN in parallel with the corresponding models employing ND. The baseline models are known as Ince's model [32], the stacked residual dilated convolutional neural network (SRDCNN) [18] and the Deep Convolutional Neural Networks with Wide First-layer Kernels (WDCNN) [15]. Although numerous other fault diagnosis models exist, these were chosen due to their simple and effective architectures. For example, WDCNN has been shown to produce the best bearing fault diagnosis results with slight modifications as an ensemble [16] and with an additional RNN-path [17]. However, the contrast in the results between models employing ND and BN can be sufficiently shown with these models without additional modifications.

This section is divided into three parts. Section 3.1 visits briefly the baseline model architectures. Then, Section 3.2 describes the ND practical implementation details. Finally, some general training algorithmic design choices are presented in Section 3.3.

3.1. Model Architectures

Ince's model [32] was one of the first CNN-based models proposed for vibration-based fault diagnosis of a rotating system. The original study showed that the model could accurately detect bearing faults from induction motor currents. The original model architecture consists of three CNN layers (Conv1D) and two fully-connected layers (FCL). The original model was slightly modified for the experiments in this study. Table 1 details the modified model architecture. Furthermore, Figure 2 shows the corresponding feature maps between the model layers. The modified version of Ince's model only employs one fully connected layer. The output space spans over 10 probabilities for every bearing health state in the CWRU dataset. In addition, the output space can include only one value corresponding to the probability of a fault, if the model is optimised for the binary thruster fault detection tasks. Furthermore, BN was placed after every CNN layer, despite BN not being mentioned in the original publication proposing Ince's model.

Table 1. Ince's model architecture.

Layer	Kernel Size	Channels in	Filters	Stride	Padding
Conv1D	9×1	1 or 2	60	5	18
Conv1D	9×1	60	40	5	4
Conv1D	9×1	40	40	9	3
FCL	1×1	400	1 or 10	N/A	N/A

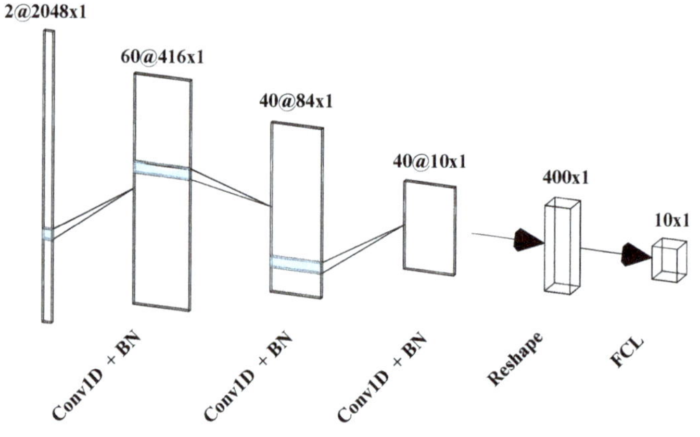

Figure 2. Feature maps of the Ince's model employed in this study. These feature maps correspond to a model that diagnoses the probability of 10 health states from vibration data measured with two vibration sensors.

WDCNN is an accurate model for vibration based condition monitoring [15]. The model consists of two levels. The first level includes five 1D-CNN, BN and pooling layers employed for feature extraction. The second level includes two fully connected layers with BN for fault recognition. Table 2 details the WDCNN architecture. Furthermore, Figure 3 shows the corresponding feature maps between the model layers. The first layer filters consist of wider 64 × 1 kernels. Each filter includes a kernel for every input channel. The rest of the CNN layers consist of 3 × 1 kernels. After every CNN layer, there is a BN layer, max-pooling layer and a (ReLU) activation function, in this order. All max-pooling layers apply 2 × 1 kernel with a stride of 2. The final fully connected layers compute the probabilities for the system health states.

Table 2. WDCNN architecture.

Layer	Kernel Size	Channels in	Filters	Stride	Padding
Conv1D	64 × 1	1 or 2	16	16	24
Conv1D	3 × 1	16	32	1	1
Conv1D	3 × 1	32	64	1	1
Conv1D	3 × 1	64	64	1	1
Conv1D	3 × 1	64	64	1	1
FCL	1×1	192	18	N/A	N/A
FCL	1×1	18	1 or 10	N/A	N/A

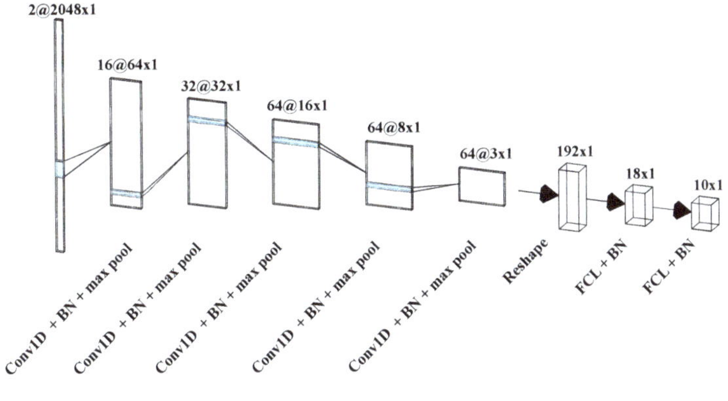

Figure 3. Feature maps of the WDCNN employed in this study. These feature maps correspond to a model that diagnoses the probability of 10 health states from vibration data measured with two vibration sensors.

SRDCNN [18] is a promising model, which achieved relatively high accuracies in bearing fault diagnosis tests in the original study. Similar to Ince's model and WDCNN, SRDCNN extracts features with 1D convolutional layers and then computes the probabilities for the system health with fully-connected layers. Table 3 lists the main components of SRDCNN architecture. Furthermore, Figure 4 shows the corresponding feature maps between the model layers. The model consists of five convolutional layers and two fully-connected layers. However, the convolutional layers of SRDCNN differ from the convolutional layers of WDCNN and Ince's model. SRDCNN applies dilated convolutions. Furthermore, each convolutional layer includes two adjacent convolutional sublayers and a residual connection. These adjacent sublayers are structured similarly to the input gates in the recurrent neural network type known as long short-term memory (LSTM). The activation values of these sublayers are multiplied element-wise together and then added element-wise to the residual values. The residual values are the input values to the layer passed through a third adjacent 1D-convolutional sublayer with 1 × 1 kernels. These dilated convolutional layers were named residual dilated convolutional layers (RDConv1D) in the original publication. BN is employed after every convolutional sublayer and fully-connected layer except the convolutional sublayers with 1×1 kernels for residual connections.

Table 3. SRDCNN architecture.

Layer	Kernel Size	Channels in	Filters	Stride	Padding	Dilation
RDConv1D	64×1	1 or 2	32	2	31	1
RDConv1D	32×1	32	32	2	31	2
RDConv1D	16×1	32	64	2	30	4
RDConv1D	8×1	64	64	2	28	8
RDConv1D	4×1	64	64	2	24	16
FCL	1×1	4096	100	N/A	N/A	N/A
FCL	1×1	100	1 or 10	N/A	N/A	N/A

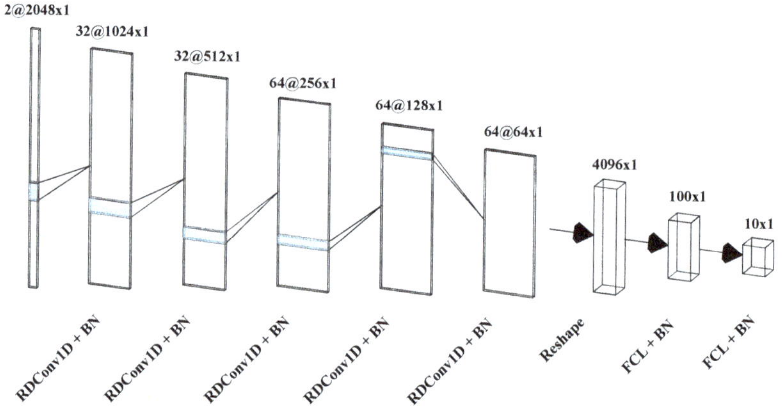

Figure 4. Feature maps of the SRDCNN employed in this study. These feature maps correspond to a model that diagnoses the probability of 10 health states from vibration data measured with two vibration sensors.

All these models can function with vibration data from an arbitrary number of sensors. The number of input sensors corresponds to the number of input channels in the first layer of the model. Tables 1–3 show that the number of the first layer input channels in all the models in this study is either one or two because the datasets in this study contain vibration data measured with one or two accelerometers. Furthermore, all these models can compute an arbitrary number of probabilities for the health states of the rotor system. The tables in this section show that the output dimensions of the final fully-connected layers of the models can be either 1 or 10. These dimensions correspond to the health states in the two datasets in this study.

Depending on the number of probabilities, this study employs two classification functions computing the diagnosed health state from the probability values. Softmax function, Equation (10), processes the 10 model output values into a probability distribution of 10 probabilities that sum to 1. The diagnosed health state of the system is the label with the highest probability. Sigmoid function, Equation (11), computes the model output value into a probability between [0, 1]. This probability corresponds to the probability of a fault occurring in the system.

$$S(\mathbf{z}) = \frac{e^{\mathbf{z}}}{\sum_{j=0}^{N} e^{z_j}} \quad (10)$$

$$S(z) = \frac{1}{1+e^{-z}} \tag{11}$$

3.2. Whitening CNN Inputs

ND, as proposed in [31], employs the matrix multiplication composition of a convolutional layer, as explained in Section 2.1. ND performs the whitening of the layer input $\mathbf{X}$ by subtracting its mean, and then by multiplying it with the inverse square root of the corresponding covariance matrix. Subtracting the mean centres the layer input, and multiplying with the inverse square root of the covariance matrix decorrelates the layer input local area-wise and channel-wise. Ideally, after ND the layer inputs have a mean of zero and the covariance matrix is approximately an identity matrix. The computations related to this whitening operation are shown in the following equations:

$$\mathbf{Cov} = \frac{1}{N}(\mathbf{X} - \mu)^T(\mathbf{X} - \mu) \tag{12}$$

$$\mathbf{D} \approx (\mathbf{Cov})^{-\frac{1}{2}} \tag{13}$$

$$\mathbf{y}_j = (\mathbf{X} - \mu) \cdot \mathbf{D} \cdot \mathbf{w_j} + \mathbf{b_j}. \tag{14}$$

In Equation (12), the covariance of layer input data is computed. $\mathbf{X}$ is the transformed input data matrix and μ are the mean of N values in the columns of $\mathbf{X}$, i.e., the mean of values multiplied by an arbitrary weight. N depends on the number of samples in a mini-batch and the number of local areas. $\mathbf{D}$ is the deconvolution kernel in Equation (13), which is an approximation of the inverse square root of the covariance matrix. Equation (14) shows the computation of the output values $\mathbf{y}_j$ of the j-th filter with the centered and transformed input $\mathbf{X} - \mu$, the deconvolution kernel $\mathbf{D} \approx \mathbf{COV}^{-\frac{1}{2}}$, the filter weights $\mathbf{w}_j$ and the filter bias terms $\mathbf{b}_j$.

The whitening computations, as presented above, may decelerate the optimisation of a deep neural network excessively. Therefore, computation acceleration techniques for ND were also proposed [31]. These techniques include subsampling the layer input matrix $\mathbf{X}$ for lighter covariance matrix computation, coupled Newton-Schulz iteration for the inverse square root of the covariance matrix approximation, and implicit decorrelation of layer inputs. This work optimised these acceleration algorithms for the 1D-CNN-based fault diagnosis models. The remainder of this subsection explains the practical implementation of ND and the required acceleration techniques.

After the layer input formulation to matrix $\mathbf{X}$, as shown in Figure 1, the covariance matrix is computed as expressed in Equation (12). Since the covariance matrix computation is performed for every layer and during every forward pass, subsampling the layer input matrices $\mathbf{X}^l$ likely decreases the required training time. That is, the number of rows N in a layer input matrix $\mathbf{X}$, consisting of local areas from all mini-batch samples, decreases by subsampling the rows. Subsampling is likely to have a small effect on the covariance matrix because the number of input values N is relatively high compared to the covariance matrix dimensions.

To whiten the layer inputs, the inverse square root of the covariance matrix needs to be computed. Several techniques exist for computing the inverse square root of a matrix. However, the coupled Newton-Schulz iteration was shown to be both a numerically stable and fast algorithm for approximating the inverse square root of the covariance matrix [31]. The iteration starts by initialising matrices $\mathbf{Y}_0 = \mathbf{Cov} + \epsilon \cdot \mathbf{I}$ and $\mathbf{Z}_0 = \mathbf{I}$. The matrices $\mathbf{Y}_k$ and $\mathbf{Z}_k$ are updated every iteration with Equations (15) and (16), respectively. The matrices converge to approximate values of the square root and the inverse square root of the covariance matrix, as shown in Formulas (17) and (18).

$$\mathbf{Y}_{k+1} = \frac{1}{2}\mathbf{Y}_k(3\mathbf{I} - \mathbf{Z}_k\mathbf{Y}_k) \tag{15}$$

$$\mathbf{Z}_{k+1} = \frac{1}{2}(3\mathbf{I} - \mathbf{Z}_k\mathbf{Y}_k)\mathbf{Z}_k \tag{16}$$

$$\mathbf{Y}_{k+1} \rightarrow \mathbf{Cov}^{\frac{1}{2}} \tag{17}$$

$$\mathbf{Z}_{k+1} \rightarrow \mathbf{Cov}^{-\frac{1}{2}} \tag{18}$$

Once the inverse square root of the covariance matrix has been approximated, the inverse correction can be applied to the layer input matrix $\mathbf{X}$. However, ND performs this whitening correction implicitly by correcting the weights $\mathbf{w}$ of the convolutional layers instead of decorrelating the input data. This whitening can be considered as decorrelating the weights of each kernel in a filter. During training, a running mean of the deconvolution matrix $\mathbf{D} \approx (\mathbf{Cov} + \epsilon \cdot \mathbf{I})^{-\frac{1}{2}}$ is collected for each layer. A small constant ϵ is added for numerical stability and regulatory effect. After training has finished, the running average of the deconvolution kernels $\mathbf{D}^l$ are frozen and kept constant during testing to reduce the computation time. This implicit deconvolution is expressed mathematically on the right-hand side of Equation (19).

$$\mathbf{y}_j^l = (\mathbf{X}^l - \mu^l) \cdot (\mathbf{D}^l \cdot \mathbf{w}_j^l) + \mathbf{b}_j^l = \mathbf{X}^l \cdot \mathbf{D}^l \cdot \mathbf{w}_j^l + \mathbf{b}_j^l - \mu^l \cdot \mathbf{D}^l \cdot \mathbf{w}_j^l \tag{19}$$

3.3. Training the Models

The training convergence of a deep neural network depends heavily on the training algorithm design. With suitable choices, the sample efficiency and the test performance are likely to increase. This work deployed various techniques, such as time window division, learning rate scheduling and early stopping. The following discusses briefly the major choices. The repository for this study is linked in Appendix A for further evaluation.

A disadvantage of deep neural network solutions for fault diagnosis originates from their need for a large number of training samples in order to converge to a satisfying optimum. Fortunately, the number of training samples can be increased with data augmentation. This work employed overlapping time window division for data augmentation. That is, the time series samples were split into shorter time windows including time steps over multiple rotor revolutions. Figure 5 demonstrates this overlapping time window division technique. The extracted time windows correspond to an input sample of 2048 time steps in this study.

The loss function for multi-categorical fault diagnosis tasks is cross-entropy loss (CE loss), as shown in Equation (20). The CE loss is a measure for the difference of the target distribution and the estimated distribution over K categories averaged over N samples in a batch. In Equation (20), $y_j^n \in \{0,1\}$ are the K values in the target distribution with the correct category encoded as 1 and $f_j^n \in [0,1]$ are the K probabilities in the estimated distribution. The loss function for binary fault detection tasks is the binary cross-entropy loss (BCE loss), as shown in Equation (21). Similarly to CE loss, the BCE loss is averaged over the N samples in the batch. In Equation (21), $y^n \in \{0,1\}$ is the correct label and $f^n \in [0,1]$ is the probability of a fault.

$$CE\ loss = -\frac{1}{N}\sum_{n=1}^{N}\sum_{j=1}^{K} y_j^n log(f_j^n) \tag{20}$$

$$BCE\ loss = -\frac{1}{N}\sum_{n=1}^{N}(y^n log(f^n) + (1-y^n)(1-log(f^n))) \tag{21}$$

The gradient optimisation steps of all models were controlled with Adam optimiser [42] and decaying learning rate. The learning rate decayed by half every tenth epoch. Furthermore, all models were optimised with early stopping and checkpoints. That is, at the end of every epoch, if the validation loss decreases, the model weights are saved. If the validation loss increases, the previous best weights are loaded to the model. The optimisation ends after a maximum number of epochs or after the validation loss increases seven times. A maximum number of epochs and other training and model related hyperparameters are detailed in Appendix B.

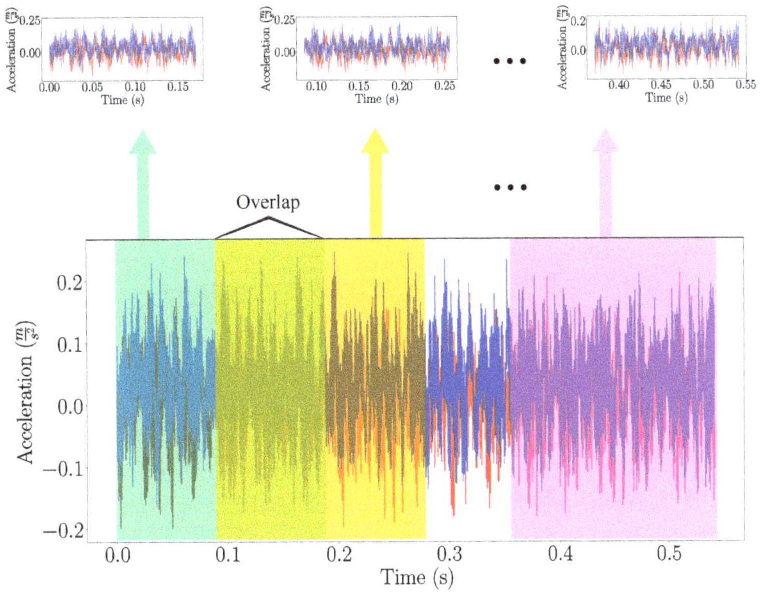

Figure 5. Time series sample consisting of two input signals divided to overlapping training samples.

4. Validation of ND for Fault Diagnosis

This section presents the performance of the baseline models relying on BN and the modified models relying on ND under two different tasks. The first task in Section 4.1 relates to the extensively studied benchmark dataset for bearing fault diagnosis. The dataset consists of rotor system vibration data sampled at different motor loads. The second task in Section 4.2 demonstrates the model's performance at detecting faults from vibration data acquired in more diverse operating conditions. The dataset of this task consists of thruster vibration data sampled in real operation conditions.

4.1. Case 1: Bearing Fault Diagnosis under Varied Load Conditions

The CWRU bearing fault dataset [33] is a well-established machine fault classification benchmark. The vibration dataset includes samples of healthy and faulty bearings placed in the test rig in Figure 6. There are four different bearing health conditions in the dataset: healthy (H), ball fault (B), inner race fault (I) and outer race fault (O). Each fault type was machined with three different diameters: 0.1778 mm ($*_L$), 0.3556 mm ($*_M$) and 0.5334 mm ($*_H$). Thus, the number of different health states in the dataset is 10. Each fault type was measured at three different motor loads: 0.746 kW (1 hp), 1.491 kW (2 hp) and 2.237 kW (3 hp). Each time series sample was measured with two accelerometers at the drive-end and the fan-end of the motor. The sampling frequency was 12 kHz. Earlier related studies have mostly trained the fault diagnosis models with the vibration data acquired with the drive-end sensor only [15,18,19]. However, often condition monitoring systems include multiple sensors. Therefore, this subsection also presents the fault diagnosis experiments employing both, the drive-end and the fan-end sensor data as model inputs.

Figure 6. Bearing fault test rig [33].

Table 4 shows the details related to the bearing fault dataset. The training samples were acquired by sampling overlapping time windows from the 10 time series samples corresponding to the health states. Each training sample is 2048 timesteps long. The shift between adjacent training samples is 32 timesteps. Test samples share the length with training samples, however, they do not overlap.

Table 4. Number of training and test samples per bearing health state and motor load.

Load	Split	H	B_L	B_M	B_H	I_L	I_M	I_H	O_L	O_M	O_H
1 hp	Train	1980	1980	1980	1980	1980	1980	1980	1980	1980	1980
	Test	59	59	59	59	59	59	59	59	59	59
2 hp	Train	1980	1980	1980	1980	1980	1980	1980	1980	1980	1980
	Test	59	59	59	59	59	59	59	59	59	59
3 hp	Train	1980	1980	1980	1980	1980	1980	1980	1980	1980	1980
	Test	59	59	59	59	59	59	59	59	59	59

The baseline models with BN and the modified models with ND were trained to recognise the health state of the bearing from the vibration data. Every model was trained on each motor load domain and then evaluated on the other motor load domains. These tests were repeated 10 times for each model and load domain. Furthermore, these experiments were conducted with data from both accelerometers and with data from the drive-end accelerometer only. Figure 7 presents the means and standard deviations of the model accuracies when only the data from the drive-end accelerometer was available. Figure 8 presents the results from repeated experiments with data from both accelerometers.

Figure 7 shows that all models diagnose the bearing health states with over 80% accuracy on average from the drive-end accelerometer data. In the same experiments, the modified WDCNN and SRDCNN models achieve more than 5 percentage points (pp) better average classification accuracies than the corresponding baseline models. The accuracy of the modified Ince's model is 0.35 pp less than the corresponding baseline. Overall the modified models achieve similar or significantly better diagnosis accuracies than the corresponding baselines in these experiments.

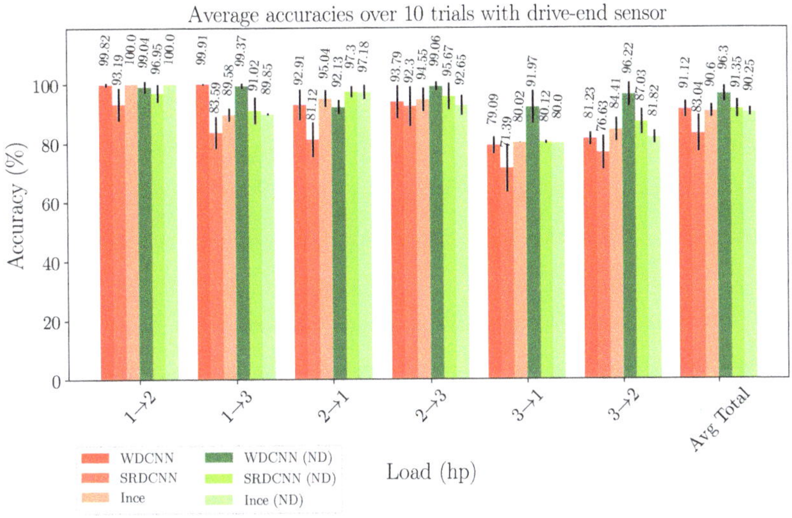

Figure 7. Means and standard deviations of the accuracies of the baseline models with BN (**red**) and the same models with ND (**green**) on six different load domain shift problems over ten trial runs. The models diagnosed the bearing health state from the drive-end sensor data. The test data was drawn from the motor load domains the arrows point and the training data was drawn from the motor load domains the arrows point from.

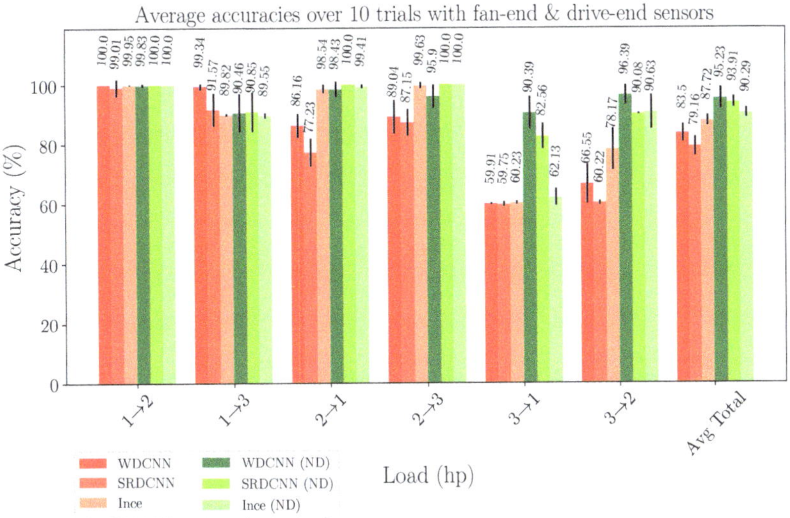

Figure 8. Means and standard deviations of the accuracies of the baseline models with BN (**red**) and the same models with ND (**green**) on six different load domain shift problems over ten trial runs. The models diagnosed the bearing health state from the drive-end and the fan-end sensors simultaneously. The test data was drawn from the motor load domains the arrows point and the training data was drawn from the motor load domains the arrows point from.

Figure 8 shows that the average diagnosis accuracies of the models decreased after introducing data from both accelerometers to the task. Only modified Ince's model and modified SRDCNN increased the diagnostic accuracy compared to the results in Figure 7. Especially the baseline models performed significantly worse when they were trained with data acquired with the motor load of 3 hp. Overall, the average diagnosis accuracies of the modified models were significantly higher than the corresponding baseline counterparts.

4.2. *Case 2: Azimuth Thruster Fault Detection*

Three azimuth thrusters of a similar configuration of the same drill ship were monitored frequently from mid-2018 to the end of 2019. An azimuth thruster is a rotor system which ships may use for movement or for preserving position. The three thrusters were operated in diverse environments at various rotating speeds and thrusting angles. Figure 9 shows the rotating speed distribution of the vibration samples in the dataset. Each vibration sample in the dataset is a time series sample including four revolutions sampled at 1024 distinct encoder positions totalling 4096 sampling points. Therefore, the time dimension differs between the vibration samples measured at different rotating speeds.

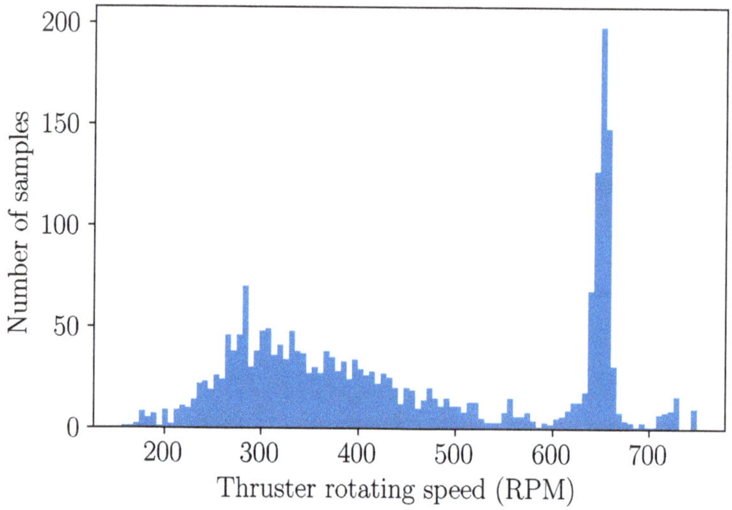

Figure 9. Thruster rotating speed varied between the acquired vibration samples in the range between 100 RPM and 750 RPM.

The vibration samples were acquired with accelerometers in similar positions near the input shafts (IS) of the thrusters. During the monitoring period, the thrusters were healthy in the beginning but suffered malfunctions in matching components. The faults were related to the bearing near the gear end of the pinion shaft (B) and the gear pinion and the gear wheel (G). Figure 10 shows the thruster assembly, the fault locations and the sensor position. All faults occurred in all three thrusters during the period of observations. The faults in the dataset were recognised by condition monitoring specialists.

Some samples with abnormal data were filtered from the dataset with a quality control function. Appendix C describes the quality control function in detail. The resulting dataset is described in Table 5, where the components were either labelled as healthy or faulty. The severity of the faults in a single thruster changes between the samples, due to the long observation period. That is, vibration samples were collected over a long period of time before and after the malfunctions were first noticed.

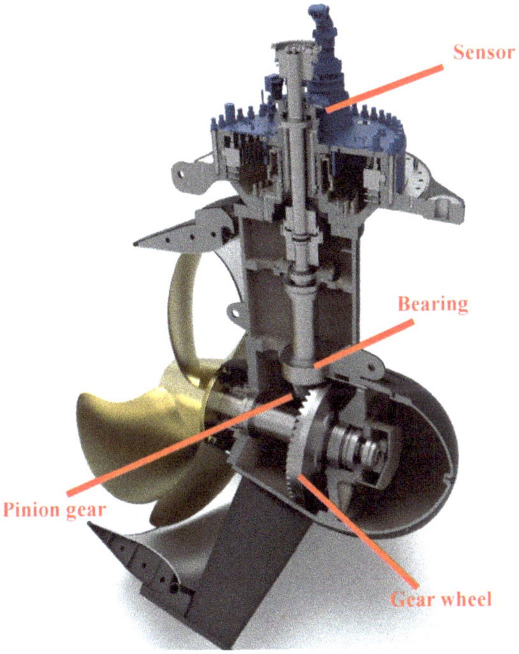

Figure 10. The azimuth thruster vibration was measured with an accelerometer sensor near the input shaft. The positions of the sensor and the faulty components are pointed with red lines.

The lowest row in Table 5 shows the number of samples drawn and augmented to training, validation and test datasets. The relatively high number of training, validation and test samples is due to data augmentation with time window division. Each time window was 2048 time steps long. The time windows were overlapped during training data and validation data augmentation, but not overlapped during test data augmentation. The same number of samples were drawn randomly 10 times for each trial consisting of training and evaluation of all models. Furthermore, each set holds an equal number of healthy and faulty samples.

Table 5. Azimuth thruster dataset statistics.

Thruster	Condition	B	G
1	Healthy	263	283
	Faulty	468	448
2	Healthy	108	200
	Faulty	843	751
3	Healthy	125	216
	Faulty	405	314
Total	Healthy	496	699
	Faulty	1716	1513
Data splits	Train	48,230	77,740
	Val	11,960	19,110
	Test	368	592

The baseline models with BN and the modified models with ND were optimised to recognise faulty behaviour in a specific component. Therefore, the models were subjected to binary classification tasks. All models were trained and then evaluated 10 times for each task with the hyperparameters listed in Appendix B. Figure 11 shows the average test classification accuracies of the models in the fault diagnosis tasks. All models achieved similar diagnosis accuracies between 84% and 91% in both tasks. Overall, the modified models with ND performed slightly better. The modified SRDCNN and Ince's model diagnosed the bearing condition less than 1 pp more accurately than the corresponding baseline models. Moreover, the modified WDCNN and SRDCNN diagnosed the bearing condition less than 2 pp more accurately than the corresponding baseline models.

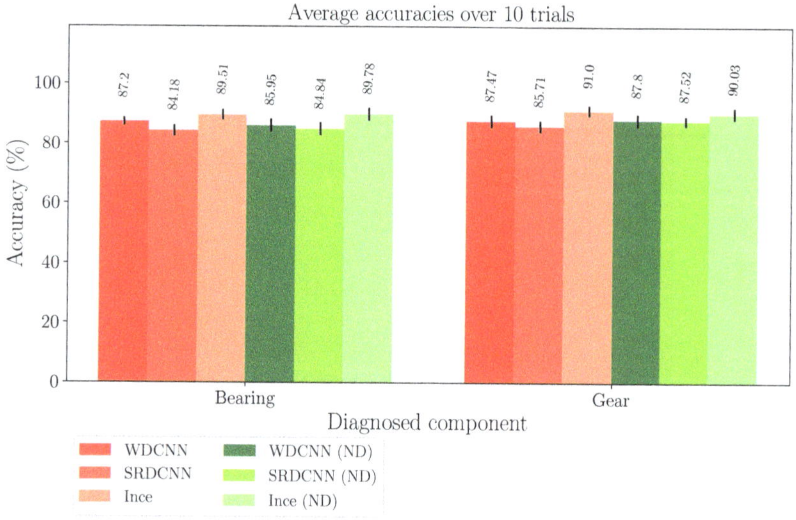

Figure 11. Mean and standard deviation of accuracies of the baseline models with BN (**red**) and the modified models with ND (**green**) on both binary fault detection problems over 10 trial runs. Datasets were randomly drawn for each trial separately. Every model was tested with the same randomly drawn set of samples.

5. Discussion

Based on the results, ND seems like a competitive solution for BN in CNN-based machine fault diagnosis from vibration data. In Section 4.1, the modified models with ND were compared to the baseline models with a well-established benchmark dataset for bearing fault diagnosis. In this multi-categorical bearing fault recognition task, the modified models with ND mostly outperformed the baseline models with BN in terms of the average accuracy of all experiments. Whitening seemed to especially improve WDCNN performance. The average accuracy of modified WDCNN was 5.18 pp and 11.73 pp higher than the baseline in results shown in Figures 7 and 8, respectively. Furthermore, the modified WDCNN and modified SRDCNN outperformed remarkably the corresponding baselines in experiments with training data drawn from the vibration data sampled at a 3 hp motor load.

In Section 4.2, the modified models and the baseline models were compared by using a real world dataset consisting of ship thrusters in diverse environments. In these thruster fault detection tasks, all models achieved relatively high accuracies of over 84%. However, there were no significant differences between the fault detection accuracies of the compared models. Based on these thruster fault detection tasks, ND can be considered as good as BN for normalising the activations of CNN-based fault detection models.

Although ND is a promising technique for whitening the features between CNN layers, it introduces a few extra hyperparameters for fault diagnosis model training. Moreover, the models relying on ND can be very sensitive toward these hyperparameters. That is, the sampling stride, the number of coupled Newton-Schulz iterations and the regularisation term ϵ, for example, may affect optimisation results and require careful tuning. For convenience, Appendix D shows accuracies at different subsampling strides and batch sizes. Furthermore, Appendix E provides some examples of the deconvolution matrix **D** after a different number of coupled Newton-Schulz iterations. Fortunately, similar ND hyperparameters seemed to perform well in both model validation case studies, even though the data was significantly different due to the measurement circumstances and due to the health state spaces. Therefore, the values searched in this work for ND hyperparameters are likely suitable for other vibration diagnosis tasks.

Overall, whitening the layer inputs seems to consistently provide high test performance for CNN-based fault diagnosis models. By whitening the layer inputs, the model learns uncorrelated features containing less redundant information than correlated features. With uncorrelated features, the domain adaptation of the model improves on average, as shown in Section 4.1. The difference in domain adaptation between whitened features and batch normalised features is significant, especially when shifting from the higher load domains to lower load domains. Furthermore, decor-related features seem to significantly increase the accuracies of the diagnosis models compared to the baseline models when data from two sensors were employed, as Figure 8 shows. This indicates that decorrelating CNN-based model features may increase fault diagnosis accuracy of condition monitoring systems with many sensors.

6. Conclusions

This study demonstrated the effect of whitening the features of 1D-CNN-based fault diagnosis models. The features of three commonly known and highly accurate fault diagnosis models were whitened with network deconvolution. Network deconvolution is a recently proposed, implicit and approximative whitening technique. The models modified with network deconvolution were compared to the originally proposed models relying on batch normalisation under two validation case studies. In the first case study, the models were evaluated on a well established bearing fault dataset under varied load domains. The second case study evaluated the model performances in more challenging real thruster fault detection tasks. The first case study showed that whitened features increased the 1D-CNN model performances on average. Furthermore, the same case study showed that the models with whitened features were significantly more accurate at diagnosing the bearing health state from the vibration data acquired with two sensors. However, the second case study showed that the models with whitened features achieved similar fault detection accuracies to the corresponding baseline models. Overall, this study shows that whitening 1D-CNN-based fault diagnosis model features may improve the diagnosis performance. These results are significant for CNN-based fault diagnosis algorithms since the whitening technique employed in this study can replace all batch normalisation layers in any CNN-based fault diagnosis model.

Author Contributions: Conceptualization, J.M., R.-P.N. and J.K.-R.; methodology, J.M.; software, J.M.; validation, J.M., R.-P.N., J.K.-R., F.F. and T.T.; formal analysis, J.M.; investigation, J.M.; resources, J.M.; data curation, J.M., R.-P.N. and J.K.-R.; writing—original draft preparation, J.M.; writing—review and editing, J.M., R.-P.N., J.K.-R., F.F., T.T., S.S. and R.V.; visualization, J.M.; supervision, J.K.-R., F.F., T.T., S.S. and R.V; project administration, J.K.-R. and R.V.; funding acquisition, J.K.-R. and R.V. All authors have read and agreed to the published version of the manuscript.

Funding: This research was funded by Business Finland as part of the Reboot IoT project (grant number 4356/31/2019) and by the Academy of Finland as part of the AI-ROT research project (grant number 335717).

Institutional Review Board Statement: Not applicable.

Data Availability Statement: Data sharing concerning the thruster dataset is not applicable to this article due to legal issues. Publicly available datasets were analyzed in this study. This data, concerning the bearing fault dataset, can be found here: https://engineering.case.edu/bearingdatacenter.

Conflicts of Interest: The authors declare no conflict of interest. The funders had no role in the design of the study; in the collection, analyses, or interpretation of data; in the writing of the manuscript, or in the decision to publish the results.

Abbreviations

The following abbreviations are used in this manuscript:

IFD	Intelligent Fault Diagnosis
BN	Batch Normalization
ND	Network Deconvolution
CNN	Convolutional Neural Network
DL	Deep Learning
ML	Machine Learning
DBN	Deep Belief Network
AE	Autoencoder
RNN	Recurrent Neural Network
WDCNN	Deep Convolutional Neural Networks with Wide First-layer Kernels
SRDCNN	Stacked Residual Dilated Convolutional Neural Network
ReLU	Rectified Linear Unit
LSTM	Long Short-Term Memory
CE	Cross-Entropy
BCE	Binary Cross-Entropy
pp	Percentage Point

Appendix A. Source Code

The repository linked below contains the source code related to this study.
https://github.com/miettij/Intelligent-fault-diagnosis; accessed on 4 April 2022.

Appendix B. Model Specific Hyperparameters

Before the model optimisation, some of the training related and model related hyperparameters were optimised for every model separately. Table A1 lists the hyperparameters employed in the bearing fault diagnosis experiments in Section 4.1. Table A2 details the hyperparameters of the thruster experiments in Section 4.2. The models marked with 'ND' in parenthesis refer to the models modified with network deconvolution. First layer iterations refers to the number of coupled Newton-Schulz iterations at the first convolutional layer. Deconv iterations refers to the number of coupled Newton-Schulz iterations on other model layers. ϵ is the small constant for regularisation and numerical stability of the iteration. Sampling stride defines the subsampling factor for the layer input matrix $\mathbf{X}$.

Table A1. Hyperparameters deployed in bearing fault experiments *.

Param	Ince	SRDCNN	WDCNN	Ince (ND)	SRDCNN (ND)	WDCNN (ND)
Batch size	32	64	64	8	128 (8)	8
Learning rate	0.001	0.0001	0.001	0.0001	0.1 (0.0001)	0.0001
Max epochs	60	60	70	70	40	70
Bias	False	True	True	True	True	True
First layer iterations	N/A	N/A	N/A	15	15	15
Deconv iterations	N/A	N/A	N/A	5	5	5
ϵ	N/A	N/A	N/A	10^{-5}	10^{-5}	10^{-5}
Sampling stride	N/A	N/A	N/A	5	5	5

* Hyperparameters employed in experiments with the drive-end and the fan-end sensors are in parentheses if different.

Table A2. Hyperparameters deployed in thruster fault experiments.

Param	Ince	SRDCNN	WDCNN	Ince (ND)	SRDCNN (ND)	WDCNN (ND)
Batch size	32	64	64	8	8	8
Learning rate	0.001	0.0001	0.001	0.0001	0.0001	0.0001
Max epochs	60	60	70	70	70	70
Bias	False	True	True	True	True	True
First layer iterations	N/A	N/A	N/A	15	15	25
Deconv iterations	N/A	N/A	N/A	5	5	5
ϵ	N/A	N/A	N/A	10^{-5}	10^{-5}	10^{-5}
Sampling stride	N/A	N/A	N/A	5	5	36

Appendix C. Quality Control Function for Filtering Abnormal Samples

Although the thruster data was sampled in diverse environments and the time series samples differed, some samples containing outliers were removed from the dataset. Outlier samples originated likely due to many reasons, such as faulty sensor or heavy storm conditions. For this purpose, a quality control algorithm was developed to reject the outlying samples based on three checks. Firstly, the data sample consisting of 4096×1 time series was divided into sliding time windows of 100×1, with the step size of 1. A mean value was then computed for all the sliding windows. The sample was rejected if the difference between the maximum and the minimum mean value was higher than 0.2×9.81 m/s^2. Secondly, the sample was rejected if the maximum and minimum values of the time series were the same. Thirdly, the sample was rejected if the absolute mean of the time series was over 0.5×9.81 m/s^2. If the sample passed each check, it was accepted for further processing.

Appendix D. Batch Size and Sampling Stride Effect on ND

The batch size and sampling stride both affect the number of values in the layer input $\mathbf{X}$, as in Figure 1. With larger batch sizes, the number of values in each column increases. With higher sampling strides, the number of values in each column decreases. The number of values in each column correlates with the representability of the covariance matrix, and thus affects the decorrelation reliability. With a low number of inputs per neuron, the covariance matrix might not represent the true input distribution over the whole dataset. Therefore, the sampling stride and batch size were searched. Figure A1 shows three different grid search results for batch size, sampling stride and learning rate. The model in this grid search was WDCNN and the input data included vibration data from the fan-end and the drive-end sensors. Each accuracy in the figure corresponds to average accuracy of six load domain shift tasks, as in Section 4.1. The experiments were repeated 10 times with less than 20 training epochs. Each standard deviation in the figure corresponds to the distribution of all load domain shift test accuracies over the ten experiments. In addition, Figure A2 visualises covariance matrices of the WDCNN first layer inputs corresponding to a random sample with drive-end and fan-end data from the bearing fault dataset. The covariance matrices are computed with different sampling strides. Figure A2 shows that the covariance between the inputs decreases as the sampling stride increases.

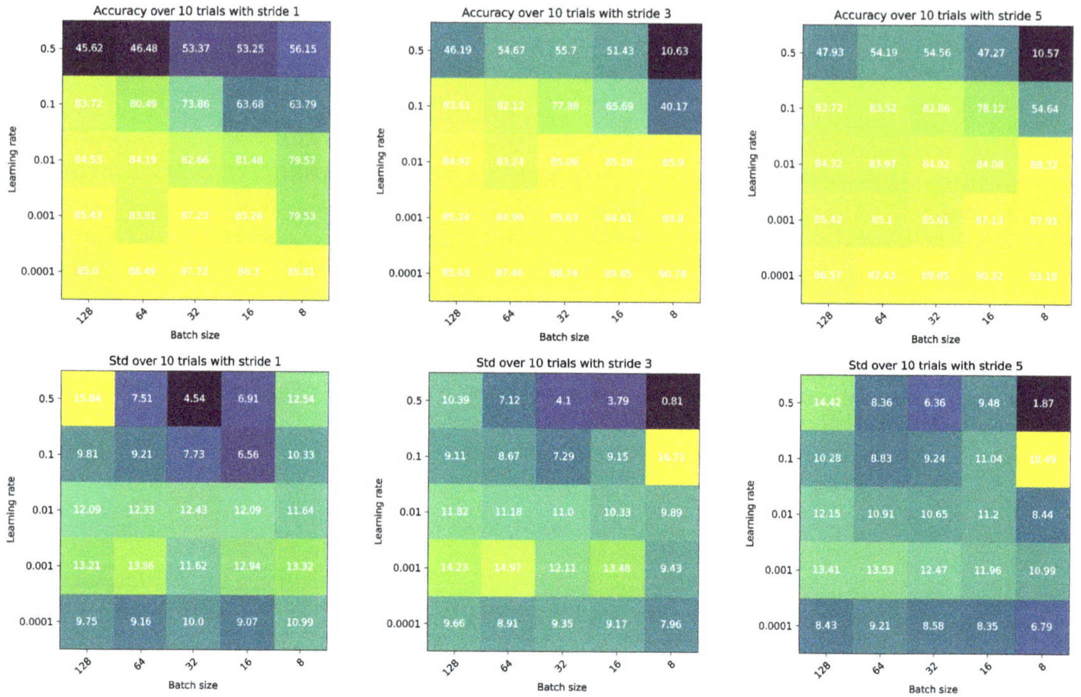

Figure A1. Mean and standard deviations of WDCNN test accuracies over 10 trials of load domain shift tests with the bearing fault dataset. Specifically, each accuracy and standard deviation in the figure is the total average of the six load domain shift results, similar to the ones in Section 4.1.

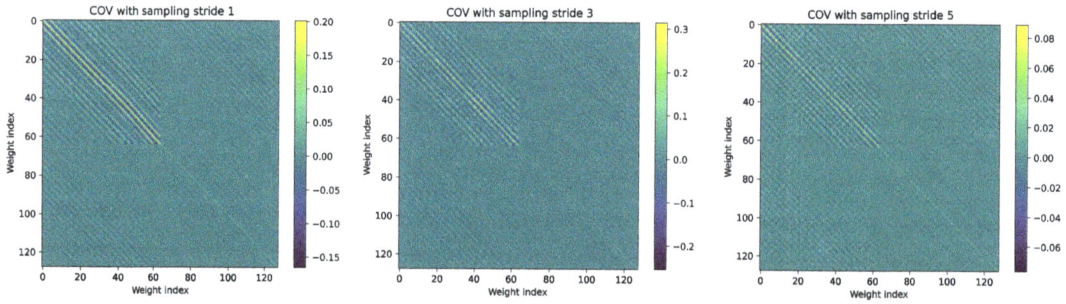

Figure A2. Covariance matrices of the first layer input related to a batch of vibration samples with two channels (fan-end and drive-end sensors) from the bearing fault dataset. The sampling stride corresponds to the sampling strides in Figure A1. The covariance is highest between inputs in the same channel (diagonal corner quarters of the heatmaps) and between the nearby weights within a kernel. The first layer filter of WDCNN has two kernels of size 64×1, which explains the covariance matrix dimension of 128×128.

Appendix E. Iteration Count Effect on the Approximation of the Deconvolution Kernel

The coupled Newton-Schulz iteration for approximating the inverse square root of the covariance of layer input matrix $\mathbf{X}$ converges to values with more contrast as the number of iterations increases. Figure A3 shows these deconvolution matrices approximated with different number of iterations.

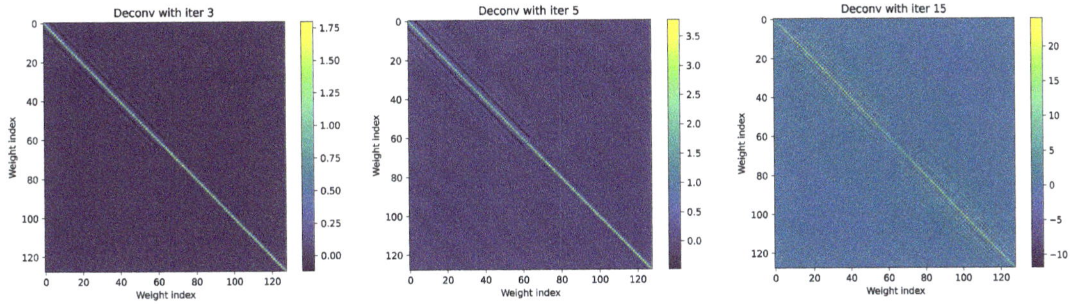

Figure A3. Three deconvolution matrices with different number of iterations approximated from the leftmost covariance matrix in Figure A2. The deconvolution matrix approximation grow significantly sharper as the number of iterations increase.

References

1. Lei, Y.; Yang, B.; Jiang, X.; Jia, F.; Li, N.; Nandi, A.K. Applications of machine learning to machine fault diagnosis: A review and roadmap. *Mech. Syst. Signal Process.* **2020**, *138*, 106587. [CrossRef]
2. Liu, R.; Yang, B.; Zio, E.; Chen, X. Artificial intelligence for fault diagnosis of rotating machinery: A review. *Mech. Syst. Signal Process.* **2018**, *108*, 33–47. [CrossRef]
3. Lei, Y.; Zuo, M.J.; He, Z.; Zi, Y. A multidimensional hybrid intelligent method for gear fault diagnosis. *Expert Syst. Appl.* **2010**, *37*, 1419–1430. [CrossRef]
4. Yang, B.S.; Di, X.; Han, T. Random forests classifier for machine fault diagnosis. *J. Mech. Sci. Technol.* **2008**, *22*, 1716–1725. [CrossRef]
5. Widodo, A.; Yang, B.S. Support vector machine in machine condition monitoring and fault diagnosis. *Mech. Syst. Signal Process.* **2007**, *21*, 2560–2574. [CrossRef]
6. Witczak, M.; Korbicz, J.; Mrugalski, M.; Patton, R.J. A GMDH neural network-based approach to robust fault diagnosis: Application to the DAMADICS benchmark problem. *Control Eng. Pract.* **2006**, *14*, 671–683. [CrossRef]
7. Hinton, G.E. Learning multiple layers of representation. *Trends Cogn. Sci.* **2007**, *11*, 428–434. [CrossRef] [PubMed]
8. Li, C.; Sanchez, R.V.; Zurita, G.; Cerrada, M.; Cabrera, D.; Vásquez, R.E. Multimodal deep support vector classification with homologous features and its application to gearbox fault diagnosis. *Neurocomputing* **2015**, *168*, 119–127. [CrossRef]
9. Lu, C.; Wang, Z.Y.; Qin, W.L.; Ma, J. Fault diagnosis of rotary machinery components using a stacked denoising autoencoder-based health state identification. *Signal Process.* **2017**, *130*, 377–388. [CrossRef]
10. Zhao, R.; Yan, R.; Chen, Z.; Mao, K.; Wang, P.; Gao, R.X. Deep learning and its applications to machine health monitoring. *Mech. Syst. Signal Process.* **2019**, *115*, 213–237. [CrossRef]
11. Khan, S.; Yairi, T. A review on the application of deep learning in system health management. *Mech. Syst. Signal Process.* **2018**, *107*, 241–265. [CrossRef]
12. Shao, H.; Jiang, H.; Zhang, H.; Duan, W.; Liang, T.; Wu, S. Rolling bearing fault feature learning using improved convolutional deep belief network with compressed sensing. *Mech. Syst. Signal Process.* **2018**, *100*, 743–765. [CrossRef]
13. Malhotra, P.; Ramakrishnan, A.; Anand, G.; Vig, L.; Agarwal, P.; Shroff, G. LSTM-based Encoder-Decoder for Multi-sensor Anomaly Detection. *arXiv* **2016**, arXiv:1607.00148.
14. Zhang, S.; Zhang, S.; Wang, B.; Habetler, T.G. Deep Learning Algorithms for Bearing Fault Diagnostics—A Comprehensive Review. *IEEE Access* **2020**, *8*, 29857–29881. [CrossRef]
15. Zhang, W.; Peng, G.; Li, C.; Chen, Y.; Zhang, Z. A New Deep Learning Model for Fault Diagnosis with Good Anti-Noise and Domain Adaptation Ability on Raw Vibration Signals. *Sensors* **2017**, *17*, 425. [CrossRef]
16. Zhang, W.; Li, C.; Peng, G.; Chen, Y.; Zhang, Z. A deep convolutional neural network with new training methods for bearing fault diagnosis under noisy environment and different working load. *Mech. Syst. Signal Process.* **2018**, *100*, 439–453. [CrossRef]
17. Shenfield, A.; Howarth, M. A Novel Deep Learning Model for the Detection and Identification of Rolling Element-Bearing Faults. *Sensors* **2020**, *20*, 5112. [CrossRef]
18. Zhuang, Z.; Lv, H.; Xu, J.; Huang, Z.; Qin, W. A Deep Learning Method for Bearing Fault Diagnosis through Stacked Residual Dilated Convolutions. *Appl. Sci.* **2019**, *9*, 1823. [CrossRef]
19. Hendriks, J.; Dumond, P.; Knox, D. Towards better benchmarking using the CWRU bearing fault dataset. *Mech. Syst. Signal Process.* **2022**, *169*, 108732. [CrossRef]
20. Janssens, O.; Slavkovikj, V.; Vervisch, B.; Stockman, K.; Loccufier, M.; Verstockt, S.; Van de Walle, R.; Van Hoecke, S. Convolutional Neural Network Based Fault Detection for Rotating Machinery. *J. Sound Vib.* **2016**, *377*, 331–345. [CrossRef]
21. Jing, L.; Zhao, M.; Li, P.; Xu, X. A convolutional neural network based feature learning and fault diagnosis method for the condition monitoring of gearbox. *Measurement* **2017**, *111*, 1–10. [CrossRef]

22. Zhao, D.; Wang, T.; Chu, F. Deep convolutional neural network based planet bearing fault classification. *Comput. Ind.* **2019**, *107*, 59–66. [CrossRef]
23. Han, T.; Liu, C.; Yang, W.; Jiang, D. A novel adversarial learning framework in deep convolutional neural network for intelligent diagnosis of mechanical faults. *Knowl.-Based Syst.* **2019**, *165*, 474–487. [CrossRef]
24. Guo, L.; Lei, Y.; Xing, S.; Yan, T.; Li, N. Deep Convolutional Transfer Learning Network: A New Method for Intelligent Fault Diagnosis of Machines With Unlabeled Data. *IEEE Trans. Ind. Electron.* **2019**, *66*, 7316–7325. [CrossRef]
25. Yang, B.; Lei, Y.; Jia, F.; Xing, S. An intelligent fault diagnosis approach based on transfer learning from laboratory bearings to locomotive bearings. *Mech. Syst. Signal Process.* **2019**, *122*, 692–706. [CrossRef]
26. Ioffe, S.; Szegedy, C. Batch Normalization: Accelerating Deep Network Training by Reducing Internal Covariate Shift. *arXiv* **2015**, arXiv:cs.LG/1502.03167.
27. Huang, L.; Qin, J.; Zhou, Y.; Zhu, F.; Liu, L.; Shao, L. Normalization techniques in training DNNs: Methodology, analysis and application. *arXiv* **2020**, arXiv:2009.12836.
28. LeCun, Y.A.; Bottou, L.; Orr, G.B.; Müller, K.R. Efficient backprop. In *Neural networks: Tricks of the Trade*; Springer: Berlin/Heidelberg, Germany, 2012; pp. 9–48. [CrossRef]
29. Huang, L.; Zhou, L.Z.Y.; Zhu, F.; Liu, L.; Shao, L. An investigation into the stochasticity of batch whitening. In Proceedings of the IEEE Computer Society Conference on Computer Vision and Pattern Recognition, Seattle, WA, USA, 14–19 June 2020; pp. 6438–6447. [CrossRef]
30. Huang, L.; Yang, D.; Lang, B.; Deng, J. Decorrelated Batch Normalization. In Proceedings of the IEEE Conference on Computer Vision and Pattern Recognition (CVPR), Salt Lake City, UT, USA, 18–23 June 2018.
31. Ye, C.; Evanusa, M.; He, H.; Mitrokhin, A.; Goldstein, T.; Yorke, J.A.; Fermuller, C.; Aloimonos, Y. Network Deconvolution. In Proceedings of the International Conference on Learning Representations, Addis Ababa, Ethiopia, 26–30 April 2020.
32. Ince, T.; Kiranyaz, S.; Eren, L.; Askar, M.; Gabbouj, M. Real-Time Motor Fault Detection by 1-D Convolutional Neural Networks. *IEEE Trans. Ind. Electron.* **2016**, *63*, 7067–7075. [CrossRef]
33. Case Western Reserve University Bearing Data Center. Case Western Reserve University Bearing Data Center Website. Available online: https://engineering.case.edu/bearingdatacenter (accessed on 5 April 2022).
34. Scherer, D.; Müller, A.; Behnke, S. Evaluation of pooling operations in convolutional architectures for object recognition. In Proceedings of the International Conference on Artificial Neural Networks, Thessaloniki, Greece, 15–18 September 2010; pp. 92–101.
35. He, K.; Zhang, X.; Ren, S.; Sun, J. Deep Residual Learning for Image Recognition. In Proceedings of the 2016 IEEE Conference on Computer Vision and Pattern Recognition (CVPR), Las Vegas, NV, USA, 27–30 June 2016; pp. 770–778. [CrossRef]
36. Huang, G.; Liu, Z.; van der Maaten, L.; Weinberger, K.Q. Densely Connected Convolutional Networks. In Proceedings of the IEEE Conference on Computer Vision and Pattern Recognition (CVPR), Las Vegas, NV, USA, 27–30 June 2016.
37. Xie, S.; Girshick, R.; Dollar, P.; Tu, Z.; He, K. Aggregated Residual Transformations for Deep Neural Networks. In Proceedings of the IEEE Conference on Computer Vision and Pattern Recognition (CVPR), Las Vegas, NV, USA, 27–30 June 2016.
38. He, K.; Gkioxari, G.; Dollar, P.; Girshick, R. Mask R-CNN. In Proceedings of the IEEE International Conference on Computer Vision (ICCV), Venice, Italy, 22–29 October 2017.
39. Desjardins, G.; Simonyan, K.; Pascanu, R.; Kavukcuoglu, K. Natural Neural Networks. In Proceedings of the NIPS'15: 28th International Conference on Neural Information Processing Systems, Montreal, QC, Canada, 7–12 December 2015; Volume 2, pp. 2071–2079.
40. Luo, P. Learning Deep Architectures via Generalized Whitened Neural Networks. In Proceedings of the 34th International Conference on Machine Learning, Sydney, Australia, 6–11 August 2017; Volume 70, pp. 2238–2246.
41. Huang, L.; Zhou, Y.; Zhu, F.; Liu, L.; Shao, L. Iterative Normalization: Beyond Standardization Towards Efficient Whitening. In Proceedings of the IEEE/CVF Conference on Computer Vision and Pattern Recognition (CVPR), Long Beach, CA, USA, 15–20 June 2019.
42. Kingma, D.P.; Ba, J. Adam: A Method for Stochastic Optimization. In Proceedings of the International Conference on Learning Representations (ICLR), San Diego, CA, USA, 7–9 May 2015. [CrossRef]

applied sciences

MDPI

Review

Is the Artificial Pollination of Walnut Trees with Drones Able to Minimize the Presence of *Xanthomonas arboricola* pv. *juglandis*? A Review

Ioannis Manthos [1], Thomas Sotiropoulos [2] and Ioannis Vagelas [3,*]

[1] Department of Nut Trees, Institute of Plant Breeding & Genetic Resources, Hellenic Agricultural Organization (ELGO)-DIMITRA, Neo Krikello, 35100 Lamia, Greece; jmanthos@elgo.gr
[2] Department of Deciduous Fruit Trees, Institute of Plant Breeding & Genetic Resources, Hellenic Agricultural Organization (ELGO)-DIMITRA, 59200 Naoussa, Greece; thsotiropoulos@elgo.gr
[3] Laboratory of Plant Pathology, Department of Agriculture Crop Production and Rural Environment, School of Agricultural Sciences, University of Thessaly, 38446 Volos, Greece
* Correspondence: vagelas@uth.gr

Abstract: Walnut (*Juglans regia* L.) is a monoecious species and although it exhibits self-compatibility, it presents incomplete overlap of pollen shed and female receptivity. Thus, cross-pollination is prerequisite for optimal fruit production. Cross-pollination can occur naturally by wind, insects, artificially, or by hand. Pollen has been recognized as one possible pathway for *Xanthomonas arboricola* pv. *juglandis* infection, a pathogenic bacterium responsible for walnut blight disease. Other than the well-known cultural and chemical control practices, artificial pollination technologies with the use of drones could be a successful tool for walnut blight disease management in orchards. Drones may carry pollen and release it over crops or mimic the actions of bees and other pollinators. Although this new pollination technology could be regarded as a promising tool, pollen germination and knowledge of pollen as a potential pathway for the dissemination of bacterial diseases remain crucial information for the development and production of aerial pollinator robots for walnut trees. Thus, our purpose was to describe a pollination model with fundamental components, including the identification of the "core" pollen microbiota, the use of drones for artificial pollination as a successful tool for managing walnut blight disease, specifying an appropriate flower pollination algorithm, design of an autonomous precision pollination robot, and minimizing the average errors of flower pollination algorithm parameters through machine learning and meta-heuristic algorithms.

Keywords: cross-pollination; *Juglans regia*; literature review; self-compatibility; walnut blight disease; aerial pollination; artificial pollination technologies; pollination drone

Citation: Manthos, I.; Sotiropoulos, T.; Vagelas, I. Is the Artificial Pollination of Walnut Trees with Drones Able to Minimize the Presence of *Xanthomonas arboricola* pv. *juglandis*? A Review. *Appl. Sci.* **2024**, *14*, 2732. https://doi.org/10.3390/app14072732

Academic Editor: Luis Javier Garcia Villalba

Received: 14 January 2024
Revised: 15 March 2024
Accepted: 19 March 2024
Published: 25 March 2024

1. Introduction

The process of pollination involves the transfer of pollen grains from the anther, the male portion of a flower, to the female part (stigma) of the same or another plant. There are two types of pollination: (i) self-pollination (autogamy), in which pollen is deposited on the stigma of the same or another flower on the same plant; and (ii) cross-pollination (allogamy), in which pollen is transferred from one plant to the flower of a genetically different plant or cultivar. Walnut trees are self-compatible, but they require cross-pollination with another walnut tree to produce nuts due to being protandrous, meaning that the male flowers mature—release pollen—before the female flowers become receptive, and pollen shedding occurs before female bloom begins, or being protogynous, meaning that the female flower begins opening—become receptive—prior to pollen shedding. Cross-pollination involves transferring pollen from the male flowers of one walnut tree to the female flowers of another. This can occur naturally, with the help of the wind (wind-blown pollen) or insects such as bees, or artificially through the process of hand pollination [1].

On walnut trees, the pollen is produced in catkins, which may also be colonized with *Xanthomonas arboricola* pv. *juglandis*, the causative agent of walnut blight disease [2,3]. Mainly the disease can affect the leaves, stems, and nuts of the tree, leading to reduced yield and poor-quality nuts. *Xanthomonas arboricola* pv. *juglandis* is primarily spread by water, either through rain or irrigation, and can be more severe during warm and wet weather [4,5].

Once the bacterium enters the tree tissues, it can survive and spread within the tree through the sap. To prevent and control *X. arboricola* pv. *juglandis*, farmers can use a combination of cultural and chemical control measures. This may include removing infected plant material, managing irrigation practices to reduce water on the foliage, and applying copper-based fungicides during the dormant season or at the first signs of infection. Here, it is important to note that the overuse of chemical control measures can lead to the development of resistant strains of the bacterium, so it is important to use a holistic approach to disease management that incorporates a variety of methods. Additionally, early detection and rapid response to infected trees can help to limit the spread of the disease to other trees in the orchard.

Research has shown that inoculum of *X. arboricola* pv. *juglandis* is also disseminated through pollen [3,6]. This evidence-based early detection of developmental-behavioral problems from primary infection of *X. arboricola* pv. *juglandis* in symptomless plant materials, such as catkins and pollen, should be considered besides that in symptomatic materials (leaves, fruit, and other plant debris).

Pathogenic bacteria and pollen are two distinct biological entities that are not directly related to each other. While pathogenic bacteria and pollen are not directly related, they can sometimes interact in certain situations. For example, pollen can sometimes serve as a carrier for pathogenic bacteria. Pollen of *Actinidia* spp. is a good substrate for *Pseudomonas syringae* pv. *actinidiae* colonization, survival, and a pathway for its spread [7]. Therefore, pollen may be a conduit for the spread of *P. syringae* pv. *actinidiae* and kiwifruit bacterial canker [7]. Further, pollen dispersal has been presented for *Erwinia amylovora* of pome fruit [8] and for *X. arboricola* pv. *juglandis* of walnut [9,10]. Moreover, pollen was recognized as a possible pathway for *X. arboricola* pv. *juglandis*, although further studies were suggested to confirm if pollen could spread the pathogen [3]. Viable pathogenic bacteria such as *X. arboricola* pv. *juglandis* have often been isolated from pollen, and infected pollen also represents a potential route of introduction into healthy walnut groves even in case of mechanical pollination [3,6]. Walnut cv. Chandler and cv. Serr results showed that pollen was recognized as a possible pathway for *X. arboricola* pv. *juglandis* [3].

Therefore, the survival of the bacterium *X. arboricola* pv. *juglandis* in catkin buds and catkins should be checked before the bacterium overwinters in blighted leaf and catkin buds. When water carries the bacteria to the leaves and stigmatic surfaces of the flowers, blight spreads from these reservoirs. When catkins open and staminate flowers release pollen, the disease may also spread through the air. Contaminated pollen may be carried by wind and deposited on any young growing parts of trees [4].

Artificial pollination technologies have been developed to address various challenges in natural pollination, including the issue of contaminated pollen or contributing to possible disease outbreaks from contaminated pollen [11,12]. Artificial pollination systems have been developed to supplement natural pollination and provide yield security even in poor pollination scenarios. These technologies include various methods for pollen collection and application, such as hand pollination, handheld and vehicle-mounted devices, unmanned aerial vehicles (UAVs), and robotic and autonomous pollinators. These systems have been found to perform adequately for certain crops, including kiwifruit, olive, date palm, walnut, and tomato [13,14].

Moreover, artificial pollination technologies have seen significant advancements, with the integration of machine learning and artificial intelligence (AI) playing a crucial role in the development of innovative solutions for future farming. Especially, AI and machine learning are being integrated into pollination technologies to develop autonomous pollination systems [15,16]. Based on the above, researchers are developing various drone-based pollination technologies, such as the use of tiny drones equipped with artificial intelligence to autonomously navigate and carry pollen between plants [17,18].

In our view, the parameters are important and will be further analyzed in this review paper. Further, while pollen-mediated transmission of bacterial pathogens has been suggested for *Xanthomonas arboricola* pv. *juglandis*, we will try to answer what are the advantages of pollination drones and how they can help to prevent or reduce the risk of walnut blight disease. In the end, we have designed a path-planning algorithm for a pollination robot that involves determining the disease inoculum and an optimal route for the robot to pollinate flowers efficiently.

2. Walnut Blight Prevention

Walnut Blight and Conditions

Typically, the cycles of walnut blight bacteria are dependent upon weather conditions and rainfall during the growing season. Infrequent rainfall during the spring may lead to monocyclic progress, while frequent spring rainfall tends to favor polycyclic disease epidemics. Rainfalls during late spring (after leaf growth) have been reported to favor the spread of *X. arboricola* pv. *juglandis* bacterium, which causes serious damage to trees and is responsible for significant crop losses, which can reach more than 50% of nut drop [19].

All aerial walnut organs, including catkins, female flowers, leaves, and fruit, are infected [3]. Necrotic lesions on the fruit, twigs, and foliage are characteristic disease symptoms. Leaf lesions consist of small water-soaked spots, surrounded by chlorotic halos that extend to become brown necrotic lesions. Fruit lesions begin as tiny, water-soaked spots and develop into pericarp and inner nut tissue necrosis, which results in early fruit drop. After shell hardening, infections often only impact the epicarp [20].

Cankers serve as a source of inoculum for leaves and nutlet infections [4,21,22]. Populations of *X. arboricola* pv. *juglandis* found on dormant buds serve as the primary inoculum for nut infections [21]. Tissues that have recently been infected can act as secondary sources of inoculum for the pathogen. Pollen released from infected catkins plays a role in pathogen dissemination [2,21]. The bacterium is transmitted through moisture, particularly through the combined action of wind and rain [23]. The cultivars Chandler and Vina exhibit significant susceptibility to *X. arboricola* pv. *juglandis*, thus demonstrating the potential of these cultivars to be infected with *X. arboricola* pv. *juglandis* under conditions favorable for the disease [5,21,24]. The terminal fruitfulness cultivars Milotai, Marbot, Sibisel, and Ronde de Montignac and the lateral fruitfulness cultivars Chandler, Sunland, and Techama were found to be highly susceptible cultivars, making it possible to serve as host responses to bacterial blight infections at different leaf and fruit growth stages [20].

Overall, the degree of infection caused by *X. arboricola* pv. *juglandis* bacterium depends on: (a) the quantity of the pathogen present in individual catkin buds and catkins (inoculum); (b) the quantity of walnut blight cankers present on certain walnut varieties; (c) the environmental conditions, such as rain, which play a significant role in spreading bacteria and aiding infection; and (d) the variety, with early leafing varieties being most severely affected.

Besides the favorable conditions for the disease, research suggests that pollen released from infected catkins plays a role in pathogen dissemination [21,22]. Aerial dissemination of infected pollen from diseased catkins may also transmit the bacterium *X. arboricola* pv. *juglandis* to pistillate flowers. However, this source of inoculum might be region specific [25] or due to different origins of the propagation material [3]. Up to date new evidence provides data that infections depend on pollen, especially in walnut orchards with varieties for which the catkins emerge before the pistillate flowers, i.e., cv. Chandler. Indeed, pollen is important for spreading bacteria and aiding infection [3]. Even more, the isolation of *X. arboricola* pv. *juglandis* in late winter-early spring led to the finding that the primary inoculum is present in buds (overwintering), catkins, and female flowers [4,21].

So, it is crucial to select walnut varieties resistant to bacterial blight and to implement good orchard management techniques, such as pruning and fertilization, to keep trees healthy and less susceptible to disease. Moreover, one should be aware of pollen released from infected catkins, which contributes to the spread of the pathogen, *X. arboricola* pv. *juglandis*. If bacterial blight is present in the orchard, it may be necessary to apply fungicides or use other treatments to prevent the disease from spreading, such as artificial techniques for cross-pollination, which probably directly causes or prevents bacterial blight in walnut trees. Apart from the infection of catkins with *X. arboricola* pv. *juglandis*, which plays a role in pathogen dissemination, walnuts produce pollen that is desiccation intolerant. Pollen that does not have homeostatic mechanisms for maintaining a constant water content dies rapidly after opening of the anther or after pollen dispersal [26]. The previously described 'partially hydrated' or, more precisely, desiccation-sensitive pollen of this type may serve as the connection point with *X. arboricola* pv. *juglandis* when the environmental conditions such as temperature and relative humidity affect pollination processes or are highly favorable for pathogen growth in plants [26].

However, the relationship between this pollen property and walnut blight disease during the flower cycle when the daily temperature and leaf wetness are more favorable for *X. arboricola* pv. *juglandis* has not been supported with detailed experimental data. The epiphytic colonization of the stigmas of the kiwifruit flower after inoculation by pollen contaminated with GFPuv-labeled *Pseudomonas syringae* pv. *actinidae* (Psa), which is responsible for the bacterial canker of the kiwifruit, indicated that Psa is often transmitted to the stigma by pollen contamination [27]. Further, it is well known that plants employ sexual mimicry, and flowers mimic the mating signals of their pollinator insects. Based on the mimicry phenomenon, researchers demonstrated that fire blight, a serious disease of pear and apple trees, requires the combination of warm temperatures, open blossoms, and wet weather. The disease spreads quickly from flower to flower through wind, water, and pollinating insects. So, the specific mimic odors that serve as a tool to enhance honeybee foraging and pollination activities in pear and apple crops spread serious diseases such as a fire blight of pear and apple trees [28,29]. So, concerning walnut blight disease, the fundamental questions are: Is flower/corolla closure linked to a decrease in viability of desiccation-sensitive pollen? Is this disease related to other pollination activities or phenomena such as mimicry or dissemination by wind?

As far as walnut plants are concerned, if pollen serves as a possible pathway for the dissemination of *X. arboricola* pv. *juglandis* and walnut blight disease, to prevent the disease from spreading, apart from fungicides, it is necessary to use artificial techniques for cross-pollination, as mentioned above, with uninfected pollen (pollen that is free from the above pathogens or diseases).

3. Walnut Buds: Bloom and Pollination Events—Cross-Pollination

Walnuts are monoecious and have male and female flowers on the same tree. Male flowers are formed in structures called catkins. They develop directly on the prior year's growth and are easy to identify by eye. At leaf out, the preformed shoot develops, and compound leaves start to grow before the pistillate (female) flowers form. This explains why walnut cultivars are indicated by both their leaf out date and bloom date. Female flowers are only receptive to pollination for a short time. In particular, pollen shed from staminate (male) flowers during anthesis is spread by wind (wind-blown pollen) and remains viable for a short time, generally up to 48 h. As already mentioned, walnut is self-compatible but has adapted a mechanism called dichogamy to reduce the degree of inbreeding. Walnuts are classified as heterodichogamous; however, the majority of commercial walnut cultivars, such as Chandler and Serr, are protandrous, meaning that the male flowers mature and pollen shed occurs before the female bloom begins. So, protandrous cultivars, i.e., Serr, may be large contributors to protogynous cultivar pollination. In most walnut-growing regions, dichogamy is the reason for including pollinizers in orchards. Moreover, in certain cultivars, such as Serr, excessive pollen on pistillate flowers (too much pollen) has been identified to be the cause of pistillate flower abortion [1].

During cross-pollination, pollen is transferred from the male reproductive organ (stamen) of one plant to the female reproductive organ (pistil) of another plant of the same species, resulting in fertilization and the production of seeds. In the case of nut trees like walnuts, cross-pollination is necessary for the trees to produce nuts. Cross-pollination can occur naturally, through the action of wind or insects such as bees, or it can be performed artificially through hand pollination, in which pollen is manually transferred from one tree to another. Natural cross-pollination can be affected by factors such as the proximity of the trees, the timing of flowering, and the presence of pollinators.

Walnuts require cross-pollination for optimal nut production. Cross-pollination increases the genetic diversity of the trees and can lead to larger and more flavorful fruit. However, not all nut tree varieties are compatible for cross-pollination. It is important to choose compatible varieties and to plant them close enough for natural cross-pollination to occur. In some cases, artificial pollination may be necessary to ensure adequate pollination and fruit set. This is especially true in orchards where natural pollinators are scarce or when the weather is unfavorable for pollination. Artificial pollination involves manually transferring pollen from the male flowers of one tree to the female flowers of another. As mentioned above, walnut trees probably require cross-pollination with another walnut tree to produce nuts and minimize the risk of bacterial contamination. This can occur naturally, artificially with air vehicles, or through the process of hand pollination or the design of specific aerial pollination systems for walnut trees.

4. Artificial Pollination—Artificial Pollination Technology

Pollination is critical for many crops for successful production. To avoid pollination failure due to weather events, bloom asynchrony, insects, and wind-based pollination systems, artificial pollination systems are required that can provide yield security for crops [30].

There are various reasons for resorting to artificial pollination, including:

1. Crop yield enhancement: In agriculture, artificial pollination is sometimes employed to increase crop yields. This can be particularly important for crops where natural pollination may be insufficient [31].
2. Control of pollination: Artificial pollination allows for precise control over the pollination process. This is useful in hybrid seed production, where specific traits can be selected [32].
3. Overcoming pollination challenges: Some crops may face challenges with natural pollination due to factors like low insect activity, unfavorable weather conditions, i.e., wind, or geographic isolation. Artificial pollination can overcome these challenges [33].
4. Biotechnological research: In scientific research, artificial pollination can be used to study plant genetics, breeding, and other aspects of plant biology [34].

Artificial pollination technology involves various methods and tools designed to facilitate the pollination process in plants by assisting the natural transfer of pollen. Some of the technologies and techniques used for artificial pollination include:

1. Drones: Unmanned aerial vehicles (UAVs), or drones, equipped with special devices can be used for pollination. These devices may carry pollen and release it over crops, i.e., walnut trees, or mimic the actions of bees and other pollinators [35].
2. Robotic pollinators: Small robots designed to mimic the behaviors of natural pollinators can navigate through crops, transferring pollen between flowers. These robots are often equipped with cameras and sensors to identify and locate flowers [36].
3. Spraying devices: Some systems involve the use of sprayers to disperse pollen over crops. These devices can be mounted on tractors or other vehicles, releasing pollen in a controlled manner [37].

4. Electrostatic pollination: This method uses an electrostatic charge to adhere pollen to flowers. The charged pollen is attracted to the stigma, increasing the chances of successful pollination [38].
5. Vibrational devices: Certain crops respond well to vibrational stimulation, which can be achieved through devices that vibrate the flowers, causing the release of pollen [39].
6. Artificial flowers: In controlled environments like greenhouses, artificial flowers containing pollen can be placed strategically to enhance pollination [40].
7. Automated pollination systems: Some systems use automated robotic arms or other mechanical devices to transfer pollen between flowers. These systems can be programmed to work efficiently and quickly [41].

The development of artificial pollination technologies is driven by the need to address challenges such as declining bee populations, environmental factors, and the increasing demand for efficient and reliable pollination in agriculture. Using VOS viewer mapping software (version 1.6.20) and the Scopus bibliographic database based on the search strategy criteria "Artificial and Pollination and Technologies" (Figure 1) revealed that the above-mentioned technologies show promise, but they are still in the early stages of development (co-keyword: "artificial intelligence", Figure 1) and may vary in effectiveness (co-keyword: "optimization", Figure 1), depending on the specific crop, environmental conditions, and probably other parameters such as the disease inoculum [42–46].

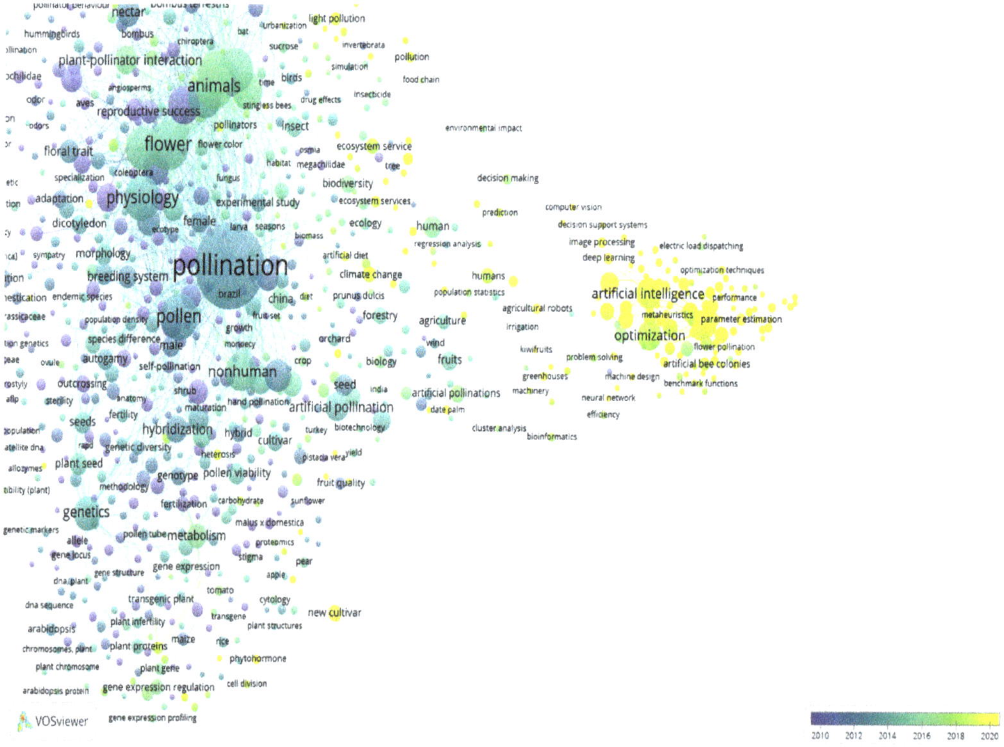

Figure 1. Co-keyword network visualization based on "Artificial" and "Pollination and Technologies".

Furthermore, it is important to note that while artificial pollination can be a useful tool in certain situations, such as for walnut trees, apart from robotics (co-keyword: "artificial robots", Figure 2), modeling (co-keyword: "MATLAB", Figure 2), and agriculture drones (co-keyword: "agriculture drones", Figure 2), pollen germination (co-keyword: "pollen germination", Figure 2) and knowledge of pollen as a possible pathway for the dissemination of bacterial diseases of other crops, such as pear and kiwifruit plants (co-keywords: "pear" and "Actinidia deliciosa", Figure 2), remain crucial information for the design and manufacture of aerial pollinator robots for walnut trees.

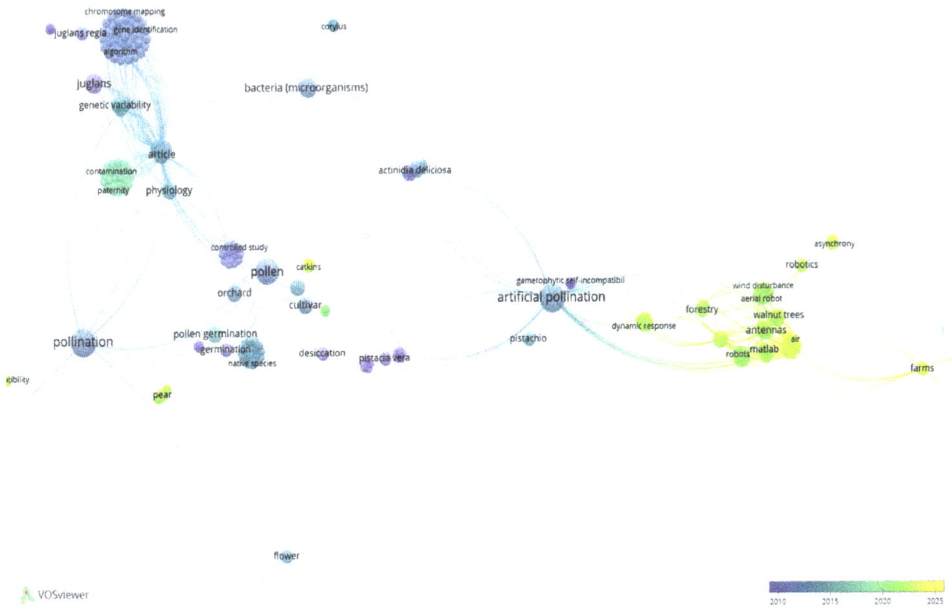

Figure 2. Co-keyword network visualization based on "Artificial" and "Pollination and Technologies and Walnut".

The keywords "Artificial" and "Pollination and Technologies and Walnut" are presented as 13 clusters defined by 310 keywords (items), which contribute to a total 100%, as presented in Figure 2.

Cluster 1 (Figure 3) is defined by 52 keywords (items), with keywords including "MATLAB", "Adams MATLAB cosimulation", "computational fluid dynamics", "cosimulation", "flight simulators", "flying robots", "quad rotors", "aerial robot", "robotics", "agricultural robots", "system stability", "vibration analysis", "vibration transmissibility", "software testing", "antennas", "artificial pollinations", "fruit production", " population growth", "population statistics", "walnut pollinator", "crop growth", "wind disturbance", etc.

Cluster 2 (Figure 4) is defined by 45 keywords (items), with keywords including "algorithms", "bacterial artificial chromosome", "chromosomes, artificial, bacterial", "contig mapping", "expressed sequence tags", "genome analysis", "genotyping techniques", "heterozygosity", "homozygosity", "physical map", "plant genome", "plant growth", "pollen sources", "population genetic structure", "sequence analysis, DNA", "single nucleotide polymorphism", "vegetative propagation", etc.

Based on the above observations in clusters 1 and 2 (Figures 3 and 4), "artificial pollination technologies" include knowledge of: (a) mechanical pollination technology, i.e., aerial vehicles (UAVs), robotics, and autonomous pollinators (hardware) and basic simulation methodologies for controlling a quadrotor (software); and (b) Mother Nature's pollination technology, i.e., pollen (pollen germination), crops (cultivars), and microorganisms (bacteria).

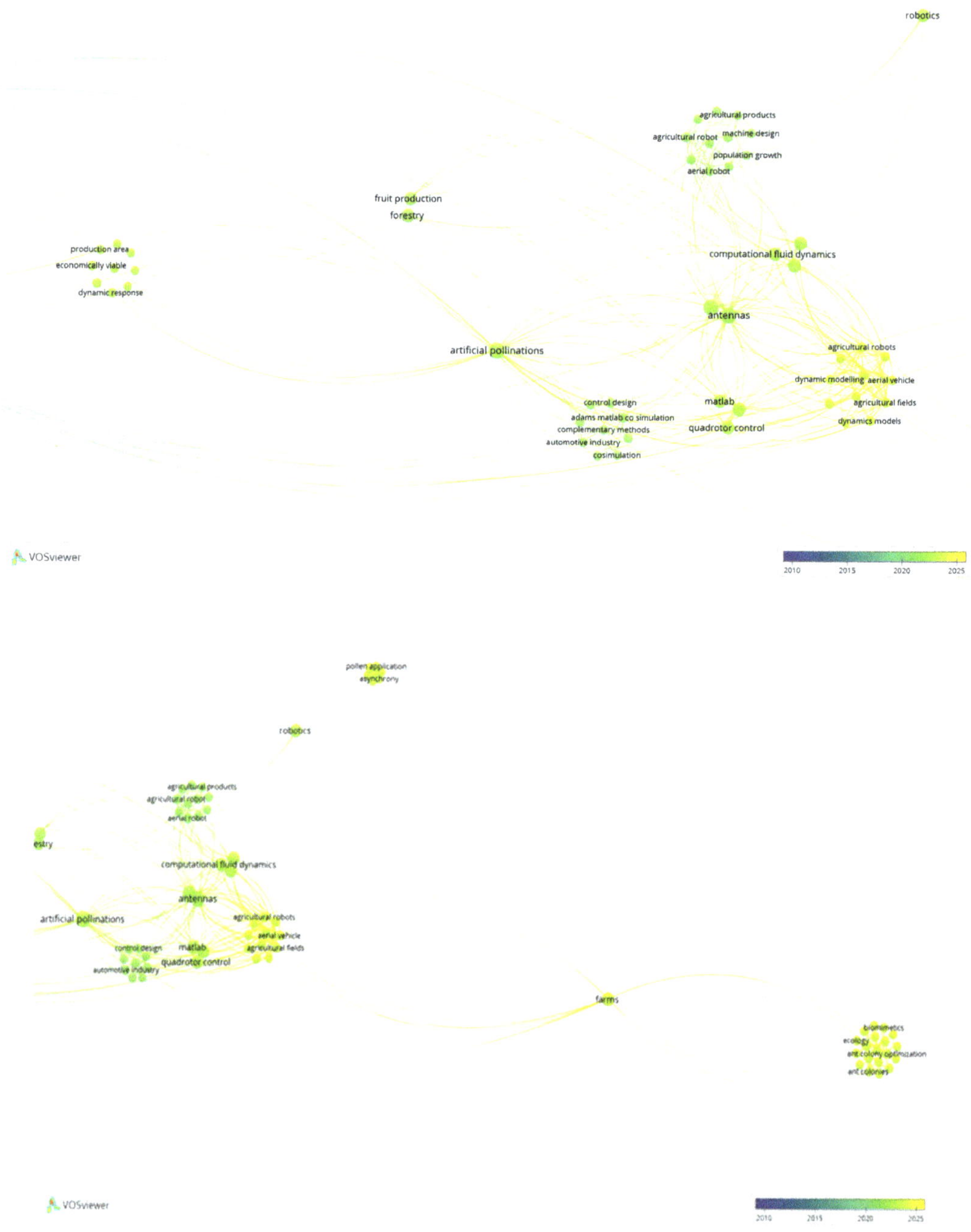

Figure 3. Co-keyword network visualization based on "Artificial" and "Pollination and Technologies and Walnut". Results are based on Cluster 1, which is defined by 52 keywords (items).

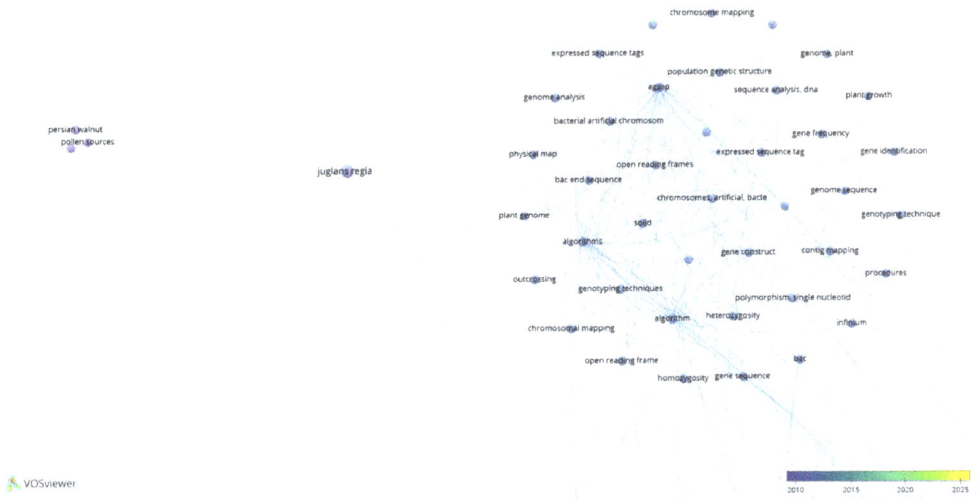

Figure 4. Co-keyword network visualization based on "Artificial" and "Pollination and Technologies and Walnut". Results are based on Cluster 2, which is defined by 45 keywords (items).

Based on simulation methodologies for controlling a quadrotor, MATLAB provides a solution for the standard flower pollination algorithm, with more information on nature optimization algorithms provided in a book entitled *Nature-Inspired Optimization Algorithms*. The flower pollination algorithm (FPA) is a type of optimization algorithm based on the behavior of flowering plants [47]. It is a population-based metaheuristic algorithm that has been modified and hybridized to perform efficiently across a range of optimization problems. One such modification involves the integration of the bee pollinator concept, which has shown promising results in solving the data clustering problem [48]. A modified version of the FPA, which utilizes the crossover technique for resolving multidimensional knapsack problems, was also developed [49]. Keeping the abovementioned facts in view, we believe that an algorithm such as the FPA should be used for a pollination robot to prevent or reduce the risk of walnut blight disease.

In addition to the FPA, the bacterial microbiota associated with flower pollen is influenced by the pollen type and exhibits a significant degree of diversity and species specificity [49]. So, for microbe–pollen interactions, presumably we must know the sequencing of 16S rRNA gene amplicon libraries to identify dominant microbial phyla and the core microbiome of pollen from different walnut cultivars. Since pollen-associated bacteria may have a potential impact on walnut blight disease, pollen microbial communities from different walnut cultivars need to be identified. This information could play a significant role in the flower pollination algorithm and development of a strategy that leads to new valuable information on walnut cultivar microbe–pollen interactions during pollination.

Moreover, considering the algorithm-based approach, it is necessary to provide criteria for the aerial robot path. Basic simulation steps helped to determine pollen streams under a quadrotor unmanned aerial vehicle [35]. These steps were the following:

1. Design and fabrication of quadrotor components For the quadrotor to be able to carry and distribute pollen over trees, the quadrotor components needed to be selected correctly, i.e., the body size was chosen based on the pollen tank. The objective of the quadrotor was to pollinate, so the tank was equipped with a nozzle with four holes to allow pollen to fall uniformly. It was recommended that the propulsion system use a motor with a lower current. The electronic device contained various sensors, such as a compass, a global positioning system (GPS), a barometer, and connections for the flight control system [35].

2. Modeling and Control Computational fluid dynamic (CFD) software was used to simulate the airflow beneath the UAV. This simulation assisted in identifying the pollen streams under the robot so that the released pollen could be directed toward the target trees. The quadrotor controller was designed and simulated in MATLAB to ensure system stability [35].
3. Pollination of walnut trees Different mixtures of pollen diluted with talcum powder were distributed over various groups of trees using the quadrotor. The results achieved on the trees were measured after a few months to evaluate the benefits of the proposed system [35].

In the context of pollination supply modeling, MATLAB is utilized to predict pollination services like pollinator visitation rates, fruit set, and pollen deposition [50]. These predictions can help to optimize pollination services in the field and support the development of effective agri-environmental schemes or conservation initiatives. Bayesian models, particularly in MATLAB, are pivotal in pollination research for various applications [51]. These models aid in reconstructing plant–pollinator networks from observational data by separating structure from noise, estimating the expected number of visits between specific plant–pollinator species pairs, and predicting pollinator abundance under different scenarios. In summary, research shows that the integration of Bayesian models with MATLAB provides a powerful tool for researchers to analyze plant–pollinator interactions, predict pollinator abundance, optimize pollination services, and make informed decisions regarding conservation strategies and agricultural practices based on reliable data-driven insights [50,51].

5. Machine Learning and Pollination

Machine learning (ML) can play a significant role in the context of pollination, offering innovative solutions and insight to address challenges and optimize pollination processes. Below are several ways in which machine learning is applied to pollination:

1. Predictive modeling: ML algorithms can analyze historical data on pollination success, environmental conditions, crop yields, and phenology to create predictive models. These models can help to predict optimal times for pollination, considering factors such as weather patterns, bloom asynchrony, and the availability of pollinators [52–54].
2. Automated monitoring: ML-powered monitoring systems can analyze images or sensor data to track the health and development of crops. This real-time monitoring allows for the early detection of issues related to pollination, such as low pollination rates or the presence of pests that could affect pollinators [55,56].
3. Optimizing pollination strategies: Machine learning algorithms can optimize artificial pollination strategies based on a variety of factors [57,58]. These include the type of crop, environmental conditions, and the efficiency of different pollination methods [59,60]. This can lead to more targeted and effective pollination efforts [61].
4. Identification of pollinator behavior: ML can be used to analyze the behavior of natural pollinators, such as bees, by processing video footage or sensor data. Understanding pollinator behavior can provide insight into their preferences, movement patterns, and efficiency in pollinating specific crops [62,63].
5. Genetic analysis: Machine learning techniques can analyze genetic data related to plant characteristics, including traits associated with pollination [64,65]. This information can contribute to breeding programs aimed at developing crops that are more resilient to environmental challenges and more compatible with artificial pollination methods [66,67].
6. Decision support systems: ML-based decision support systems can assist farmers in making informed choices related to pollination strategies. These systems can consider a range of variables and provide recommendations for optimal pollination practices [68,69].

7. Data integration: Machine learning excels at integrating and analyzing large datasets from various sources. In the context of pollination, this can include data on weather conditions, soil quality, plant health, and more. The integrated data can provide a comprehensive understanding of the factors influencing pollination success [70–72].

While machine learning holds great promise for improving pollination processes, it is essential to recognize the importance of interdisciplinary collaboration between machine learning and pollination, as presented by the VOS viewer analysis in Figure 5. Based on Figure 5, up to date knowledge as of 2022 (Figure 5 items with yellow dots) requires: "anatomy and histology", "classification of information", "classification algorithms", "image classification", "neural networks", "population statistics", "robotics", "machine learning", "deep learning", and "meta-heuristic algorithms" (Figure 5, items with yellow dots).

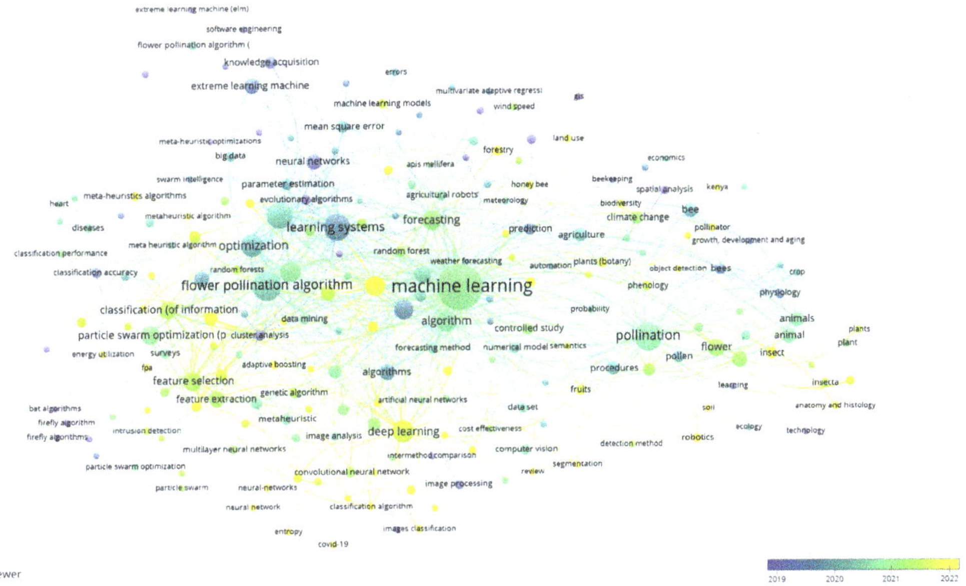

Figure 5. Co-keyword network visualization based on "Machine Learning" and "Pollination".

Even more, using VOS viewer mapping software and the Scopus bibliographic database based on the search strategy criteria "Aerial and Pollination" (Figure 6) revealed that all of the abovementioned criteria or technologies show promise, but they still require important improvements, such as "antennas", "aircraft detection", "aircraft control", "MATLAB", "internet of things", "population diversity", "flower population algorithm", "swarm intelligence algorithm", "learning algorithm", "learning systems", "deep learning", "quadrotor control", "image enhancement", "auxiliary pollination", "supplementary pollination", and "convolutional neural networks" (Figure 6, items with yellow dots).

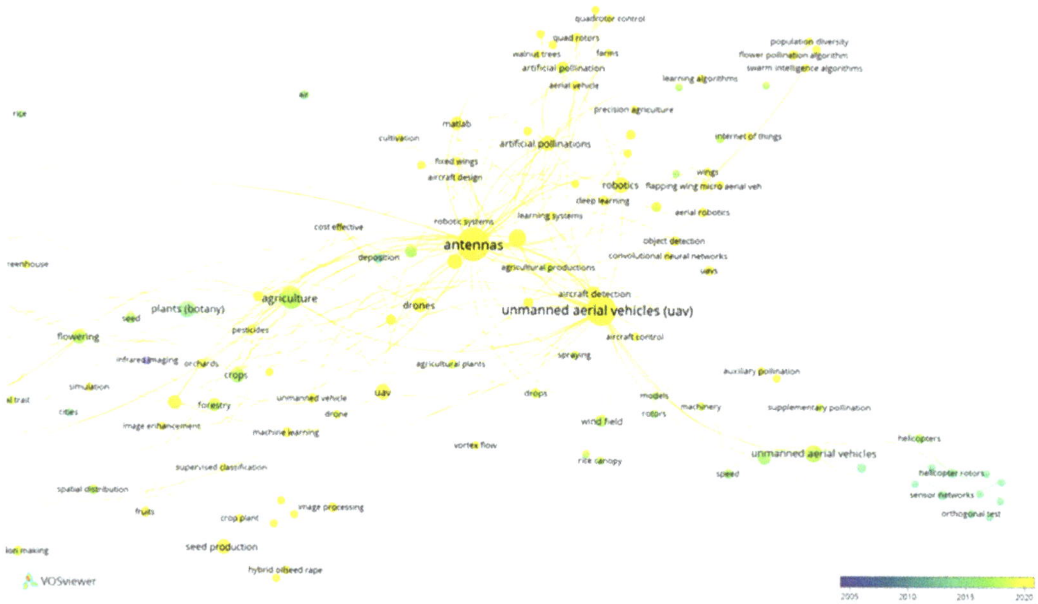

Figure 6. Co-keyword network visualization based on "Aerial" and "Pollination".

6. Walnut Pollination: Model to Prevent or Reduce the Risk of the Walnut Blight Disease (Our View)

Developing a walnut pollination model involves creating a predictive framework that considers various factors influencing the pollination of walnut trees [36,48]. Keeping in mind the success of the walnut pollination model (Figures 1–6) and based on the above paragraphs, we illustrate the following flowchart (6 steps, state of the art flowchart), which provides a general guideline for conducting a state-of-the-art analysis for a pollination robot to prevent or reduce the risk of walnut blight disease. The development of autonomous visual navigation for a flower pollination drone has been presented in a paper published in the journal *Machines* [73]. This technology could enable drones to autonomously approach flowers and perform pollination tasks.

State of the Art Flowchart

1st Step. Walnuts: budbreak, bloom, and pollination growth stages

1.1. Identify spring bud break, leaf emergence, and anthesis growth stages of the walnut cultivars.
1.2. Understand how plants grow and develop during bud break, anthesis, and pollination.
1.3. Understand protandrous and protogynous mechanisms prior to pollen shedding.

2nd Step. Study the bacterial microbiota associated with flower pollen

2.1. Identify the "core" pollen microbiota.
2.2. Compare bacterial abundance and diversity between walnut cultivars.
2.3. Assess the impact of the pollination type on the variability of the flower pollen microbiota.
2.4. Estimate the role of *X. arboricola* pv. *juglandis* in stigma exposed to contaminated pollen.

3rd Step. State of Walnut Pollination – Develop Pollination Algorithms

3.1. Check reservoir cultivars, i.e., Chandler, for the presence of inoculum.

3.2. Check for conditions that encourage the disease to spread, such as moisture, and especially the combined action of wind and rain.
3.3. Check for air-borne inoculum when catkins open.
3.4. Check for pistil-late flowers.
3.5. Collect and store uninfected pollen.

4th Step. State of Walnut Pollination – Develop Pollination Algorithms

4.1. Set genetic algorithm for 'mutation', 'selection', and 'recombination' based on pollen–microbe interaction.
4.2. Use metaheuristic algorithms, which include differential evolution.
4.3. Use the appropriate flower pollination algorithm that is suitable and inspired by the process of pollination.

5th Step. Design of an Autonomous Precision Pollination Robot

5.1. Quadrotor (pollinating drone) to carry pollen grains.
5.2. Pollinating drone to make an ideal delivery system, landing on the pistil of a flower to result in pollination.
5.3. Drone technique would need some refinement in localization, mapping, and control.
5.4. Metaheuristic optimization algorithm to find the best (feasible) solution out of all possible solutions to the pollination optimization problem.

6th Step. Algorithm Optimization

6.1. Analyze historical data on pollination success, environmental conditions, and crop yields (machine learning).
6.2. Tune flower pollination algorithm parameters (formulating the above steps, mainly steps 1 and 2, due to climate change).
6.3. Start the process from step 3 and improve the equipment at steps 4 and 5.

7. Conclusions

Evidence to date is convincing that microbes such as the bacterium *X. arboricola* pv. *juglandis* occur in pollen and influence walnut blight disease. Research shows that *X. arboricola* pv. *juglandis*, the causative agent of walnut blight, can affect the leaves, stems, and nuts of the tree, and even the pollen. In this review, we present a flow diagram of a new artificial pollinator that we assume can reduce the spread of the disease in orchards. As we have seen in this study, we can conclude that the walnut pollination model and walnut blight disease are complex problems that require solutions due to the interaction of several factors. Significant progress in understanding these dynamic processes is reported in the literature utilizing various scientific approaches. Considering the knowledge needed for a solution to overcome this bacterial plant infection, the VOS viewer results suggest that the foundation for a new, more sophisticated and efficient walnut pollination model to prevent or reduce the risk of walnut blight disease is possible. So, the purpose of the ideas presented here was to facilitate a description of such a pollination model with fundamental components, including the identification of the 'core' pollen microbiota, specifying an appropriate flower pollination algorithm, design of an autonomous precision pollination robot, and minimizing the average errors of flower pollination algorithm parameters through machine learning and meta-heuristic algorithms.

Author Contributions: Conceptualization, I.V., I.M. and T.S.; methodology, I.M. and I.V.; software, I.V.; validation, I.M. and I.V.; formal analysis, I.V.; investigation, I.M., I.V. and T.S.; resources, I.V.; data curation, I.M. and I.V.; writing—original draft preparation, I.V, T.S. and I.M.; writing—review and editing, I.V, T.S. and I.M.; visualization, I.V. and I.M.; supervision, I.M., I.V. and T.S.; project administration, I.M. and I.V.; funding acquisition, I.M. and I.V. All authors have read and agreed to the published version of the manuscript.

Funding: This work has received no external funding.

Institutional Review Board Statement: Not applicable.

Informed Consent Statement: Not applicable.

Data Availability Statement: Not applicable.

Conflicts of Interest: The authors declare no conflicts of interest.

References

1. Polito, V.S.; Pinney, K.; Weinbaum, S.; Aradhya, M.K.; Dangl, J.; Yanknin, Y.; Grant, J.A. Walnut pollination dynamics: Pollen flow in walnut orchards. *Acta Hortic.* **2005**, *705*, 465–472. [CrossRef]
2. Ark, P.A. Further evidence of pollen dissemination of walnut blight. *Phytopathology* **1944**, *34*, 329–334.
3. Kałużna, M.; Fischer-Le Saux, M.; Pothier, J.F.; Jacques, M.A.; Obradović, A.; Tavares, F.; Stefani, E. *Xanthomonas arboricola* pv. *juglandis* and pv. *corylina*: Brothers or distant relatives? Genetic clues, epidemiology, and insights for disease management. *Mol. Plant Pathol.* **2021**, *22*, 1481–1499. [CrossRef]
4. Mulrean, E.N.; Schroth, M.N. Ecology of *Xanthomonas campestris* pv. *juglandis* on Persian (English) Walnuts. *Phytopathology* **1982**, *72*, 434–438. [CrossRef]
5. Lang, M.D.; Evans, K. Epidemiology and status of walnut blight in Australia. *J. Plant Pathol.* **2010**, *92*, 49–56.
6. Giovanardi, D.; Bonneau, S.; Gironde, S.; Saux, M.F.; Manceau, C.; Stefani, E. Morphological and genotypic features of *Xanthomonas arboricola* pv. *juglandis* populations from walnut groves in Romagna region, Italy. *Eur. J. Plant Pathol.* **2016**, *145*, 1–16. [CrossRef]
7. Tontou, R.; Giovanardi, D.; Stefani, E. Pollen as a possible pathway for the dissemination of *Pseudomonas syringae* pv. *actinide* and bacterial canker of kiwifruit. *Phytopathol. Mediterr.* **2014**, *53*, 333–339. [CrossRef]
8. Van der Zwet, T.; Bell, R.L. Survival of *Erwinia amylovora* on apple and pear pollen. *Acta Hortic.* **1992**, *338*, 111–112. [CrossRef]
9. Garcin, A.; El-Maataoui, M.; Tichadou, S.; Prunet, J.P.; Ginibre, T.; Penet, C. Walnut blight, new knowledge for an old disease: Summary of research (1995–2000). *Infos-Ctifl* **2001**, *171*, 27–30.
10. Giovanardi, D.; Dallai, D.; Stefani, E. Population features of *Xanthomonas arboricola* pv. *juglandis* and epidemiology of walnut blight in Romagna (Italy). In Proceedings of the Petria 13th Congress of the Mediterranean Phytopathological Union, Rome, Italy, 20–25 June 2010; Volume 20, pp. 96–97.
11. Matsumoto, D.; Shimizu, S.; Shimazaki, A.; Ito, K.; Taira, S. Effects of Self-pollen Contamination in Artificial Pollination on Fruit Set of 'Fuji Murasaki' Akebia trifoliata. *Hortic. J.* **2022**, *91*, 431–436. [CrossRef]
12. Everett, K.; Cohen, D.; Pushparajah, I.; Vergara, M.; Curtis, C.; Larsen, N.; Jia, Y. Heat treatments to kill *Pseudomonas syringae* pv *actinidiae* on contaminated pollen. *N. Z. Plant Prot.* **2012**, *65*, 8–18. [CrossRef]
13. Dingley, A.; Anwar, S.; Kristiansen, P.; Warwick, N.W.; Wang, C.; Sindel, B.M.; Cazzonelli, C.I. Precision Pollination Strategies for Advancing Horticultural Tomato Crop Production. *Agronomy* **2022**, *12*, 518. [CrossRef]
14. Hiraguri, T.; Kimura, T.; Endo, K.; Ohya, T.; Takanashi, T.; Shimizu, H. Shape classification technology of pollinated tomato flowers for robotic implementation. *Sci. Rep.* **2023**, *13*, 2159. [CrossRef] [PubMed]
15. Sánchez-Molina, J.; Rodríguez, F.; Moreno, J.; Sánchez-Hermosilla, J.; Giménez, A. Robotics in greenhouses. Scoping review. *Comput. Electron. Agric.* **2024**, *219*, 108750. [CrossRef]
16. Gudowska, A.; Cwajna, A.; Marjańska, E.; Moroń, D. Pollinators enhance the production of a superior strawberry—A global review and meta-analysis. *Agric. Ecosyst. Environ.* **2024**, *362*, 108815. [CrossRef]
17. Rice, C.R.; McDonald, S.T.; Shi, Y.; Gan, H.; Lee, W.S.; Chen, Y.; Wang, Z. Perception, Path Planning, and Flight Control for a Drone-Enabled Autonomous Pollination System. *Robotics* **2022**, *11*, 144. [CrossRef]
18. Yamada, N.; Hiraguri, T.; Shimizu, H.; Kimura, T.; Shimada, T.; Shibasaki, A.; Takemura, Y. Drone Flight Experiment using RTK Positioning for Pear Pollination. In Proceedings of the 2023 International Conference on Consumer Electronics—Taiwan (ICCE-Taiwan), PingTung, Taiwan, 17–19 July 2023; pp. 655–656. [CrossRef]
19. Chevallier, A.; Bray, O.; Prunet, J.P.; Giraud, M. Factors influencing walnut blight symptoms emergence and development. *Acta Hortic.* **2010**, *861*, 473–478. [CrossRef]
20. Vagelas, I.; Rumbos, C.I.; Tsiantos, J.A. Variation in disease development among persian walnut cultivars, selections and crosses when inoculated with *Xanthomonas arboricola* pv. *juglandis* in Greece. *J. Plant Pathol.* **2012**, *94*, 57–61. [CrossRef]
21. Moragrega, C.; Llorente, I. Effects of leaf wetness duration, temperature, and host phenological stage on infection of walnut by *Xanthomonas arboricola* pv. *juglandis*. *Plants* **2023**, *12*, 2800. [CrossRef]
22. Lindow, S.; Olson, W.; Buchner, R. Colonization of dormant walnut buds by *Xanthomonas arboricola* pv. *juglandis* is predictive of subsequent disease. *Phytopathology* **2014**, *104*, 1163–1174. [CrossRef]
23. Buchner, R.P.; Gilles, C.; Olson, W.H.; Adaskaveg, J.E.; Lindow, S.E.; Koutsoukis, R. Spray timing and materials for walnut blight (*Xanthomonas campestris* pv. *juglandis*, *Xanthomonas arboricola* pv. *juglandis*) control in northern California USA. *Acta Hortic.* **2010**, *861*, 457–464. [CrossRef]
24. Adaskaveg, J.E.; Förster, H.; Thompson, D.; Enns, J.; Connell, J.; Buchner, R. Epidemiology and management of walnut blight. *Walnut Res. Rep.* **2009**, 241–257.
25. Miller, P.W.; Bollen, W.B. *Walnut Bacteriosis and Its Control*; Agricultural Experiment, Station Technical Bulletin 9; United States Department of Agriculture Bureau of Plant Industry, Soils and Agricultural Engineering, Oregon State College: Corvallis, OR, USA, 1946.

26. Franchi, G.G.; Piotto, B.; Nepi, M.; Baskin, C.C.; Baskin, J.M.; Pacini, E. Pollen and seed desiccation tolerance in relation to degree of developmental arrest, dispersal, and survival. *J. Exp. Bot.* **2011**, *62*, 5267–5281. [CrossRef] [PubMed]
27. Donati, I.; Cellini, A.; Sangiorgio, D.; Vanneste, J.; Scortichini, M.; Balestra, G.; Spinelli, F. *Pseudomonas syringae* pv. *actinidiae*: Ecology, infection dynamics and disease epidemiology. *Microb. Ecol.* **2020**, *80*, 81–102. [CrossRef] [PubMed]
28. Farina, W.M.; Arenas, A.; Díaz, P.C.; Susic Martin, C.; Corriale, M.J. In-hive learning of specific mimic odours as a tool to enhance honey bee foraging and pollination activities in pear and apple crops. *Sci. Rep.* **2022**, *12*, 20510. [CrossRef] [PubMed]
29. Pedroncelli, A.; Puopolo, G. This tree is on fire: A review on the ecology of *Erwinia amylovora*, the causal agent of fire blight disease. *J. Plant Pathol.* **2023**. [CrossRef]
30. Broussard, M.A.; Coates, M.; Martinsen, P. Artificial pollination technologies: A review. *Agronomy* **2023**, *13*, 1351. [CrossRef]
31. Castro, H.; Siopa, C.; Casais, V.; Castro, M.; Loureiro, J.; Gaspar, H.; Castro, S. Pollination as a key management tool in crop production: Kiwifruit orchards as a study case. *Sci. Hort.* **2021**, *290*, 110533. [CrossRef]
32. Wurz, A.; Grass, I.; Tscharntke, T. Hand pollination of global crops—A systematic review. *Basic Appl. Ecol.* **2021**, *56*, 299–321. [CrossRef]
33. Shimizu, H. Advanced technologies for pollination in plant factories. In *Plant Factory Using Artificial Light*; Elsevier: Amsterdam, The Netherlands, 2019; pp. 185–192. [CrossRef]
34. Frachon, L.; Stirling, S.; Schiestl, F.P.; Dudareva, N. Combining biotechnology and evolution for understanding the mechanisms of pollinator attraction. *Curr. Opin. Biotechnol.* **2021**, *70*, 213–219. [CrossRef]
35. Mazinani, M.; Zarafshan, P.; Dehghani, M.; Vahdati, K.; Etezadi, H. Design and analysis of an aerial pollination system for walnut trees. *Biosyst. Eng.* **2023**, *225*, 83–98. [CrossRef]
36. Potts, S.G.; Neumann, P.; Vaissière, B.E.; Vereecken, N.J. Robotic bees for crop pollination: Why drones cannot replace biodiversity. *Sci. Total Environ.* **2018**, *642*, 665–667. [CrossRef]
37. Chen, P.; Douzals, J.; Lan, Y.; Cotteux, E.; Delpuech, X.; Pouxviel, G.; Zhan, Y. Characteristics of unmanned aerial spraying systems and related spray drift: A review. *Front. Plant Sci.* **2022**, *13*, 870956. [CrossRef]
38. Zhang, Y.; Huang, X.; Lan, Y.; Wang, L.; Lu, X.; Yan, K.; Deng, J.; Zeng, W. Development and prospect of UAV-based aerial electrostatic spray technology in China. *Appl. Sci.* **2021**, *11*, 4071. [CrossRef]
39. Ge, C.; Dunno, K.D.; Singh, M.; Yuan, L.; Lu, L. Development of a drone's vibration, shock, and atmospheric profiles. *Appl. Sci.* **2021**, *11*, 5176. [CrossRef]
40. Russell, A.L.; Papaj, D.R. Artificial pollen dispensing flowers and feeders for bee behaviour experiments. *J. Pollinat. Ecol.* **2016**, *18*, 13–22. [CrossRef]
41. Li, K.; Huo, Y.; Liu, Y.; Shi, Y.; He, Z.; Cui, Y. Design of a lightweight robotic arm for kiwifruit pollination. *Comput. Electron. Agric.* **2022**, *198*, 107114. [CrossRef]
42. Eck, N.J.; Waltman, L. Software survey: VOSviewer, a computer program for bibliometric mapping. *Scientometrics* **2009**, *84*, 523–538. [CrossRef]
43. Orduña-Malea, E.; Costas, R. Link-based approach to study scientific software usage: The case of VOSviewer. *Scientometrics* **2021**, *126*, 8153–8186. [CrossRef]
44. Arruda, H.; Silva, É.R.; Lessa, M.; Proença, D.; Bartholo, R. VOSviewer and Bibliometrix. *J. Med. Libr. Assoc.* **2022**, *110*, 392–395. [CrossRef] [PubMed]
45. Vagelas, I.; Leontopoulos, S. A bibliometric analysis and a citation mapping process for the role of soil recycled organic matter and microbe interaction due to climate change using scopus database. *Agric. Eng.* **2023**, *5*, 581–610. [CrossRef]
46. Lykas, C.; Vagelas, I. Innovations in agriculture for sustainable Agro-systems. *Agronomy* **2023**, *13*, 2309. [CrossRef]
47. Mergos, P.E.; Yang, X. Flower pollination algorithm parameters tuning. *Soft Comput.* **2021**, *25*, 14429–14447. [CrossRef] [PubMed]
48. Wang, R.; Zhou, Y.; Qiao, S.; Huang, K. Flower pollination algorithm with bee pollinator for cluster analysis. *Inf. Proc. Lett.* **2016**, *116*, 1–14. [CrossRef]
49. Ambika Manirajan, B.; Ratering, S.; Rusch, V.; Schwiertz, A.; Geissler-Plaum, R.; Cardinale, M.; Schnell, S. Bacterial microbiota associated with flower pollen is influenced by pollination type, and shows a high degree of diversity and species-specificity. *Environ. Microbiol.* **2016**, *18*, 5161–5174. [CrossRef] [PubMed]
50. Akwasi, A.M.; Wei, X.; Duku, O.A. Observer controller-based structure for a modified flower pollination algorithm for wind power generation. *Int. J. Autom. Control* **2024**, *18*, 53–86. [CrossRef]
51. Hemalatha, S.; Johny Renoald, A.; Banu, G.; Indirajith, K. Design and investigation of PV string/central architecture for bayesian fusion technique using grey wolf optimization and flower pollination optimized algorithm. *Energy Convers. Manag.* **2023**, *286*, 117078. [CrossRef]
52. Campbell, D.R. Predicting plant reproductive success from models of competition for pollination. *Oikos* **1986**, *47*, 257–266. [CrossRef]
53. Sáez, A.; di Virgilio, A.; Tiribelli, F.; Geslin, B. Simulation models to predict pollination success in apple orchards: A useful tool to test management practices. *Apidologie* **2018**, *49*, 551–561. [CrossRef]
54. Stock, M.; Piot, N.; Vanbesien, S.; Meys, J.; Smagghe, G.; Baets, B.D. Pairwise learning for predicting pollination interactions based on traits and phylogeny. *Ecol. Model.* **2021**, *451*, 109508. [CrossRef]
55. Pegoraro, L.; Hidalgo, O.; Leitch, I.J.; Pellicer, J.; Barlow, S.E. Automated video monitoring of insect pollinators in the field. *Emerg. Top Life Sci.* **2020**, *4*, 87–97. [CrossRef] [PubMed]

56. Ngo, T.N.; Rustia, D.J.; Yang, E.; Lin, T. Automated monitoring and analyses of honey bee pollen foraging behavior using a deep learning-based imaging system. *Comput. Electron. Agric.* **2021**, *187*, 106239. [CrossRef]
57. DeVetter, L.W.; Chabert, S.; Milbrath, M.O.; Mallinger, R.E.; Walters, J.; Isaacs, R.; Galinato, S.P.; Kogan, C.J.; Brouwer, K.; Melathopoulos, A.; et al. Toward evidence-based decision support systems to optimize pollination and yields in highbush blueberry. *Front. Sustain. Food Syst.* **2022**, *6*, 1006201. [CrossRef]
58. Menzel, C.M. Fruit set is moderately dependent on insect pollinators in strawberry and is limited by the availability of pollen under natural open conditions. *J. Hortic. Sci. Biotechnol.* **2023**, *98*, 685–714. [CrossRef]
59. Yang, M.; Lyu, H.; Zhao, Y.; Sun, Y.; Pan, H.; Sun, Q.; Chen, J.; Qiang, B.; Yang, H. Delivery of pollen to forsythia flower pistils autonomously and precisely using a robot arm. *Comput. Electron. Agric.* **2023**, *214*, 108274. [CrossRef]
60. Hiraguri, T.; Shimizu, H.; Kimura, T.; Matsuda, T.; Maruta, K.; Takemura, Y.; Ohya, T.; Takanashi, T. Autonomous drone-based pollination system using AI classifier to replace bees for greenhouse tomato cultivation. *IEEE Access* **2023**, *11*, 99352–99364. [CrossRef]
61. Cong, W.; Dupont, Y.L.; Søegaard, K.; Eriksen, J. Optimizing yield and flower resources for pollinators in intensively managed multi-species grasslands. *Agric. Ecosyst. Environ.* **2020**, *302*, 107062. [CrossRef]
62. Wajnberg, E.; Tel-Zur, N.; Shapira, I.; Lebber, Y.; Lev-Yadun, S.; Zurgil, U.; Reisman-Berman, O.; Keasar, T. Pollinator behavior drives sexual specializations in the hermaphrodite flowers of a heterodichogamous tree. *Front. Plant Sci.* **2019**, *10*, 1315. [CrossRef]
63. Knauer, A.C.; Kokko, H.; Schiestl, F.P. Pollinator behaviour and resource limitation maintain honest floral signalling. *Funct. Ecol.* **2021**, *35*, 2536–2549. [CrossRef]
64. Yuan, Y.; Byers, K.J.; Bradshaw, H.D. The genetic control of flower-pollinator specificity. *Curr. Opin. Plant Biol.* **2013**, *16*, 422–428. [CrossRef]
65. Rose, J.P.; Sytsma, K.J. Complex interactions underlie the correlated evolution of floral traits and their association with pollinators in a clade with diverse pollination systems. *Evolution* **2021**, *75*, 1431–1449. [CrossRef]
66. Feigs, J.T.; Holzhauer, S.I.; Huang, S.; Brunet, J.; Diekmann, M.; Hedwall, P.; Kramp, K.; Naaf, T. Pollinator movement activity influences genetic diversity and differentiation of spatially isolated populations of clonal forest herbs. *Front. Ecol. Evol.* **2022**, *10*, 908258. [CrossRef]
67. Opedal, Ø.H.; Pérez-Barrales, R.; Brito, V.L.; Muchhala, N.; Capó, M.; Dellinger, A.S. Pollen as the link between floral phenotype and fitness. *Am. J. Bot.* **2023**, *110*, e16200. [CrossRef]
68. Barons, M.J.; Shenvi, A. Where the bee sucks—A dynamic bayesian network approach to decision support for pollinator abundance strategies. *arXiv* **2022**, arXiv:2212.03179. [CrossRef]
69. Lonsdorf, E.V.; Kremen, C.; Ricketts, T.H.; Winfree, R.; Williams, N.M.; Greenleaf, S.S. Modelling pollination services across agricultural landscapes. *Ann. Bot.* **2009**, *103*, 1589–1600. [CrossRef] [PubMed]
70. Drucker, D.P.; Salim, J.A.; Trekels, M.; Groom, Q.J.; Parr, C.S.; Soares, F.M.; Agostini, K.; Saraiva, A.; Molloy, L.; Hodson, S.; et al. Plant-pollinator interaction data: A case study of the WorldFAIR project. *Biodivers. Inf. Sci. Stand.* **2022**, *6*, e94310. [CrossRef]
71. Salim, J.A.; Zermoglio, P.F.; Drucker, D.P.; Soares, F.M.; Saraiva, A.M.; Agostini, K.; Freitas, L.; Wolowski, M.; Rech, A.R.; Maués, M.M.; et al. Plant-pollinator vocabulary—A contribution to interaction data standardization. *Biodivers. Inf. Sci. Stand.* **2021**, *5*, e75636. [CrossRef]
72. Salim, J.A.; Saraiva, A.M.; Zermoglio, P.F.; Agostini, K.; Wolowski, M.; Drucker, D.P.; Soares, F.M.; Bergamo, P.J.; Varassin, I.G.; Freitas, L.; et al. Data standardization of plant–pollinator interactions. *GigaScience* **2022**, *11*, giac043. [CrossRef] [PubMed]
73. Hulens, D.; Van Ranst, W.; Cao, Y.; Goedemé, T. Autonomous Visual Navigation for a Flower Pollination Drone. *Machines* **2022**, *10*, 364. [CrossRef]

MDPI
St. Alban-Anlage 66
4052 Basel
Switzerland
www.mdpi.com

Applied Sciences Editorial Office
E-mail: applsci@mdpi.com
www.mdpi.com/journal/applsci

www.ingramcontent.com/pod-product-compliance
Lightning Source LLC
LaVergne TN
LVHW070729100526
838202LV00013B/1197
* 9 7 8 3 7 2 5 8 1 2 1 1 0 *